SKETCHING MASTERCLASS
Copyright © 2010 Page One Publishing Pte Ltd

First published in Asia in 2010 by
Page One Publishing Pte Ltd

Third reprint of Asian edition published in 2013 by
Page One Publishing Pte Ltd
20 Kaki Bukit View
Kaki Bukit Techpark II
Singapore 415956
Tel: (65) 6742 2088
Fax: (65) 6744 2088
enquiries@pageonegroup.com
www.pageonegroup.com

First published 2010 by Page One Publishing Pte Ltd

Text copyright © 2010 Page One Publishing Pte Ltd
Images copyright © 2010 Ruzaimi Mat Rani
Design and layout copyright © 2010 Page One Publishing Pte Ltd

Editor: Wong She-reen
Designer: Zedy Wiepandy Ng

ISBN 978-981-245-935-0

All rights reserved. No part of this publication may be reproduced, stored in any retrieval system or transmitted, in any form or by any means, electronic, mechanical, photocopying, recording or otherwise, without prior permission in writing from the publisher. for information, contact Page One Publishing Pte Ltd.

Printed and bound in Singapore.

SKETCHING MASTERCLASS

Author
Ruzaimi Mat Rani
Co-author
Ezihaslinda Ngah

Illustrators
Ruzaimi Mat Rani
Mohd. Irwan Mohd. Ishak

SKETCHING MASTERCLASS

PAGE ONE

CONTENTS

		PAGE
1.0	Introduction	8
1.1	Pen and Pencil Sketches	9
1.2	Tips in Sketch	12
1.3	The Testimonial	13
2.0	Materials and Equipment	16
2.1	Pencil	17
2.2	Pen	18
2.3	Charcoal	19
2.4	Sketch Sheet and Support Tools	20
3.0	Basic Skills	22
3.1	Sketching Lines	22
3.2	The Techniques of Sketching a Straight Line	23
3.3	The Practice of Sketching	24
3.4	Sketching the Basic Shapes of 2-D	29
3.5	Sketching Complex 2-D Shapes	30
3.6	Sketching Basic 2-D Objects	31
3.7	Sketching 2-D Complex Objects	32
3.8	Sketching 3-D Basic Shapes	33
3.9	Sketching 3-D Complex Shapes	34
3.10	Sketching 3-D Basic Objects	35
3.11	Sketching 3-D Complex Objects	37
3.12	Sketching 2-D Figures	39
3.13	Sketching 3-D Figures	49
4.0	Sketch Composition	60
4.1	The Concept of Lines in Sketching	60
4.2	Lines Using Pencil	61
4.3	Sketching Lines Using a Pen	65
4.4	Composition in Sketches	68
4.5	The Concept of Good Composition in a Sketch	70
4.6	What is Perspective	76
4.7	The Concept of Perspective	77
4.8	Types of Perspectives	78
4.9	Tips in Perspectives	80
4.10	Simple Approach in Perspective	89

		PAGE
5.0	Rendering Techniques	94
5.1	Rendering Concepts	94
5.2	Medium of Rendering	95
5.3	Shade and Shadow	96
5.4	Rendering Techniques	102
6.0	A Step By Step Process	114
6.1	Introduction	114
6.2	One Point Perspective	121
6.3	Two Point Perspective	169
6.4	Three Point Perspective	201
6.5	Multi Point Perspective	209
7.0	References	225

PREFACE

Do not sketch the scenery that you can see; sketch the scenery that you cannot see. This is definitely a good advice for those who would like to learn and improve their sketching skill.

This book is written for anybody with an interest in sketching. It can be used in arts and design including architecture, interior design, industrial design, applied arts, graphic design and multimedia. It is suitable for understanding simple methods of sketching as the processes presented are concepts.

This is a fascinating book as it tries to explain trouble-free ways of sketching through a step by step process as simple as ABC. The concepts demonstrated have long existed but never been thoroughly explained. An artist or a designer will be able to perceive and comprehend the step by step illustrations attached to the explanations.

Ruzaimi Mat Rani (Miandza)

ACKNOWLEDGEMENT

To be able to realise my dream of publishing this book and to share my knowledge with readers is one of the greatest joys that I have had in my life. Indeed, my deepest gratification goes to all my teachers and others without whom I would not be able to gain as much knowledge about life and the world. My earnest pleasure also goes to my co-author, Ezihaslinda Ngah and my friends Mohd Irwan Mohd Ishak and Hasri Hasan, in assisting me to complete the book content. Also, of course, my backbone and strength, my family: Aidaliza, my beloved wife who has been with me through thick and thin in supporting me to complete this book; my adorable children, Athirah, and Hazim; my much loved parents, Haji Mat Rani and Hajjah Maznah; my dearly loved parents in-law, Haji Aga Mohd Jaladin and Hajjah Mahyah; the rest of the family members and my friends. May your unremitting support remain forever.

Good News

I have published a blog at freedrawinglesson.blogspot.com *to share my little knowledge on how to sketch using stop motion demonstration videos (demo videos). I am looking forward to producing more than 1000 demo videos to share with people around the world.*

1.0 INTRODUCTION

'How to sketch?' is a favourite question asked whenever a person is about to begin sketching. This question will always occur to those who know little or are totally clueless about sketching but would like to try. Somebody who does not know how to sketch but is interested in trying, given the right exposure, surely, eventually, they will be able to produce excellent artwork.

This book is specifically written to assist anybody who is interested in understanding and gaining the required skill of sketching. The focus of this book is on the basic techniques of sketching using pen and pencil only. Explanation and demonstration will be given beginning from the basics of sketching to perspective drawing and rendering. Details of the basics of sketching are necessary to strengthen the fundamental skills which would be the foundation for the upcoming techniques.

1.1 PEN AND PENCIL SKETCHES

Every sketch produced has its own individual characteristics that need to be well understood including the techniques of building them. The skills in empowering these techniques will make the artist better. The followings are the examples of sketches using pens, pencils and charcoal.

Example of pencil sketch (fast technique)

Example of pen sketch (fast technique).

Example of dark pencil charcoal sketch

Example of a sketch using pen

Examples of sketches done using pen rendering technique

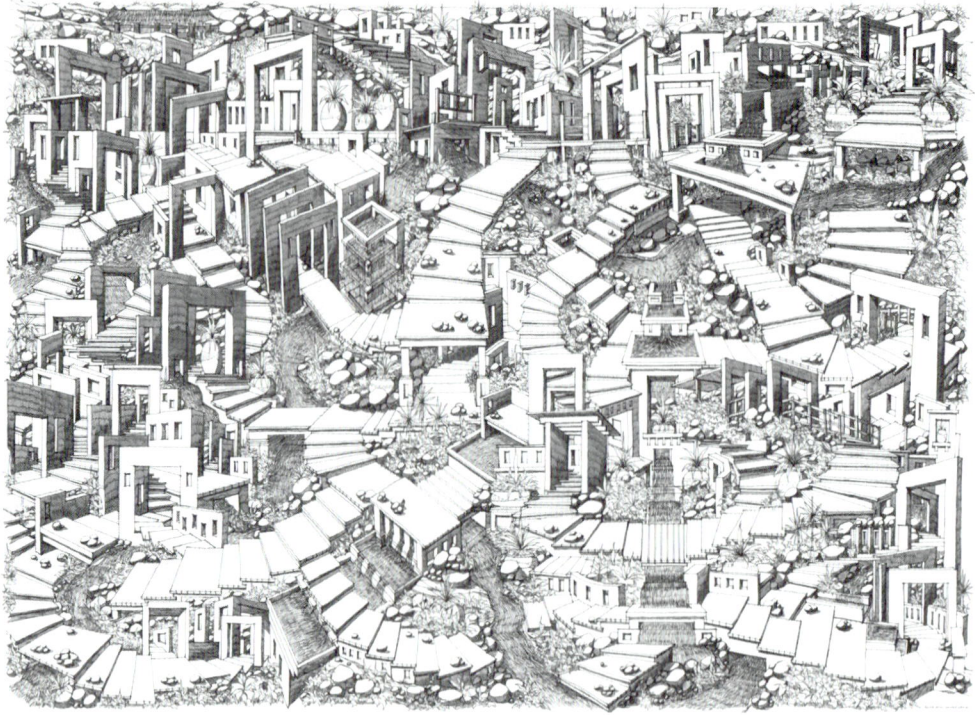
A multi-point perspective sketched by Ruzaimi Mat Rani

1.2 TIPS IN SKETCH

There are a few tips that are pivotal if one is to master the sketching skill. It has to be done consistently so that the skills acquired would be more apparent and consequently a more interesting and quality product could be constructed.

The first tip that should be possessed is the self-confidence to produce very quality sketches. This attitude could be shaped if the second and third tips later are done relentlessly following all the guidelines given in the book.

The second tip is the attitude of enthusiasm to try sketching. It is an excellent mind-set and really needed for those who would like to be skillful at sketching even if at the beginning they do not know anything about sketching. A very good example is the skill of writing. Without this inquisitive attitude surely everybody will not be able to write well and beautifully. The same process could also be applied in sketching if they would like to be an excellent artist and designer who can master the sketching skills. "Better Try than Never."

The third tip is the attitude of eagerness to try exploring new things in sketching. This is important to ensure an artist or designer understands and possesses a range of experience in which can help him to decide the best way of how to sketch or use the materials.

The fourth tip is to practise, practise and practise. This tip does not need a lengthy elaboration. The only thing that needs to be emphasized is the practice should be proceeded by all the guidelines prepared in the book.

1.3 THE TESTIMONIAL

Part 1

These are the sketches done by a participant of a class 'How to Sketch' in January 2007. The sketches were done before the techniques 'How to Sketch: As simple as ABC...' been taught to the participants.

Before

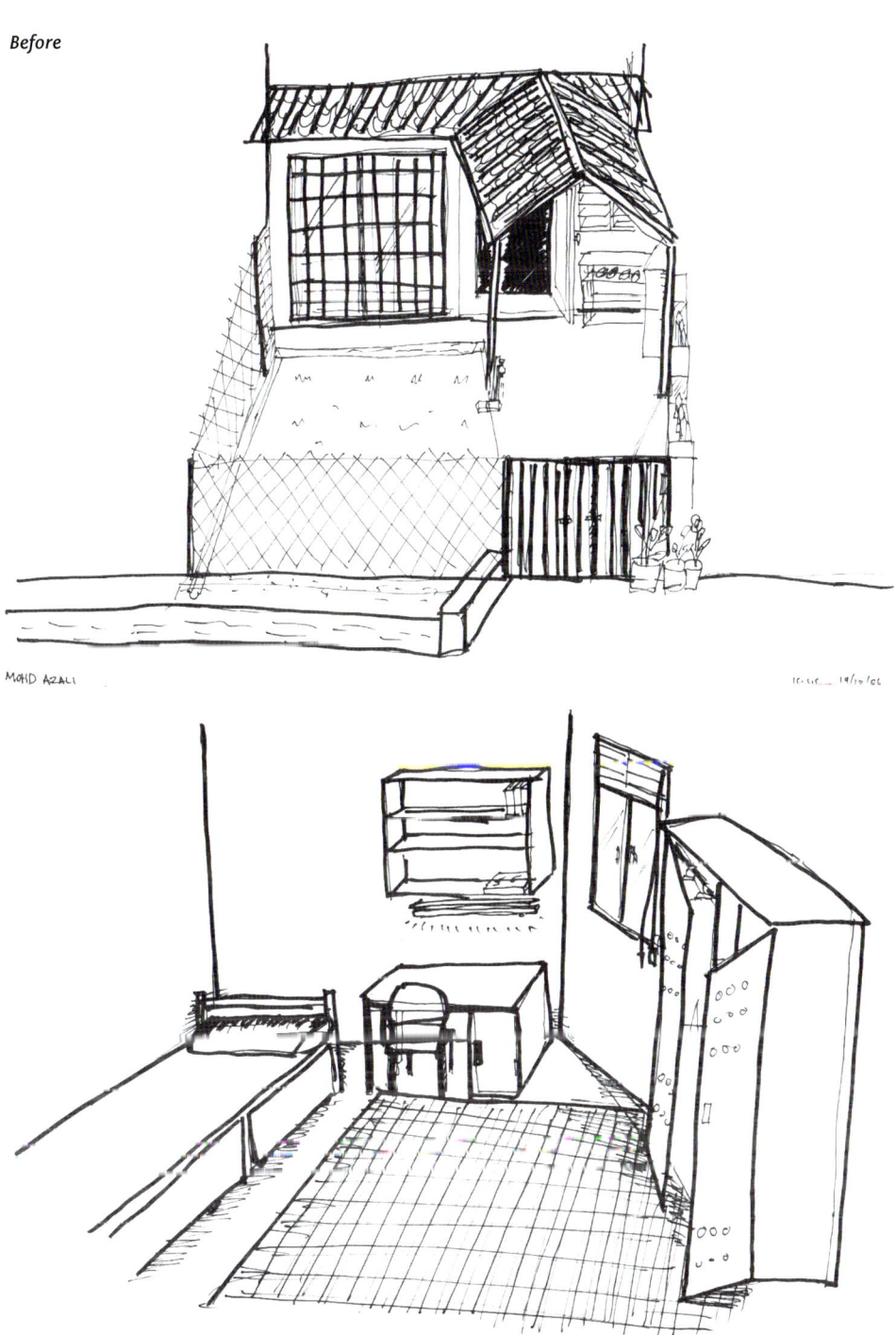

Sketches by Mohd Azali bin Mohd Nor

Part 2

These are the sketches done by the participant who applies the principles of 'How to Sketch: As simple as ABC...'. There are a lot of improvements shown by this participant throughout the class session.

After

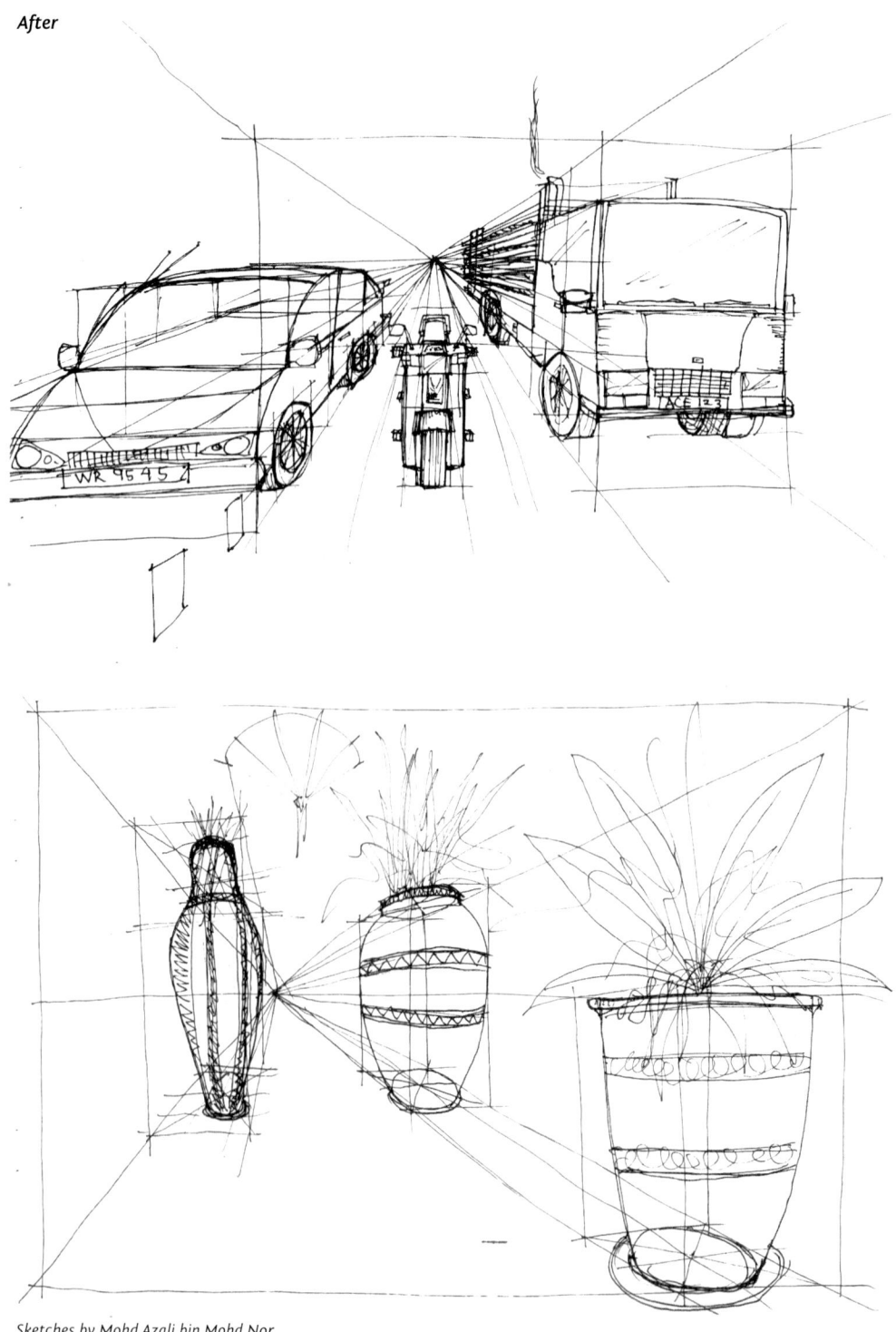

Sketches by Mohd Azali bin Mohd Nor

Part 3
Look at the two final sketches done by the participant. Do observe the significant transformation done by the participant before and after the class session 'How to Sketch: As simple as ABC...'.

After

Sketches by Mohd Azali bin Mohd Nor

INTRODUCTION 15

2.0 MATERIALS AND EQUIPMENT

The basic knowledge of materials and tools and their usage for sketching is the utmost importance in order to have quality sketches. The knowledge could be gained from a lot of readily available references in the market. This book will describe in general about the important materials and tools that need to be understood and their usage before embarking on sketching.

The basic sketching tools that are needed are a pencil or pen and a piece of paper. Apart from that support sketching tools that may be necessary are an eraser and a drawing board acting as an extra support for the drawing sheet. To be able to obtain an excellent product, please guarantee the tools and materials used are of superior quality.

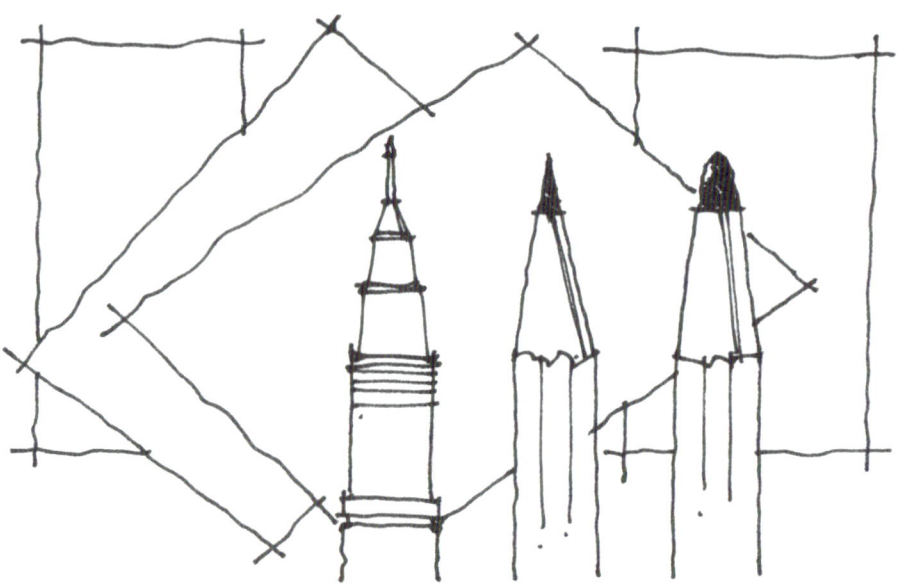

Some of the basic tools used for sketching (Paper and pen or pencil)

2.1 PENCIL

The essential knowledge about pencils that needs to be understood is the type of pencil, its grade and quality. The types of pencils are regular, coloured, water soluble and charcoal. Pencils are graded based on H and B system. H is the hard grade, 9H being the hardest. Grade B on the other hand is categorized as in the soft type where 8B is graded as the softest.

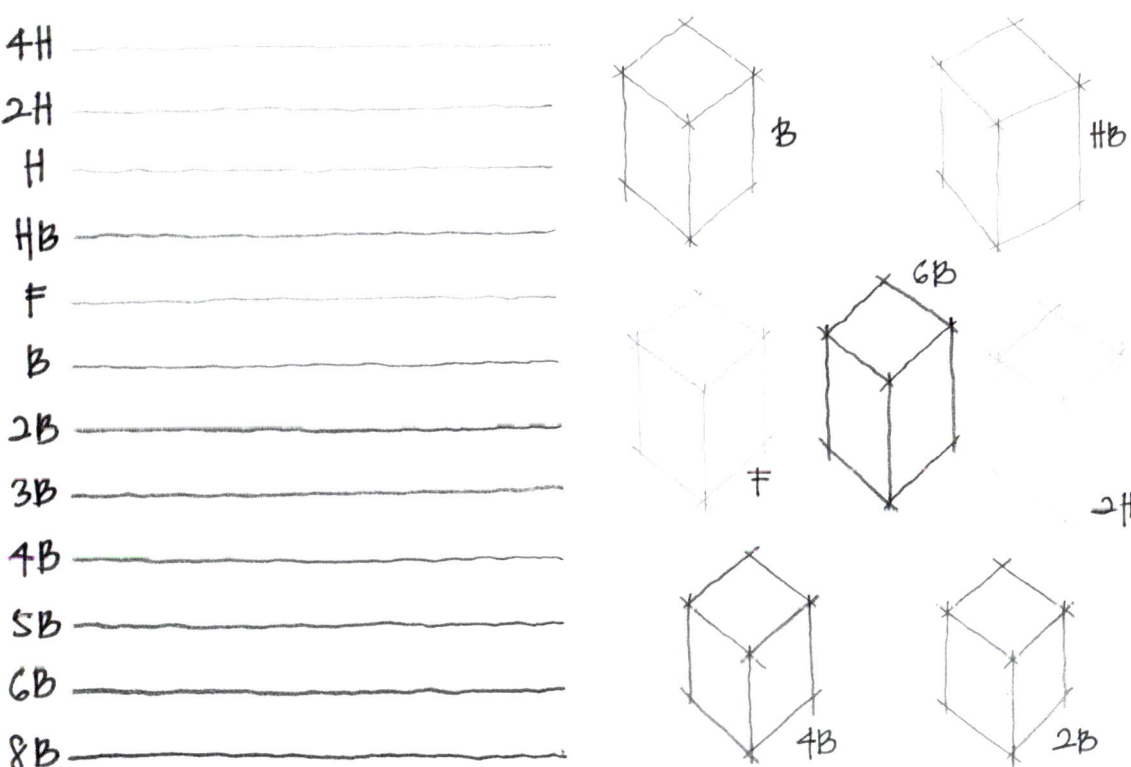

Examples of line produced by different types of pencil

Examples of 3D objects sketched with different types of pencil grade

MATERIALS AND EQUIPMENT 17

2.2 PEN

Pen is just another alternative to replace pencil for sketching. There are a few types of pens in the market such as felt tip, fountain, regular, technical and marker. These pens use two types of ink; water soluble and water proof. Water soluble pens absorb water whereas waterproof pens do not absorb water. These two types of pens have their own advantages depending on their functions.

Felt tip pens are divided into several types depending on the thickness of their felt tips. For example, 0.1, 0.2, 0.4, 0.6 and 1.0. Each type of pen has a different impact on a sketch. An artist or designer should know how to choose the types of pens for his or her sketch.

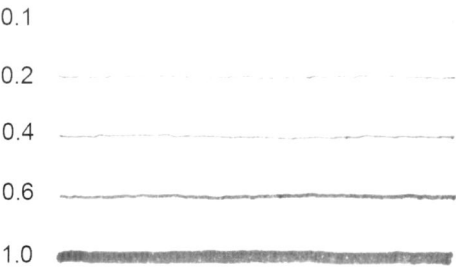

Examples of lines sketched using different thickness of felt tip pens.

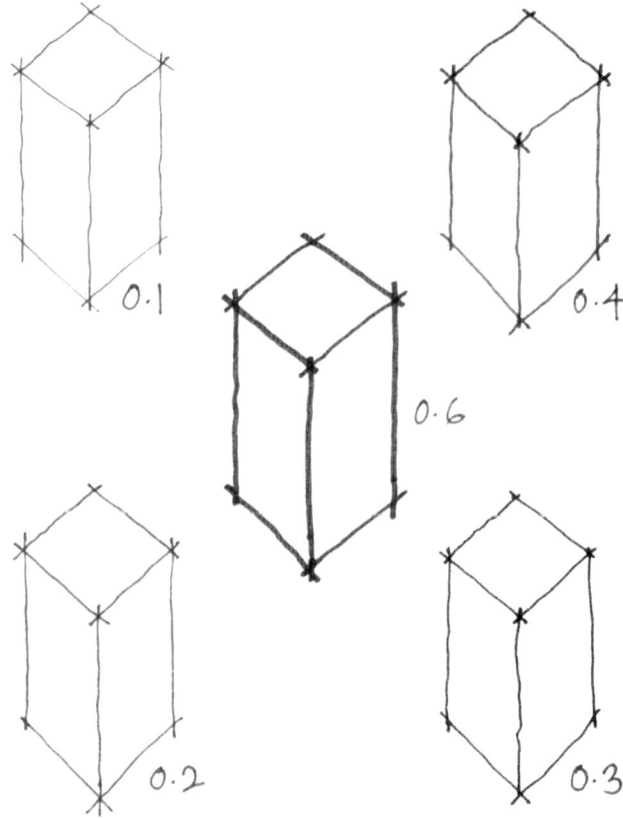

Examples of 3D objects sketched with different types of pen nibs.

18 MATERIALS AND EQUIPMENT

2.3 CHARCOAL

Charcoal is the oldest sketch tool ever used for sketching. Charcoal can be found in different thicknesses. Charcoal can also be found in pencil shapes of soft, medium and dark types. To sketch, a small size of charcoal is the most suitable one to be used. Normally, after sketching using a charcoal, a layer called a fixative is sprayed on the surface level of the sketch.

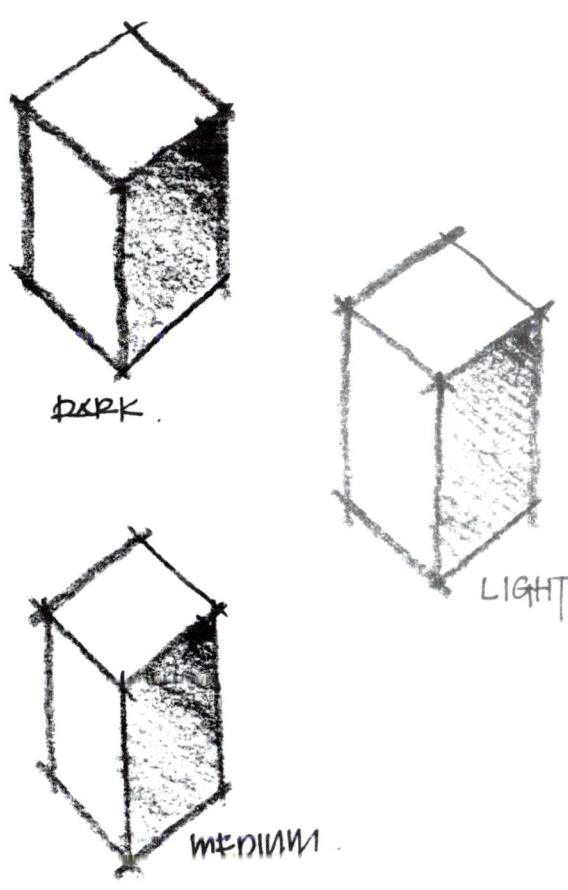

Examples of 3D objects sketched with different types of charcoal pencil

2.4 SKETCH SHEET AND SUPPORT TOOLS

A sketch sheet has to be suitable with the type of pencil, pen or charcoal used. It has various sizes, weight, textures and colours. Using the right type of sketch sheet could help in achieving a high-quality sketch. A (hot pressed) smooth sketch sheet is certainly very appropriate to be used with pencils or pens. On the other hand, a textured sketch sheet is suitable to be used with charcoal.

Texture paper 1

Texture paper 2

Texture paper 3

Texture paper 4

An example of a smooth and textured drawing sheet used for sketching.

The support tools needed in producing sketches are an eraser, a pencil sharpener, and a sketch board. An artist or designer should know how to choose the right type of eraser so as to not ruin the sketch. A good pencil sharpener on the other hand, could sharpen the pencil perfectly well without destroying the sharpened lead. As for the sketch board, it has to have a smooth surface and suitable for the size of the sketch sheet. Fixative is used to protect the surface of the sketches.

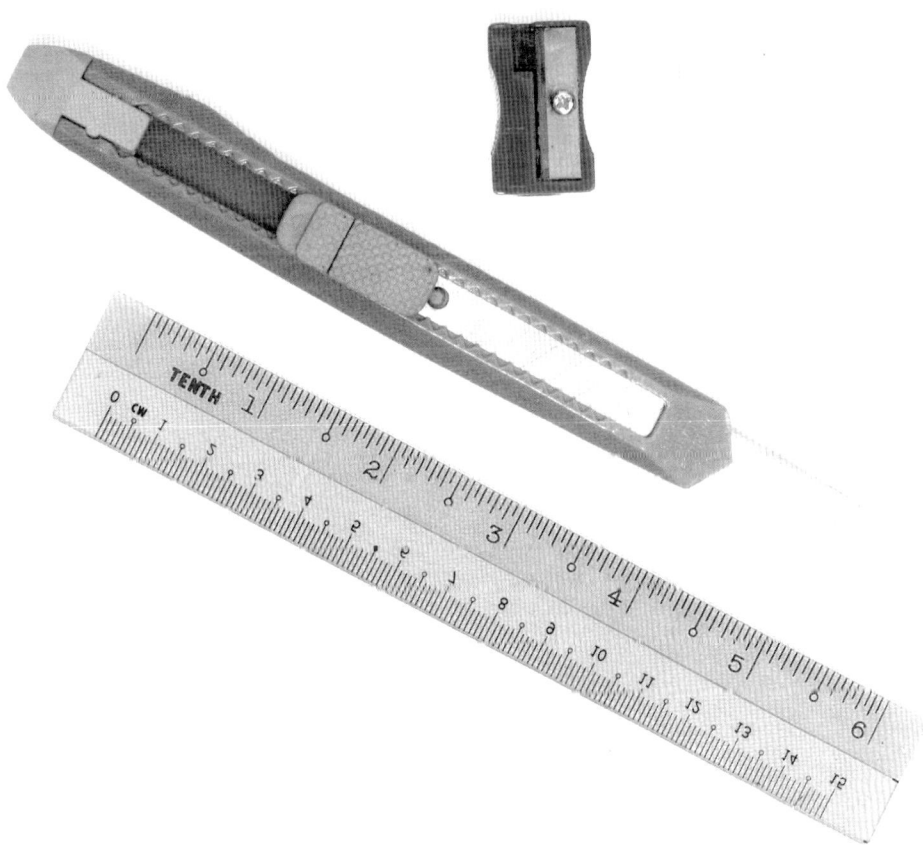

An example of support tools

3.0 BASIC SKILLS

Sketching is a basic skill that could be sharpened if the fundamental aspects are understood and practiced consistently. The must-have key principals that should be grasped by an artist or designer are sketching lines, shapes, basic forms, complex forms and basic objects.

3.1 SKETCHING LINES

The skill of sketching quality lines is one of the factors that help to produce a good sketch. It may sound easy but some specific skills are needed in order to attain a fine line. Among the skills is holding the pen or pencil correctly.

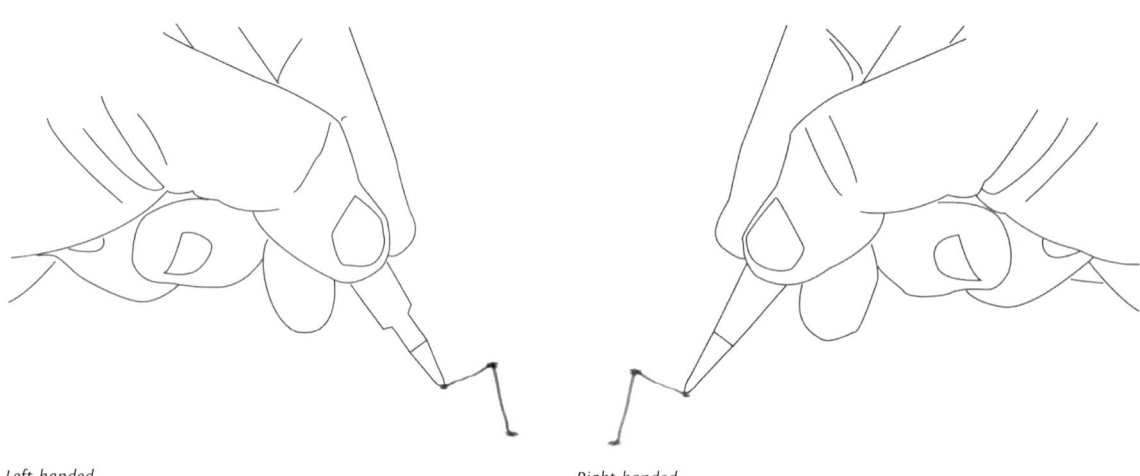

Left-handed　　　　　　　　　　　　　*Right-handed*

The right position of holding a pen or pencil during sketching session

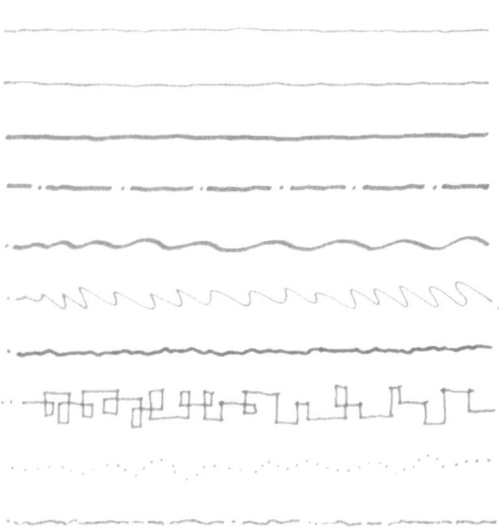

Lines types

22　BASIC SKILLS

3.2 THE TECHNIQUES OF SKETCHING A STRAIGHT LINE

The technique of sketching a line between one point to another is the best technique for creating a straight line. The points are used as the guidelines for an artist or designer to sketch a superb straight line.

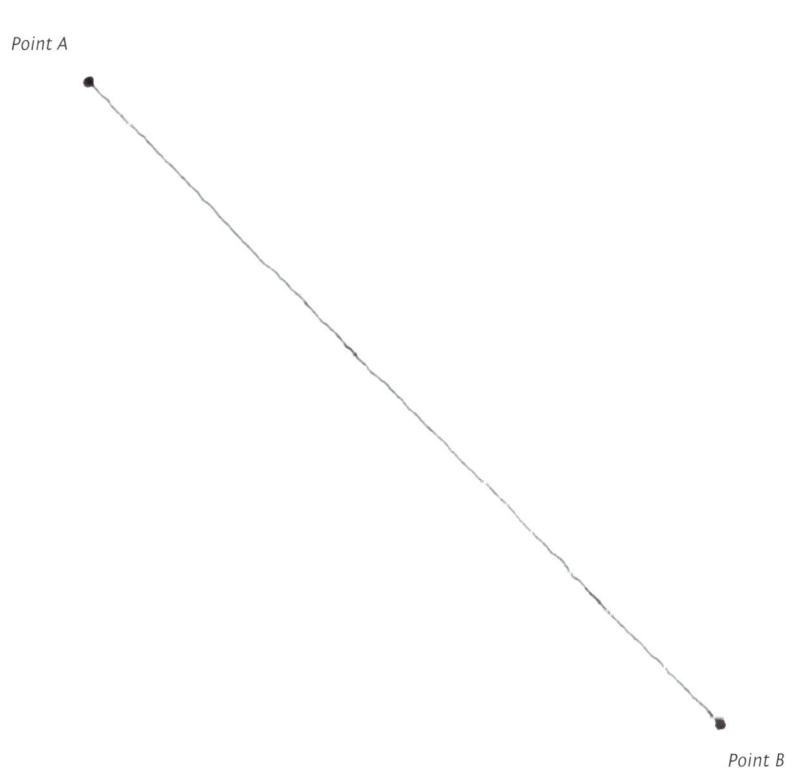

The technique of sketching a straight line from two points.

3.3 THE PRACTICE OF SKETCHING

The practice of sketching various types of lines is necessary to ensure the sketch produced is of a superior quality. Even though this may seem simple, it requires concentration and confidence to be able to produce quality lines. If each line sketched is observed carefully they all have specific categories that need to be understood by the artist or designer.

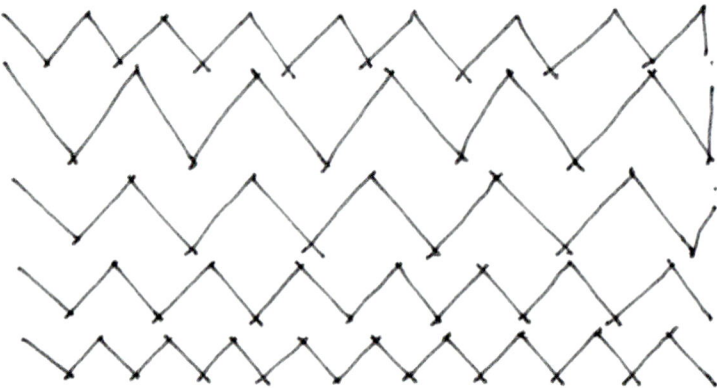

An example of practice for sketching lines: Zig Zag

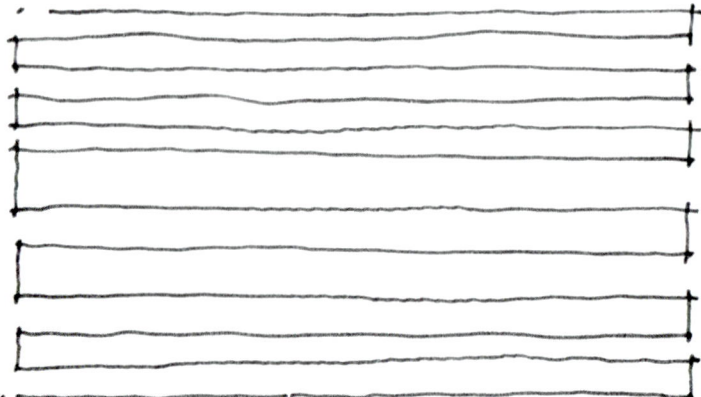

An example of practice for sketching lines: Continuity

Tip: *You have to do the practice on sketching lines repeatedly and consistently.*

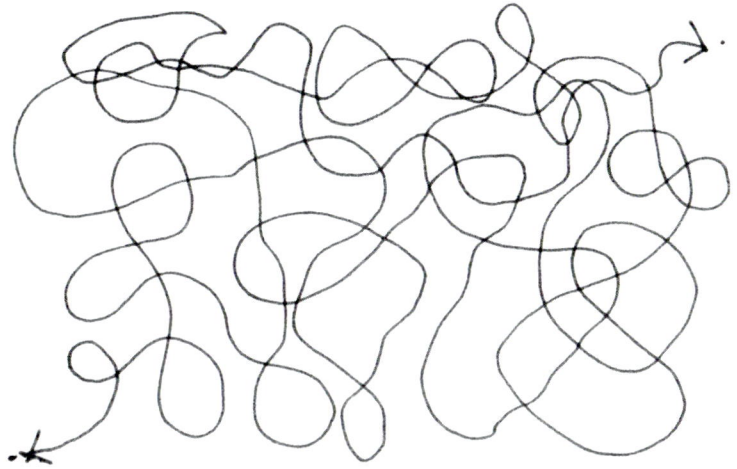

An example of practice for sketching lines: Free Lines

An example of practice for sketching lines: Staggered

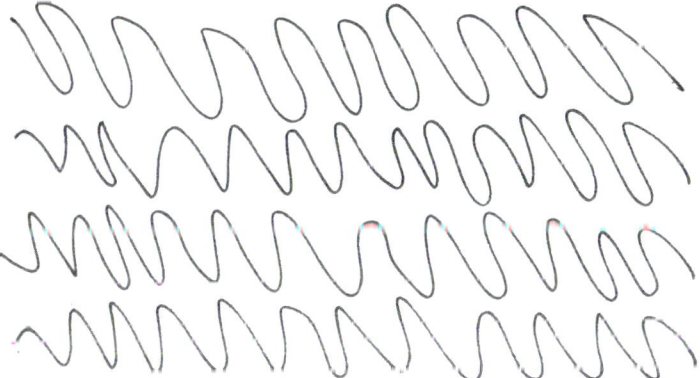

An example of practice for sketching lines: Curvy

BASIC SKILLS

An example of practice for sketching lines: Dashed

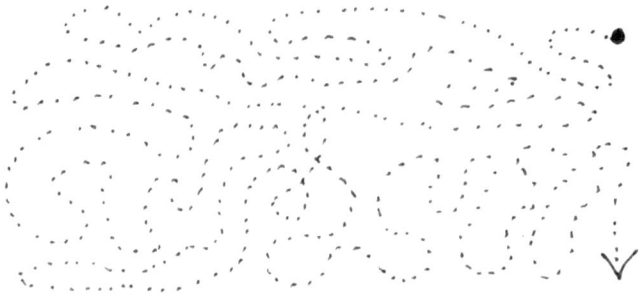

An example of practice for sketching lines: Dotted

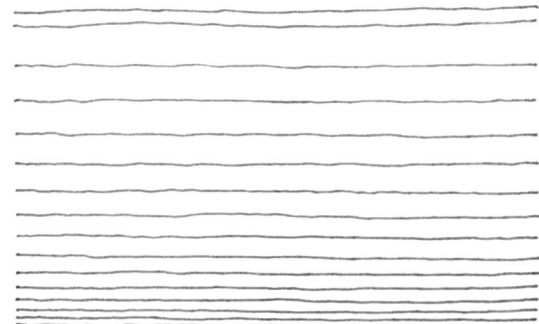

An example of practice for sketching lines: Horizontal lines

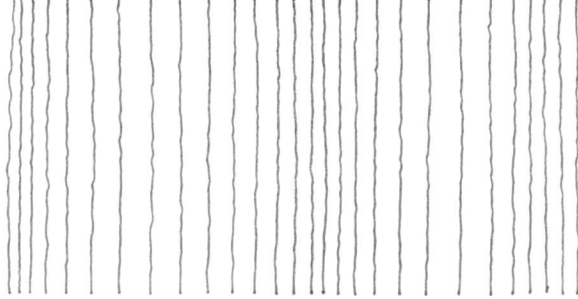

An example of practice for sketching lines: Vertical lines

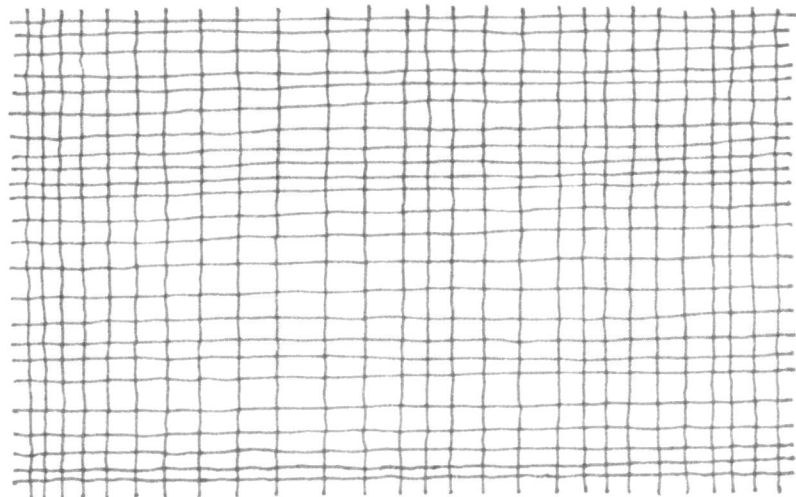

An example of practice for sketching lines: Cross lines

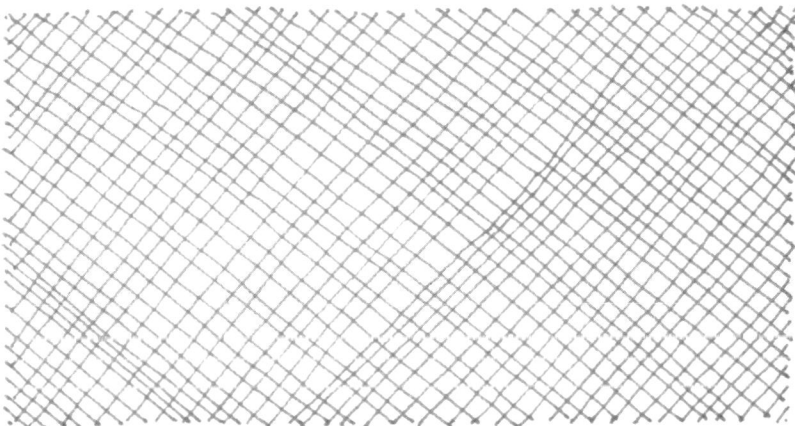

An example of practice for sketching lines: Cross angle lines

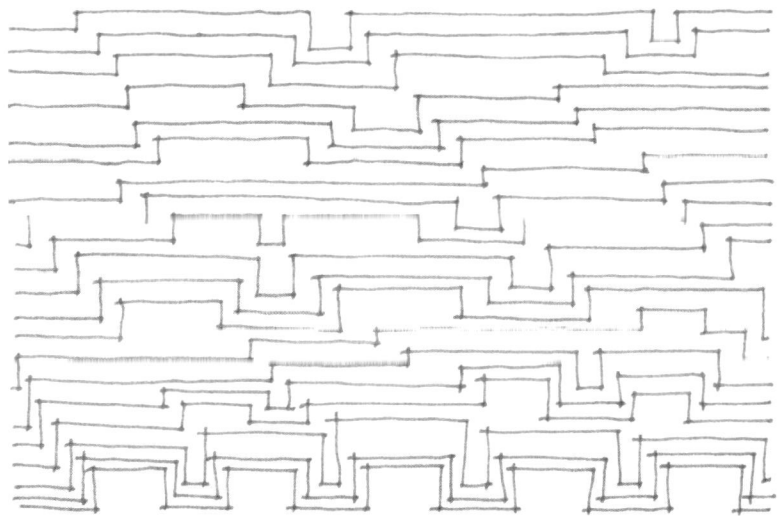

An example of practice for sketching lines: Staggered

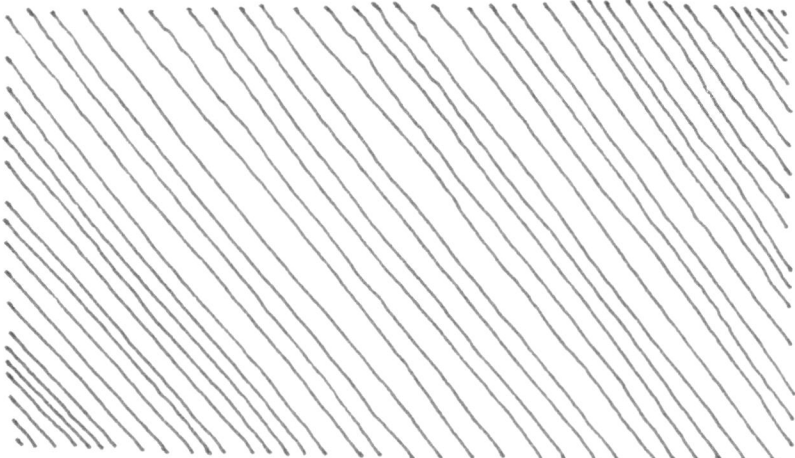

An example of practice for sketching lines: Angle

An example of practice for sketching lines: Horizontal Curvy lines

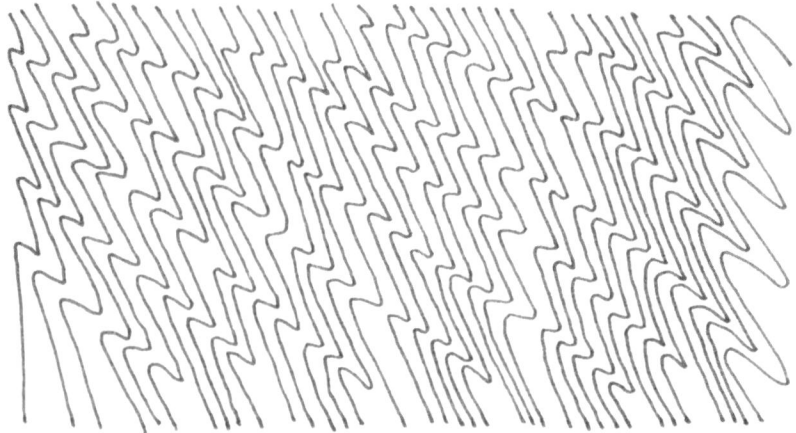

An example of practice for sketching lines: Vertical Curvy lines

3.4 SKETCHING THE BASIC SHAPES OF 2-D

The skills to sketch the basic shapes of 2-D is the second phase that needs to be understood and practiced. This skill is really needed to ensure the next stage could be mastered within a short period of time. To sketch superbly well the basic shapes of 2-D, sketching lines with superb confidence is required.

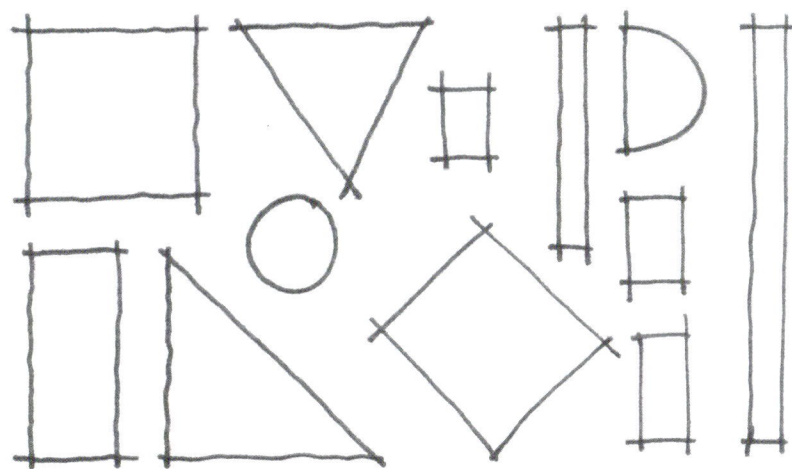

2-Dimensional (2-D) basic shapes

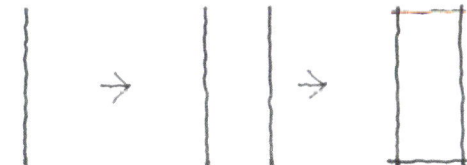

The process of sketching 2-D basic shapes: Square

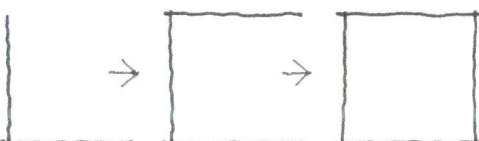

The process of sketching 2-D basic shapes: Rectangle

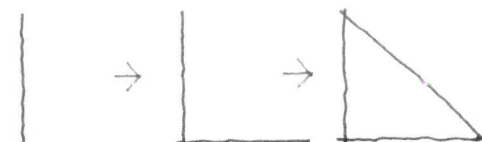

The process of sketching 2-D basic shapes: Triangle

3.5 SKETCHING COMPLEX 2-D SHAPES

The third stage is the skills of sketching complex 2-D shapes. At this stage, both skills learned on stage one and two should be mastered perfectly well. Although this may seem simple and easy to be sketched, the actual reality of producing something of an excellent quality requires appropriate basic skills.

Tip: To produce a superior quality drawing an artist should be confident and honest in sketching an item.

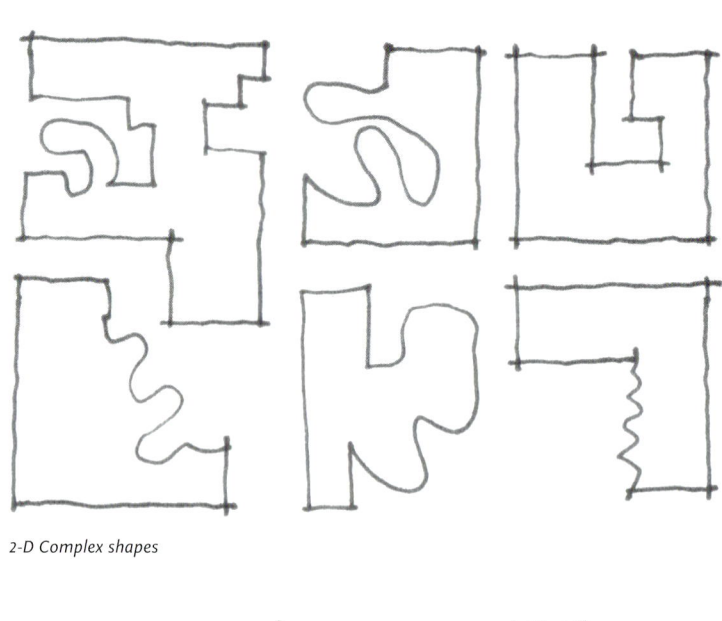

2-D Complex shapes

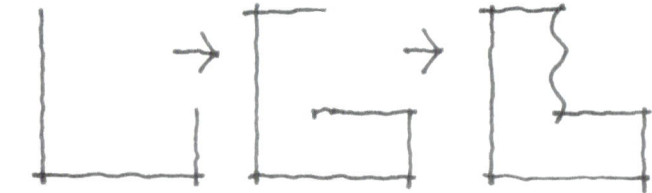

The process of sketching 2-D complex shapes: shape 1

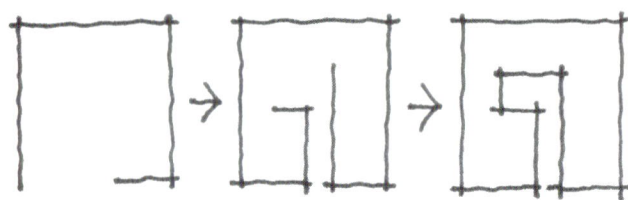

The process of sketching 2-D complex shapes: shape 2

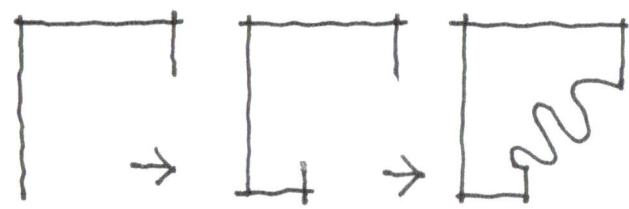

The process of sketching 2-D complex shapes: shape 3

3.6 SKETCHING BASIC 2-D OBJECTS

The fourth stage is where the artist or designer needs to sketch objects in 2-D. The sketch technique in 2-D will help an artist or designer in understanding deeply about the concept of surface and lines for each sketch produced. This technique of object sketch will use the concept of 'imaginary box'. This basic concept will ease the artist or designer in understanding and mastering the skill of sketching 2-D objects better.

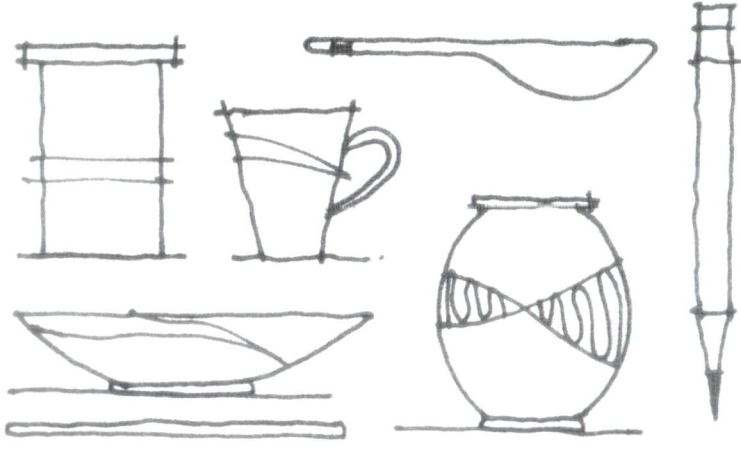

2-D basic objects

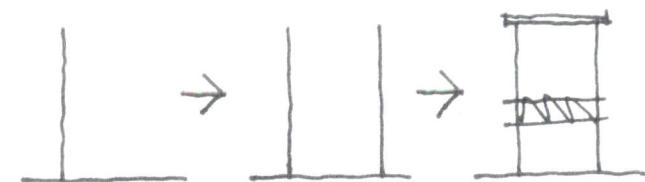

The process of sketching 2-D basic objects: object 1

The process of sketching 2-D basic objects: object 2

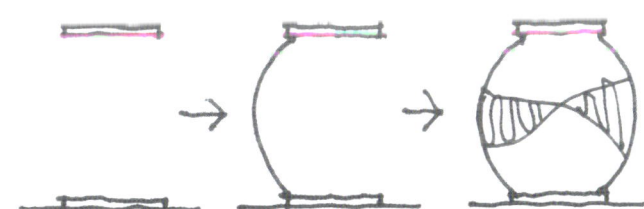

The process of sketching 2-D basic objects: object 3

BASIC SKILLS

3.7 SKETCHING 2-D COMPLEX OBJECTS

At this stage an artist or designer needs to sketch complex objects in 2-D. This process is similar to the process of sketching basic 2-D objects. But at this stage an artist or designer needs to use the skill and the strength of the mind in order to understand profoundly about 2-D sketch. The strength of the mind is required to imagine the situation of the object in 2-D. It will be easier if these techniques are practiced for a number of times.

Tip: Understand and practice until you succeed

2-D complex objects

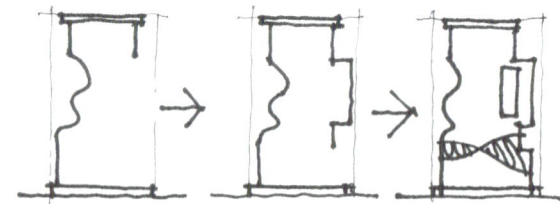

The process of sketching 2-D complex objects: object 1

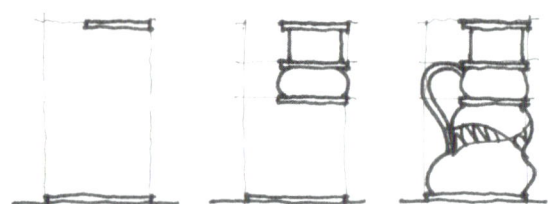

The process of sketching 2-D complex objects: object 2

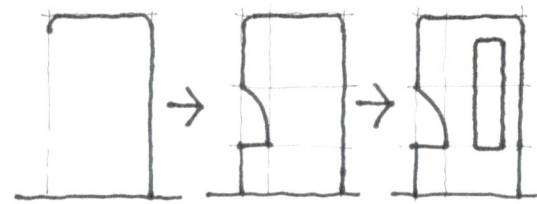

The process of sketching 2-D complex objects: object 3

3.8 SKETCHING 3-D BASIC SHAPES

The sixth stage is sketching 3-dimensional shapes (3-D). At this level an artist or designer needs the understanding in creating a shape in 3-D shape. This needs no worry as the example given will give the guidelines of how to form good basic 3-D shapes. Before embarking on this level, please ensure that the previous skills learned and practiced before this is mastered superbly well. This is vital as it will assist in understanding the skills at this level and also for the next ones.

Use the 'imaginary box' concept.

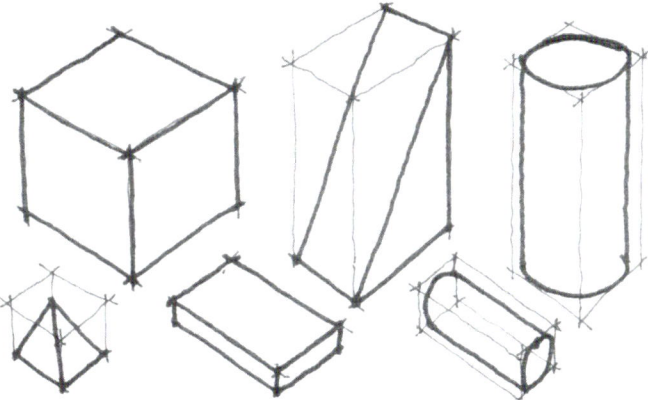

3-D Basic Shapes

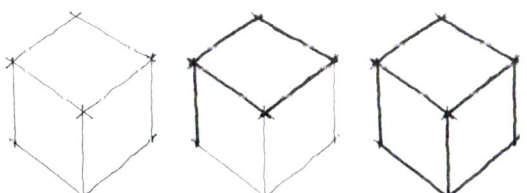

The process of sketching 3-D basic shapes: shape 1

The process of sketching 3-D basic shapes: shape 2

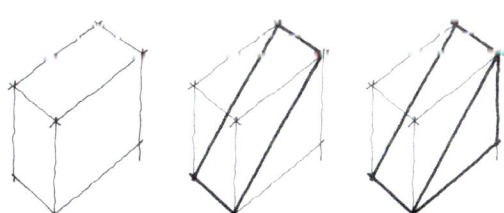

The process of sketching 3-D basic shapes: shape 3

3.9 SKETCHING 3-D COMPLEX SHAPES

The skill of sketching 3-D complex shapes is pivotal to create excellent sketches. The understanding and the use of the right techniques will certainly help in producing a high quality sketch. At this seventh stage an artist or designer is required to imagine each surface of the 3-D shape vividly using mental power. This process may seem difficult but once provided with a good understanding and with the right practice following the given concept, you will definitely be successful.

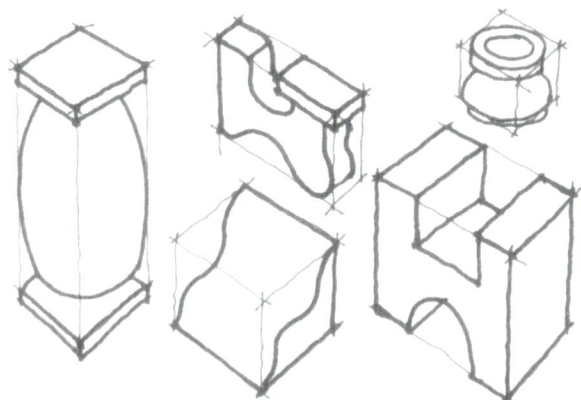

3-D complex shapes

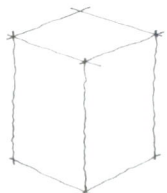 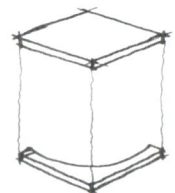 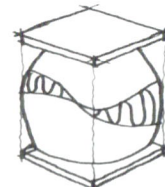

The process of sketching 3-D complex shapes: figure 1

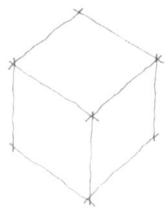  

The process of sketching 3-D complex shapes: figure 2

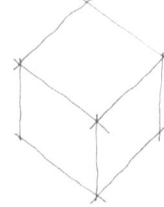 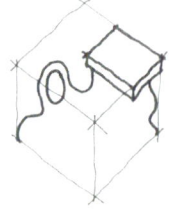 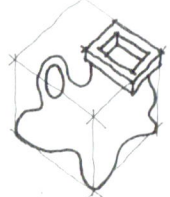

The process of sketching 3-D complex shapes: figure 3

34 BASIC SKILLS

3.10 SKETCHING 3-D BASIC OBJECTS

Sketching 3-D basic shapes is the next stage that needs to be done to ensure the skill of sketching is continuously sharpened for the next higher levels. To sketch the basic objects in 3-D, it is necessary to understand each object to be sketched begins from an 'imaginary box'. This box will be the guideline for the artist or designer to realise his or her imagination. This 'imaginary box' concept is the foundation and the stem to most effective sketching techniques and easily understood especially for sketching something based on mental picture.

Tip: Always remember the 'imaginary box'

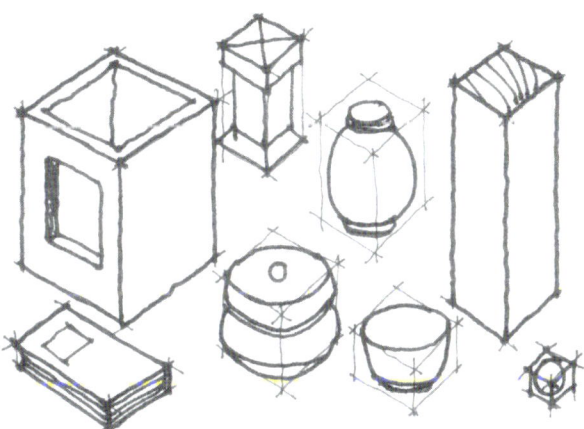

Example of objects created from an 'imaginary box"

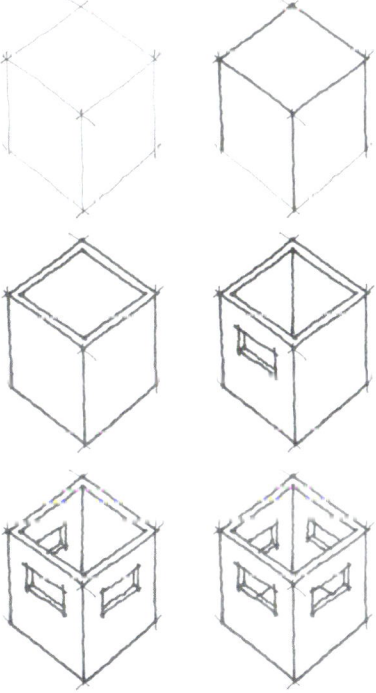

The process of sketching basic objects : 1 box

BASIC SKILLS 35

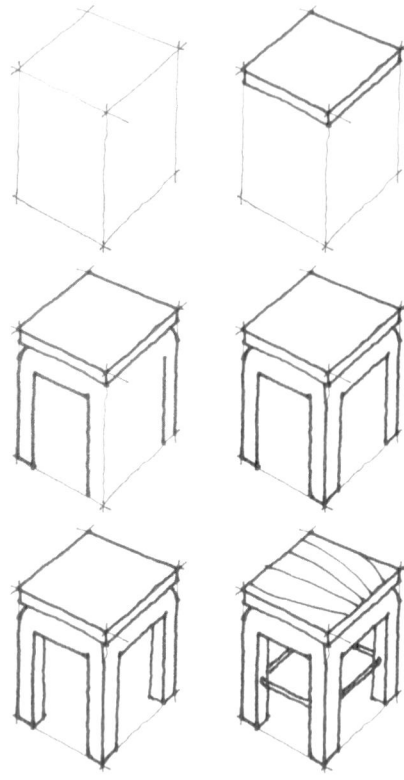

The process of sketching basic objects : 2 Chair

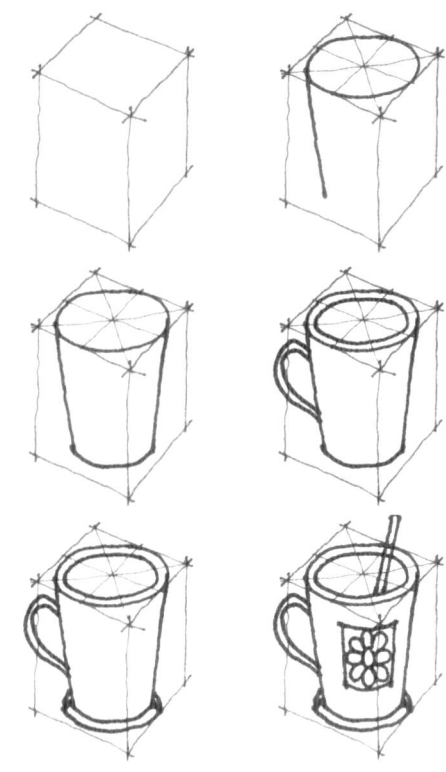

The process of sketching basic objects : 4 Glass

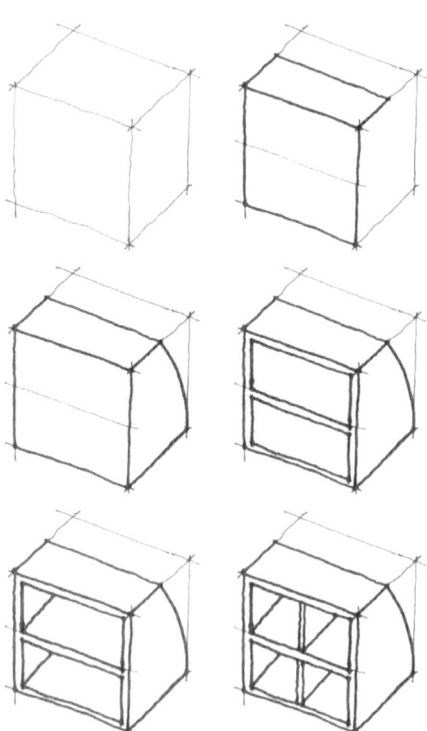

The process of sketching basic objects : 2 Bookshelf

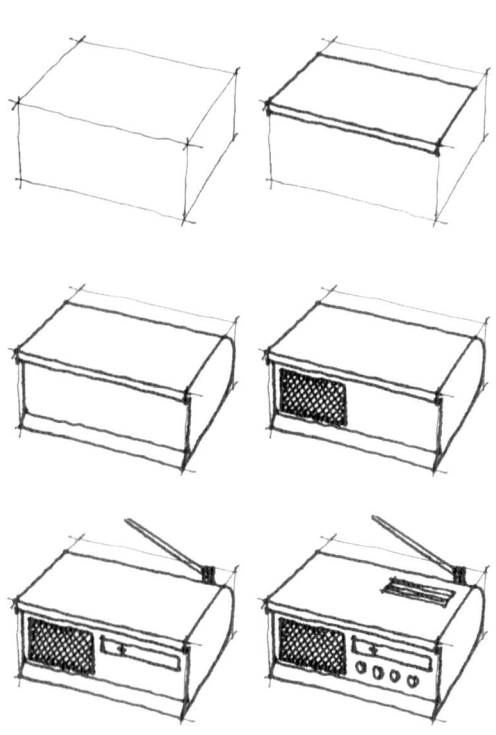

The process of sketching basic objects: 3 Radio

36 BASIC SKILLS

3.11 SKETCHING 3-D COMPLEX OBJECTS

Sketching quality 3-D objects is the goal of every artist or designer because it is the beginning of accomplishment for the next levels. The 'imaginary box' technique is still being used but requires more focus from the mind to ensure the sketches is of high quality. The mind focus is requisite in order to imagine the status of the object and its surface in 3-D shape with the intention that the process of sketching on the sketch sheet could be done perfectly well.

Tip: Always remember the 'imaginary box'

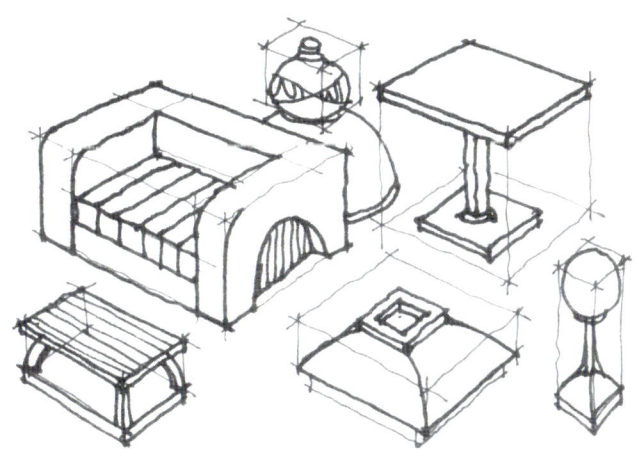

Example of complex objects from a 'box'

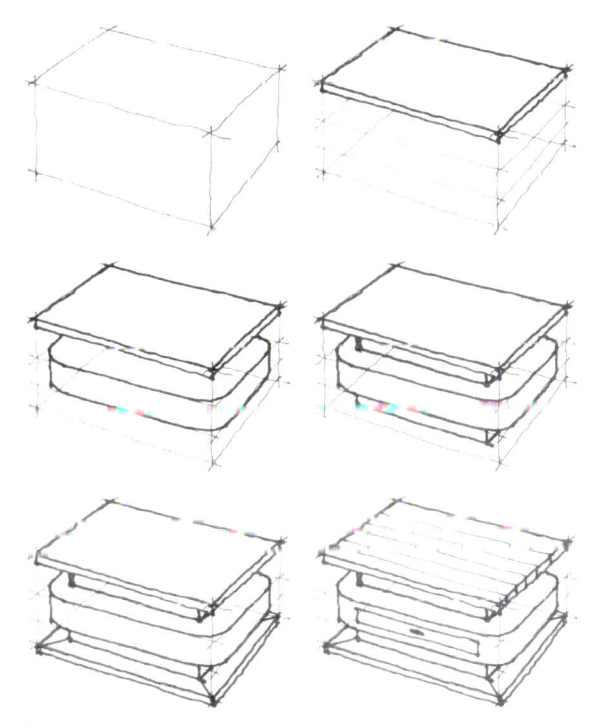

The process of sketching complex objects: table

BASIC SKILLS 37

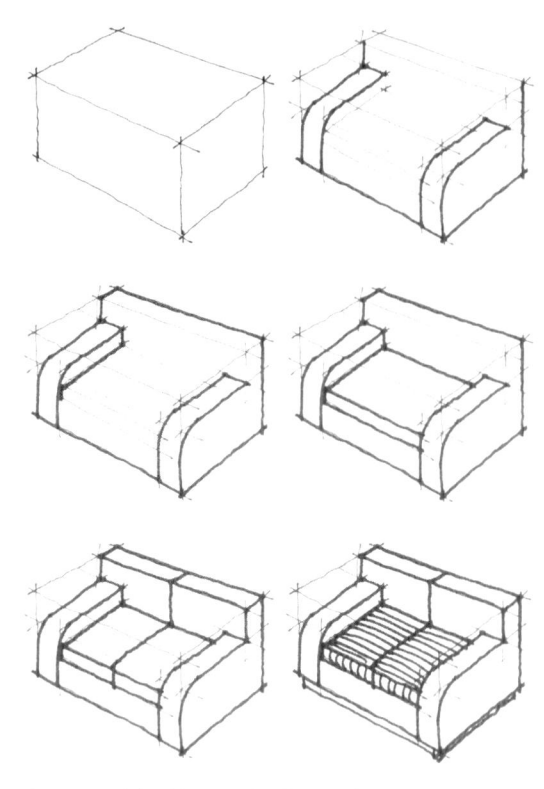

The process of sketching complex objects: sofa

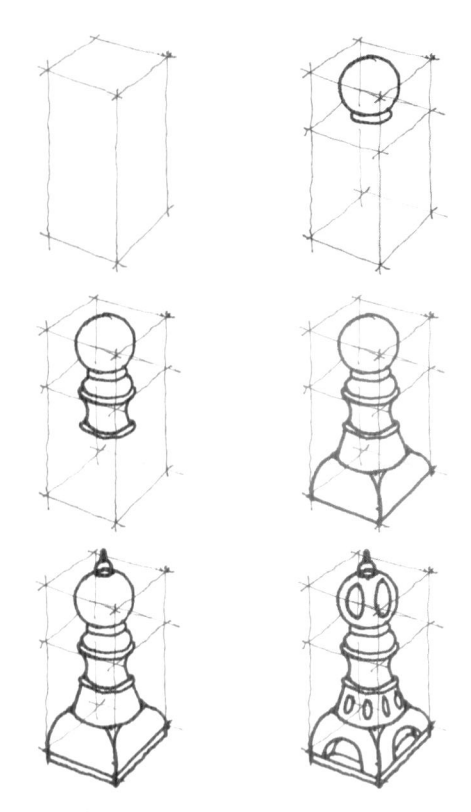

The process of sketching complex objects: 3 chess

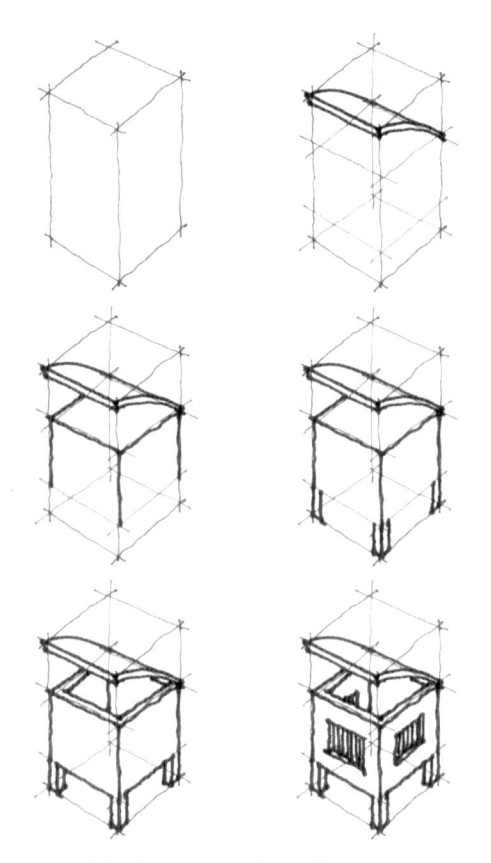

The process of sketching complex objects: safe box

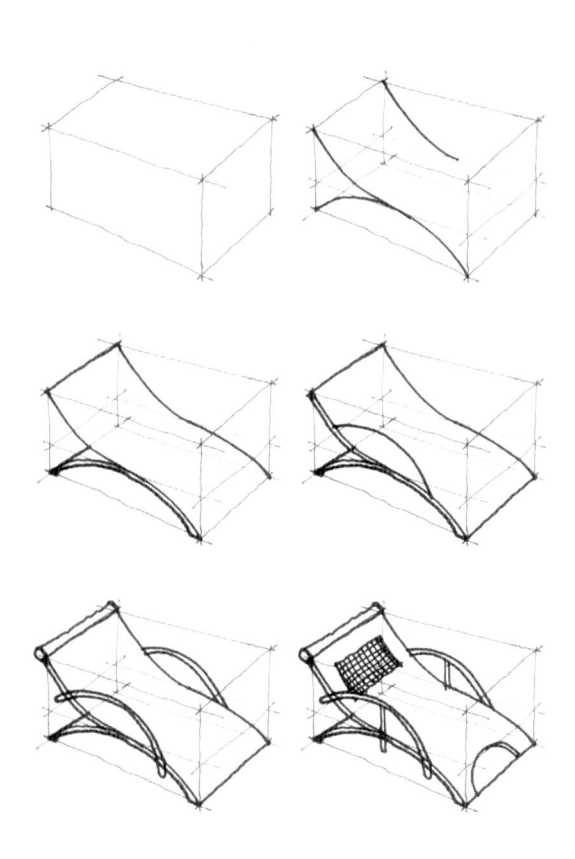

The process of sketching complex objects: resting chair

38　BASIC SKILLS

3.12 SKETCHING 2-D FIGURES

The next level that requires to be polished is the technique of sketching 2-D figures. The basic skill of sketching figures is important for an artist or designer to assist him or her in better understanding of the space sketched. In this context, an artist or designer sketching a figure in a detailed and complete shape makes himself or herself skillful in sketching the figures roughly and sufficiently to convey a message on the sketch composition itself.

2 D figures movement concept drawn by Mohamed Irwan Mohamad Ishak.

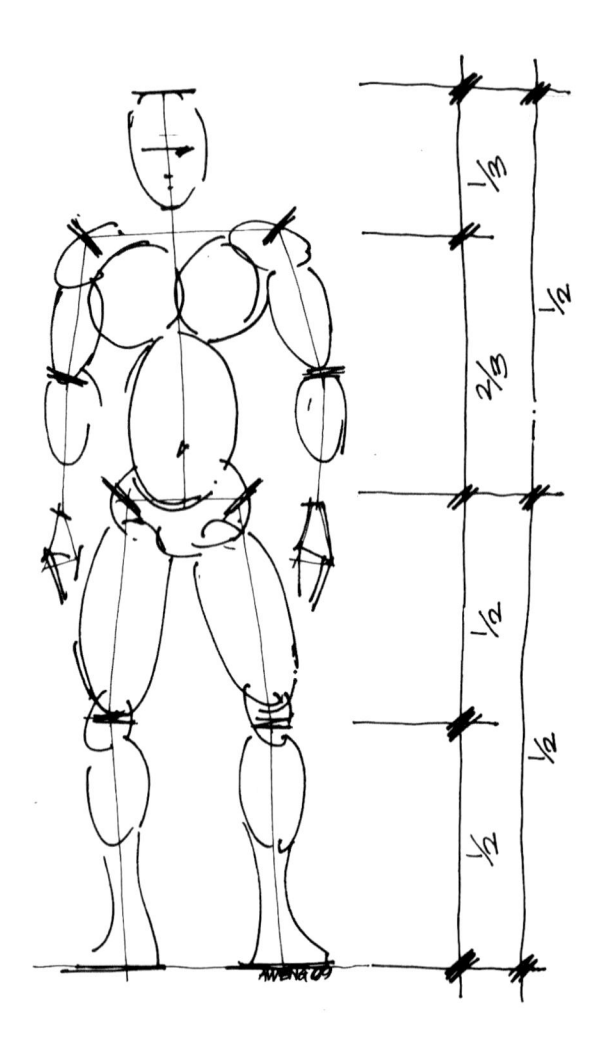

2-D figures concept drawn by Mohamed Irwan Mohamad Ishak.

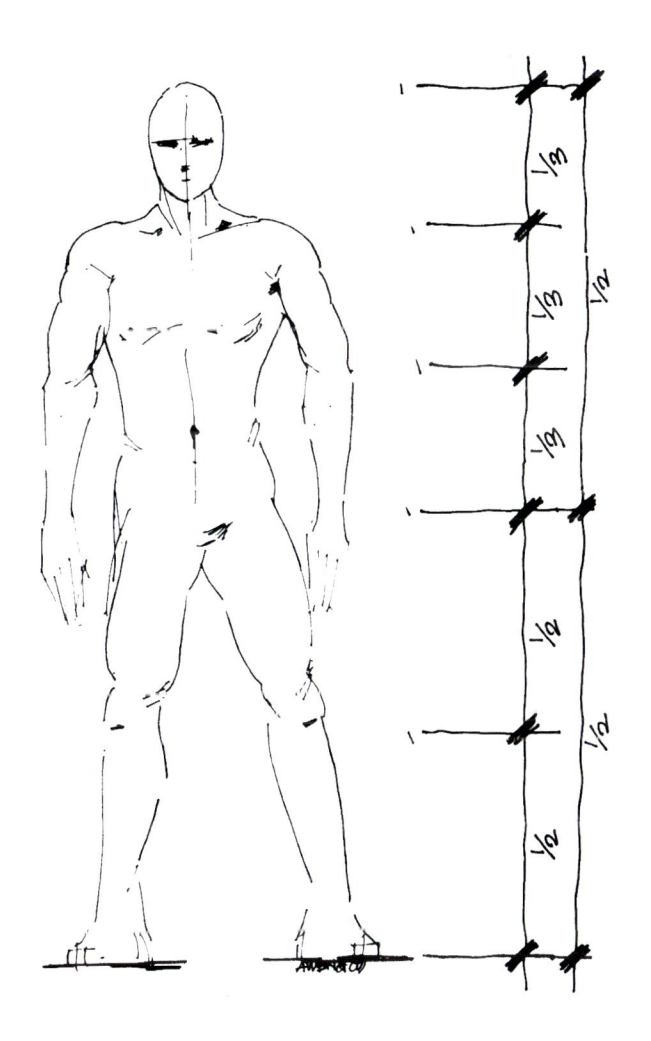

2-D figures concept drawn by Mohamed Irwan Mohamad Ishak.

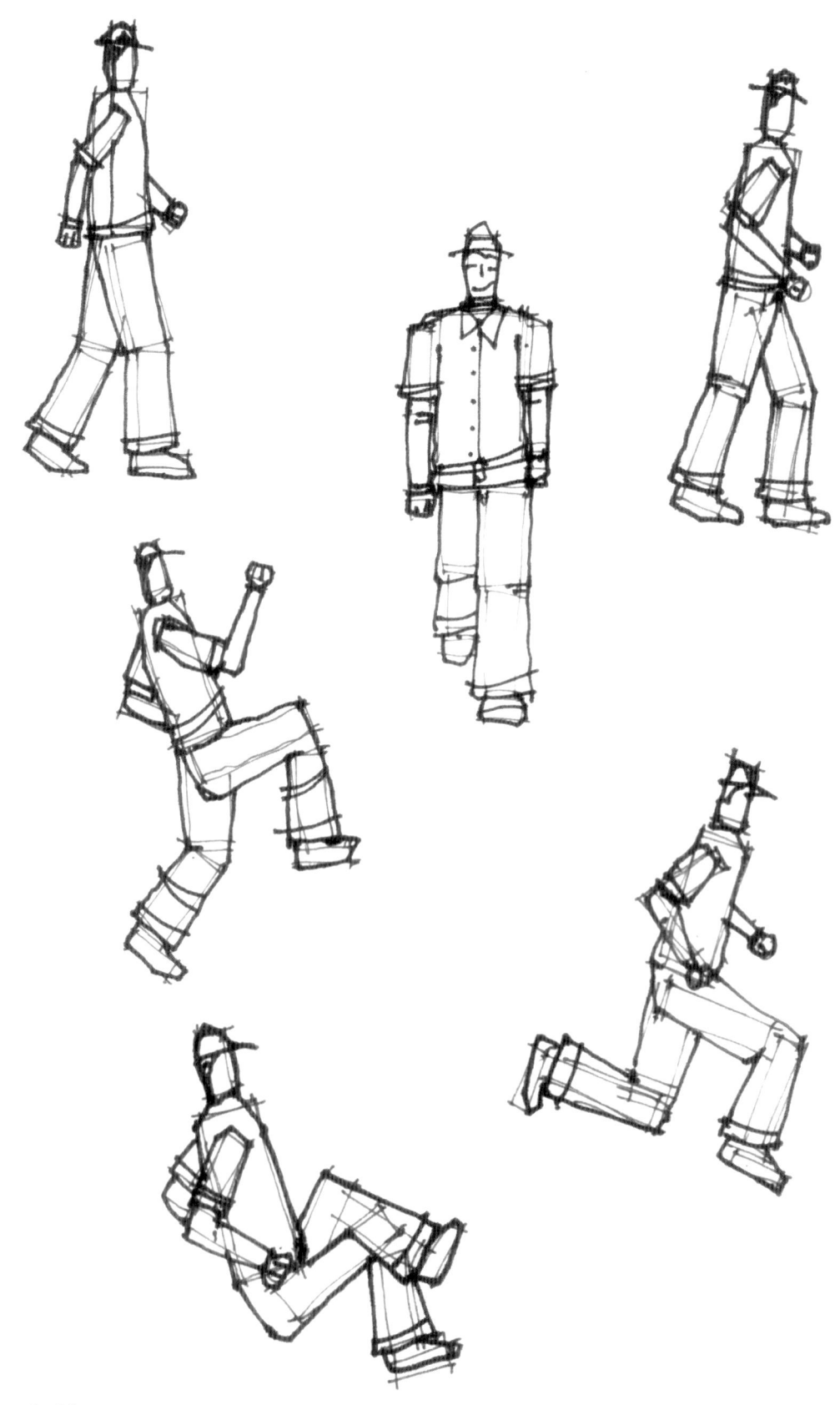

The shape of 2-D figures.

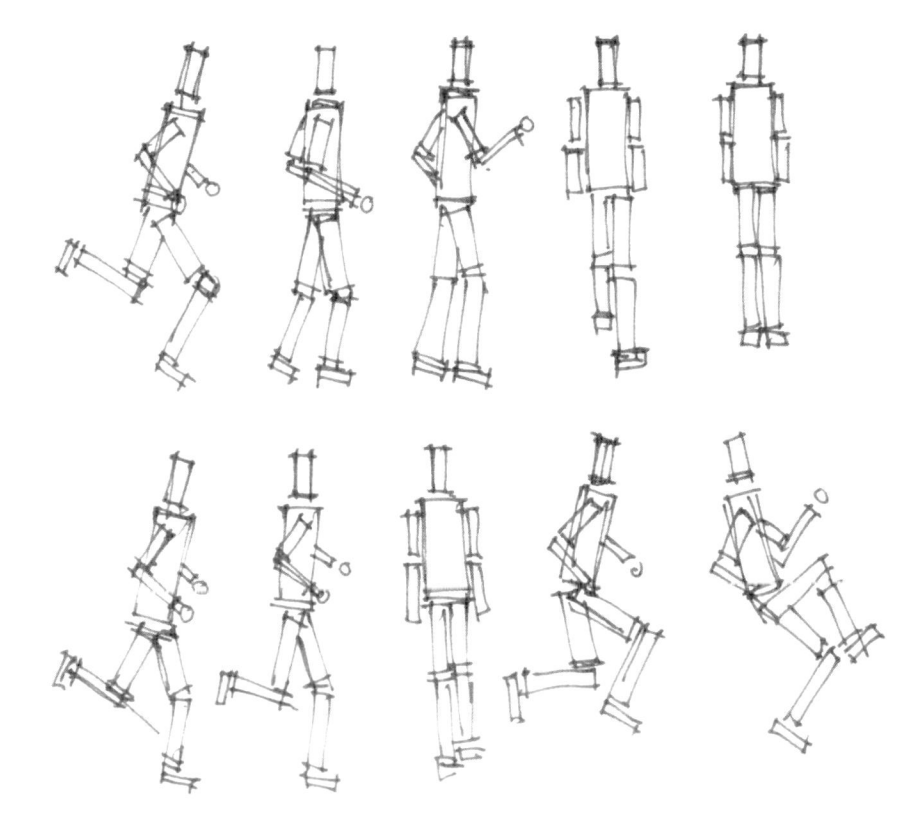

The shapes of basic figures using an 'imaginary box'.

The shapes of 2-D figures

BASIC SKILLS 43

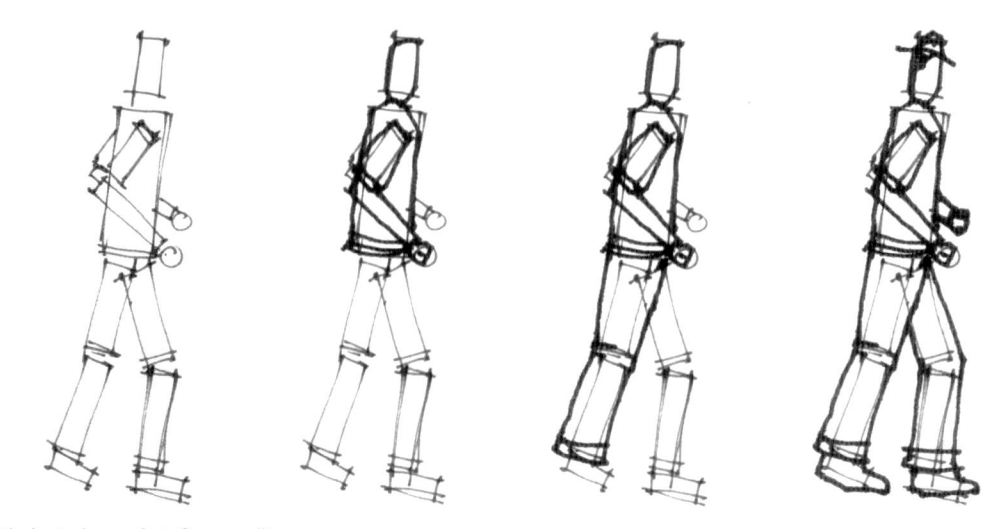

The basic shapes of 2-D figures walking

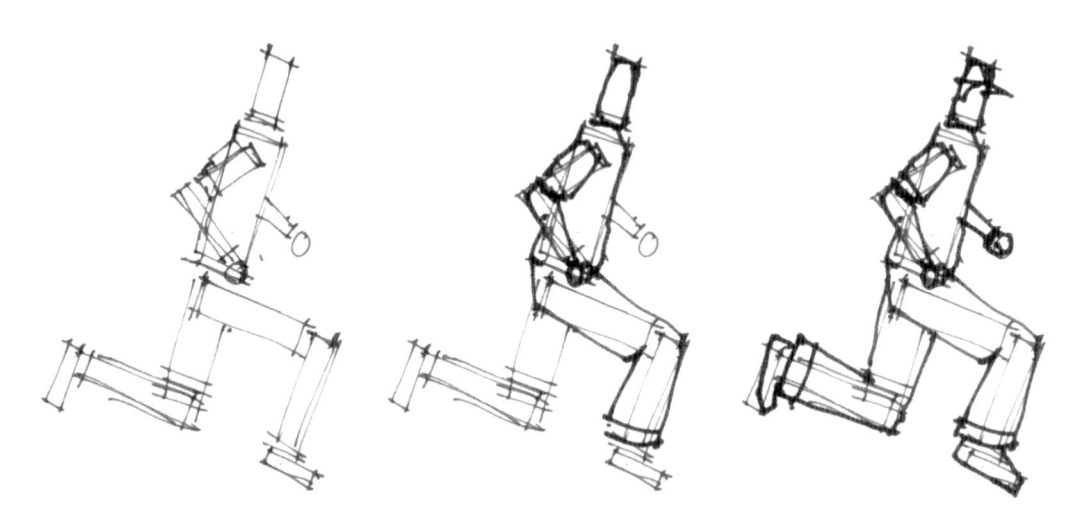

The basic shapes of 2-D figures running

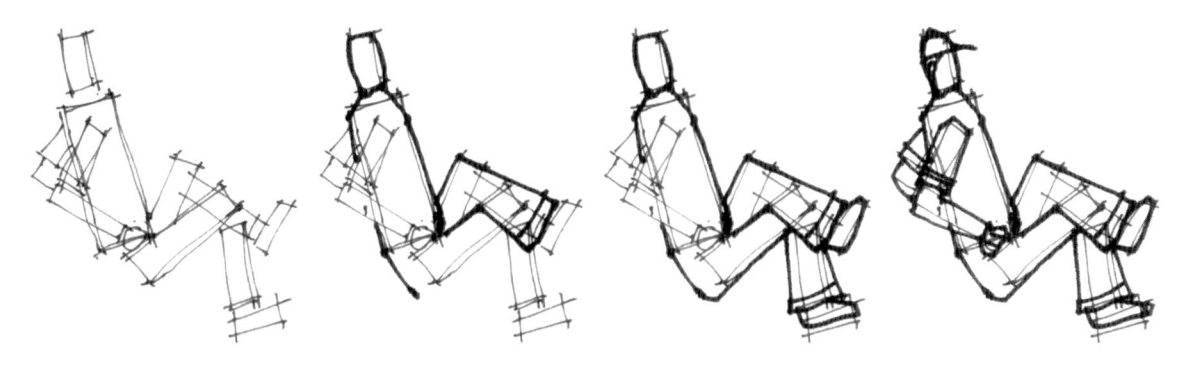

The basic shapes of 2-D figures sitting

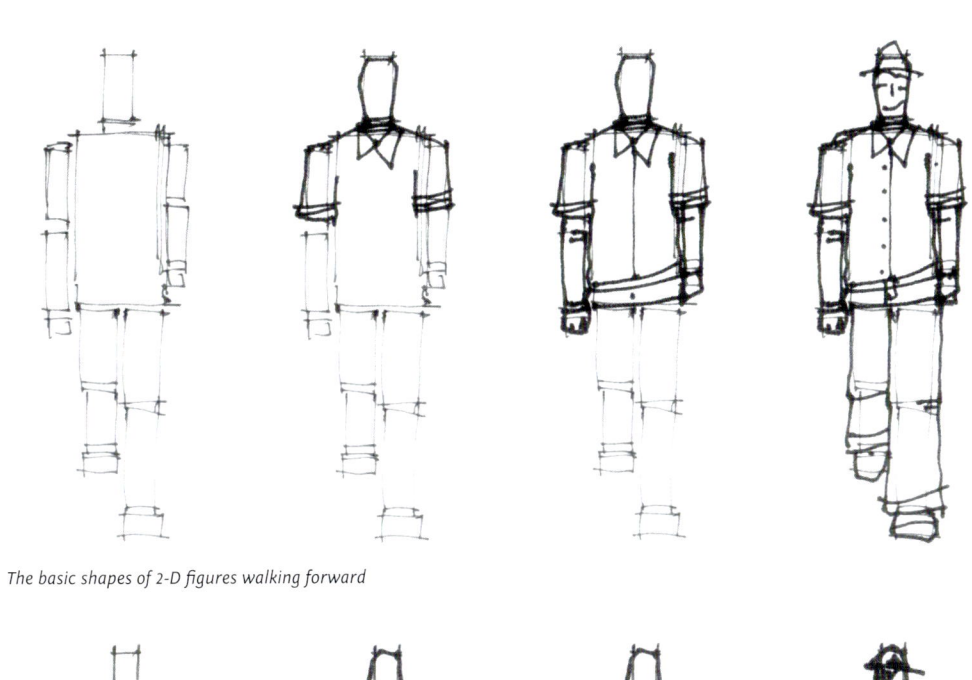

The basic shapes of 2-D figures walking forward

The basic shapes of 2-D figures slow walk

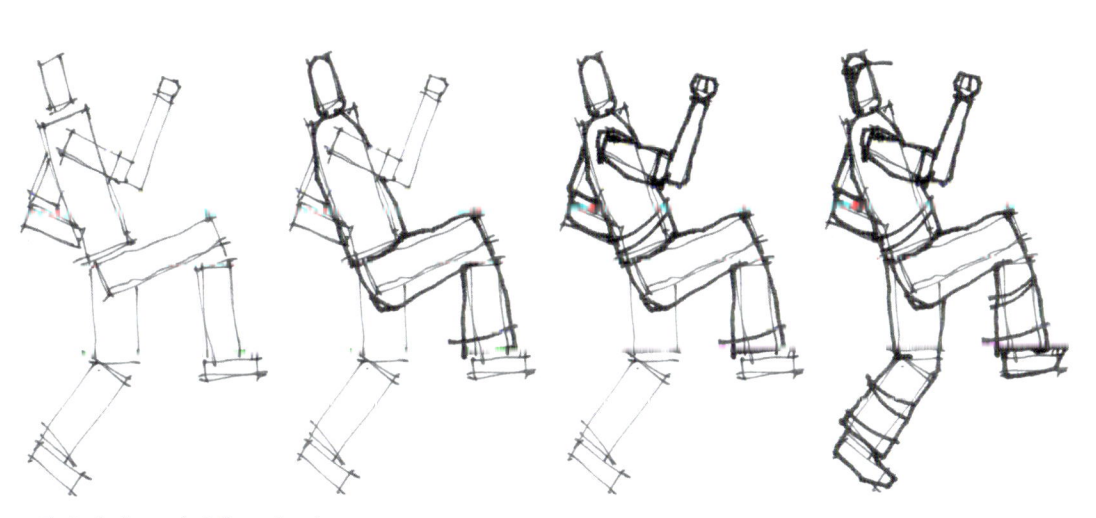

The basic shapes of 2-D figures jumping

BASIC SKILLS 45

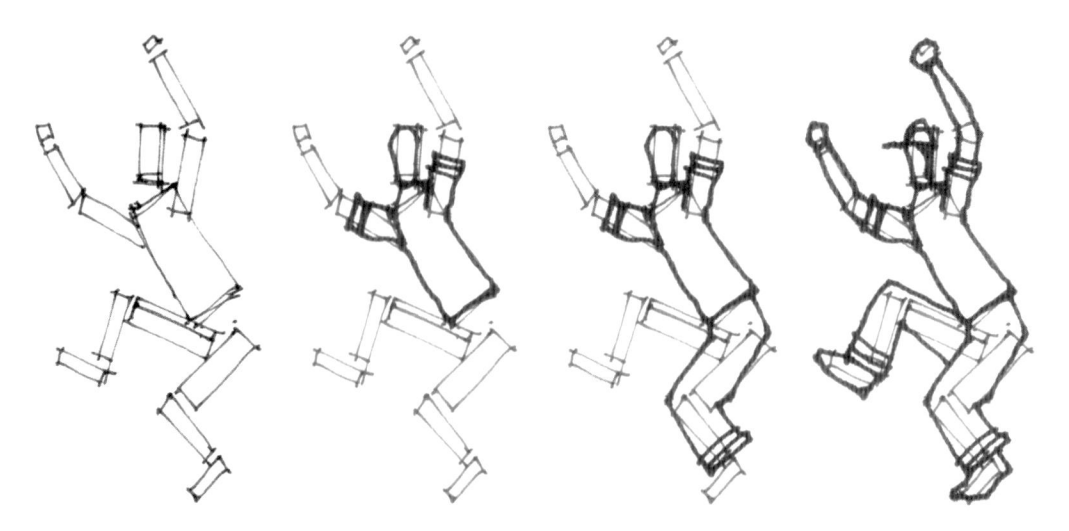

The basic shapes of 2-D figures acting 1

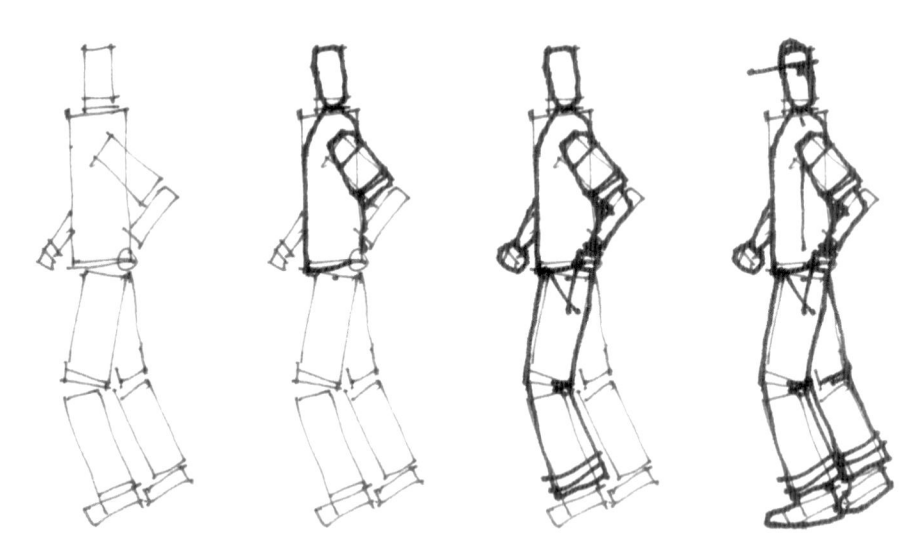

The basic shapes of 2-D figures acting 2

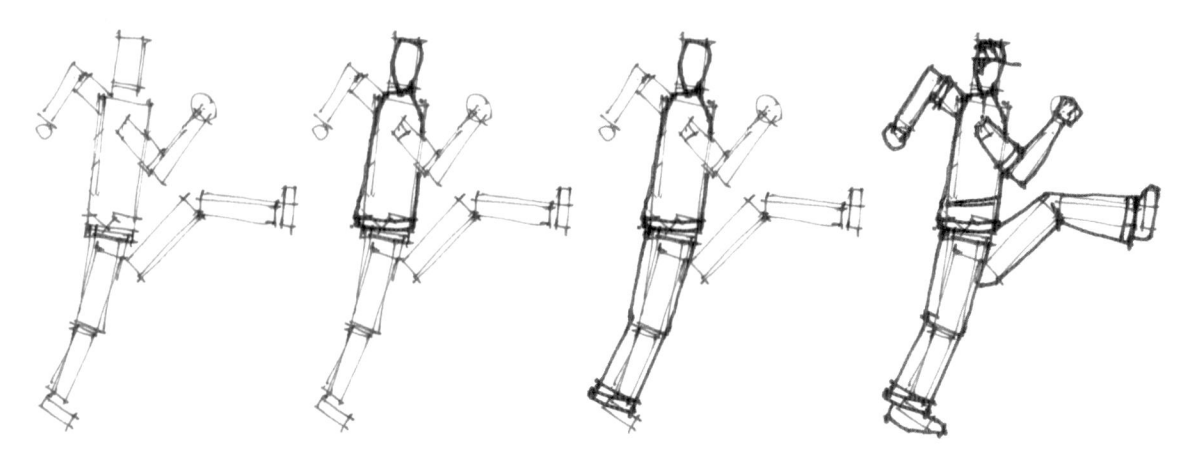

The basic shapes of 2-D figures acting 3

BASIC SKILLS

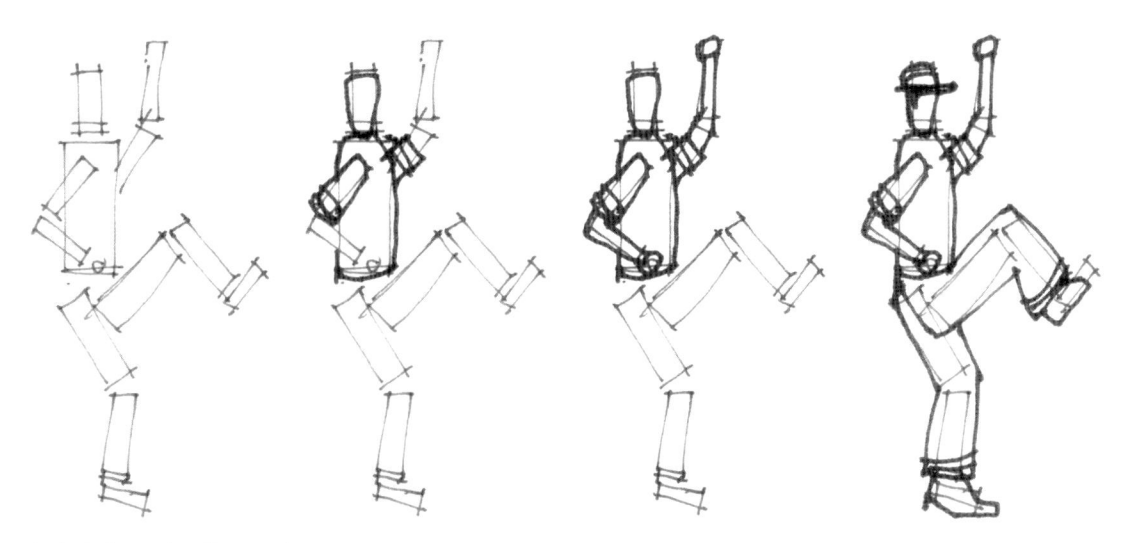

The basic shapes of 2-D figures acting 4

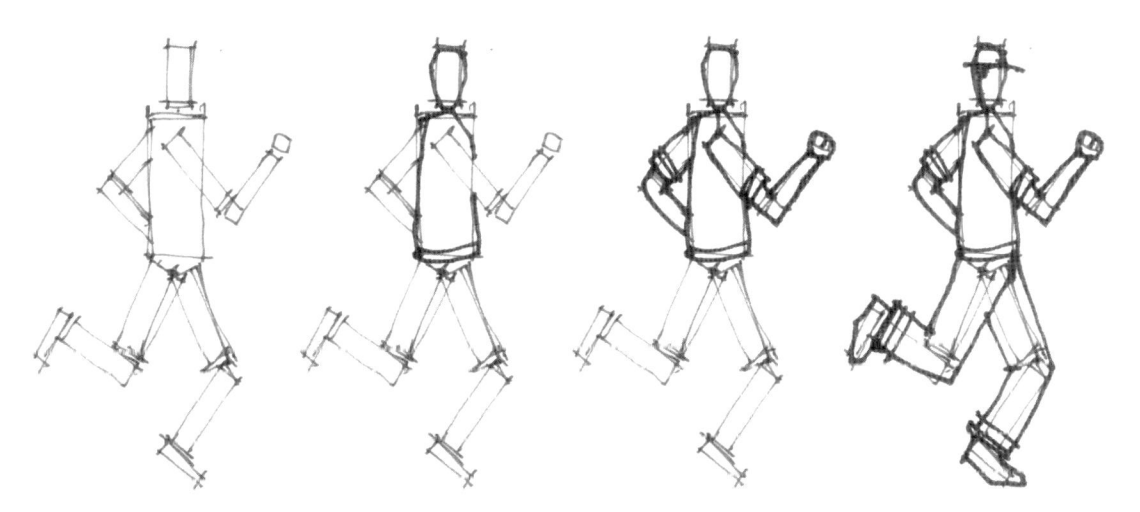

The basic shapes of 2-D figures acting 5

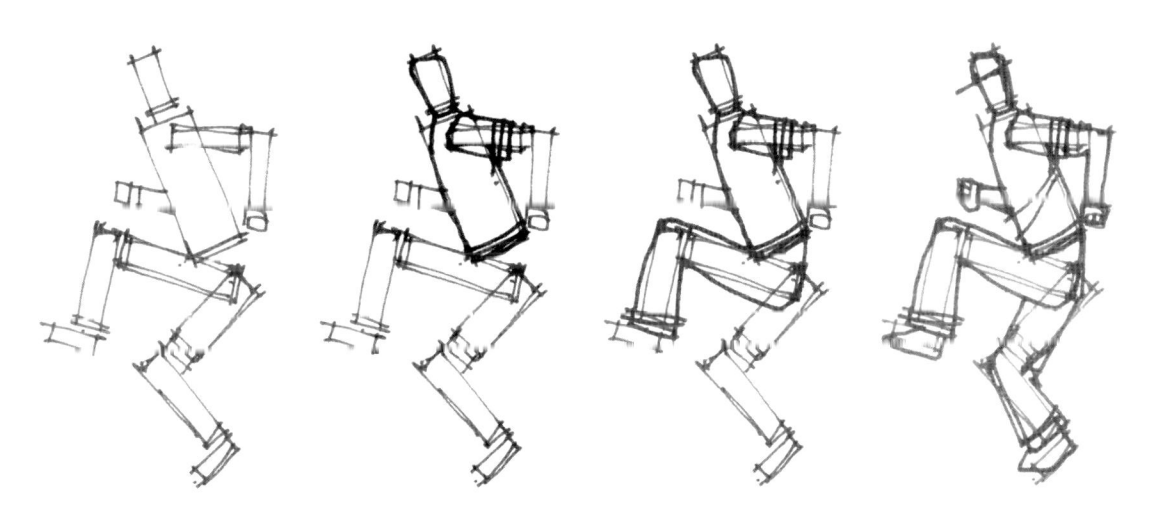

The basic shapes of 2-D figures acting 6

BASIC SKILLS 47

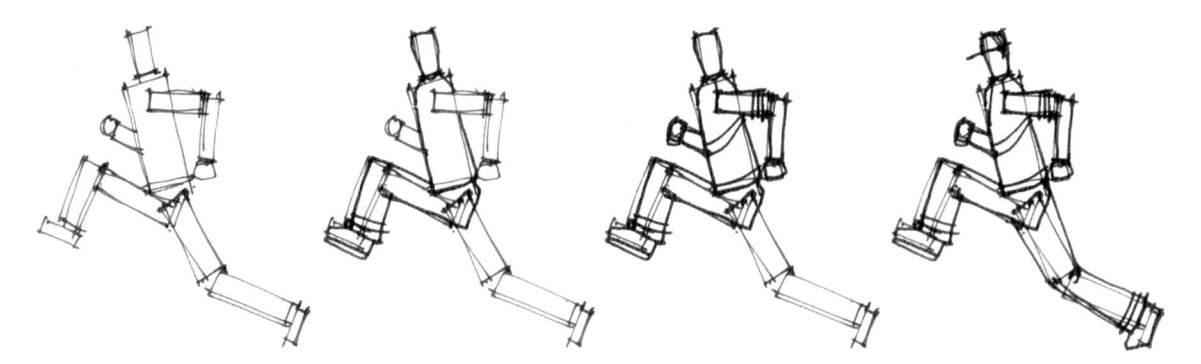

The basic shapes of 2-D figures acting 7

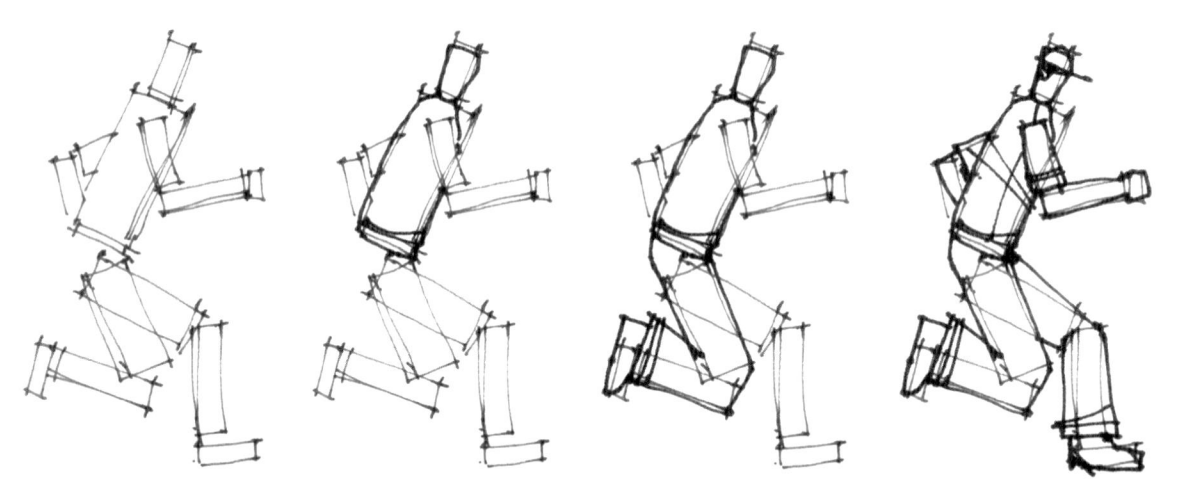

The basic shapes of 2-D figures acting 8

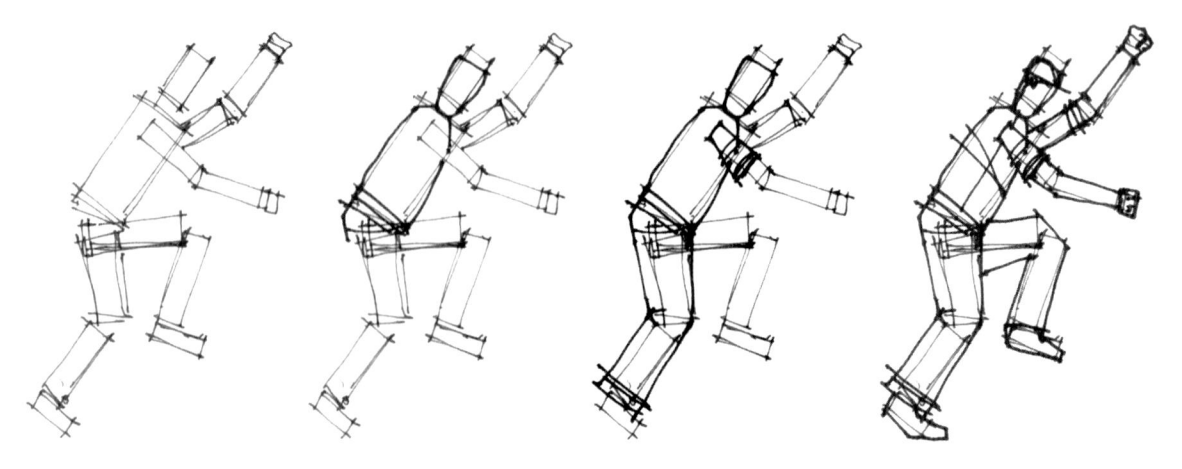

The basic shapes of 2-D figures acting 9

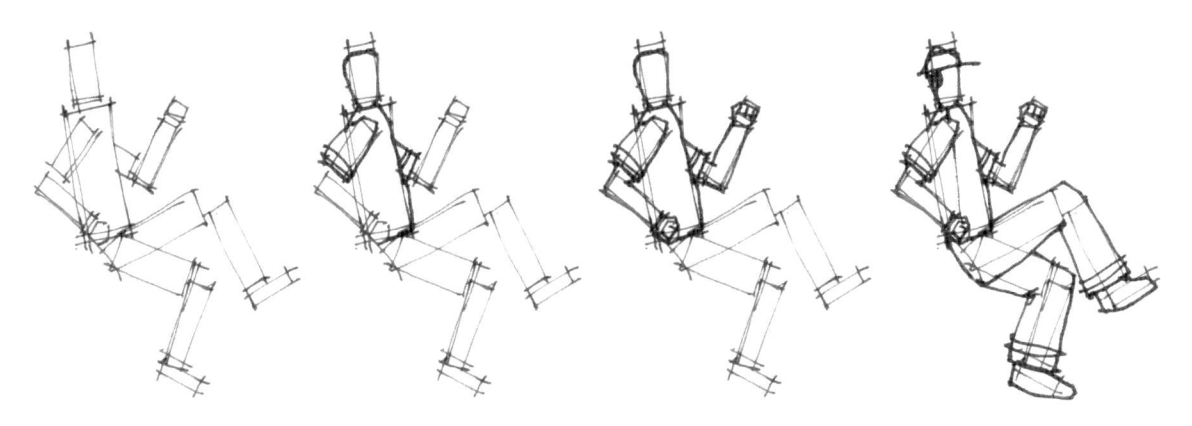

The basic shapes of 2-D figures acting 10

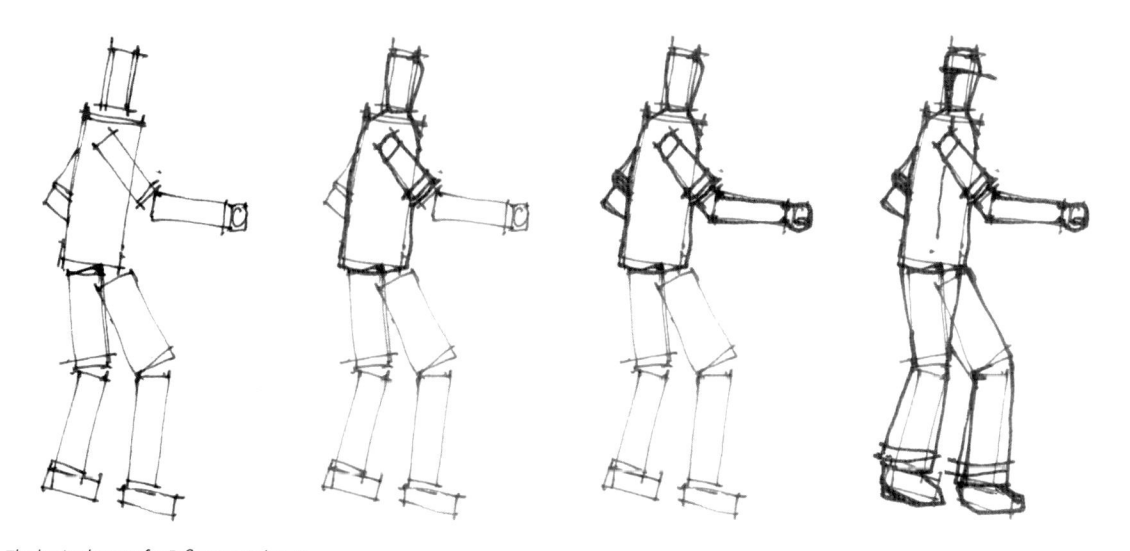

The basic shapes of 2-D figures acting 11

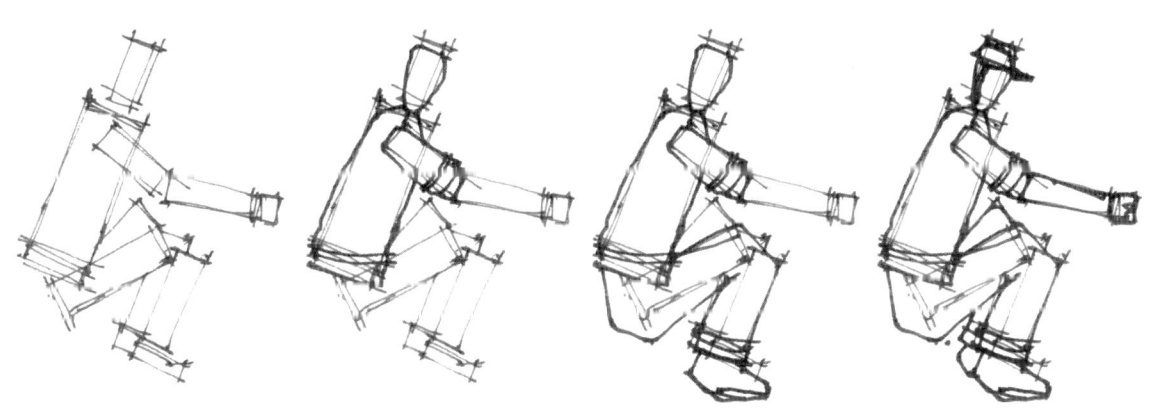

The basic shapes of 2-D figures acting 12

BASIC SKILLS 49

3.13 SKETCHING 3-D FIGURES

The skill of sketching figures in 3-D shapes will definitely assist the artist or designer to be more confident with sketches to be created, provided they are associated with figures. Sketching figures in 3-D shapes demands a vivid focus of the mind to be able to understand the movements and the surface of organs involved. The focus is necessary to ensure that the sketch to be produced is perfect and of superb quality. The sketching techniques of 3-D figures use the 'imaginary box' as the fundamental guideline in creating fabulous figures.

3-D figures concept drawn by Mohamed Irwan Mohamad Ishak.

3-D figures concept drawn by Mohamed Irwan Mohamad Ishak.

50   BASIC SKILLS

3-D figures

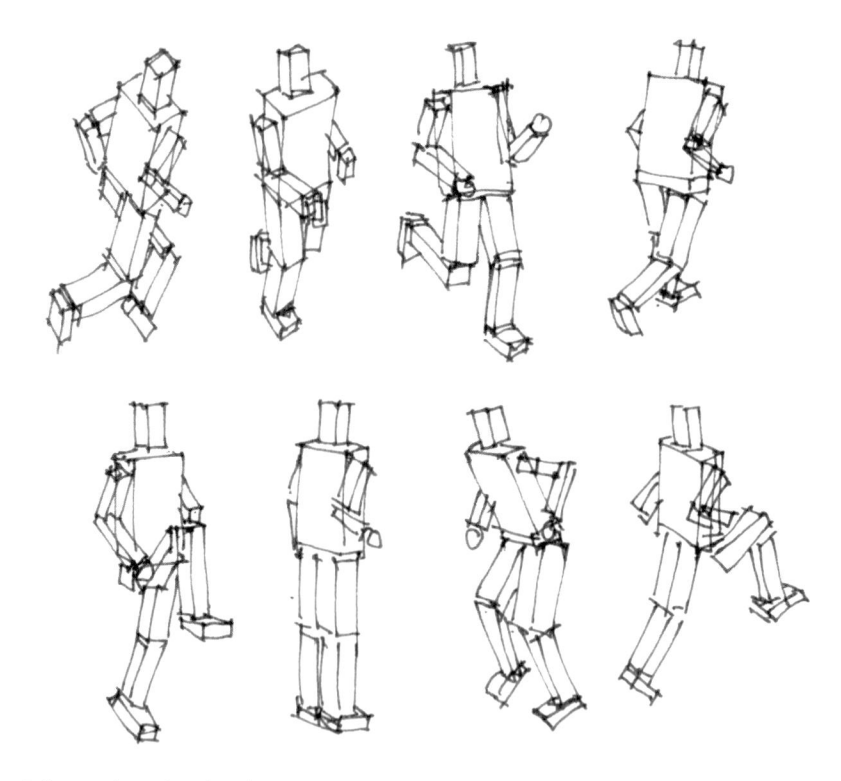

3-D figures using an 'imaginary box'

3-D figures

3-D figures: Acting 1

3-D figures: Acting 2

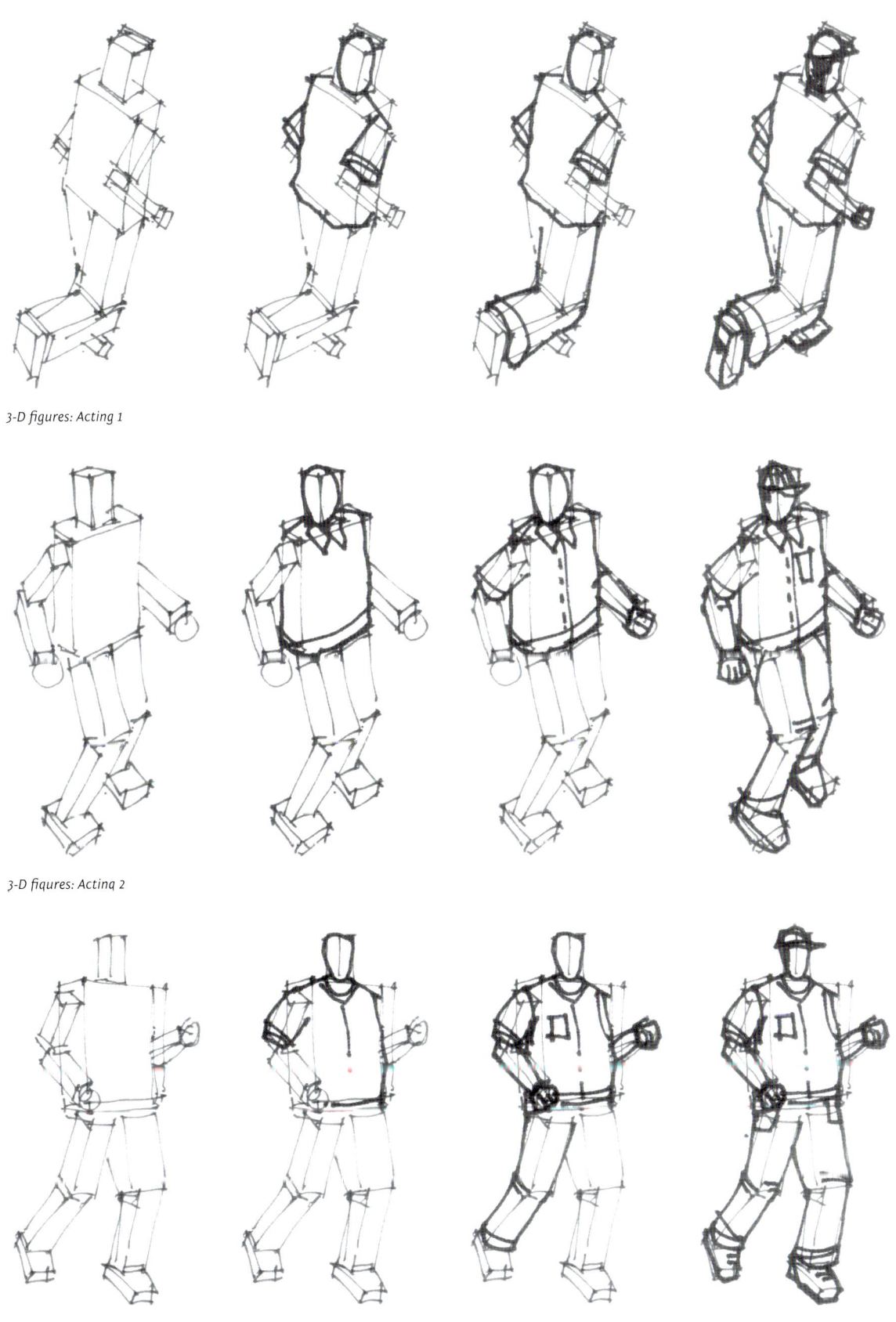

3-D figures: Acting 3

BASIC SKILLS 53

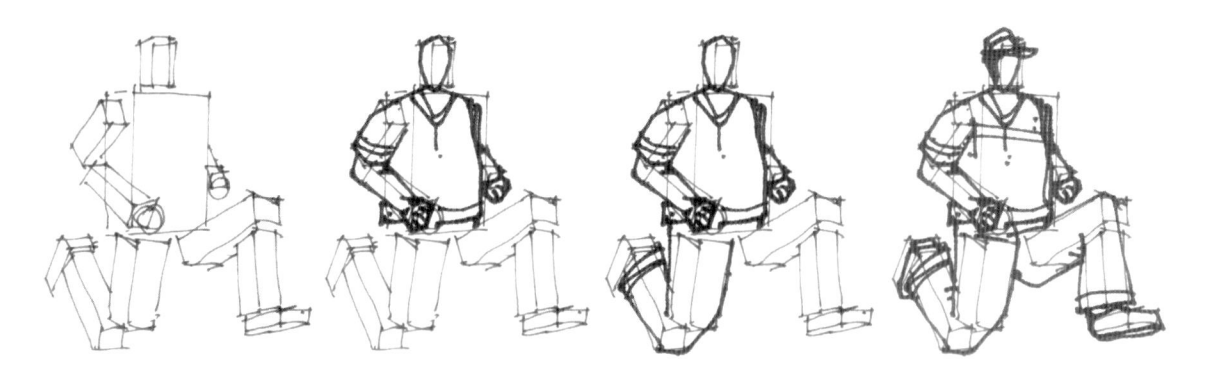

3-D figures: Acting 4

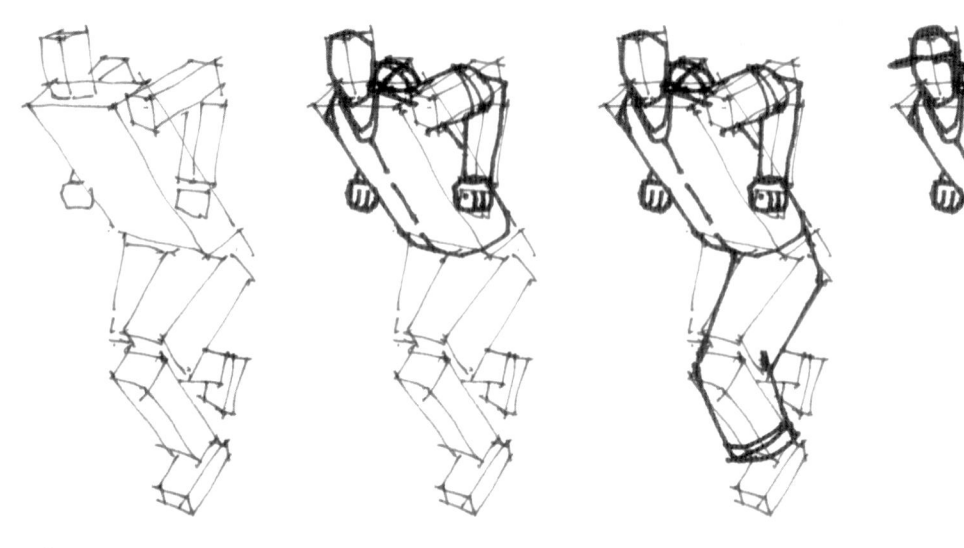

3-D figures: Acting 5

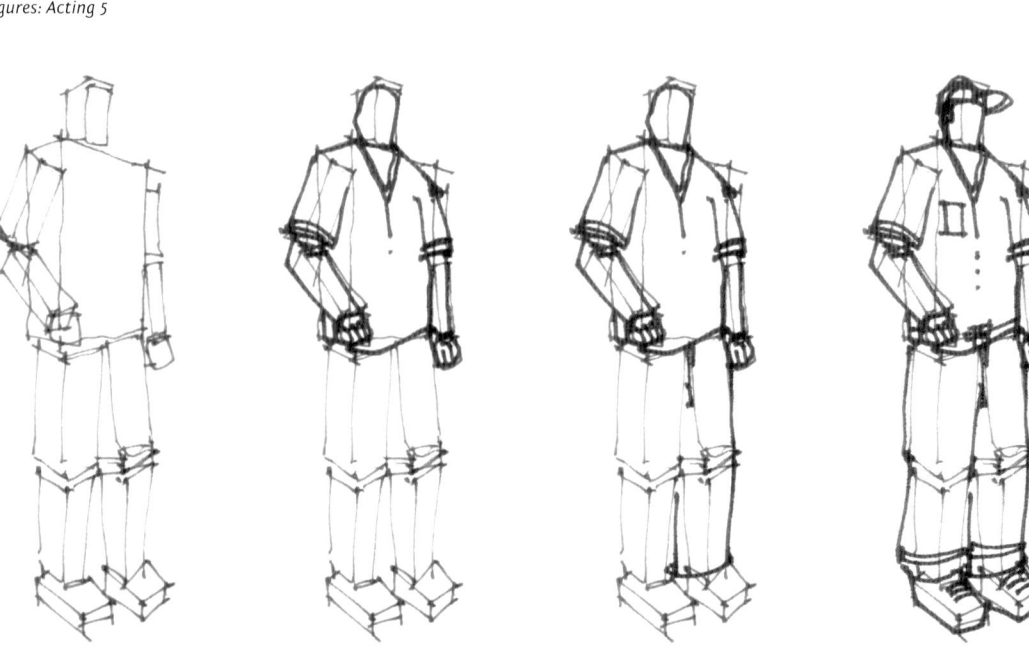

3-D figures: Acting 6

3-D figures: Acting 7

3-D figures: Acting 8

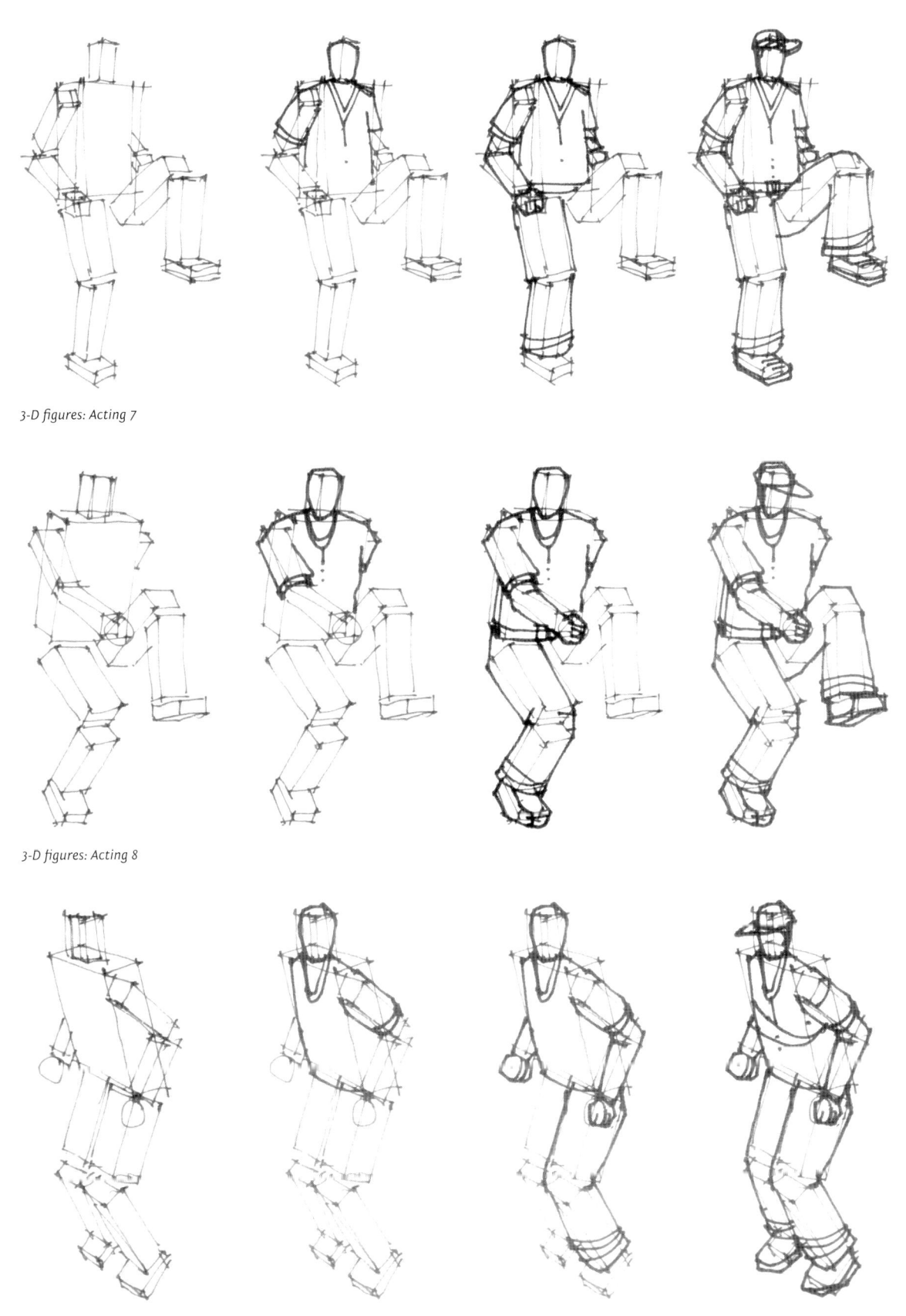

3-D figures: Acting 9

BASIC SKILLS 55

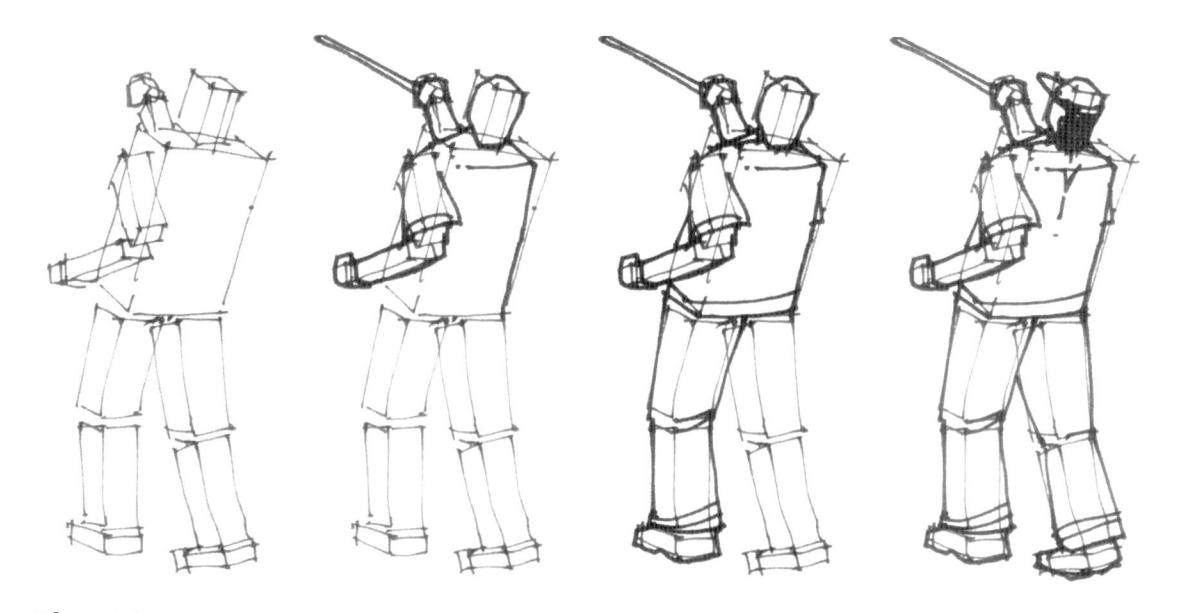

3-D figures: Acting 10

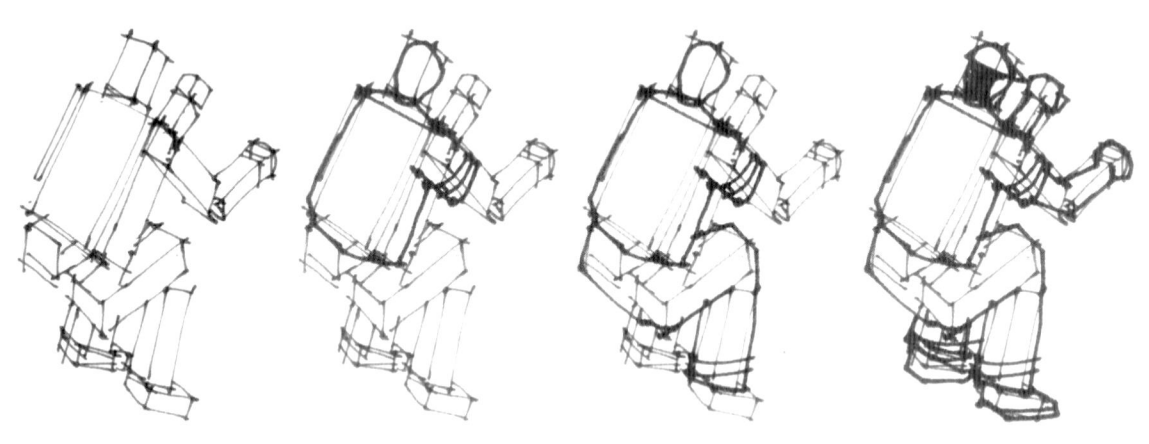

3-D figures: Acting 11

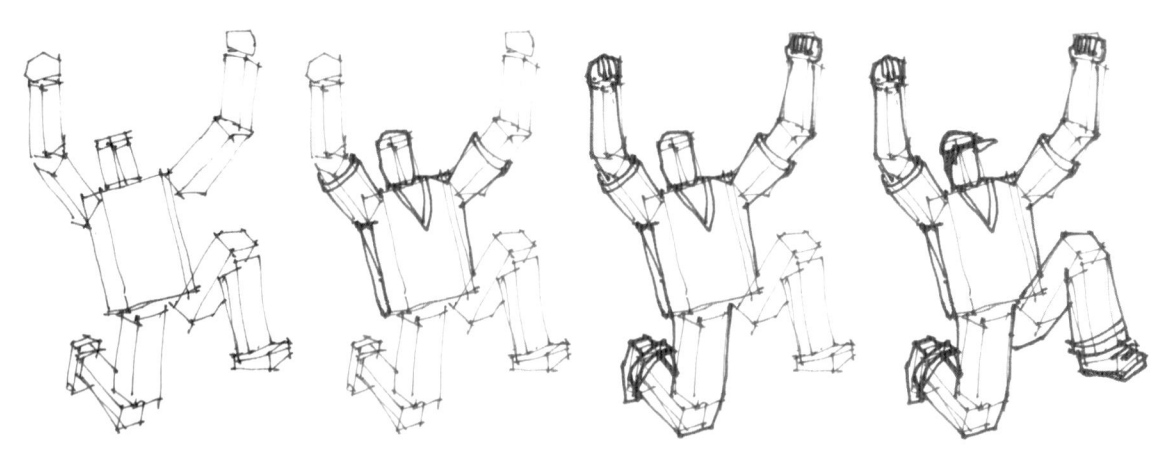

3-D figures: Acting 12

3-D figures: Acting 13

3-D figures: Acting 14

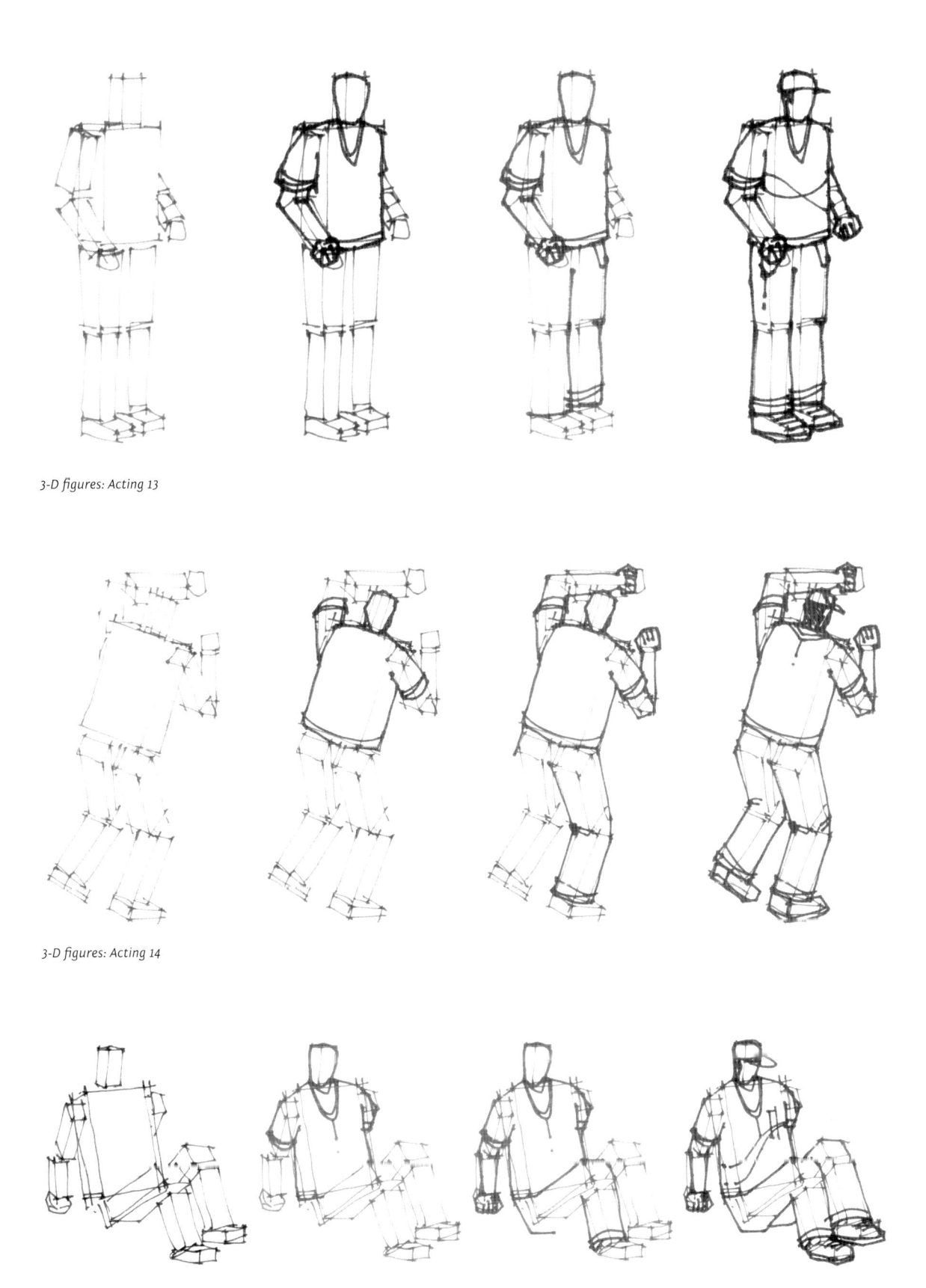

3-D figures: Acting 15

BASIC SKILLS 57

3-D figures: Acting 16

3-D figures: Acting 17

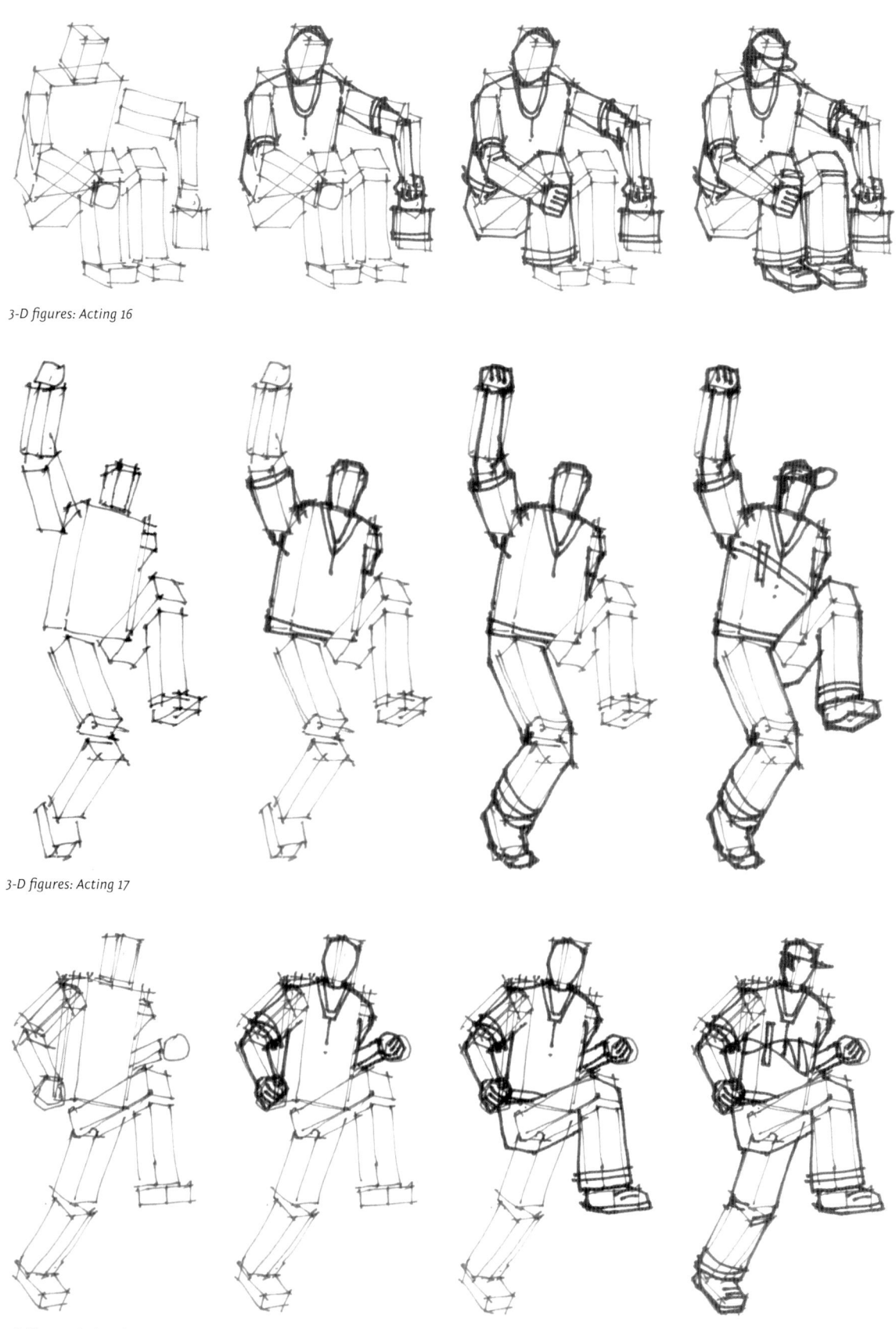

3-D figures: Acting 18

58 BASIC SKILLS

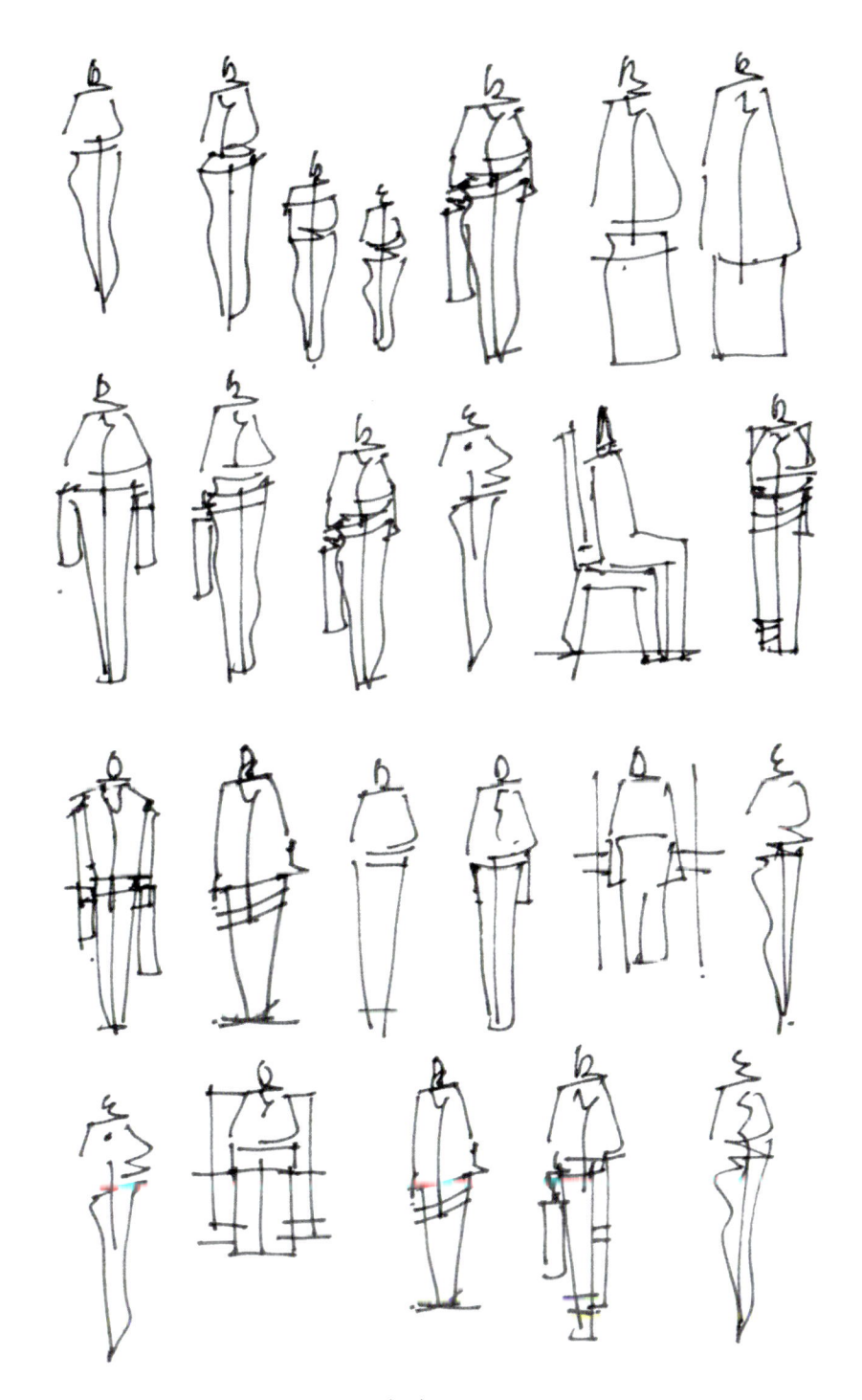

Example of fast figure can be used in 2-D or 3-D sketches.

BASIC SKILLS 59

4.0 SKETCH COMPOSITION

4.1 THE CONCEPT OF LINES IN SKETCHING

Lines are significant elements in any sketch. It derives from dots which eventually become a stretch of a long line. Lines will influence the quality of a sketch created. The knowledge and skill about the concept of lines is pivotal where each type of line will give a different effect on a sketch.

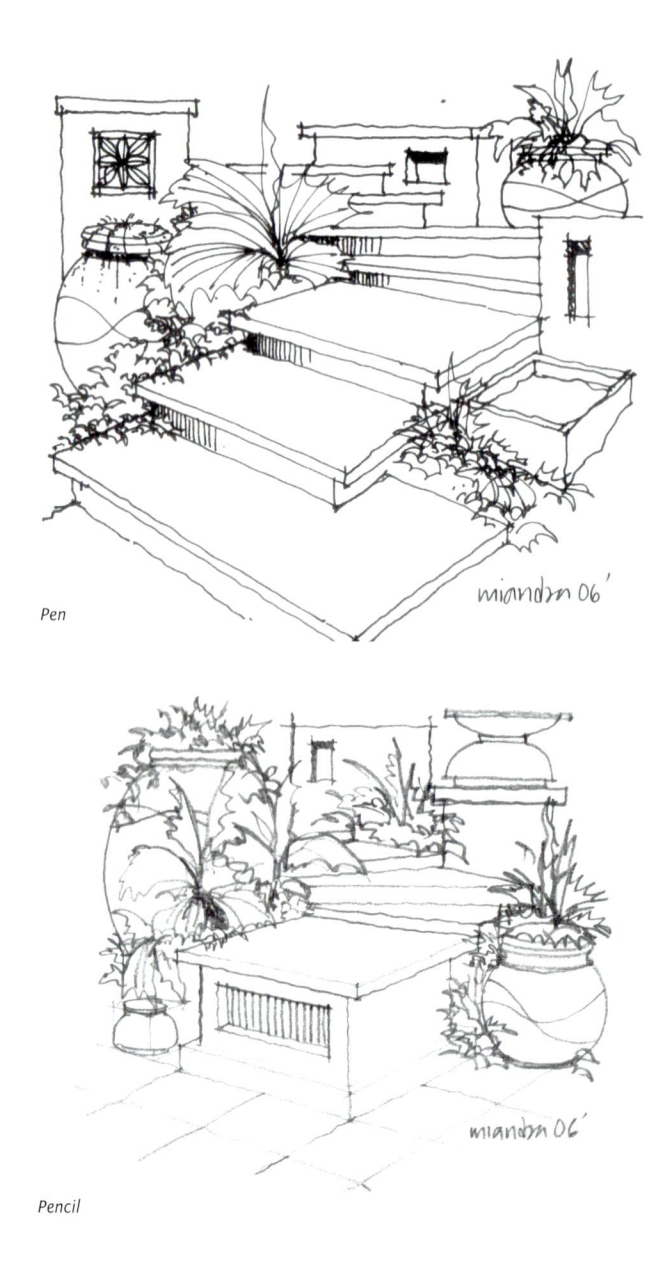

Pen

Pencil

Lines and 'mood' of sketches drawn using pencil and pen.

4.2 LINES USING PENCIL

The lines created using pencil have their own characteristics that need to be understood by an artist or designer. The nature of the lines are softer compared to the ones created using a pen. There are two grades of pencils which are the soft (HB to 9H) and the hard (B to 8B). The creating of a good quality pencil line could be done through the skill of controlling the pressure (weight) of pencil onto the sketch sheet. An artist or designer too needs to know how to combine different lines using different pressure in order to get an awesome sketch. Besides that, the way of holding a pencil and using the right type of sketch sheet too could influence the quality of sketches.

Sketch formed using 2B grade pencil

Sketch formed using 4B grade pencil

Sketch formed using 8B grade pencil

62 SKETCH COMPOSITION

Sketch formed using multiple grades of pencil and pressure.

A sketch formed using pencil charcoal with various pressures.

4.3 SKETCHING LINES USING A PEN

Knowledge and the skill of sketching lines using a pen is necessary because they have their own special characteristics depending on the type of pen, the thickness of the tip and the ink used. An artist or designer has to be smart in choosing the thickness of the pen tip to sketch because the 'mood' created by the different thickness of the lines are not the same.

A sketch using a pen with a tip of 0.2

SKETCH COMPOSITION 65

A sketch created using a pen with a tip of 0.4

A fast sketch created using a pen with a tip of 0.2

Sketch created using a combination of lines using pens with different thickness of tip.

SKETCH COMPOSITION 67

4.4 COMPOSITION IN SKETCHES

To be able to obtain an interesting composition, the understanding and skill in choosing an angle (desired angle) to sketch an object or composition is important. Choosing the right angle could help in creating a better sketch. The skill of choosing the desired angle could be practiced if the artist or designer is able to use his or her mental strength to elaborate the position of the object and understand the movements of the object surfaces. Study the examples given.

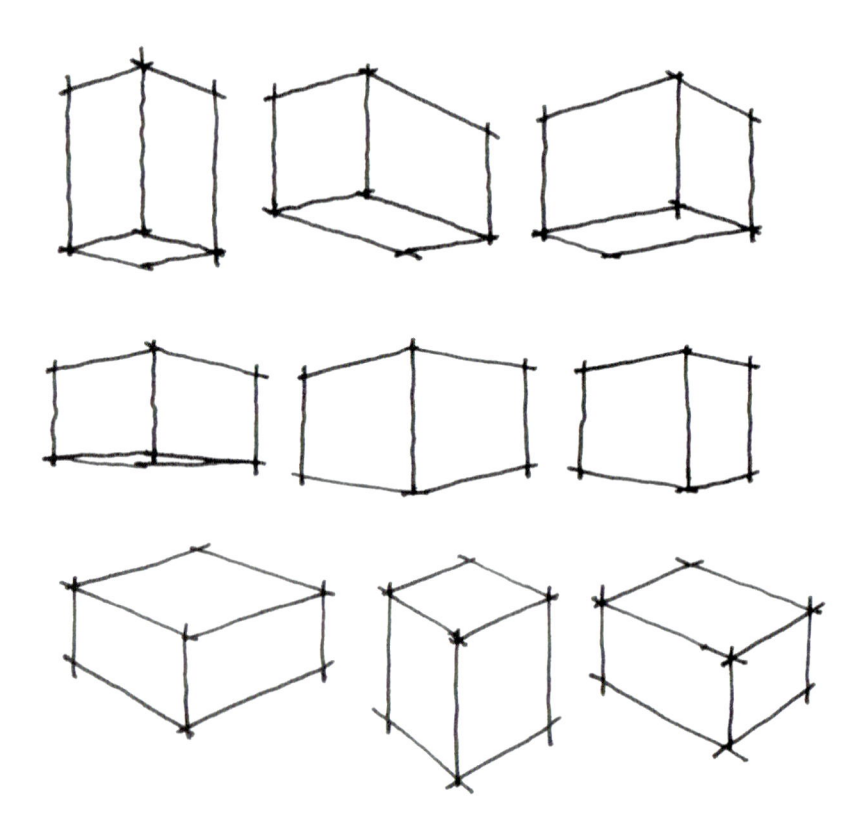

Basic shapes from different perspectives and positions. The angle of the surface changes when the view towards the object changes.

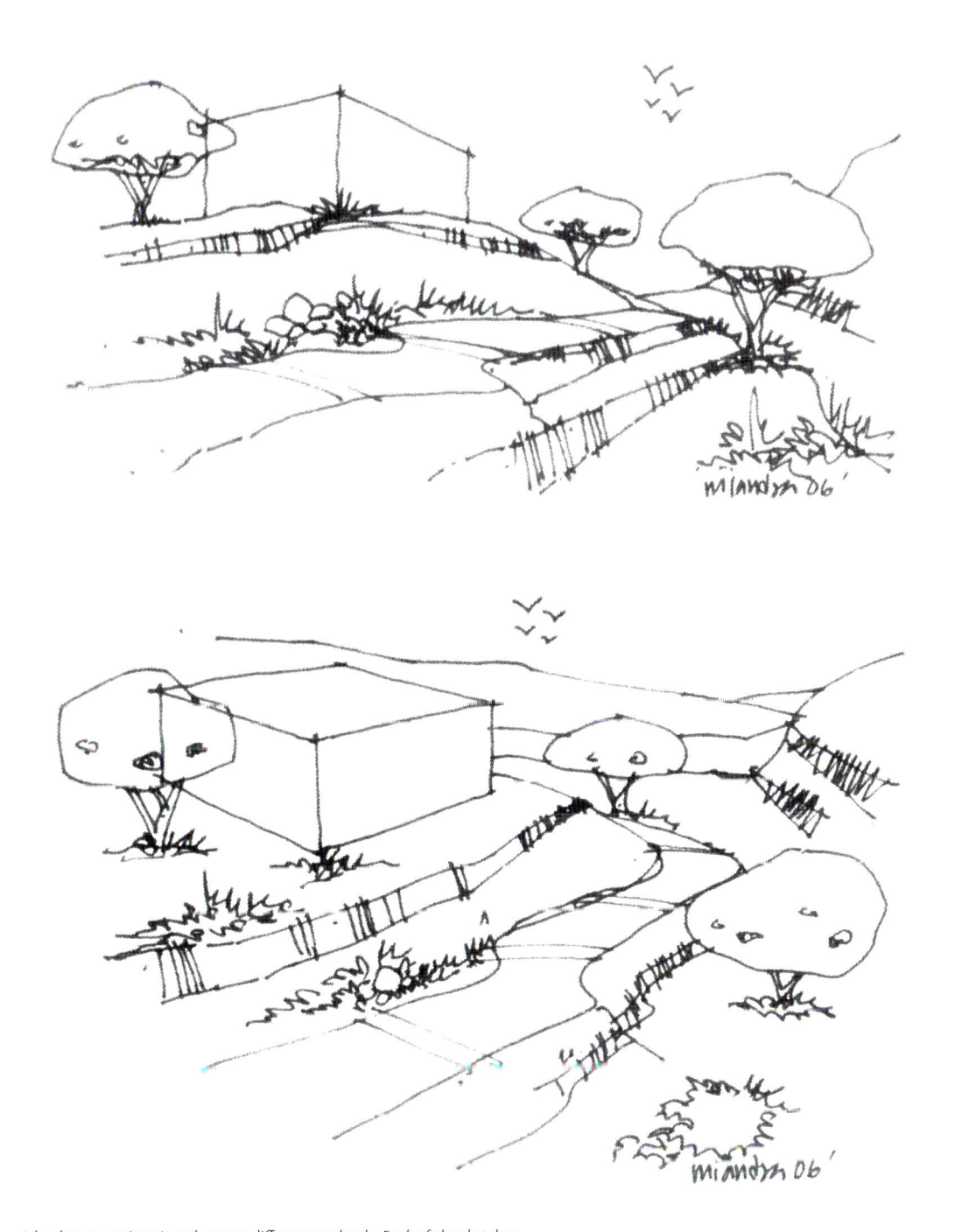

A landscape setting viewed on two different eye levels. Each of the sketches gives a different evaluation to the landscape composition.

SKETCH COMPOSITION

4.5 THE CONCEPT OF GOOD COMPOSITION IN A SKETCH

The skill of sketching an object or figure from different perspectives is crucial in ensuring the composition sketched is in the right composition. The artist or designer should clearly understand on how an object surface changes when it is viewed on different eye levels.

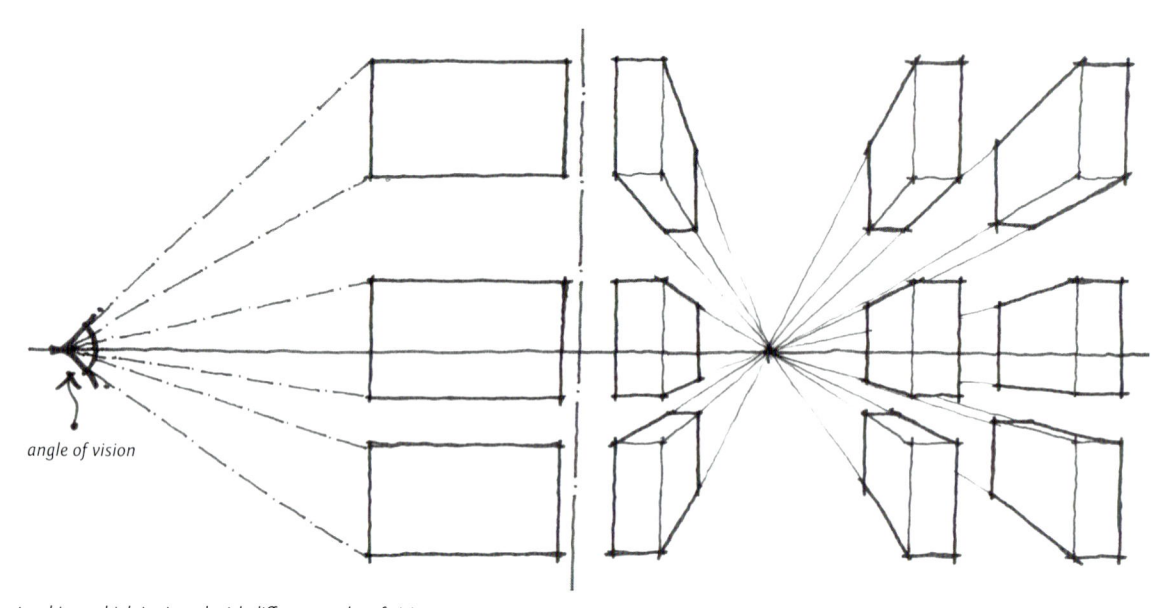

angle of vision

An object which is viewed with different angles of vision

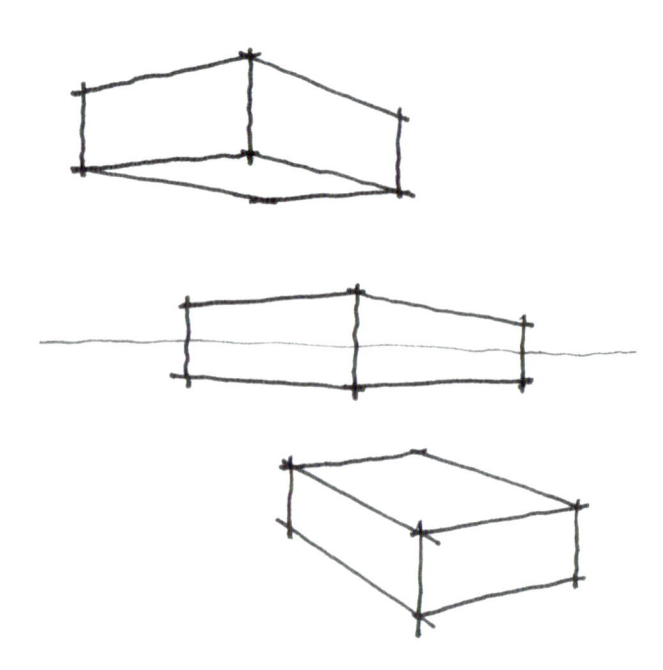

A sketch of the same basic shape view from different composition angles

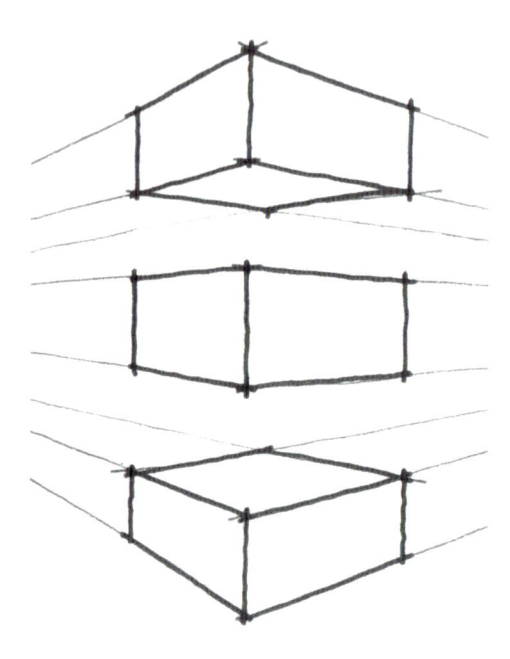

A sketch of the same basic shape viewed from different composition angles.

70   SKETCH COMPOSITION

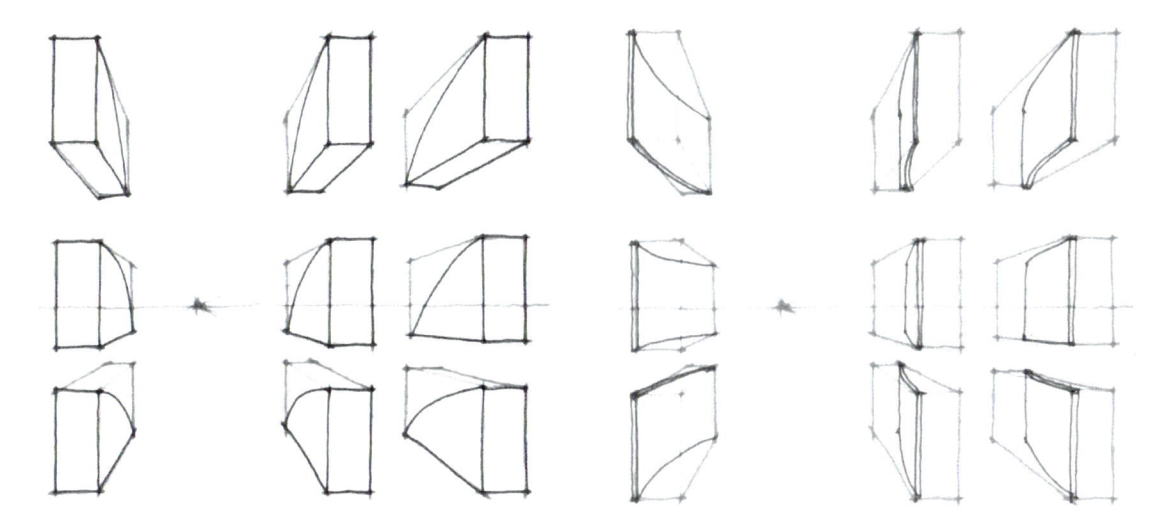

Each surface of the object changes whenever it is sketched from different composition angles

Each surface of the object changes whenever it is sketched from different composition angles

An example of figures sketched from various composition angles

SKETCH COMPOSITION 71

View 1

View 2

View 3

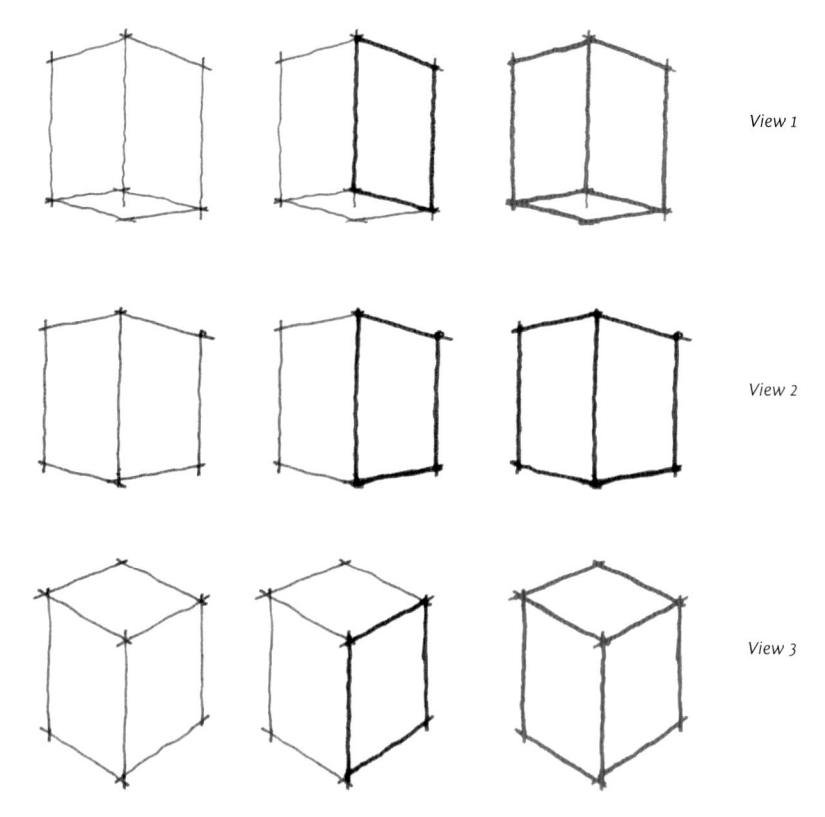

The process of sketching 'a step by step' a basic shape (a box). Views from three different composition angles.

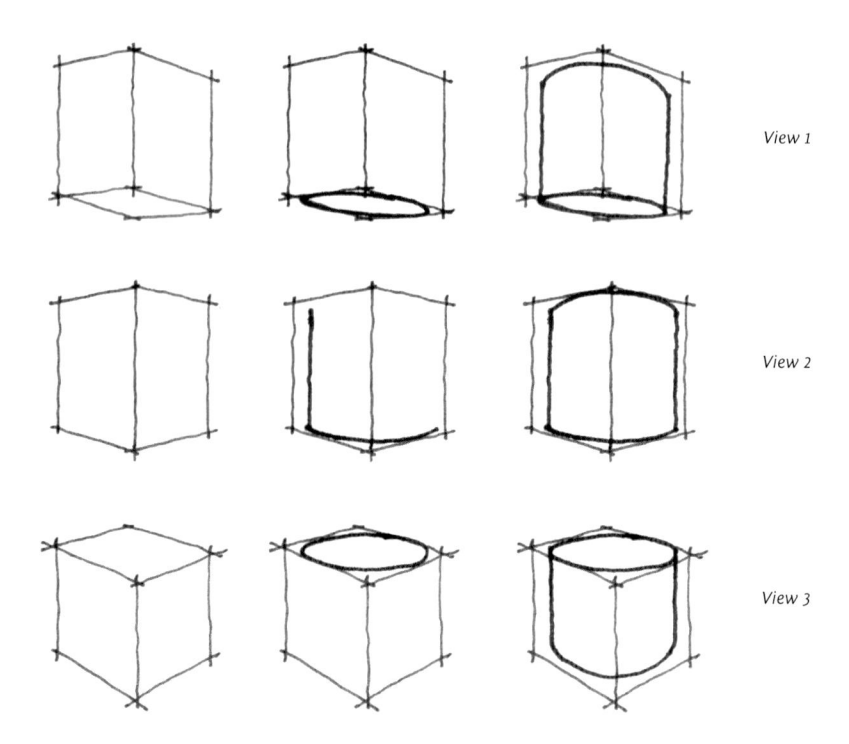

View 1

View 2

View 3

The process of sketching 'a step by step' a basic shape (a cylinder). Views from three different composition angles.

View 1

View 2

View 3

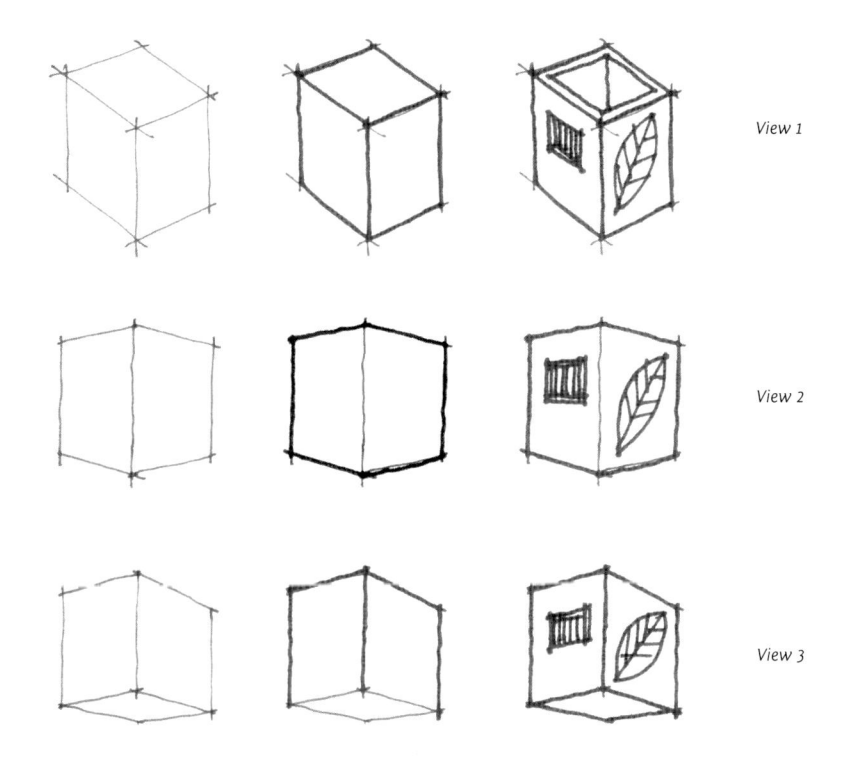

The process of sketching 'a step by step' an object (a decorative box). Views from three different composition angles.

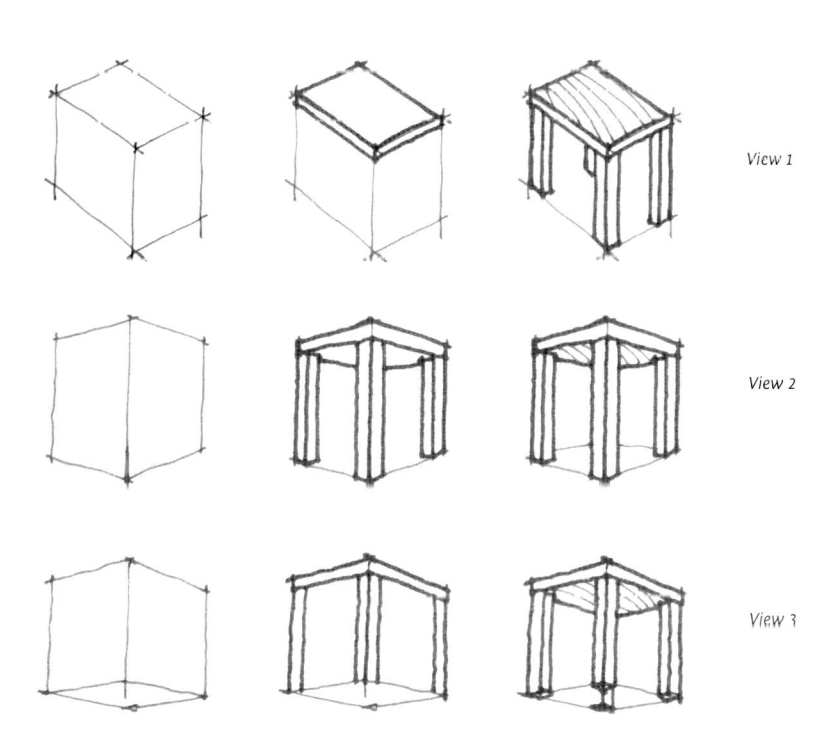

View 1

View 2

View 3

The process of sketching 'a step by step' an object (a stool). Views from three different composition angles.

SKETCH COMPOSITION 73

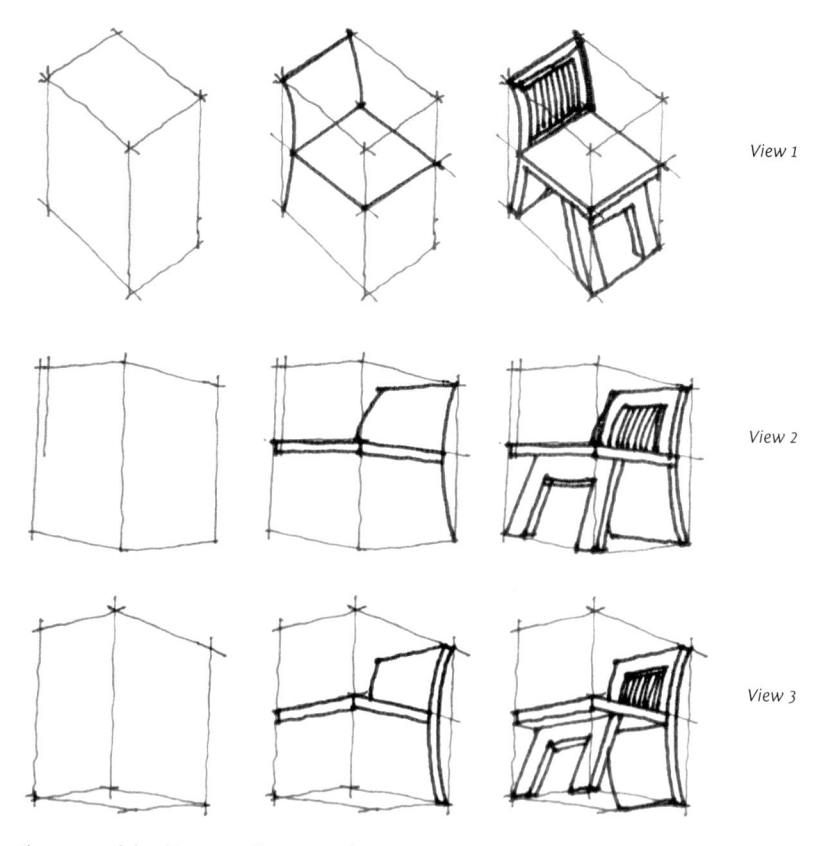

View 1

View 2

View 3

The process of sketching 'a step by step' an object
(a chair). Views from three different composition angles.

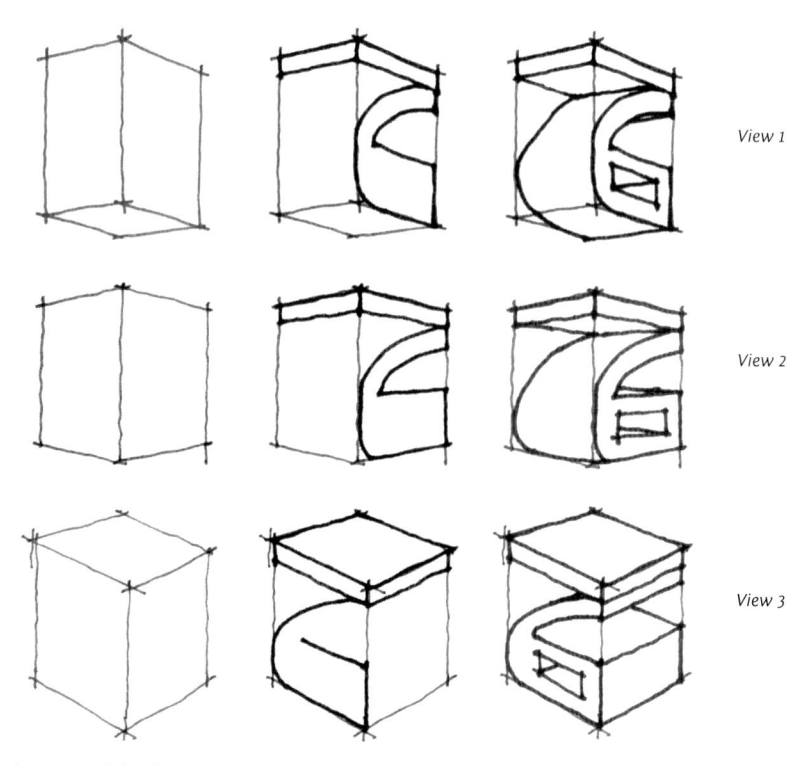

View 1

View 2

View 3

The process of sketching 'a step by step' an object
(a sculpture). Views from three different composition angles.

74   SKETCH COMPOSITION

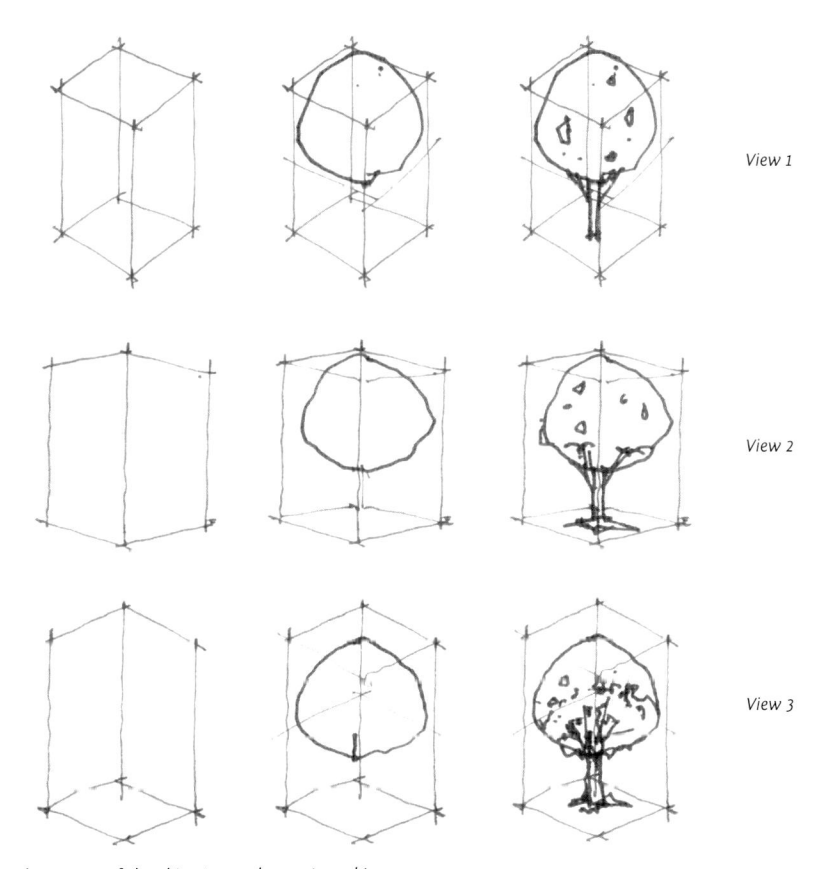

View 1

View 2

View 3

The process of sketching 'a step by step' an object (a tree). Views from three different composition angles

4.6 WHAT IS PERSPECTIVE

The skill of sketching in the right perspective could help an artist or designer to be better in creating a good sketch composition. This chapter will explain briefly the concept of perspective and the types of perspectives that are commonly used by an artist or designer. The demonstration of how to sketch will be explained in detail in order to understand the concept thoroughly.

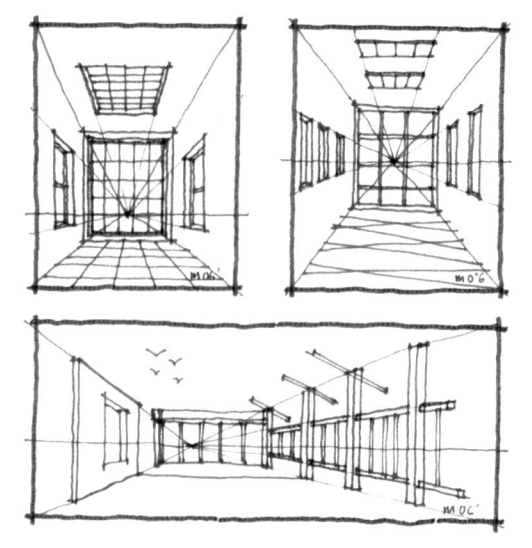

Example of fast sketch perspective

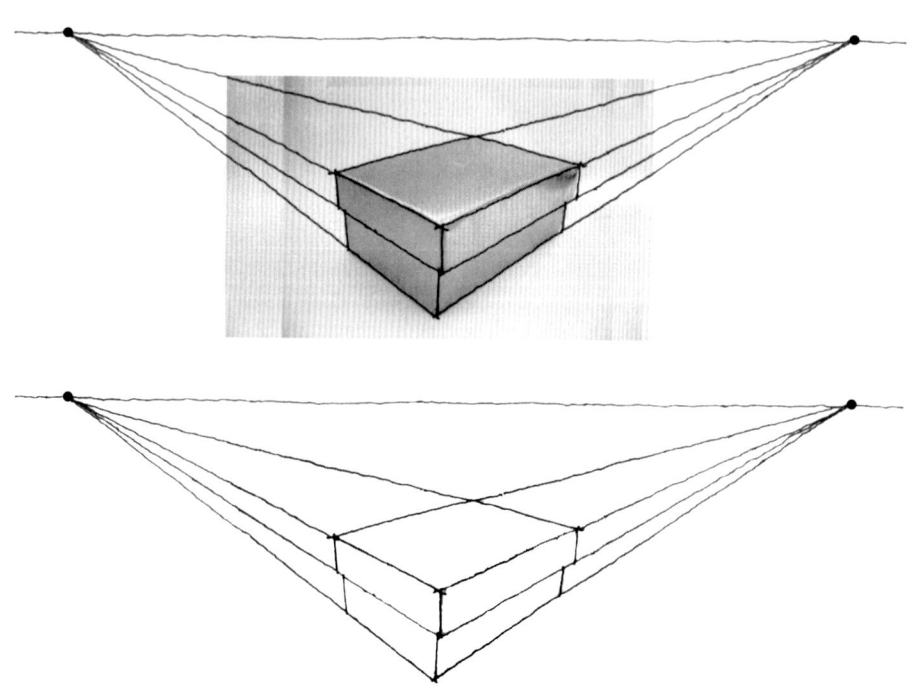

Perspective concept in photographs.

Do you know that a human being sees an object or a view based on the concept of perspectives? This happens because all objects including human beings exist three dimensionally. Try to look around us, all objects surely can be seen in three dimensions which are in perspective shapes that possess height, width and depth. An example of perspective that could easily be obtained is photographs.

4.7 THE CONCEPT OF PERSPECTIVE

The basic knowledge about perspective is vital where it will help an artist or designer in sketching easily and confidently. Among the basics are the following:

- **Picture Plane** - It is an imaginary plane like a clear sheet of glass that is used to project the image of a view before it is sketched onto its surface.

- **Vanishing Point** - is a point where parallel lines appear to converge. The number and placement of vanishing point is determined by types of perspectives such as one point perspective, two point perspective or others.

- **Horizon Line** – The imaginary line which appear across the picture and at the eye level. This line determines the perspective angle whether looking from the higher point or lower point.

- **Ground Line** – it is a line that is parallel to the picture plane base and the ground.

- **The Station Point** – the point or location where the observer views the image of the perspective.

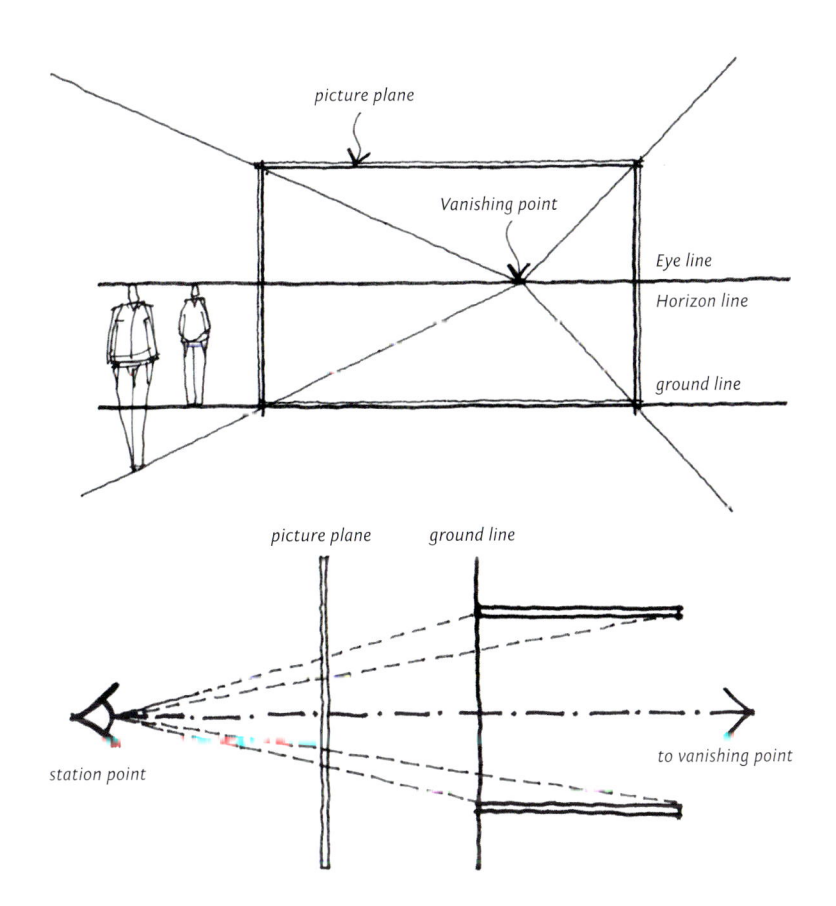

Perspective components

4.8 TYPES OF PERSPECTIVES

Perspectives could be created in various types. Among them are the following:

- **One point perspective** – it has one vanishing point. Normally used for drawing the arrangement of interiors, views of a linear object like a row of buildings, a road and many more.

- **Two point perspective** – it has two vanishing points which are right and left vanishing point. Image composition is more natural as compared to one point perspective.

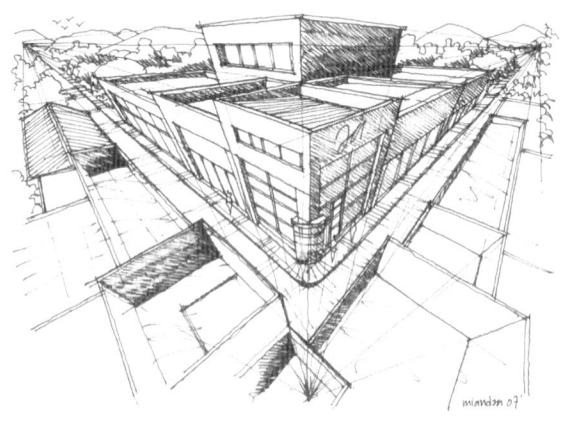

- **Three point perspective** – it has three vanishing points. This type is rarely used because the composition perspective created is quite peculiar and too complex to be understood.

- **The multiple point perspective** – is the combination of perspectives types. This type of perspective is normally used in many situations which the objects are set in different positions.

VP

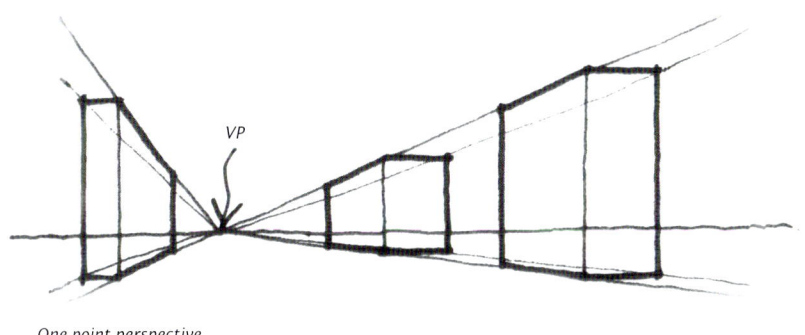

One point perspective

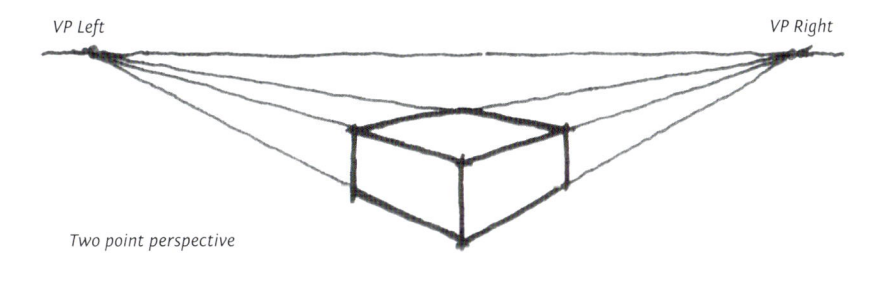

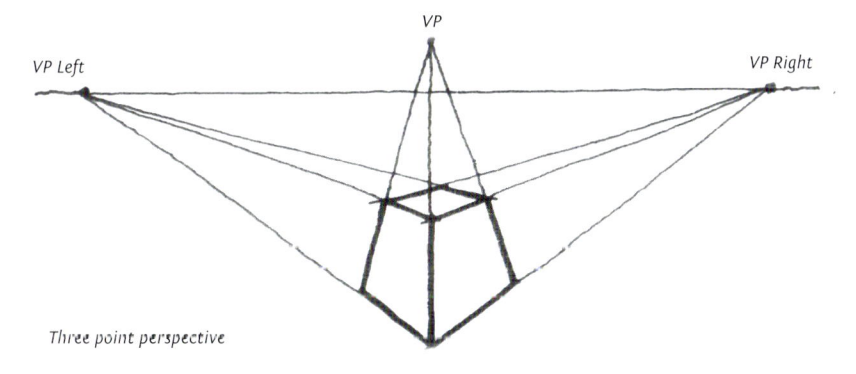

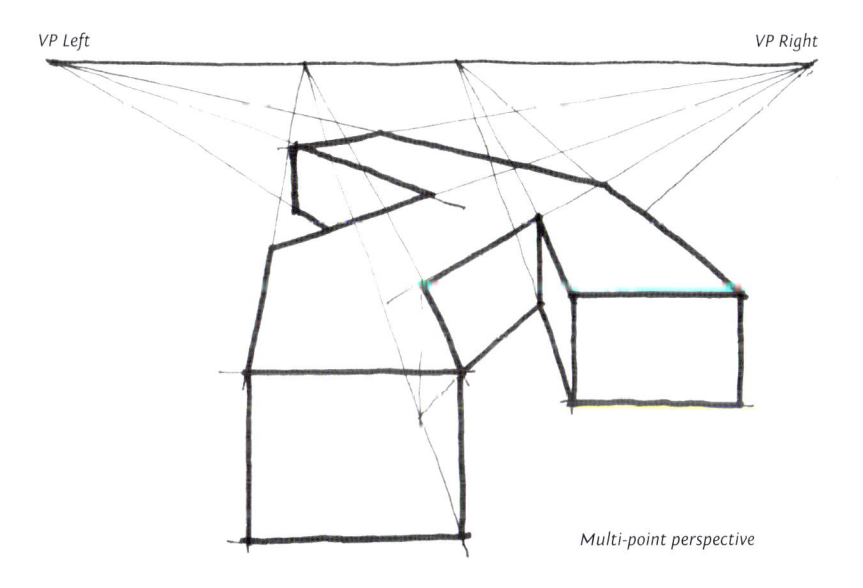

VP Left *VP Right*

Two point perspective

VP Left *VP* *VP Right*

Three point perspective

VP Left *VP Right*

Multi-point perspective

Type of perspective

SKETCH COMPOSITION 79

4.9 TIPS IN PERSPECTIVE

Apart from the basic knowledge about perspectives, there is a few other matters that ought to be understood before embarking on perspective drawing. It is important to ensure that all objects in that sketch composition hold a good scale and proportion and are suitable for the composition. Factors that need to be understood are the following:

Height, Width in Perspective
The first subject that will be discussed is height and width in perspective. All objects or elements to be sketched surely possess certain height and width. For instance, bottles, books, pails, trees and many others. The significant question is how to obtain the right height and width of an object in a perspective.

There are a number of ways that could be used to attain the right scale and proportion in perspective. One of them is the ratio concept using an element or object as a reference of height and width of a composition. Among the objects of reference that are always being used are human figures. Refer to the example of perspective to understand the concept of ratio using human figure references to composition.

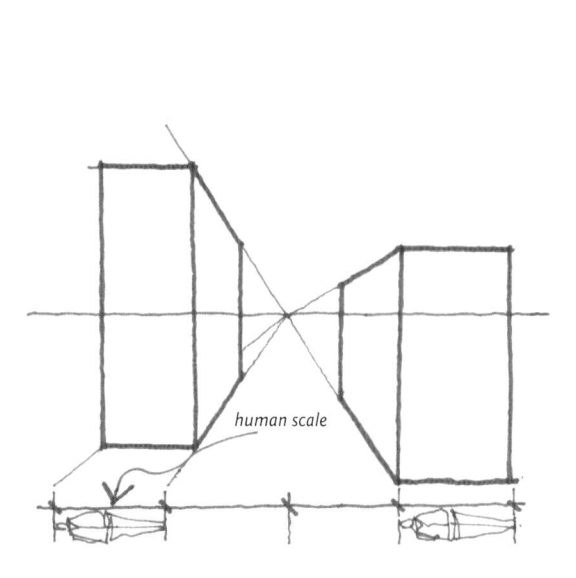

Always refer to human figures for the width setting

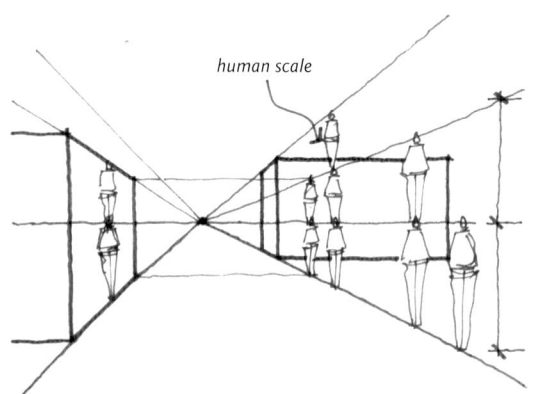

Human figures are used as scales to the height of the perspective

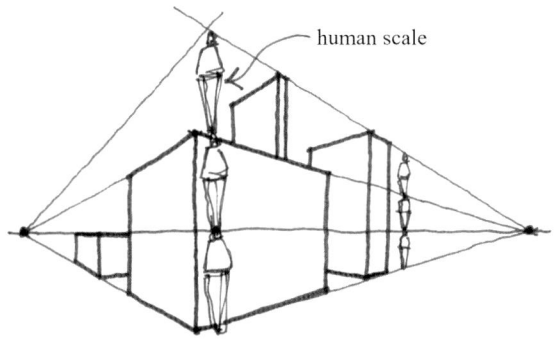

Always refer to human figures for the height setting

80 SKETCH COMPOSITION

Depth in perspective

Each 3 dimensional (3-D) perspective sketch definitely comprises depth which means the distance of an object or composition that could be sketched before the Vanishing Point (VP). A first-rate depth in perspective could be obtained through various ways and one of them is projection from the base plan. This concept could provide an appropriate proportion to the perspective composition that will be drawn in detail but not in sketches. Another concept is by assuming with scale and proportion using our own eyes. This technique is very good for sketching.

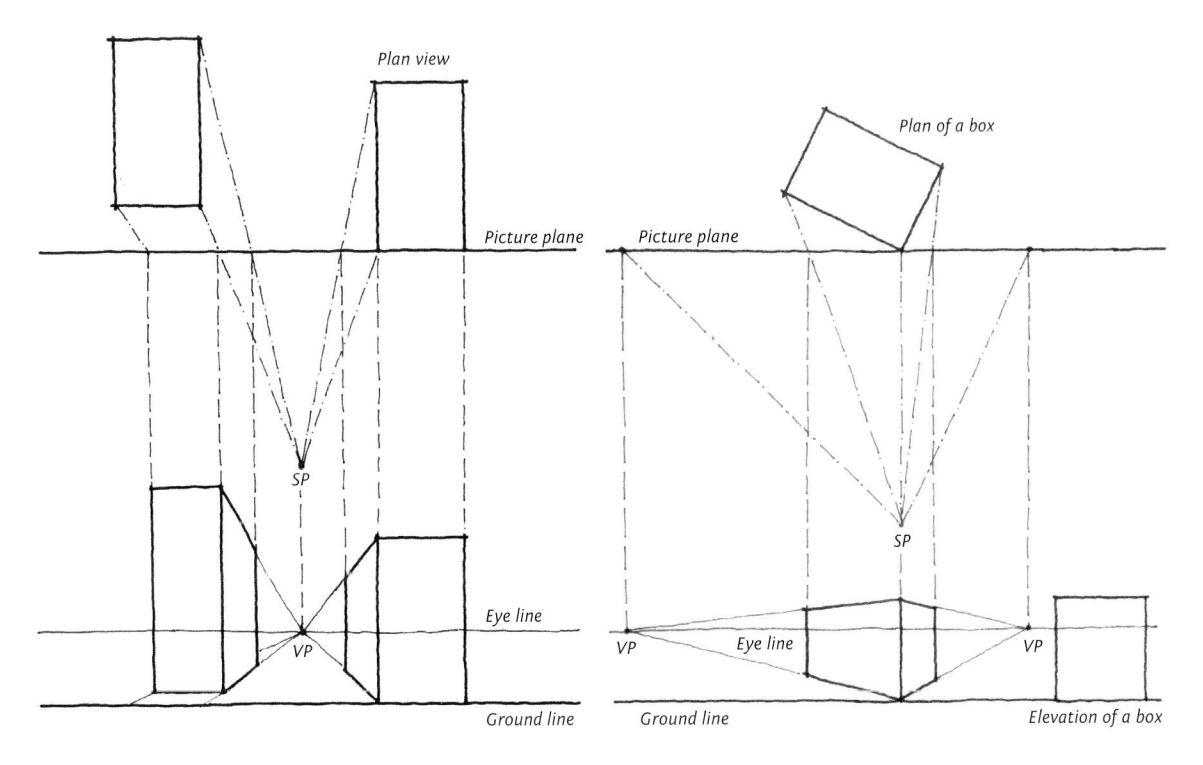

One of the solutions on how to justify 'depth' in one point perspective.

One of the solutions on how to justify 'depth' in two point perspective.

SKETCH COMPOSITION

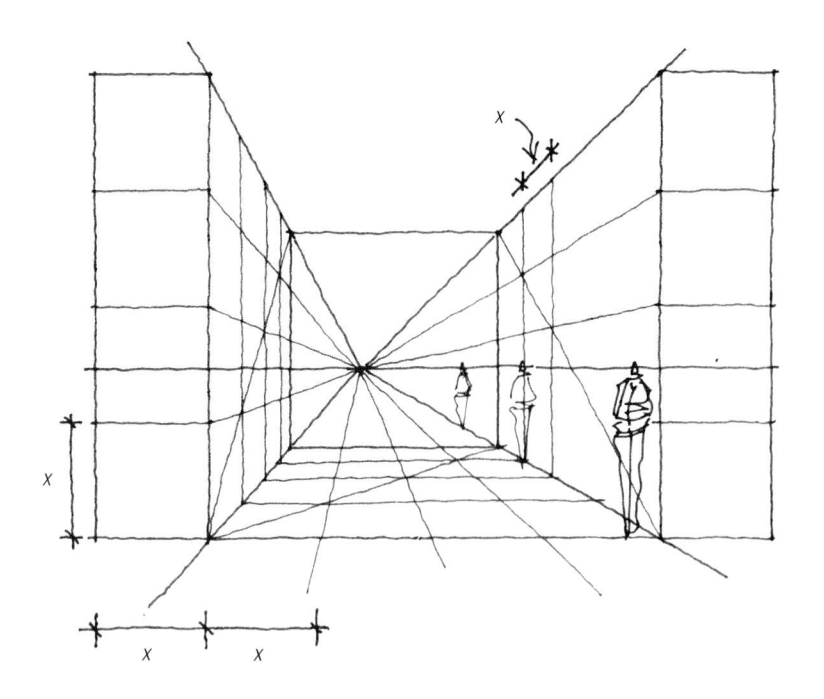

'Depth in perspective'
Human figure is used as the reference point for scale and proportion of these perspectives. Always refer to human figure to get the right 'depth' and proportion of any sketched composition.

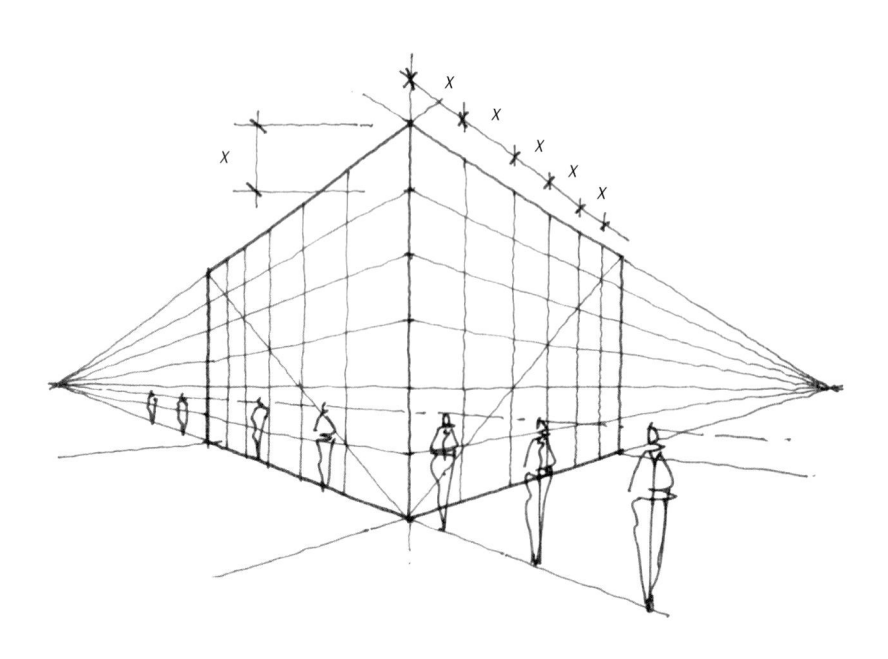

'Depth' in perspective is based on the scale and proportion techniques

Scale and Proportion in Perspective

A good sketch composition depends on the sensitivity of an artist or designer towards the right scale and proportion. They are interrelated. An artist or designer has to understand how scale could influence the proportion of a composition. The illustration below explains further.

With reference to the above explanation, the reference scale of human figures plays a vital role in influencing the sketch composition proportion. An artist or designer should familiarize him or herself in this knowledge to ensure the composition formed is accurate and will not be regarded as 'out of scale'.

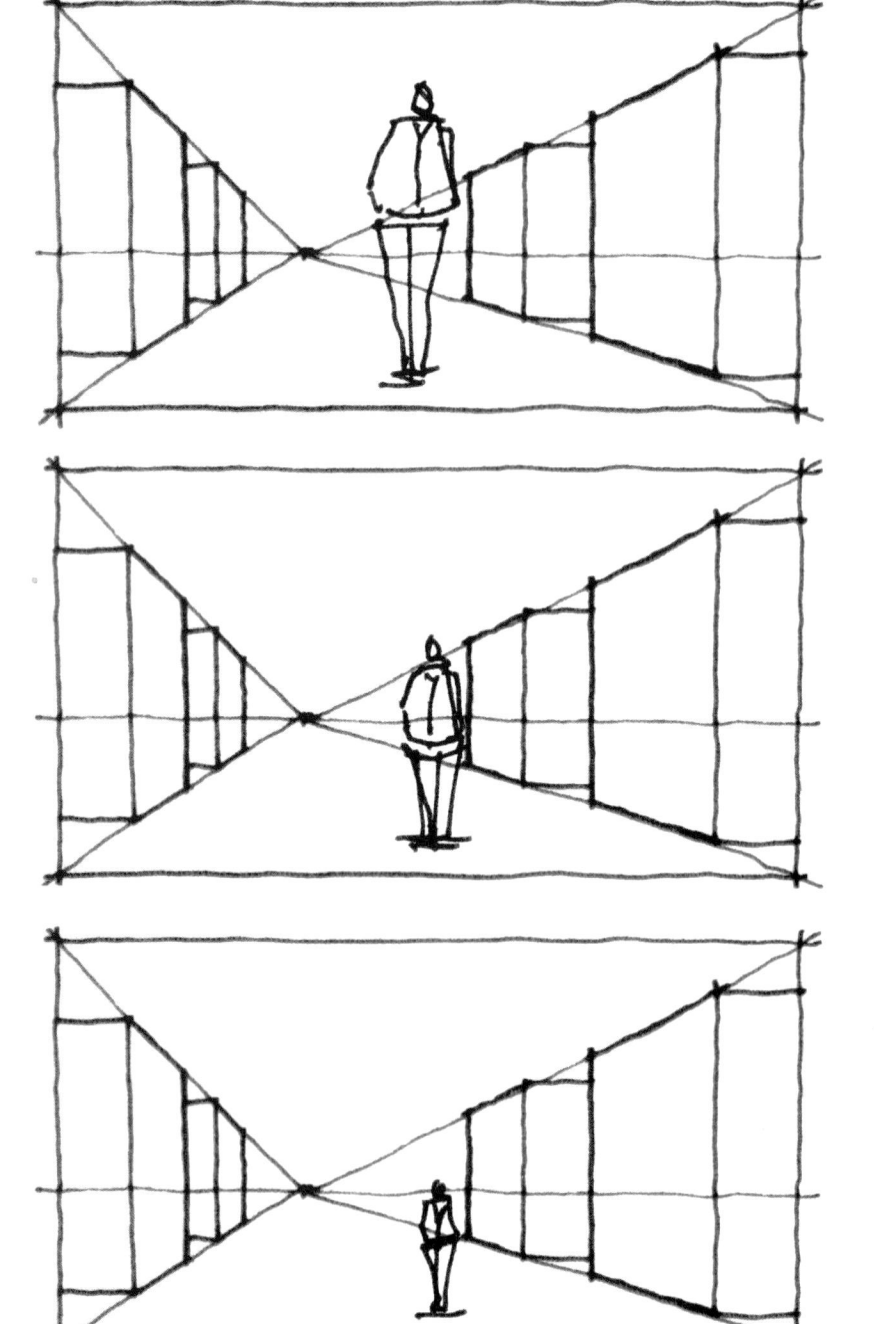

View 1
The road size is quite narrow depending on human figure scale.

View 2
The width of the road changes depending on the scale of human figure.

View 3
The use of small scale human figure makes the size of the road look really wide.

The interrelation between a human figure and surrounding objects

'Out of scale' means the drawing composition or sketch does not fulfill the required scale and proportion. The following demonstration will further explain this with the intention that it will help in better understanding of the concept.

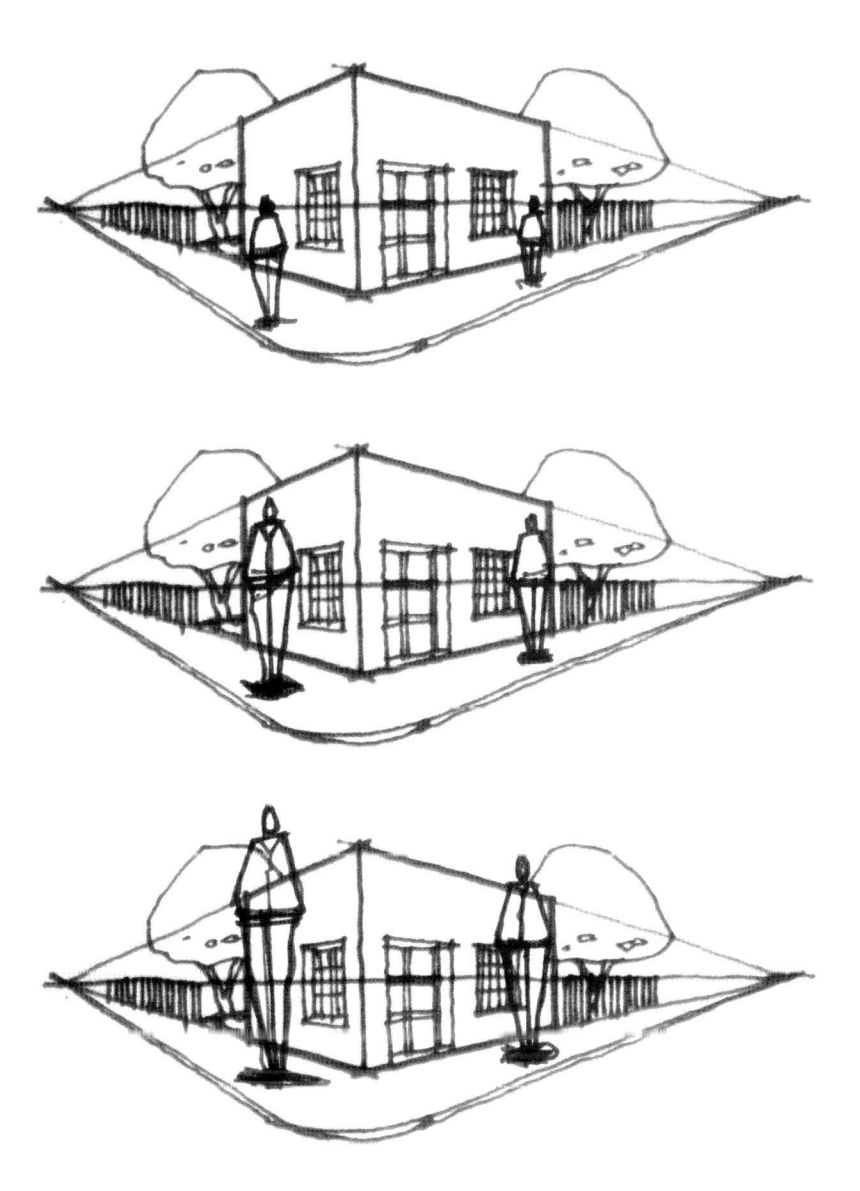

The scale and proportion concept

View in perspective

View in perspective depends on the location of eye level whether high or low depending on the requirement of the sketch composition. This could be explained through the sketch of concept view in perspective such as the subsequent illustration. The movement of eye level causes the locations of the elements such as signboards and trees change but the elements located at the horizon line such hills, birds and fence stay still.

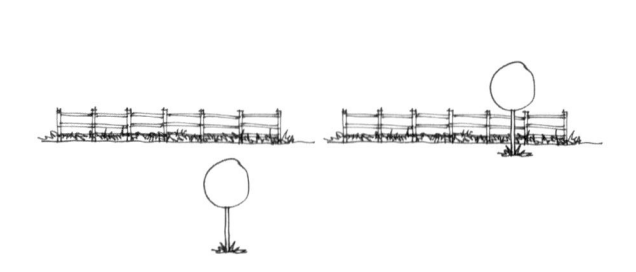

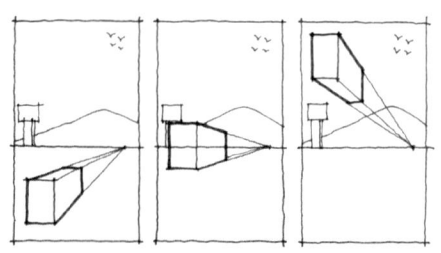

A clear example of view in perspective

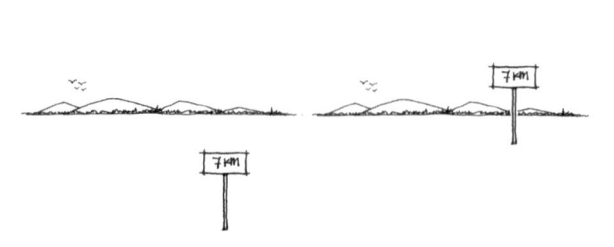

Simple sketch about concept view in perspective

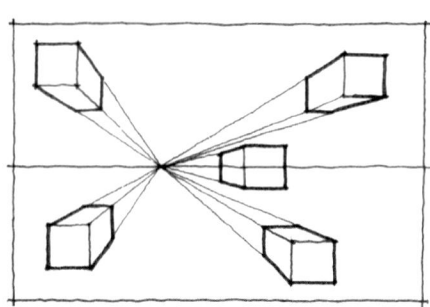

Various locations of the object could be seen in different views

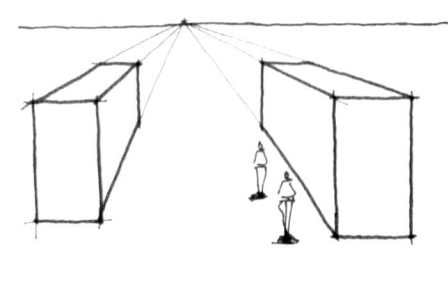

Bird's Eye View
The horizon line must be on the top of the sketch composition.

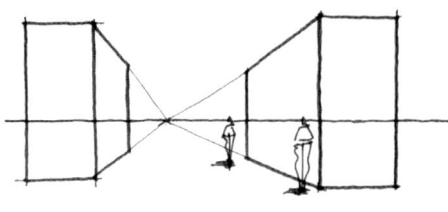

Human Eye View
The horizon line must be in the middle of the sketch composition.

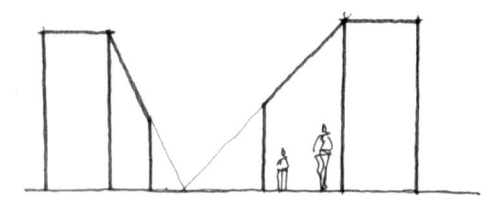

Worm's Eye View
The horizon line must be at the bottom part of the sketch composition.

Type of perspective views

SKETCH COMPOSITION

Centre point

Centre point is necessary to ensure the object sketched is in the accurate proportion. Look carefully at the demonstration exemplified below to assist in better understanding of the notion.

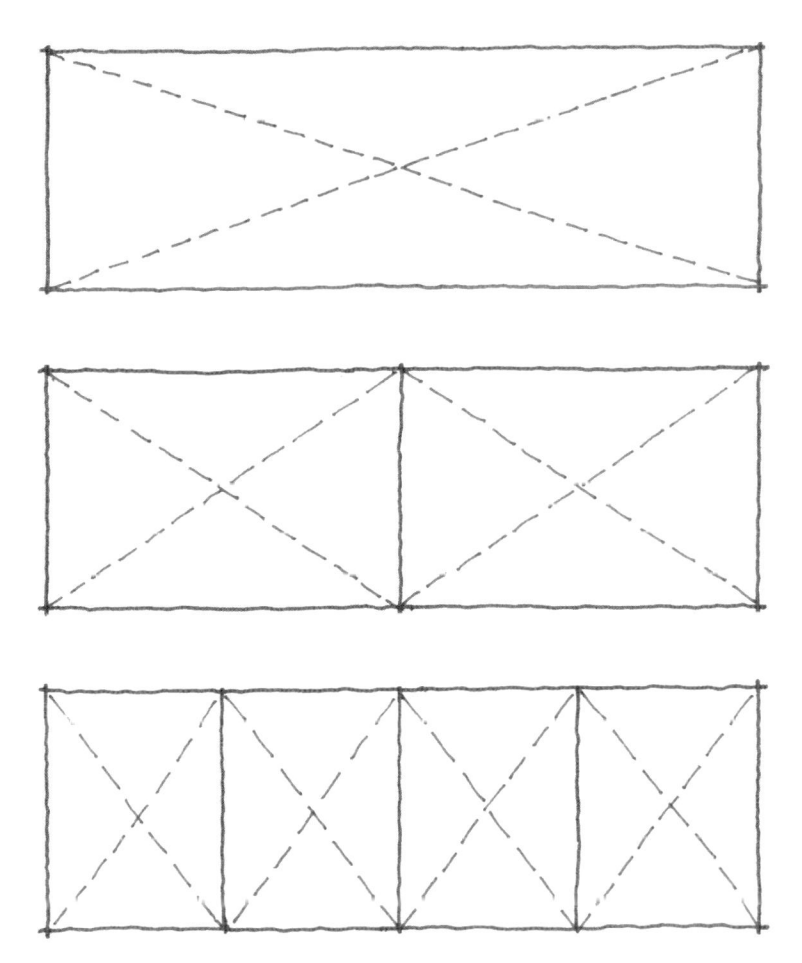

Centre Point Concept
Centre point concept can be applied in any square surfaces. Observe carefully at the process dividing a space into several parts. This concept should be clearly understood to make the process of sketching easier.

SKETCH COMPOSITION 87

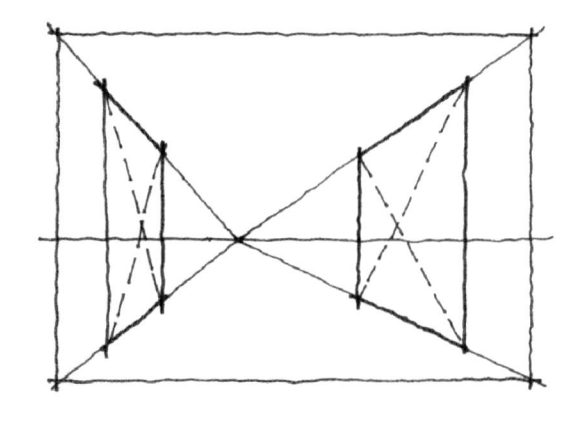

One Point Perspective
The same concept could also be applied in this perspective to obtain centre point.

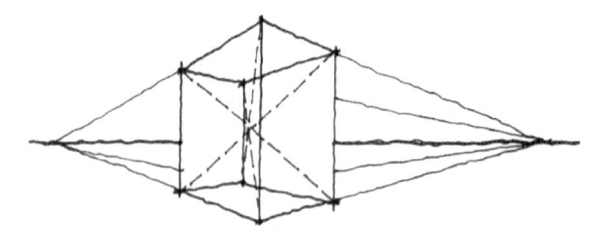

Two Point Perspective
Please observe how centre point is obtained in 3 dimensions.

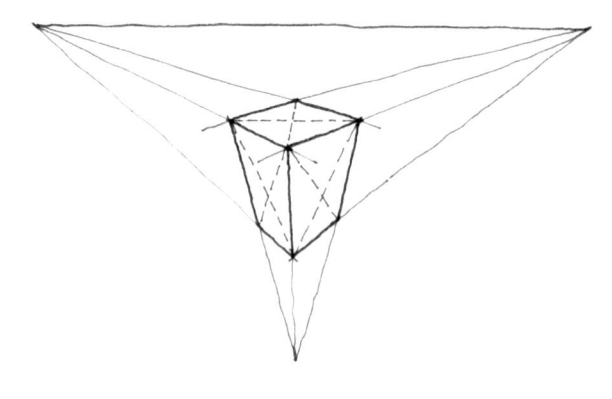

Three Point Perspective
The same concept could also be applied in this perspective to obtain centre point.

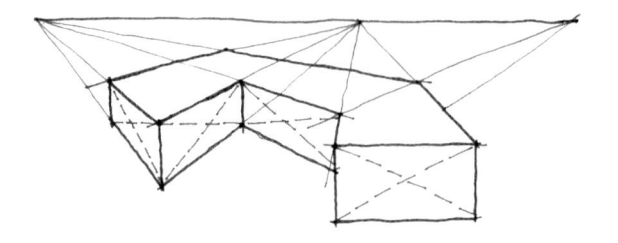

Multi Point Perspective
The same concept could also be applied in this perspective to obtain centre point.

4.10 SIMPLE APPROACH IN PERSPECTIVE

A simple quality sketch anticipates speed in creating a setting in any perspective. It could be achieved through the right and suitable approach to guarantee a composition of a sketch has a fine scale and proportion. One of the approaches is the use of ratio concept and estimation in order to attain a high-quality setting perspective.

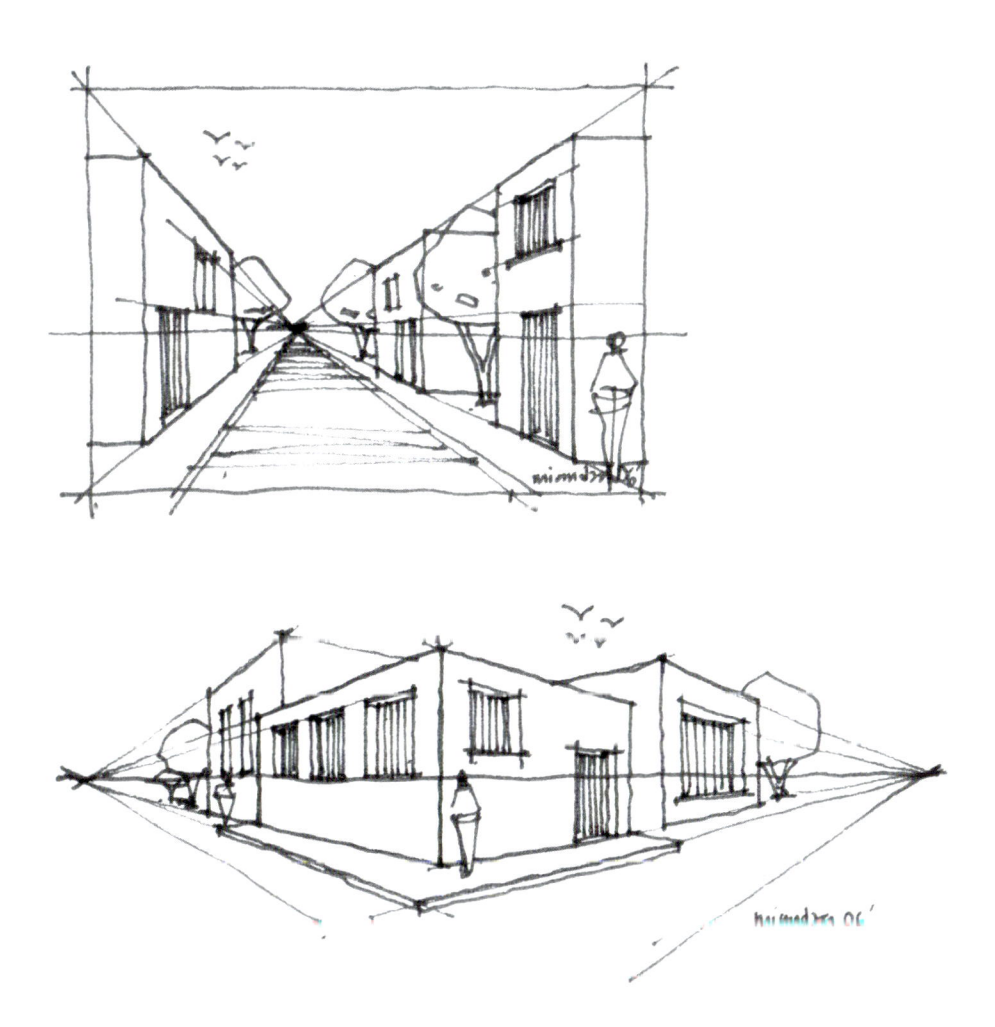

An example of a simple sketch

Step 1
- Sketch 'box' boundary on the sketch
- Human figure as a reference scale
- Sketch horizon line or eye line

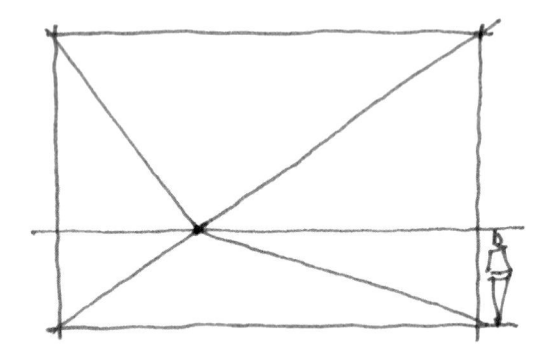

Step 2
- Locate the Vanishing Point on the eye line.
- Sketch construction line at four boundary corners.

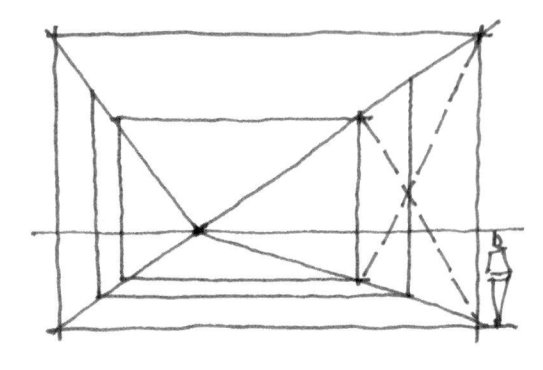

Step 3
- Estimate the suitable depth for setting.
- To obtain the same centre and depth part, cross the line to the 4 corners shown in the diagram.

Step 1
- Sketch horizon line or eye line
- Human figure as the reference scale

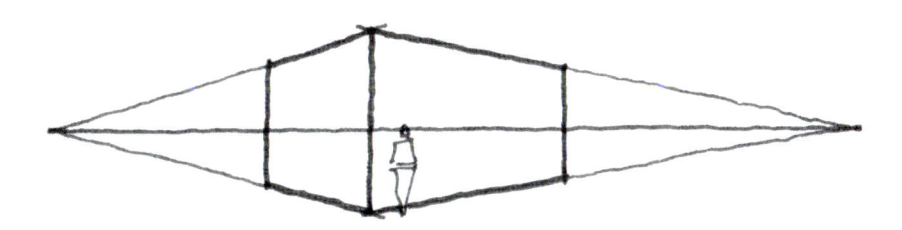

Step 2
- Estimate the depth perspective that will be used on the object sketched.
- Sketch construction line at the four boundary corners.

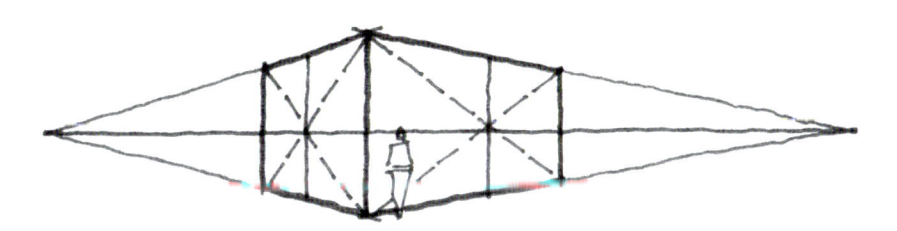

Step 3
- To be able to gain the same centre and depth, cross the line to the 4 corners shown in the diagram.

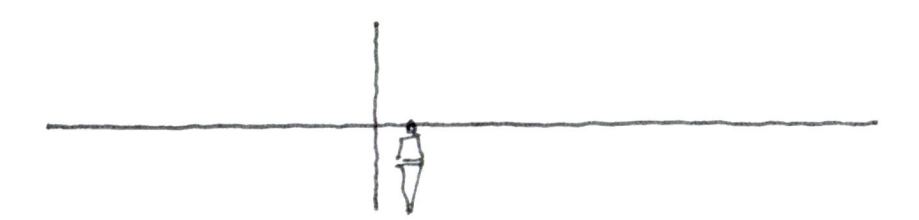

SKETCH COMPOSITION

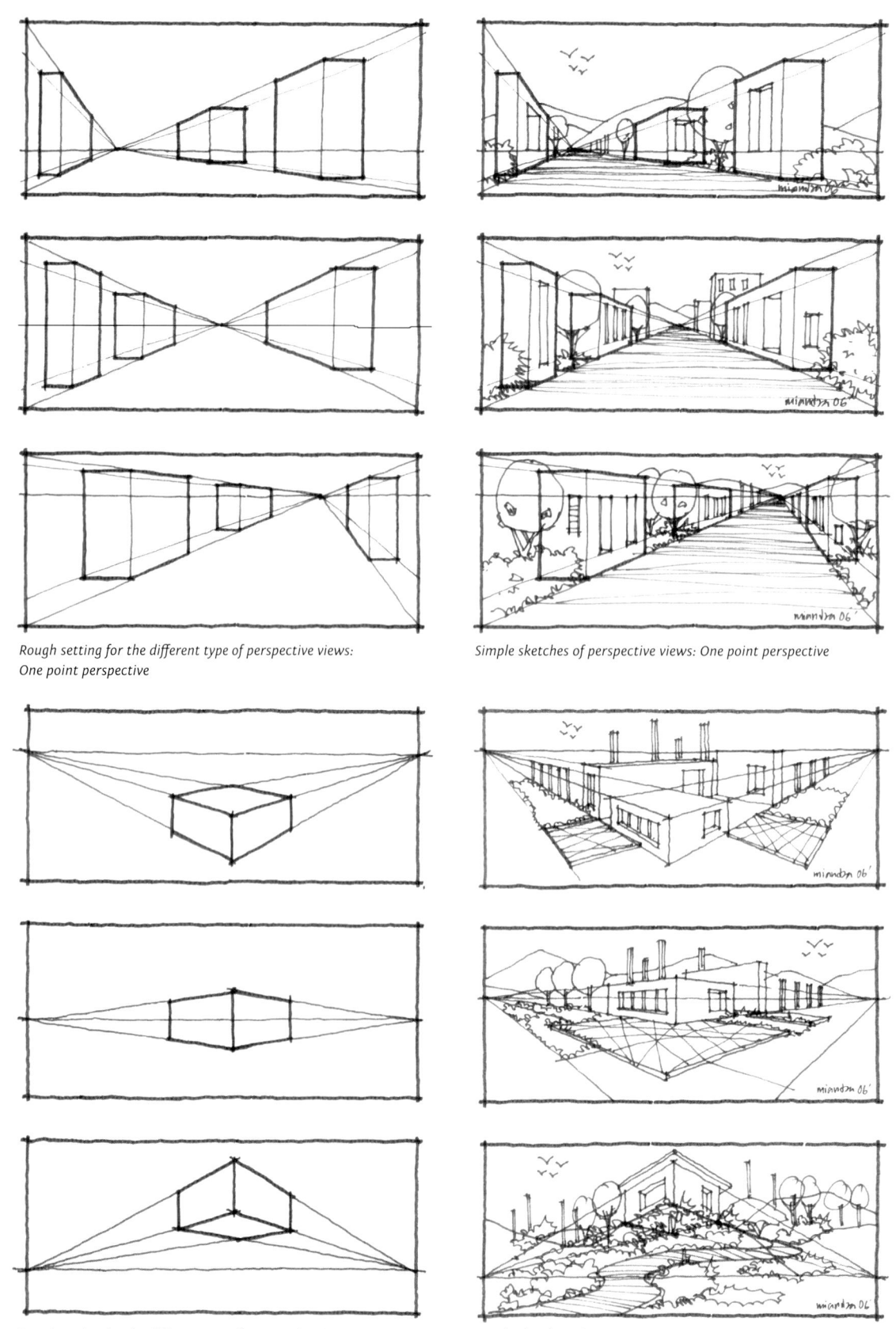

Rough setting for the different type of perspective views:
One point perspective

Simple sketches of perspective views: One point perspective

Rough setting for the different type of perspective views:
Two points perspectives

Simple sketches of perspective views: Two point perspective

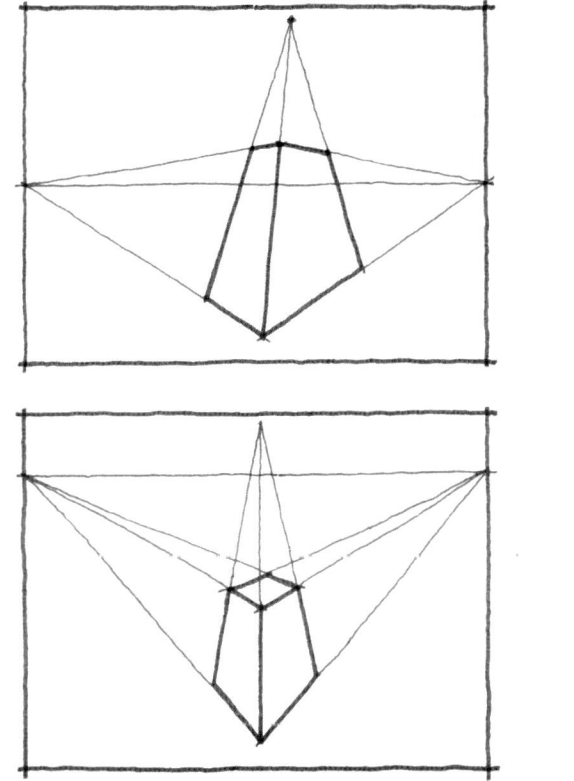

Rough setting for the different type of perspective views: Three points perspectives

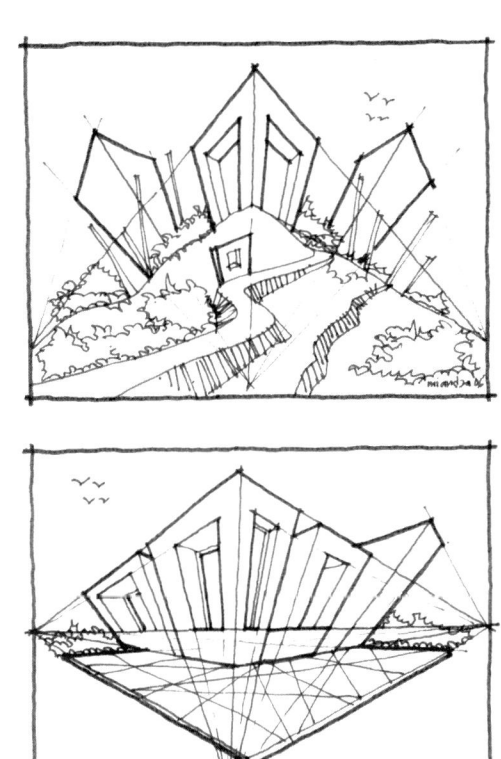

Simple sketches of perspective views: Three point perspective

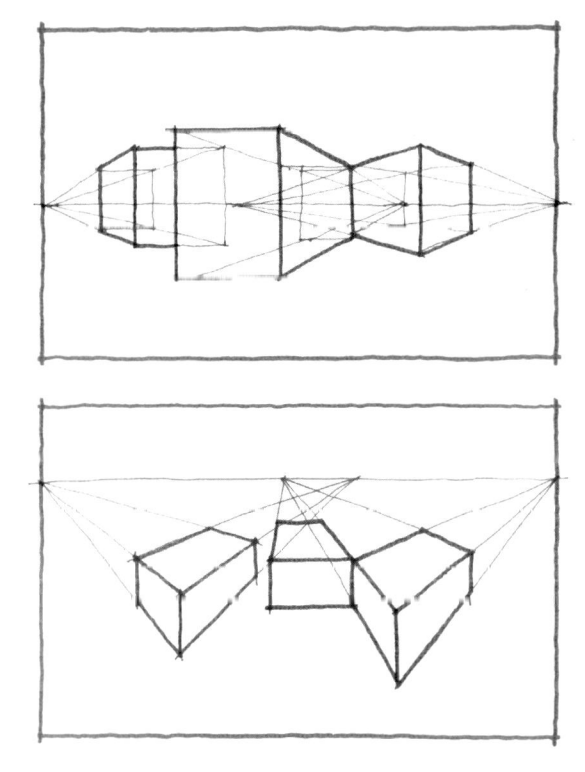

Rough setting for the different type of perspective views: Multi- points perspective

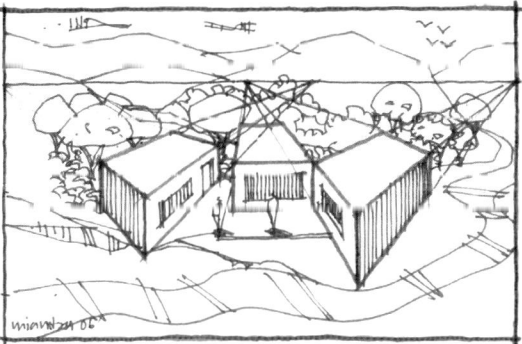

Simple sketches of perspective views: Multi- point perspective

SKETCH COMPOSITION 93

5.0 RENDERING TECHNIQUES

Rendering is the final process of a sketch. There are a lot of rendering techniques using pen, pencil and charcoal pencil. An artist or designer is free to choose an appropriate technique which is suitable with the sketch to ensure the necessary impact is successfully conveyed. Despite that, an artist or a designer too should be smart in enhancing these techniques to more fascinating and stunning ones. Generally, rendering medium is divided into three categories which are dry, semi wet and wet. This chapter will only explain dry medium technique (pencil and pen) and a few more types of rendering techniques. Apart from that, the understanding of shade and shadow is also needed to ensure the rendering produced is more realistic.

5.1 RENDERING CONCEPTS

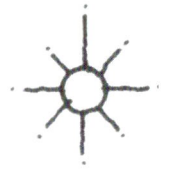

There are a few things that need to be clarified before commencing on the rendering process. They are:

- **Medium of Rendering**
- **Shade and Shadow**
- **Rendering Techniques**

5.2 MEDIUM OF RENDERING

Medium plays a significant role in ensuring the rendering product is of an excellent quality and a fine one. The medium meant here are the basic sketching tools such as pen, pencil and paper. Each one of this medium possesses its own special characteristics that need to be clearly understood by every artist or designer. The different sizes of pen tips produce different quality of rendering. The same applies to pencils that have different softness and hardness of lead.

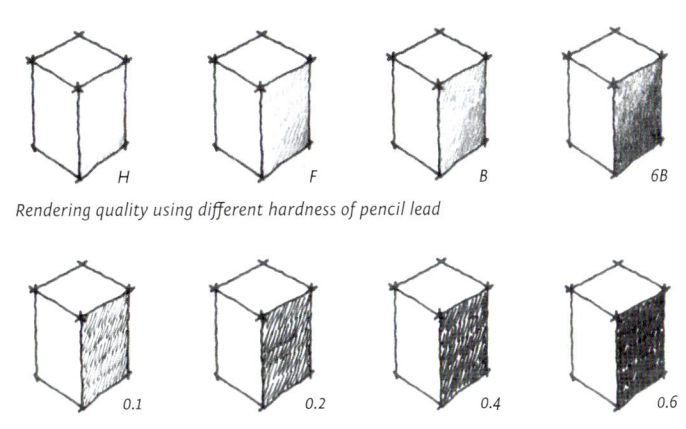

Rendering quality using different hardness of pencil lead

Different pen tips produce different rendering quality

Paper too has various textures which include soft, smooth, hard and many others. This will also influence the rendering quality of a sketch composition. Observe the sample given below where 6B pencil is used on different types of texture paper. The end product clearly differs from one to another.

RENDERING TECHNIQUES   95

5.3 SHADE AND SHADOW

Light Source & Surface Shape

The location of light source is vital in the rendering process. It differentiates the surface that is exposed to the light and vice versa. The surface that is exposed to light will be brighter as compared to the one that is sheltered. This matter is carefully observed in a few examples provided whereby light source locations vary.

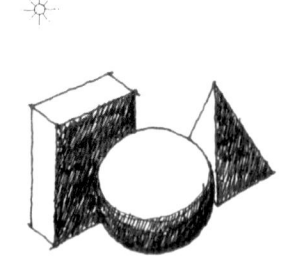

Surface that is sheltered from to light will be darker.

Light Source : Location 1

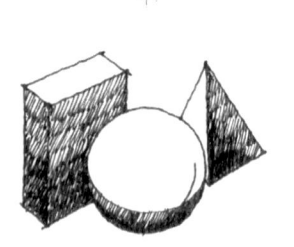

When light source is moved from one point to another, the surface brightness also differ depending upon the percentage of light exposed to each surface.

Light Source : Location 2

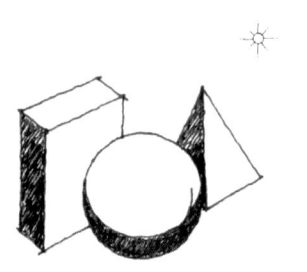

Every object possesses certain surface characteristics whereby the percentage of light exposed to the surface depends on the shape of the object surface

Light Source : Location 3

Shadow Casting

Shadow casting is one of the rendering processes. Each artist or designer is required to understand how a certain shadow is shaped depending on the movement or location of light source. Among light sources that are always being referred to are the Sun (natural source) and light bulb (artificial source). An artist or designer should practice sketching shadows beginning from the basic shapes to complex perspectives. This process is to be repeated for the artist or designer to be more sensitive to the desired shadow concept.

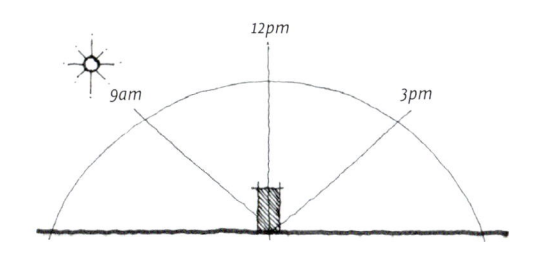

Natural sunlight source. The Sun movement affects the shadow formation of an object.

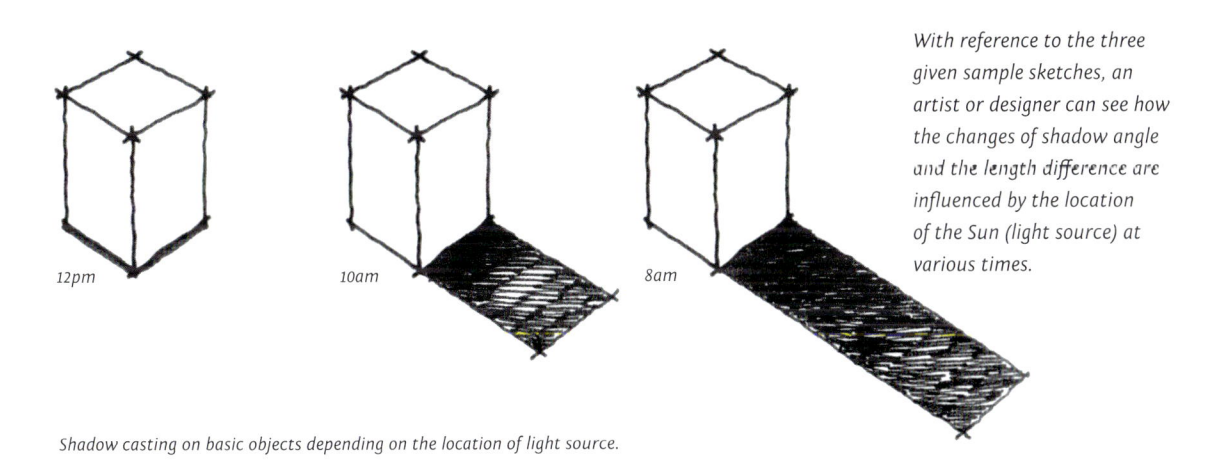

12pm   10am   8am

With reference to the three given sample sketches, an artist or designer can see how the changes of shadow angle and the length difference are influenced by the location of the Sun (light source) at various times.

Shadow casting on basic objects depending on the location of light source.

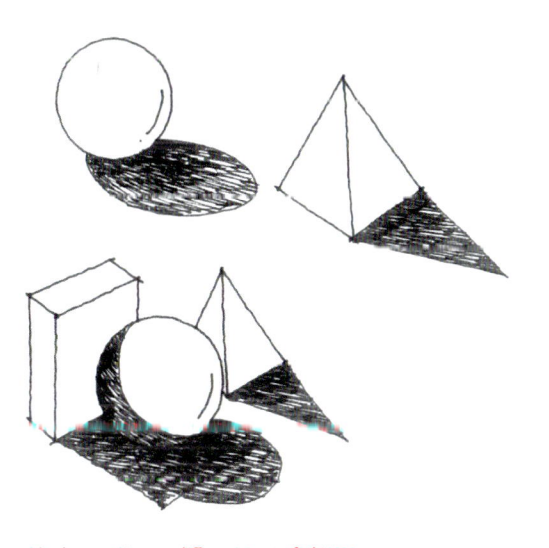

Each shadow formed depends on the shape of the object and location of light source.

Shadow casting on different type of objects

The same concept is used to form shadows on sketch composition perspectives. The variants of shadow location and its shape depend on the light source and the type of perspective used (please refer to the example provided).

Shadow Casting : One Point Perspective

Observe with attention to details on the examples given. It depends on three shadow situations following the different light source locations. The understanding of this concept is significant to ensure the shadow formed is suitable for the sketch to be produced. Then, the utmost important step to success is to try.

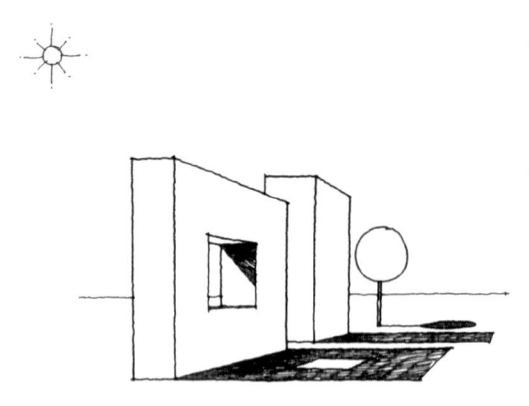

Shadow casting:
Example 1
The location of light source influences the shape of the shadow to be formed.

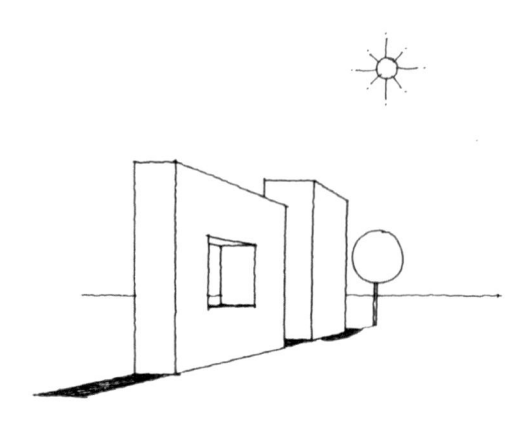

Shadow Casting : Sun Position 1

Shadow casting:
Example 2
The shadow is parallel with the location of the light source (the Sun).

Shadow Casting : Sun Position 2

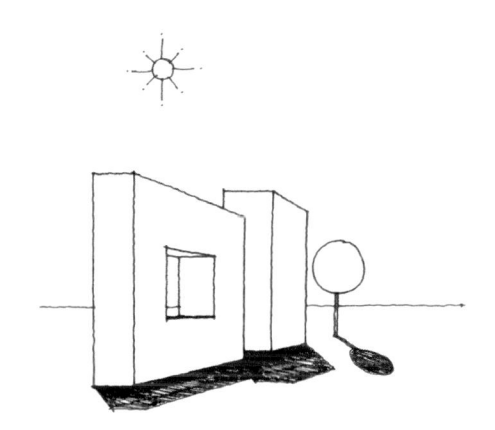

Shadow casting:
Example 3
The shadow formed is quite short when the light source is almost vertical with the object.

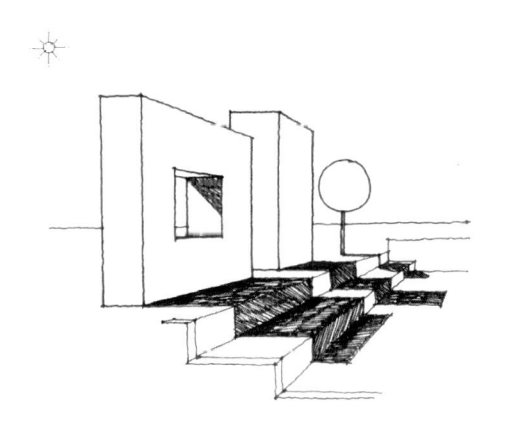

Shadow Casting : Sun Position 3

Shadow casting:
Different level
Observe the nature of the shadow when it is cast on an area with different heights.

Shadow casting : Shadow casting on different levels

Shadow Casting : Two Point Perspective

The same process which is applied for one point perspective will be used for a two point perspective. The entity that differentiates the shadow cast is the shape and the shadow location. Observe carefully how the shadow is being cast to the surface and try to compare with the one point perspective. Always refer to the vanishing points and source of light in creating shadows for any object.

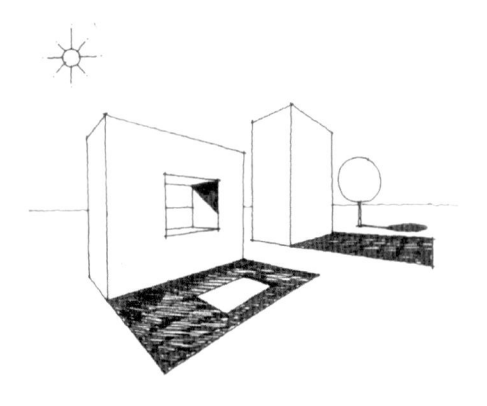

Shadow casting:
Example 1
Try to observe the shape of the shadow when the light source is on the left of the composition.

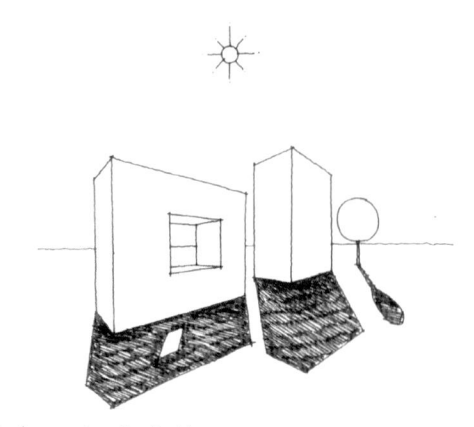

Shadow casting : Sun Position 1

Shadow casting:
Example 2
The shape of the shadow changes in line with the change in light locations.

Shadow casting : Sun Position 2

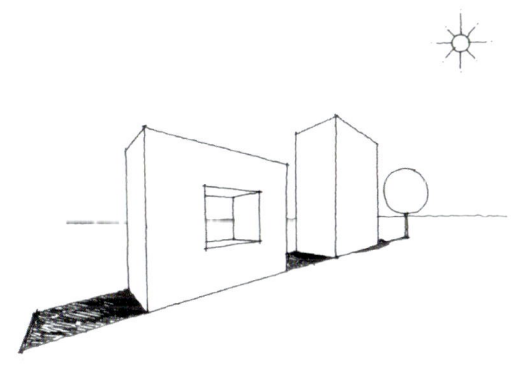

Shadow casting
Example 3
The shape of the shadow is parallel with the object if the light source also corresponds to the composition object

Shadow casting : Sun Position 3

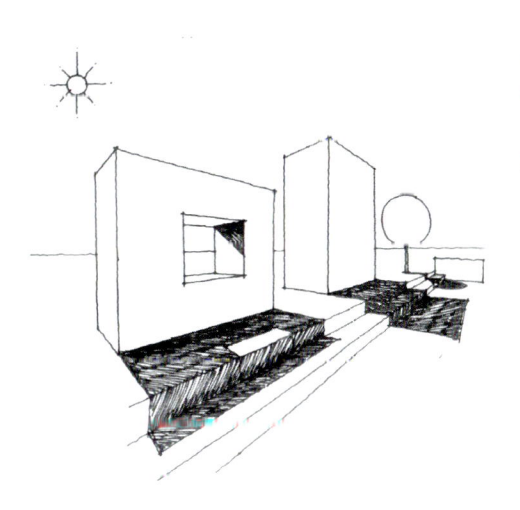

Shadow casting
Different level
The shape of the shadow formed at areas with variant heights

Shadow casting: Shadow casting on different levels

RENDERING TECHNIQUES 101

5.4 RENDERING TECHNIQUES

Pencil

The understanding of rendering techniques is imperative to ensuring the quality of sketches produced. There is a range of rendering techniques to choose from such as single hatching, cross hatching, pattern, pointillism and line and tone value. This section will only explain in great detail the techniques aforementioned.

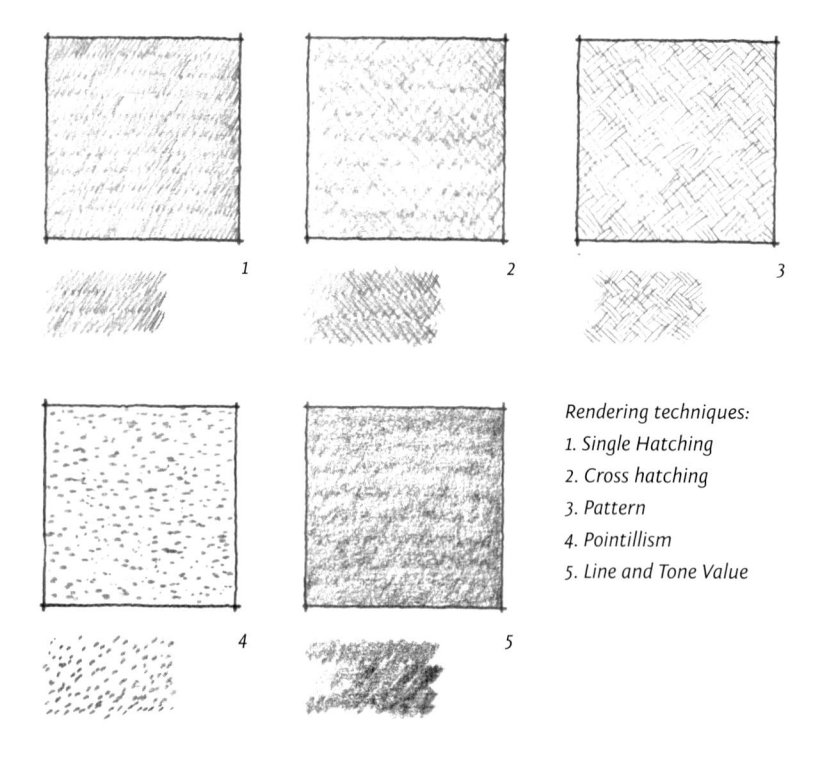

Rendering techniques:
1. Single Hatching
2. Cross hatching
3. Pattern
4. Pointillism
5. Line and Tone Value

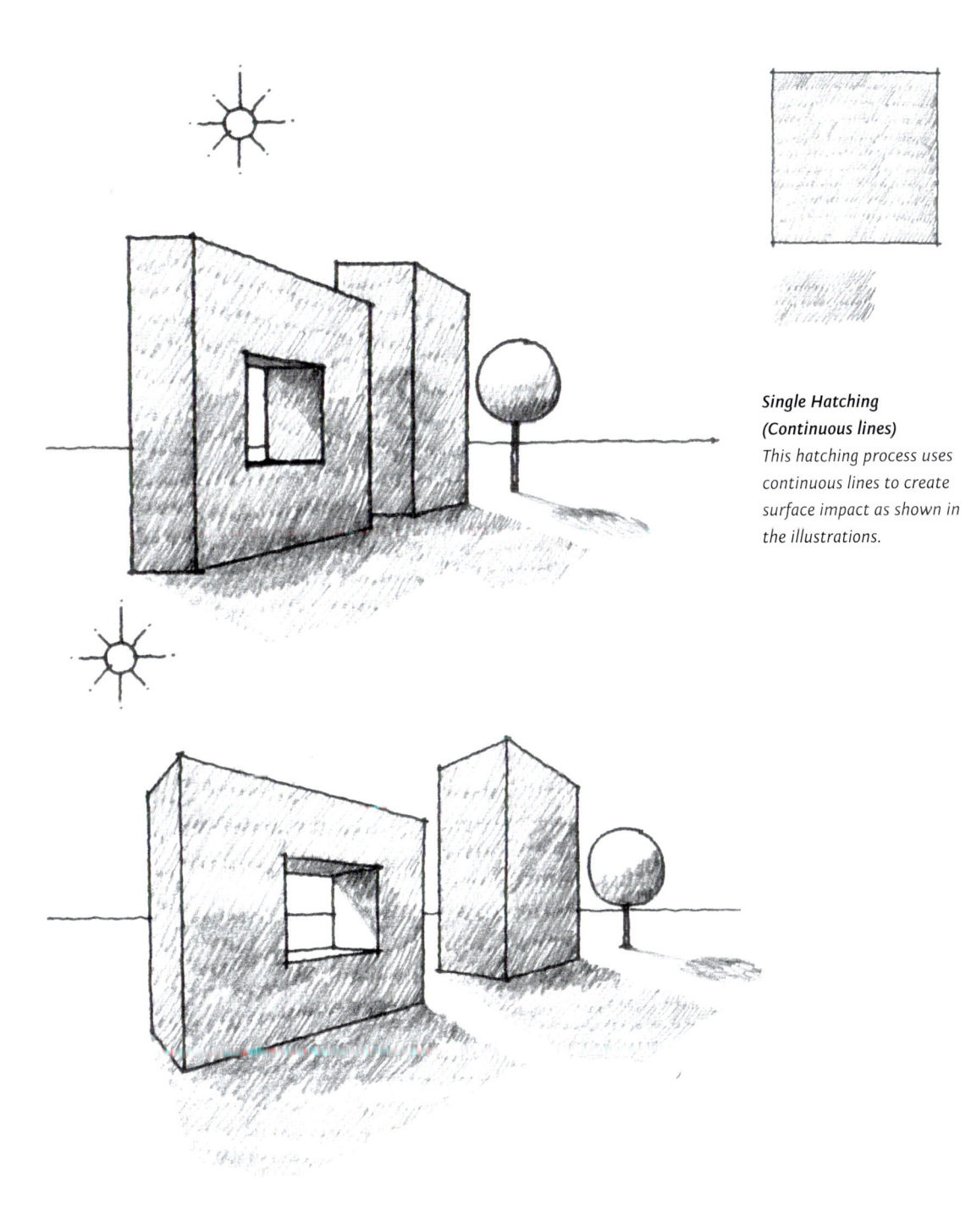

***Single Hatching
(Continuous lines)***
This hatching process uses continuous lines to create surface impact as shown in the illustrations.

RENDERING TECHNIQUES 103

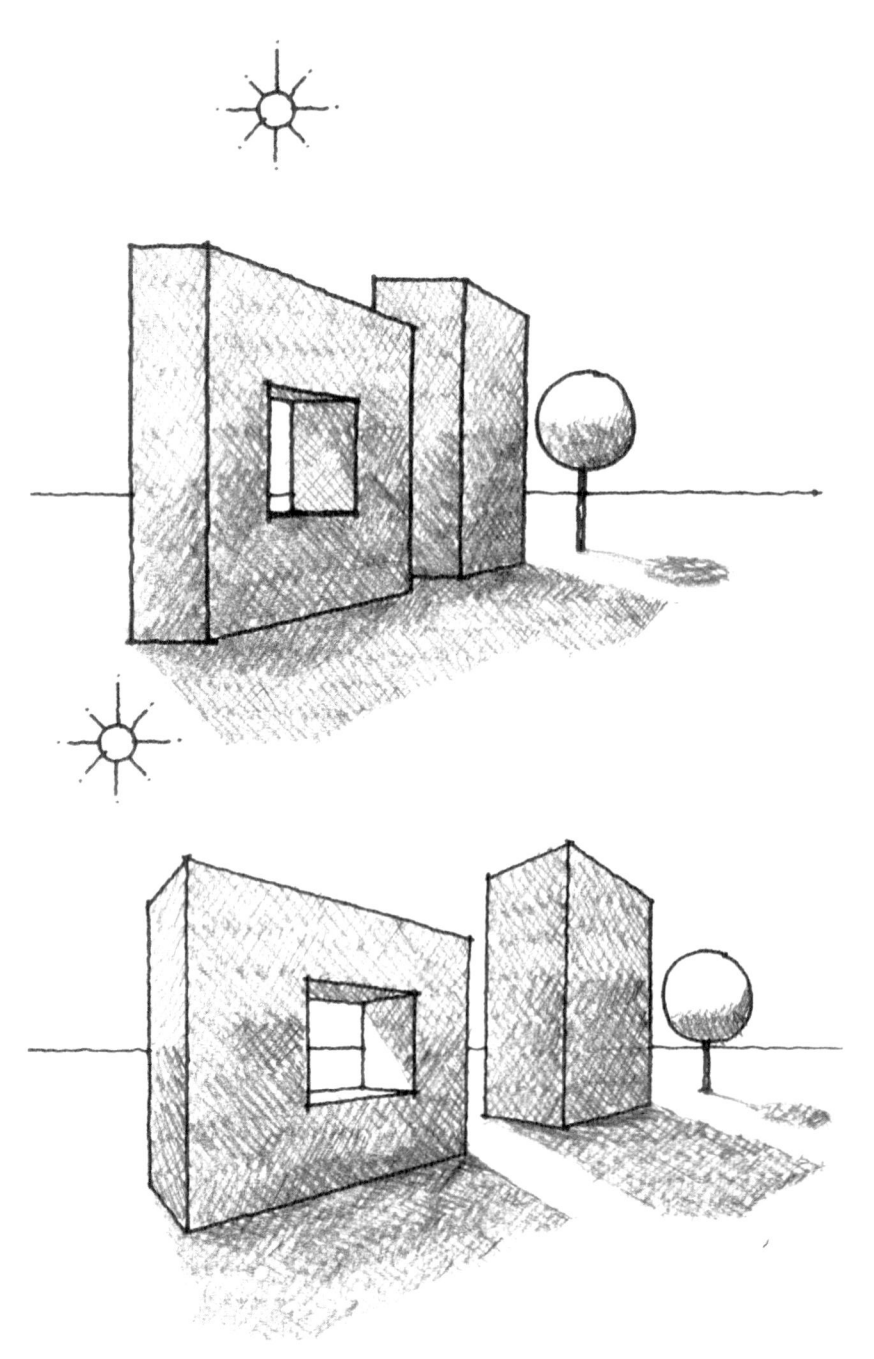

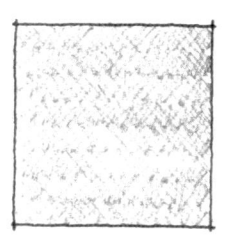

Cross Hatching
(Continuous lines)

The same process is used as in single hatching technique but the impact created on the object surface is very different compared to the surface using single hatching technique.

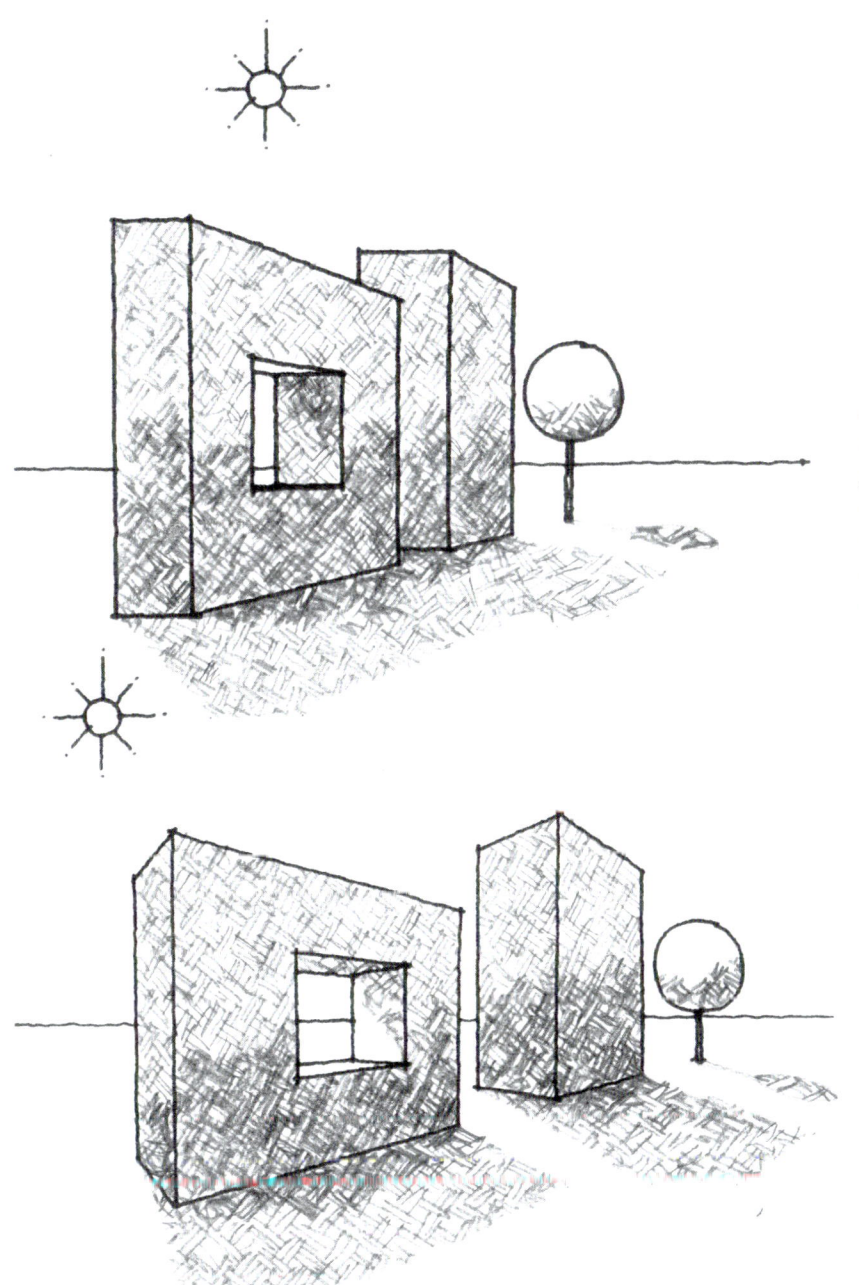

Pattern Rendering
The use of pattern in rendering process could also result in a fascinating end product, making the texture of the surface become more apparent.

RENDERING TECHNIQUES 105

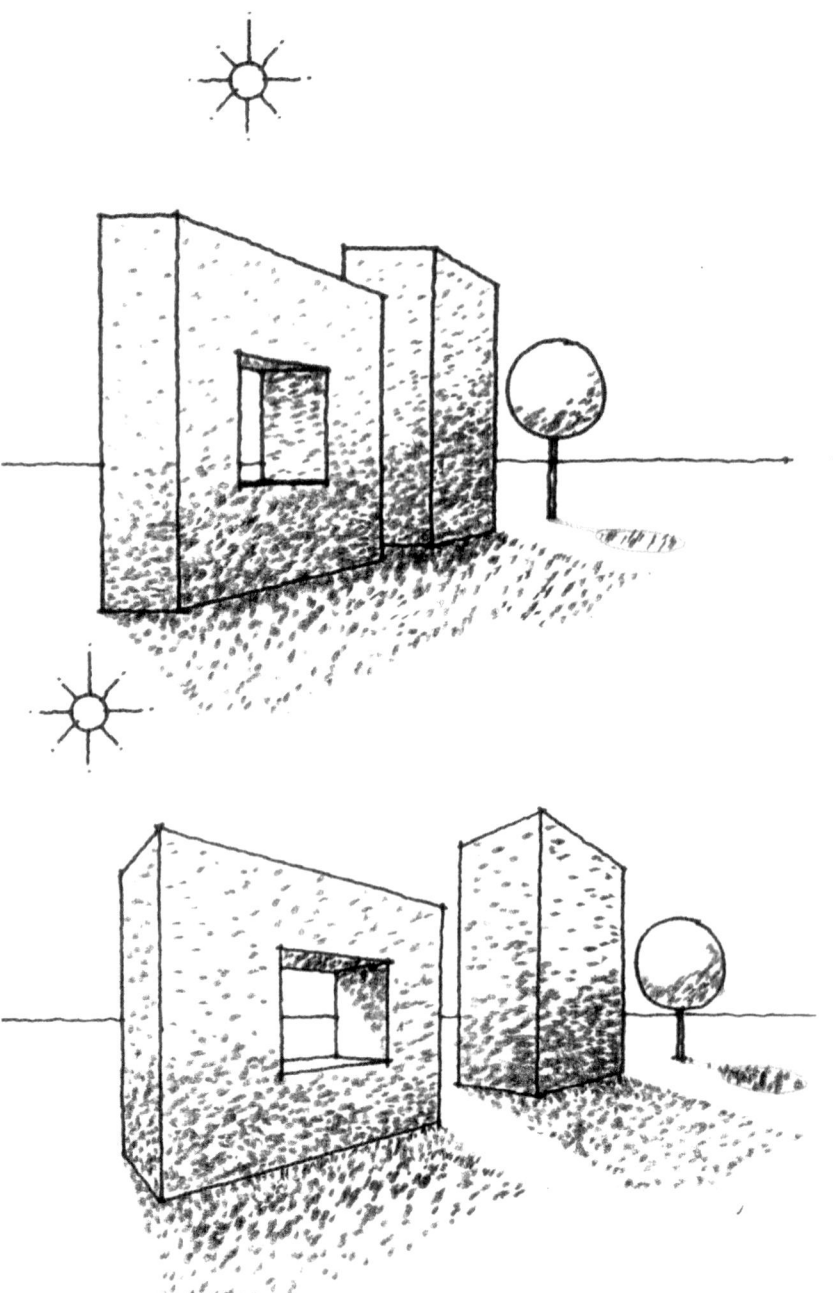

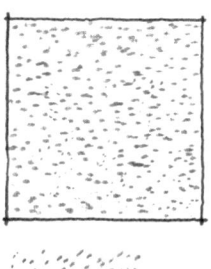

Pointillism
An interesting technique but it is very time consuming to produce a composition as compared to hatching technique.

106 RENDERING TECHNIQUES

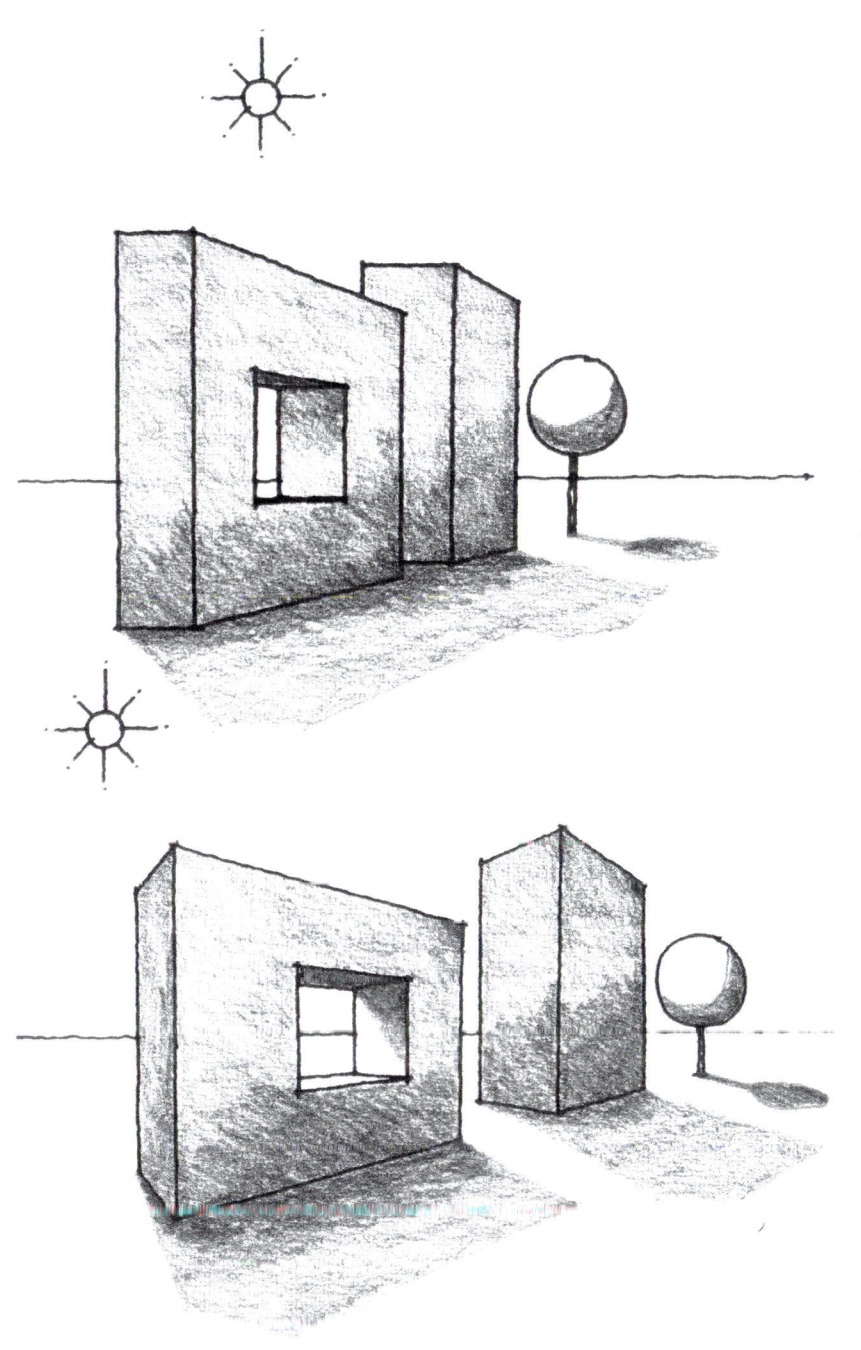

Line and Tone Value
A simple concept to be understood and practised. An artist or designer is only required to familiarize himself in determining the appropriate light zone to ensure the tone value used is the right one and suitable for the composition.

RENDERING TECHNIQUES 107

Pen

Pen is a dry medium rendering that facilitates the production of a quality sketch. The result of rendering by pen is different to pencil although the same rendering techniques are applied. Do compare the results based on the examples given.

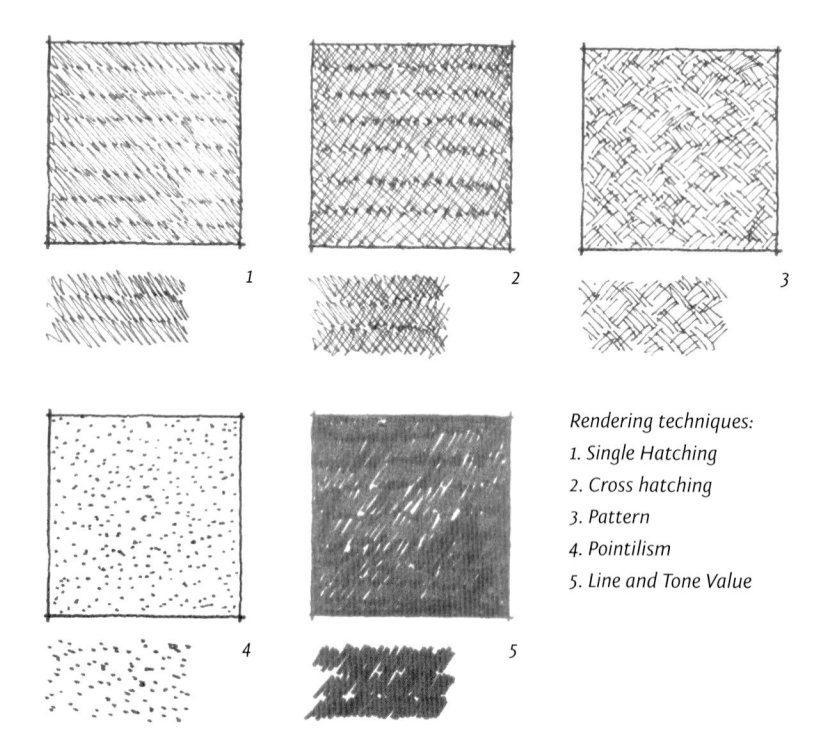

Rendering techniques:
1. Single Hatching
2. Cross hatching
3. Pattern
4. Pointilism
5. Line and Tone Value

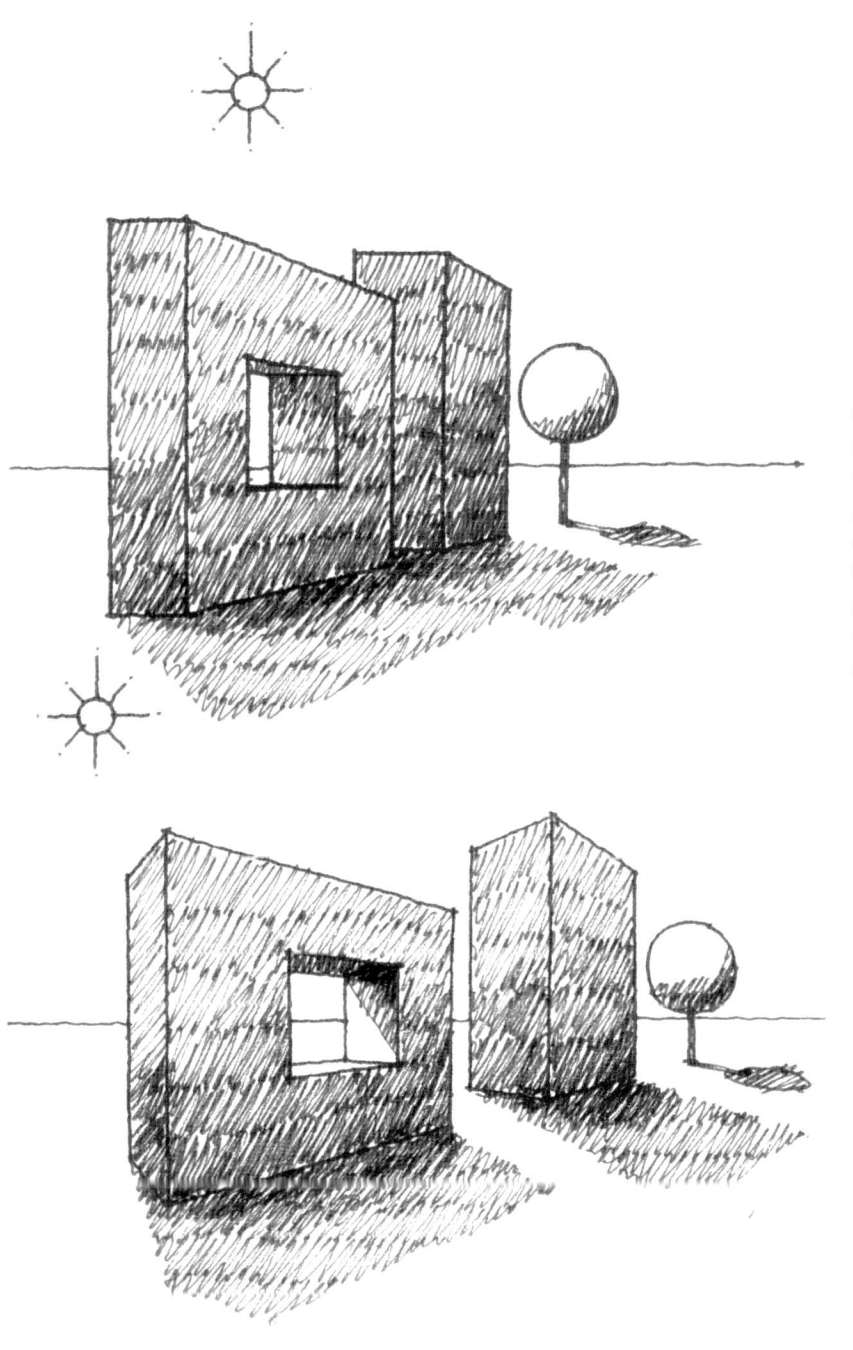

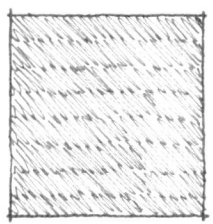

***Single Hatching
(Continuous line)***
Observe the impact of using pen and pencil rendering as compared to rendering using this technique. The impact of using a pen is more apparent as compared to the one using a pencil.

RENDERING TECHNIQUES 109

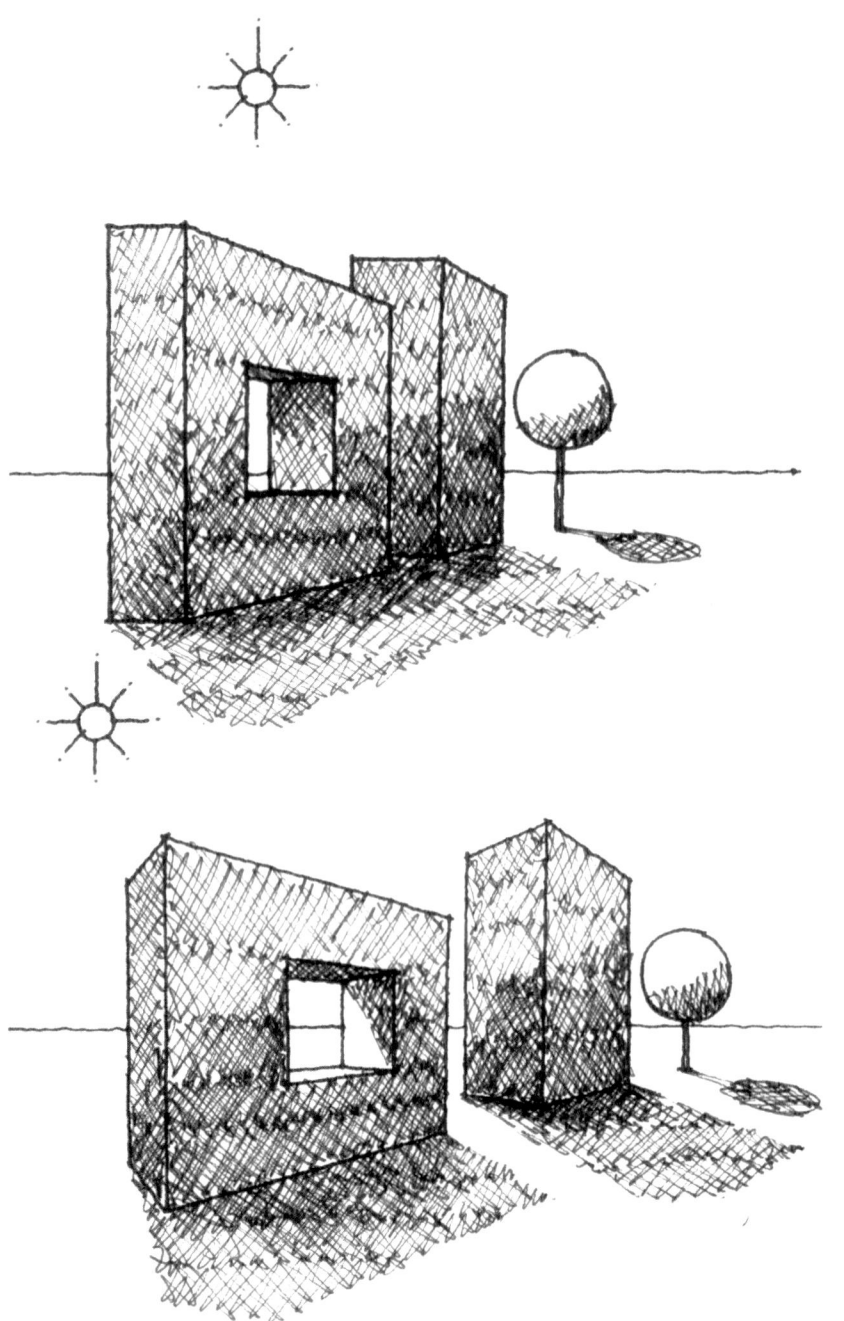

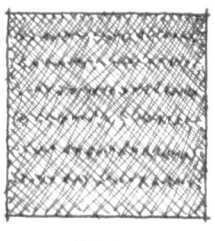

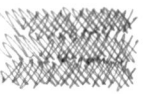

***Cross Hatching
(Continuous line)***
Observe how different impacts are created by two sketch compositions which use the same rendering concept but of different lines.

110 RENDERING TECHNIQUES

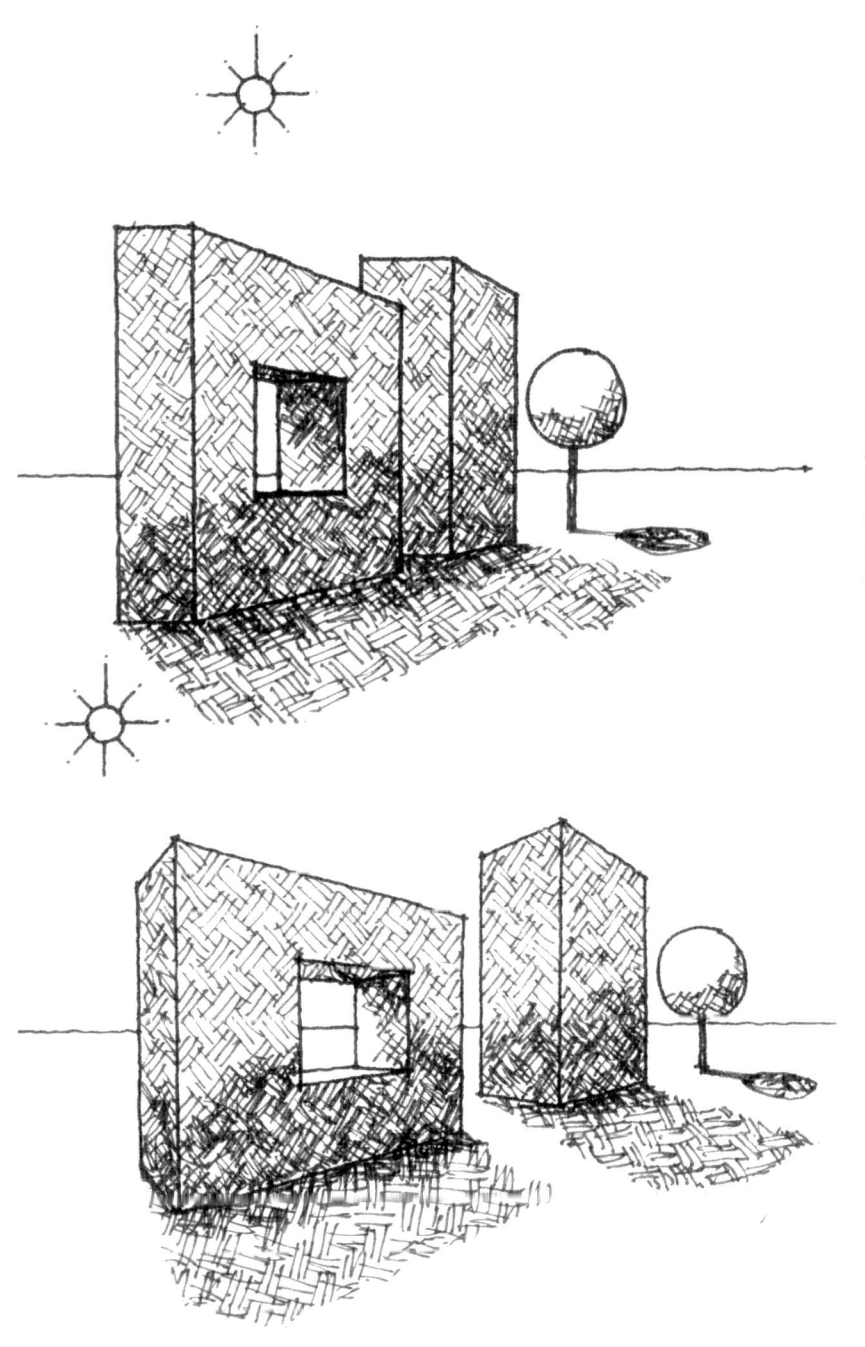

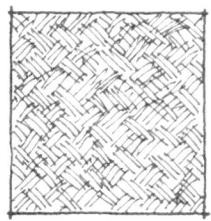

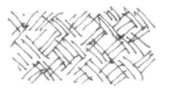

Pattern Rendering
Study how pattern rendering is used in sketch composition in the illustrations given. It could be used to give texture on the surface of an object.

RENDERING TECHNIQUES 111

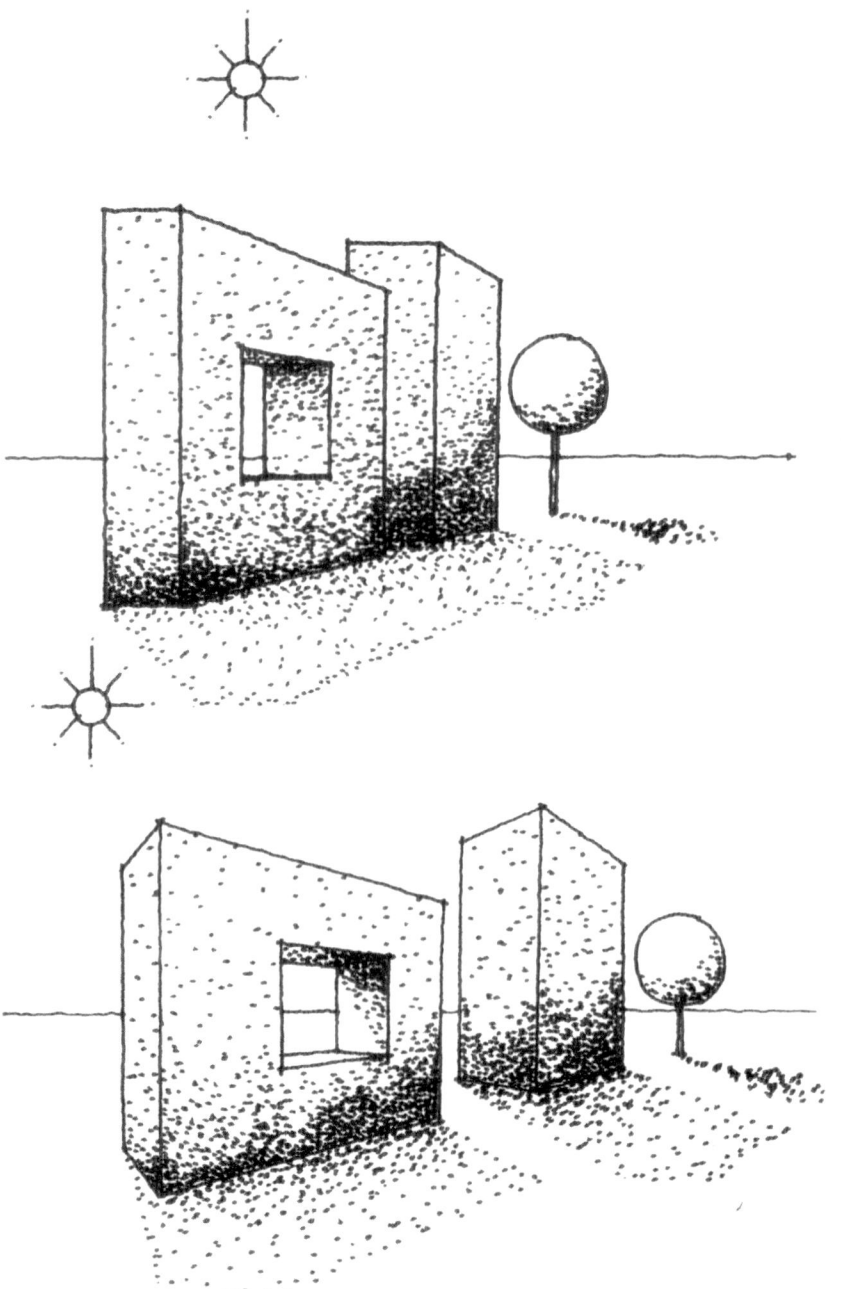

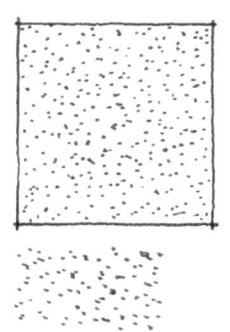

Pointillism
An artist or designer has to be smart in deciding on the focus point to differentiate the area that receives less light to the one that receives more.
This technique demands a lot of time to produce a sketch composition.

112　RENDERING TECHNIQUES

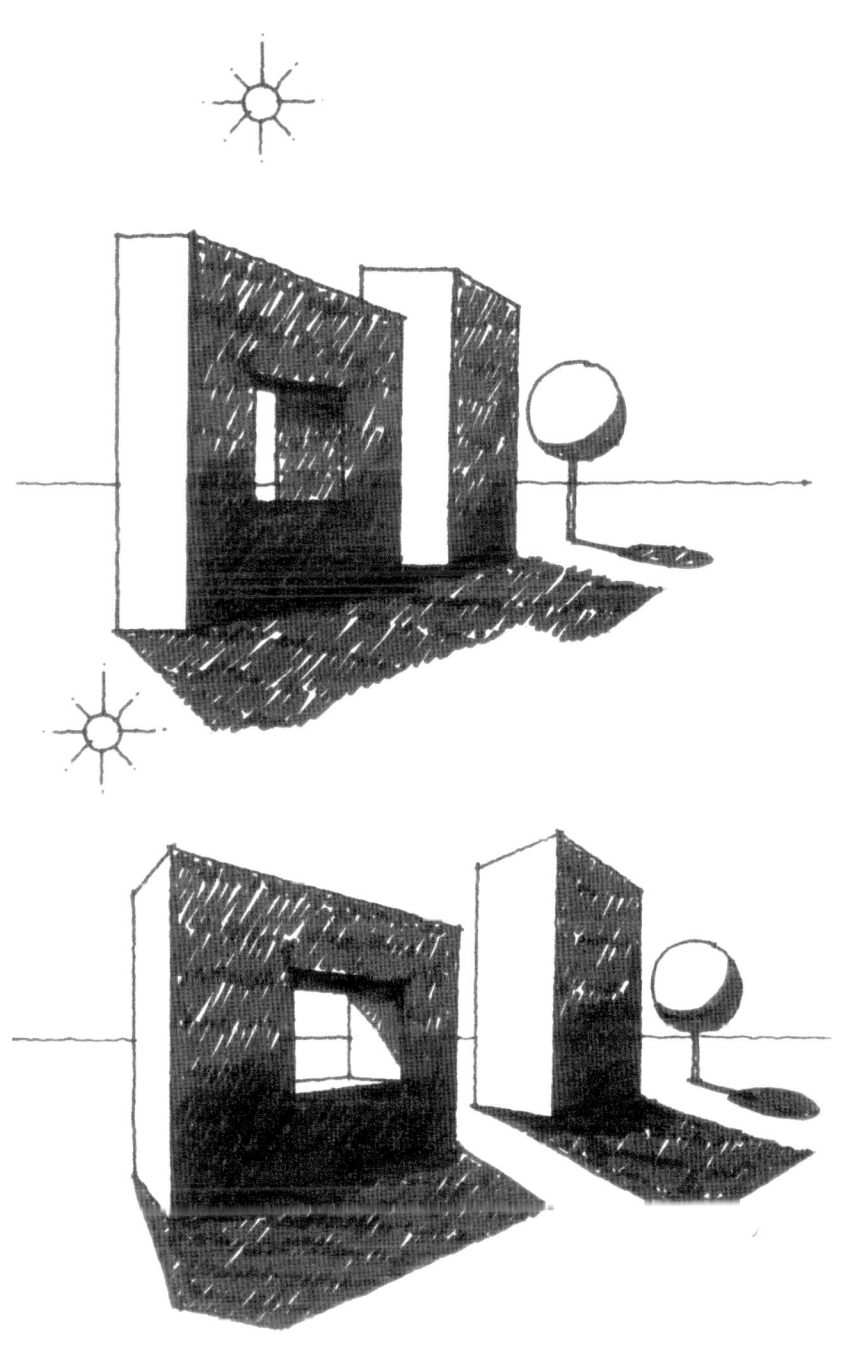

Line and Tone Value
This technique involves advance skills to guarantee the sketch composition is not overshadowed by radical rendering impact.

RENDERING TECHNIQUES 113

6.0 A STEP BY STEP PROCESS

6.1 INTRODUCTION

This chapter will demonstrate a step by step' process to creating a sketch composition. This interesting process will start from setting up the horizon line to the rendering process. The chapter is divided into three main sections which are one point, two point and multi point perspectives. Generally, all the sections will be focusing on the different types of settings such as object setting, landscape setting and urban setting. This is to give a broad perspective and understanding in creating a good quality sketch composition. Other than that, some examples will show how to set the perspective when dealing with levels and height. Do observe properly and understand how the perspective settings are done to create a good sketch composition. Enjoy the journey.

Example of one point perspective of a landscape setting composition produced from a step by step process.

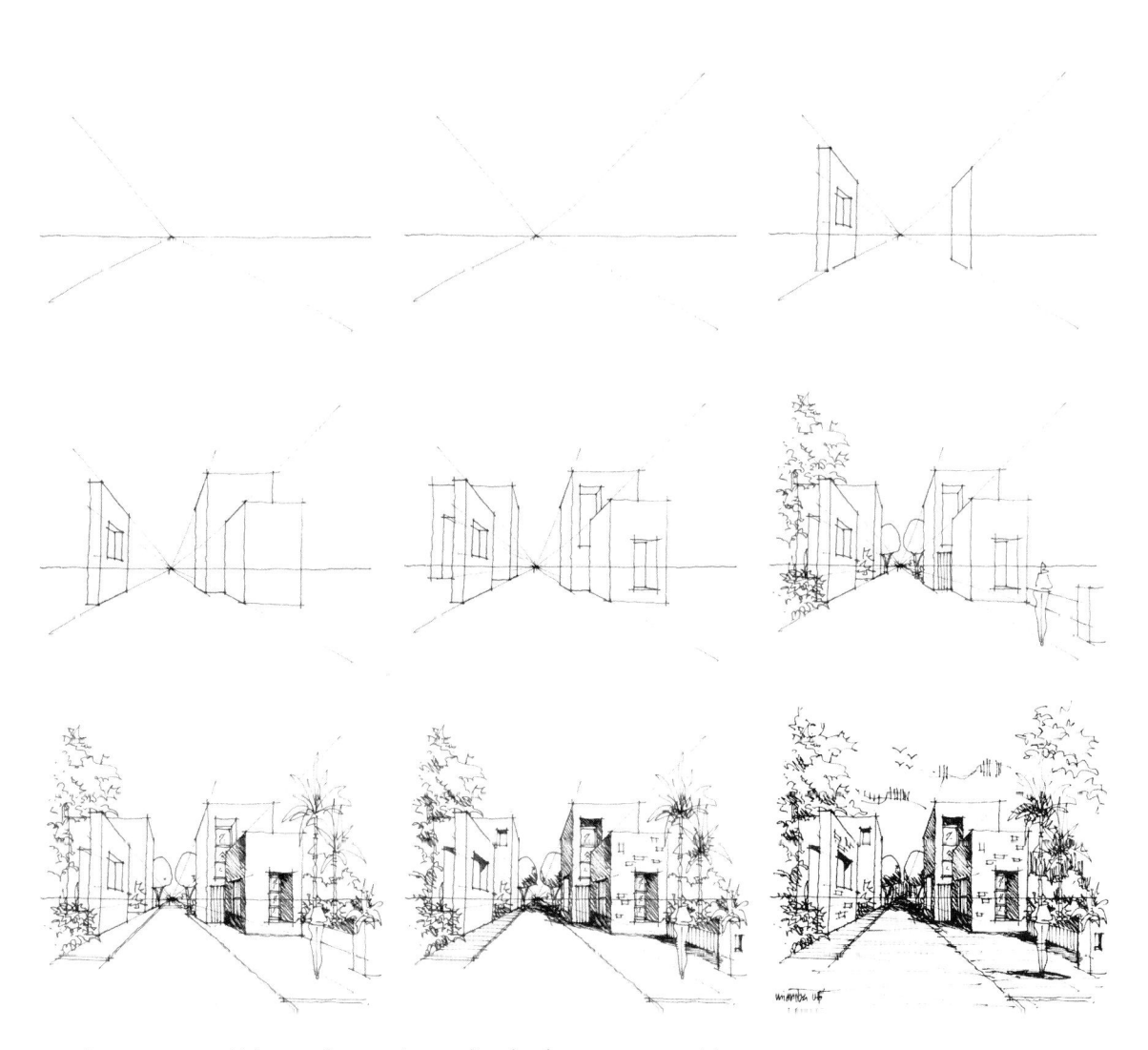

A step by step process which starts from a point to a line then becomes a composition.

- **Step by Step: One Point Perspective**

This section will demonstrate how to sketch using one point perspective with different types of environment settings starting with object setting to urban and architectural setting. Each of these settings has its own criteria that need to be identified and understood especially when dealing with rendering which involves shadow.

One point perspective: objects setting

One point perspective: interior setting

One point perspective: landscape setting

One point perspective: Urban and architectural setting

One point perspective: Height setting in perspectives

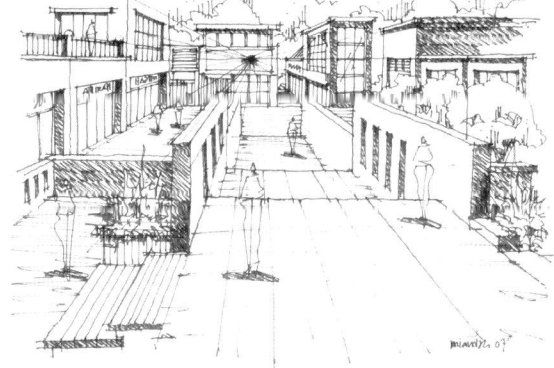

One point perspective: Level setting in perspectives

- **Step by Step: Two Point Perspective**

Different types of environment setting will be used to demonstrate a step by step process of two point perspective. Do observe the process to identify the difference between one point and two point perspective compositions.

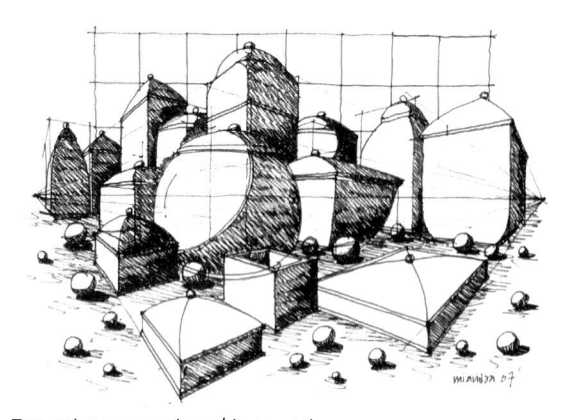

Two point perspective: objects setting

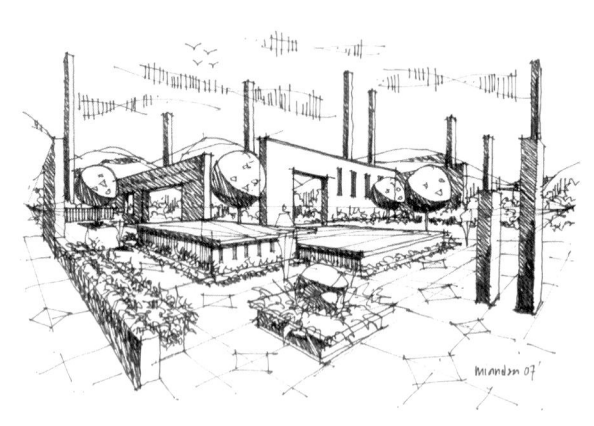

Two point perspective: landscape setting

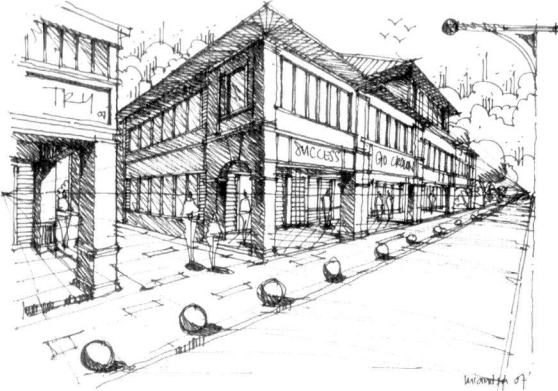

Two point perspective: Urban and architectural setting

Two point perspective: Level setting in perspectives

- **Step by Step: Three Point Perspective**

These exercises are the process to sketch a three point perspective using two samples: urban setting and landscape setting. The process is almost the same with the other perspective techniques but what makes it different is the number of vanishing points involved, which are three points.

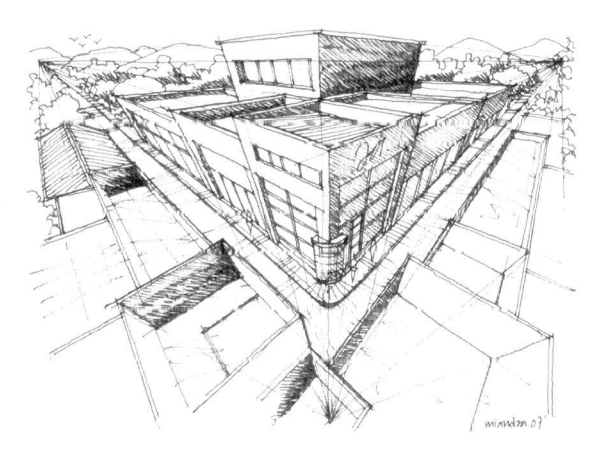

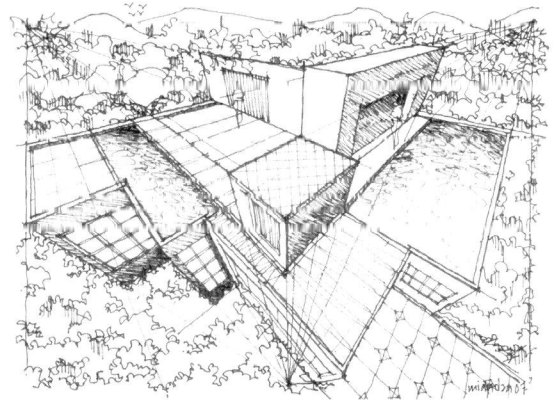

Three point perspective: Urban and landscape setting

- **Step by Step: Multi Point Perspective**

This is another interesting exercise to be explored and practised because most of the environment settings especially those related to nature are in the multi point perspective setting. It is an excellent technique that needs to be mastered by designers.

Multi point perspective: Interior and landscape setting

Multi point perspective: Urban and level setting

6.2 ONE POINT PERSPECTIVE

- Object setting 1

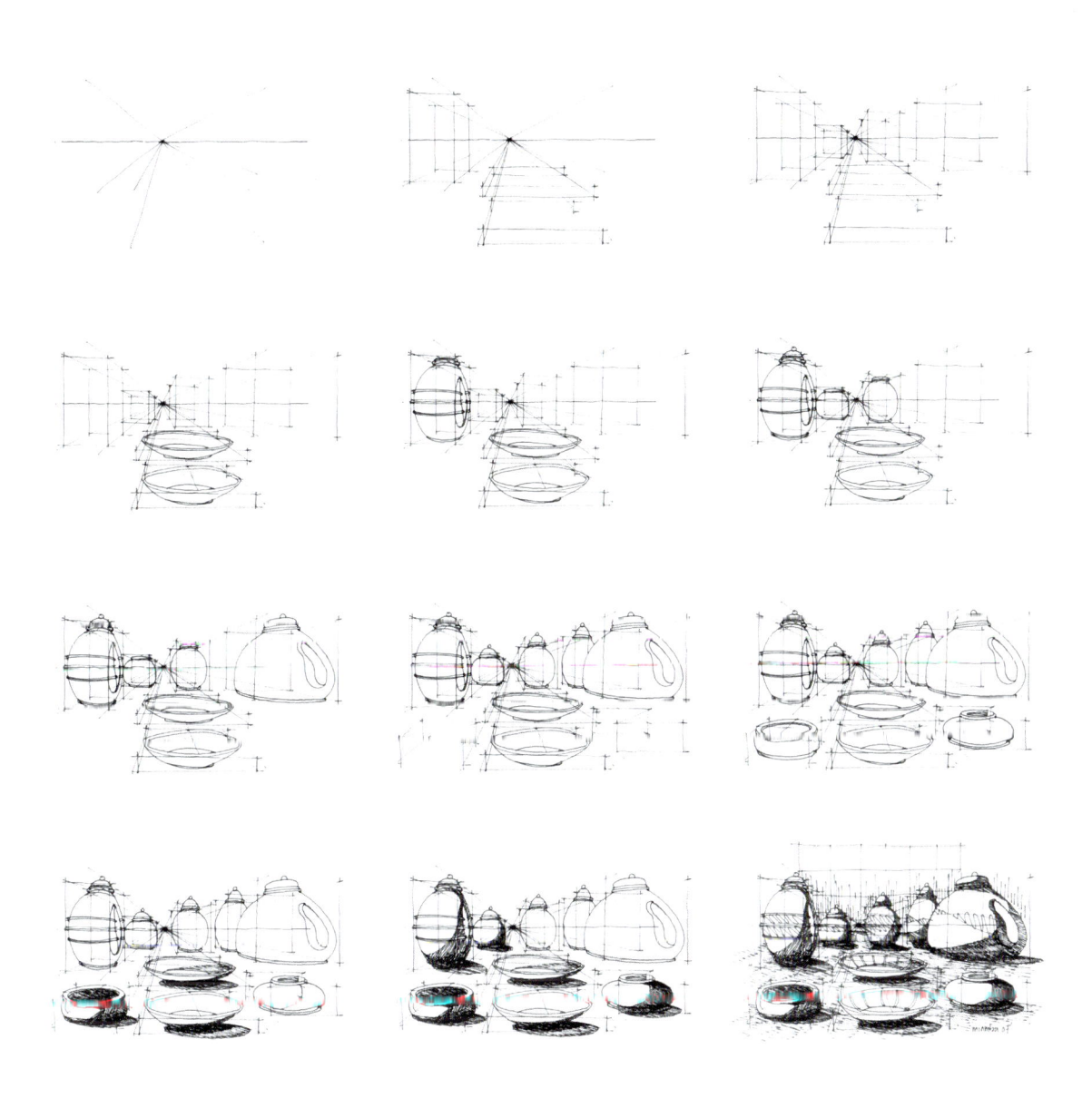

A STEP BY STEP PROCESS

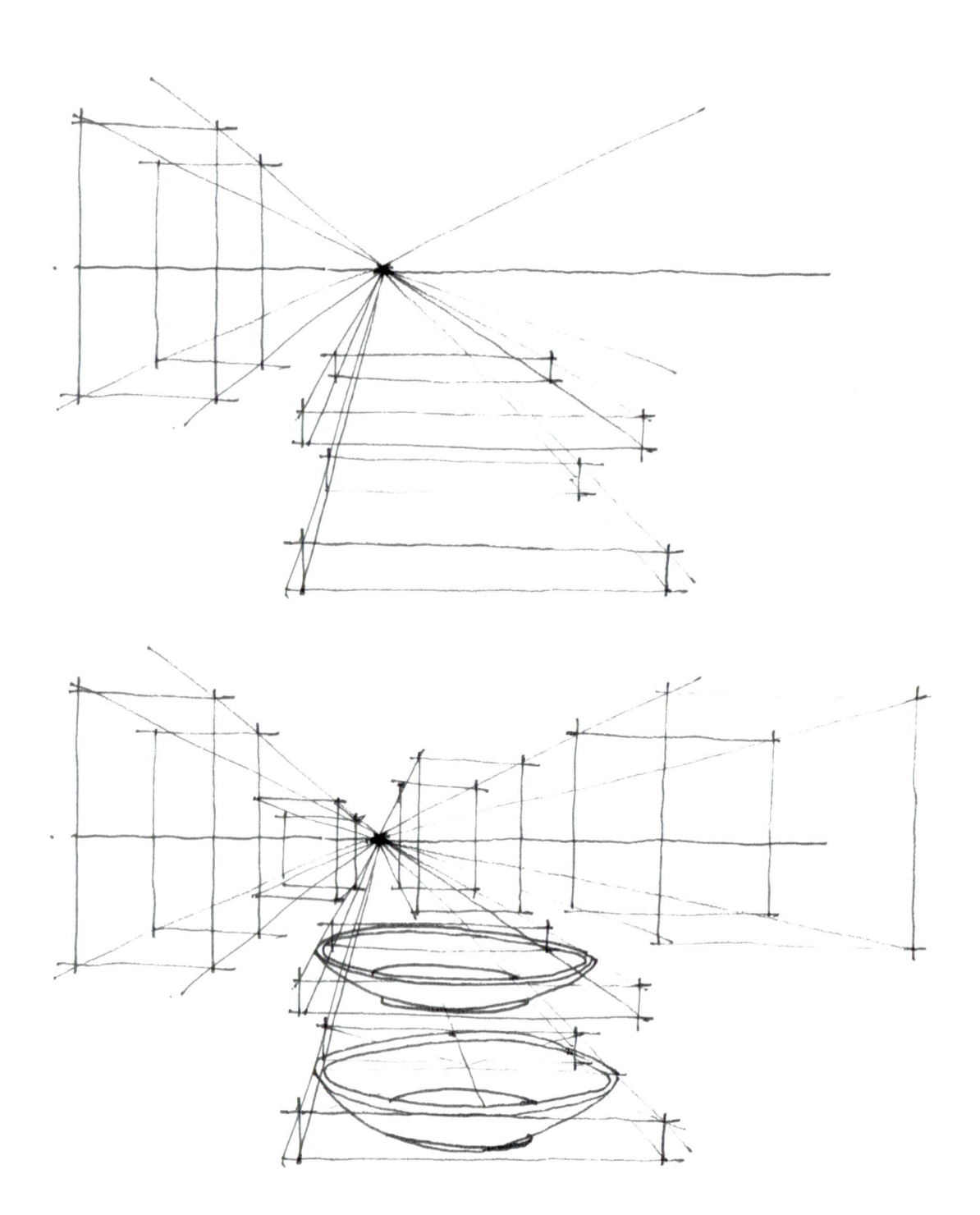

Step 1
The imaginary box is one of the main factors to create a quality sketch. Look carefully at the examples given on how these boxes work to create objects for the sketch composition.

Tip: *Remember the imaginary box.*

122   A STEP BY STEP PROCESS

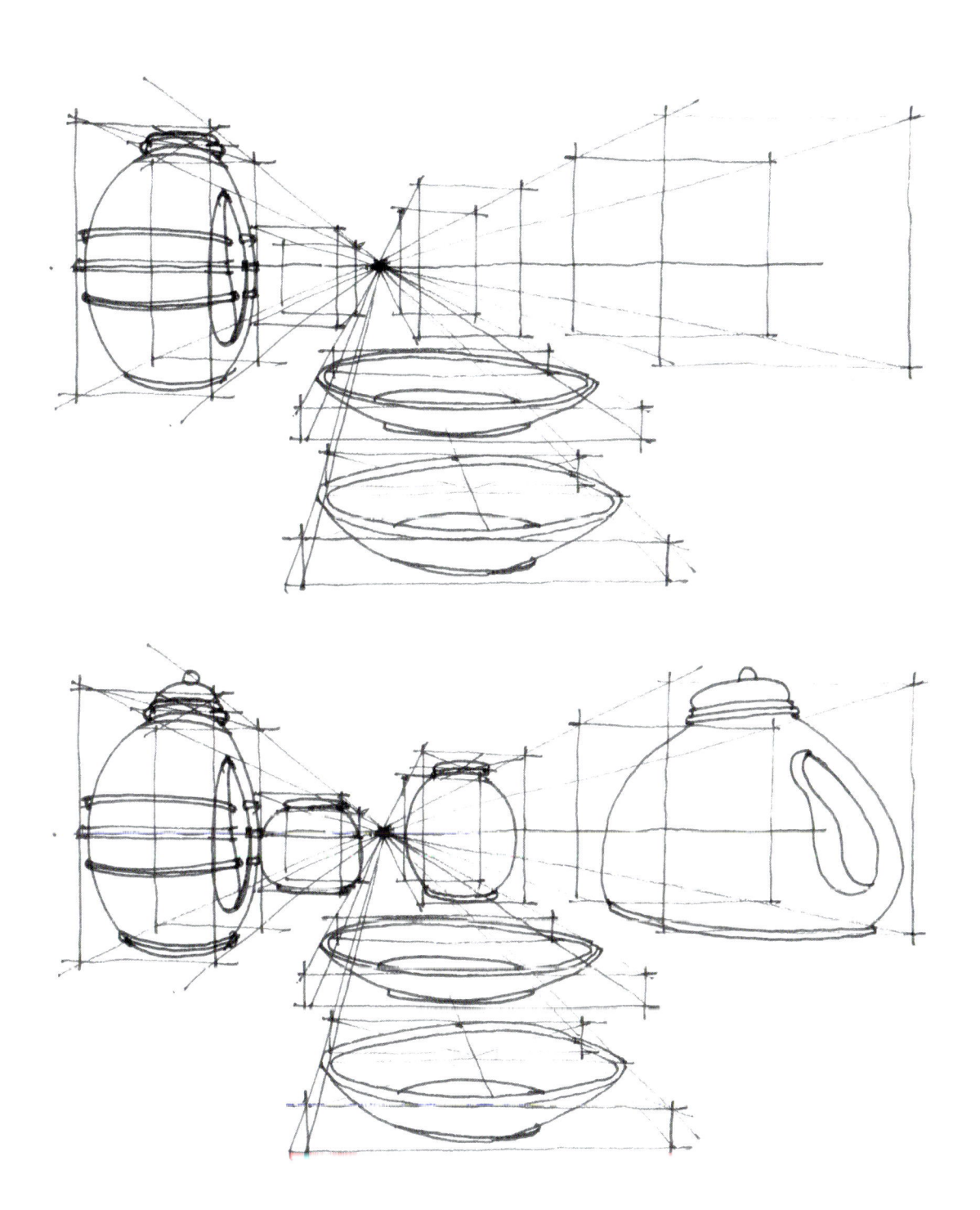

Step 2
The next step is to draw objects from within the imaginary boxes. This principle will help to control the objects' position, size, proportion and scale.

Tip: Follow the principles and you will get a quality sketch composition.

A STEP BY STEP PROCESS

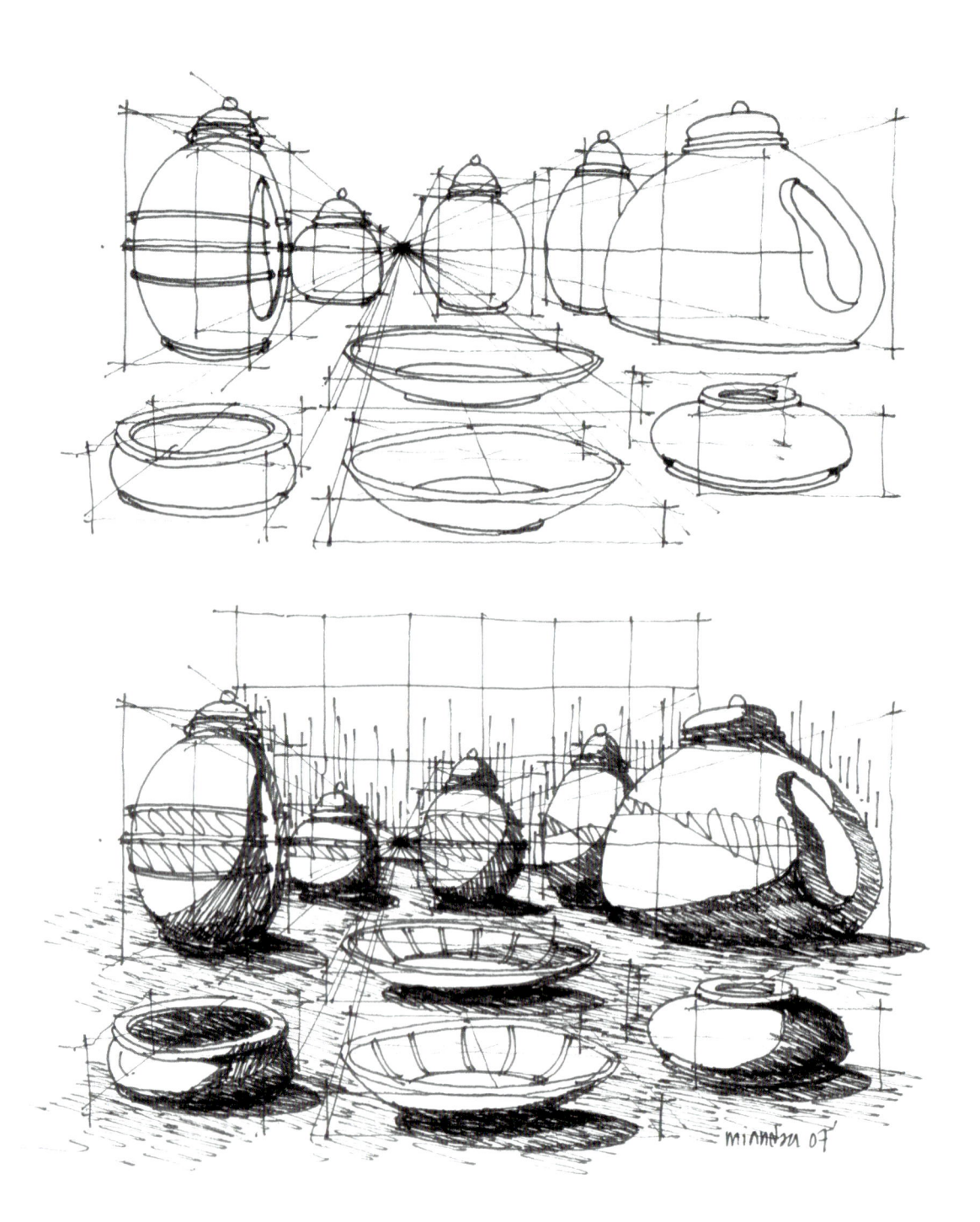

Step 3
Shade and shadow principles help to highlight the sketch composition. One of the factors that needs to be considered is the light source and its direction. From the example, the light source comes from the top left-hand side of the sketch composition.

Tip: Light source and direction need to be determined before applying shade and shadow

124 A STEP BY STEP PROCESS

• Object setting 2

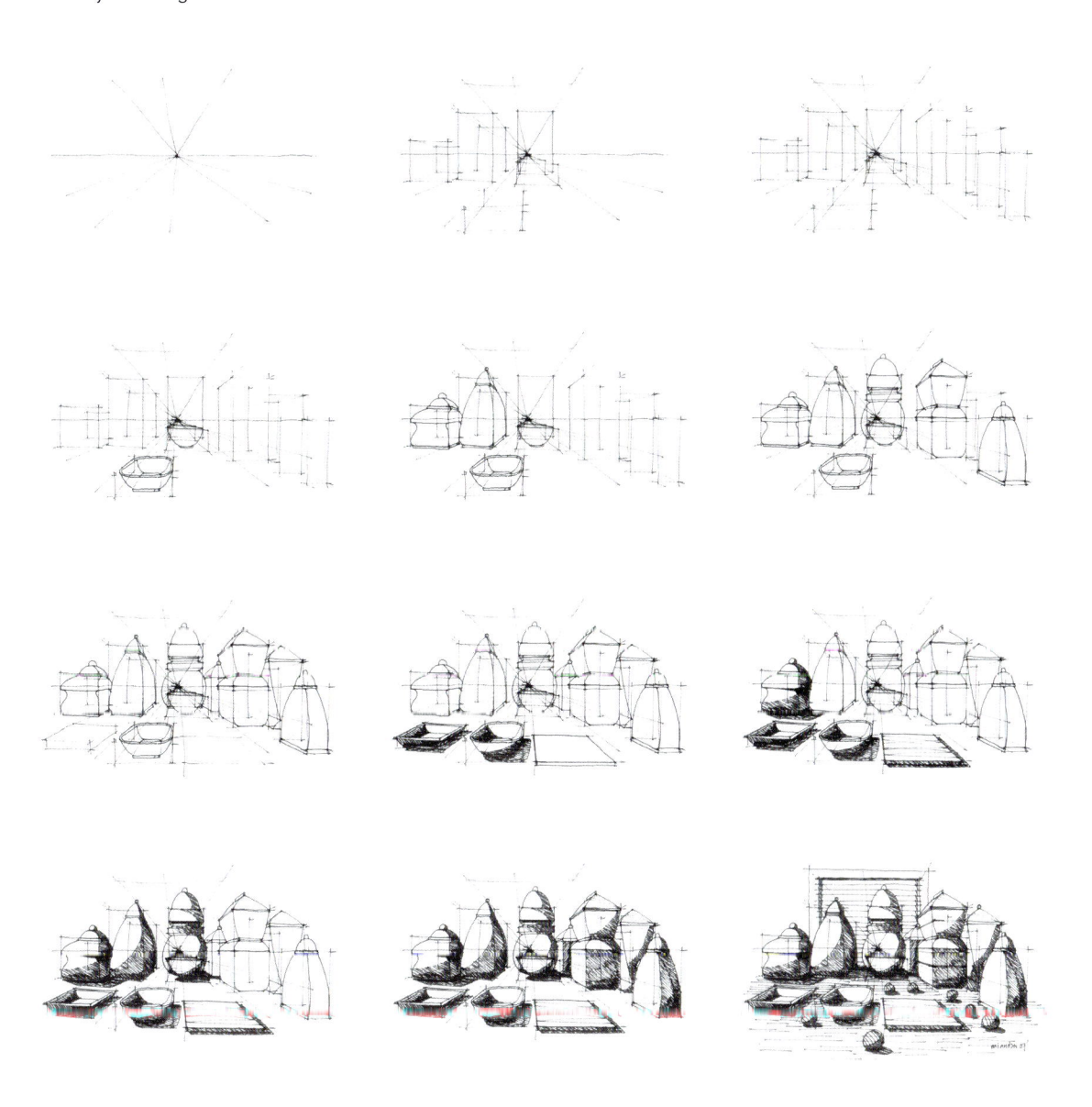

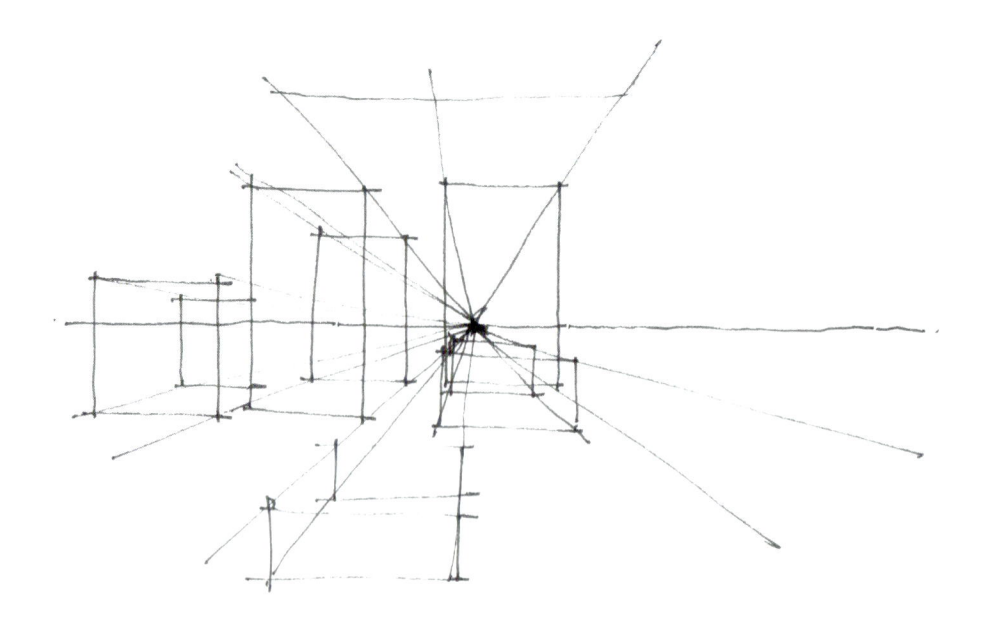

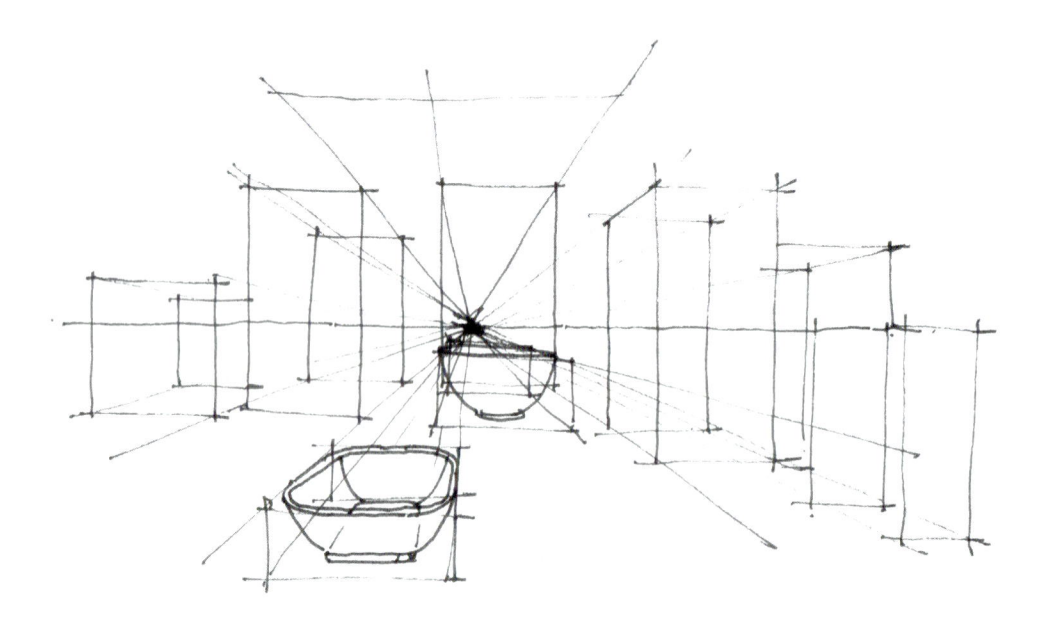

Step 1
A quality sketch is determined by the quality of lines. The designers should have confidence with the lines that they are going to suggest.

Tip: Be confident with lines.

126 A STEP BY STEP PROCESS

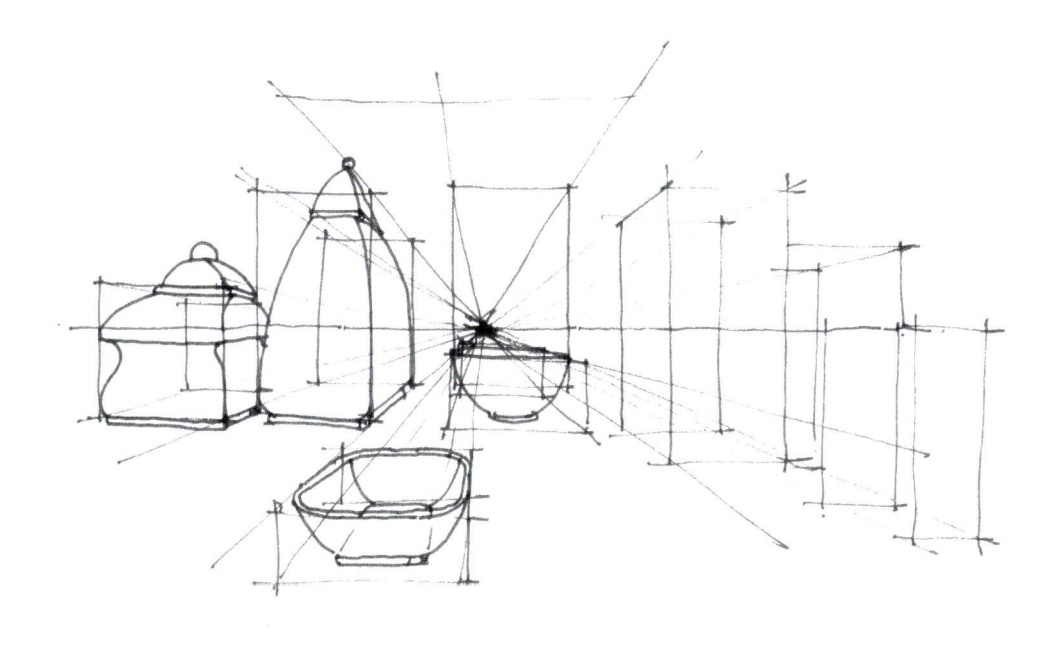

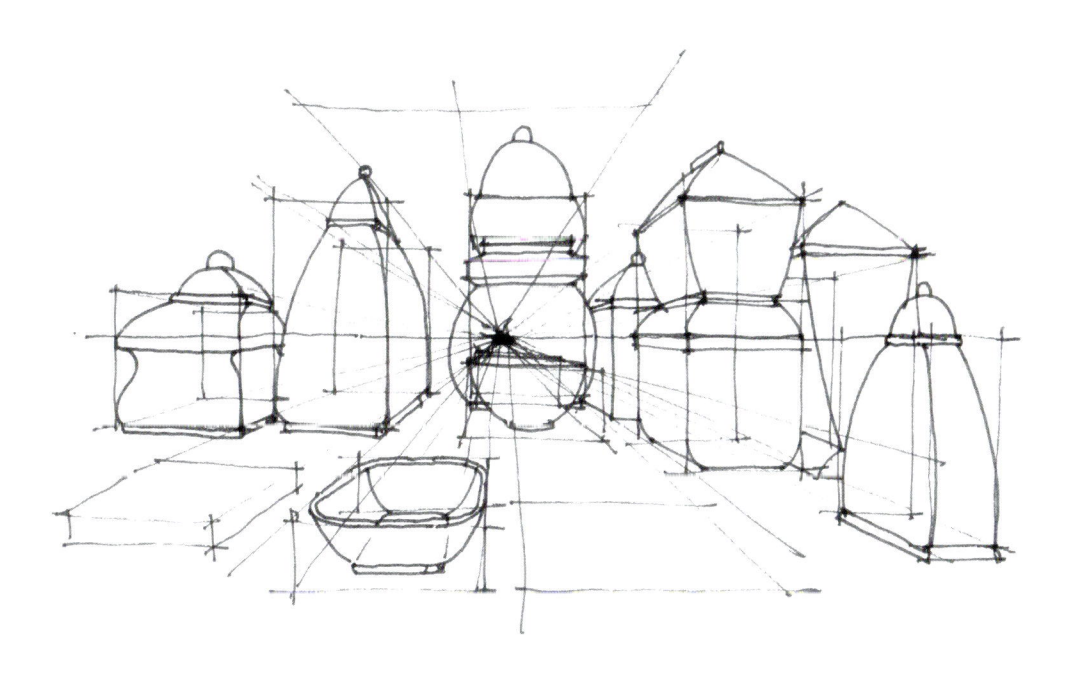

Step 2
The imaginary box does not only act as the object boundary but it also acts as the object locator to the sketch composition. The examples given clearly show the process of setting up the location of object by using the box.

Tip: *Do practise this principle*

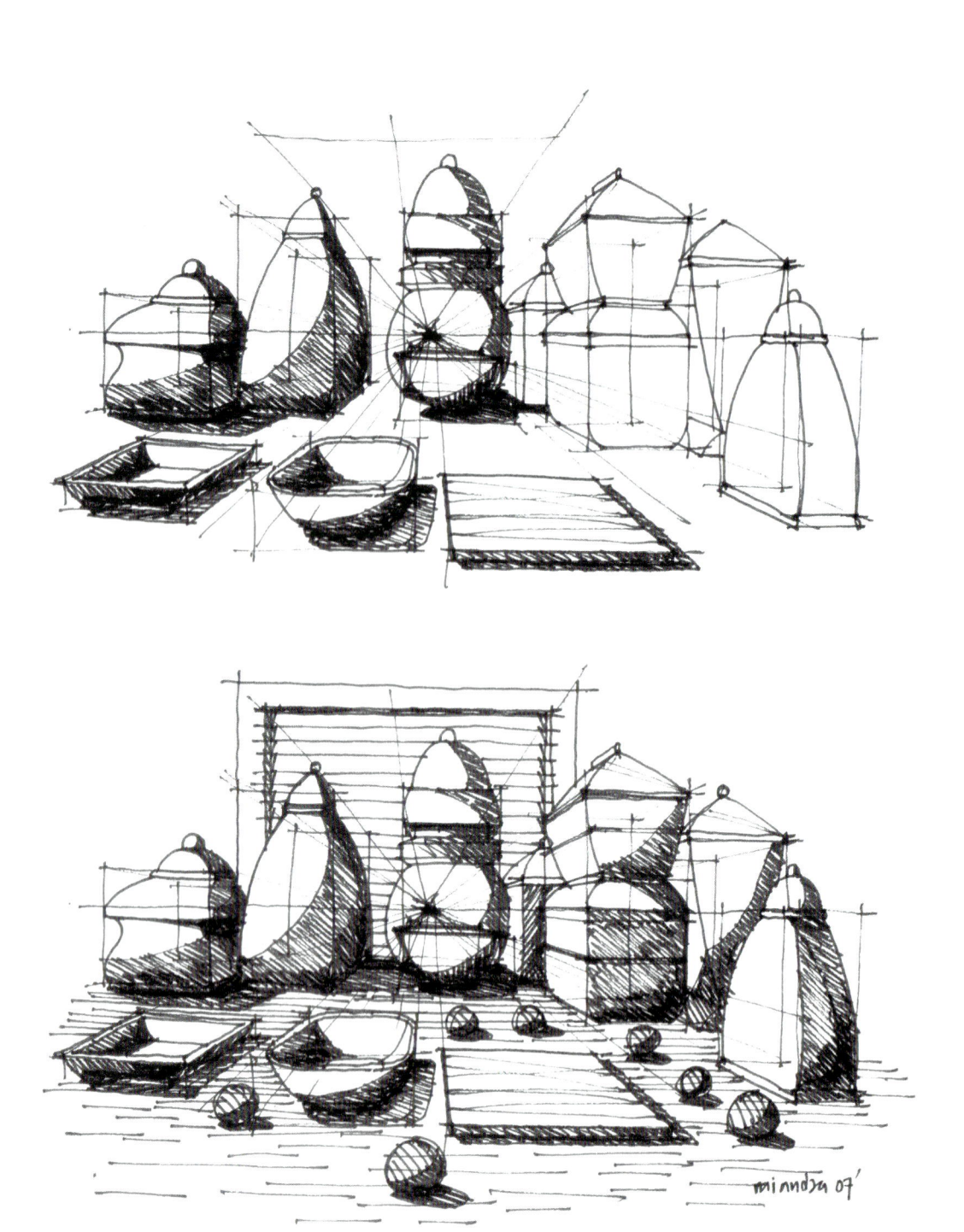

Step 3
Compare these two compositions and look at their interesting transformation. The final composition looks much better. As a conclusion, rendering is a must to get a quality sketch. Look at the process carefully, try to understand how the rendering process takes place.

Tip: *Do refer to rendering technique*

128   A STEP BY STEP PROCESS

• Interior 1 (Living room)

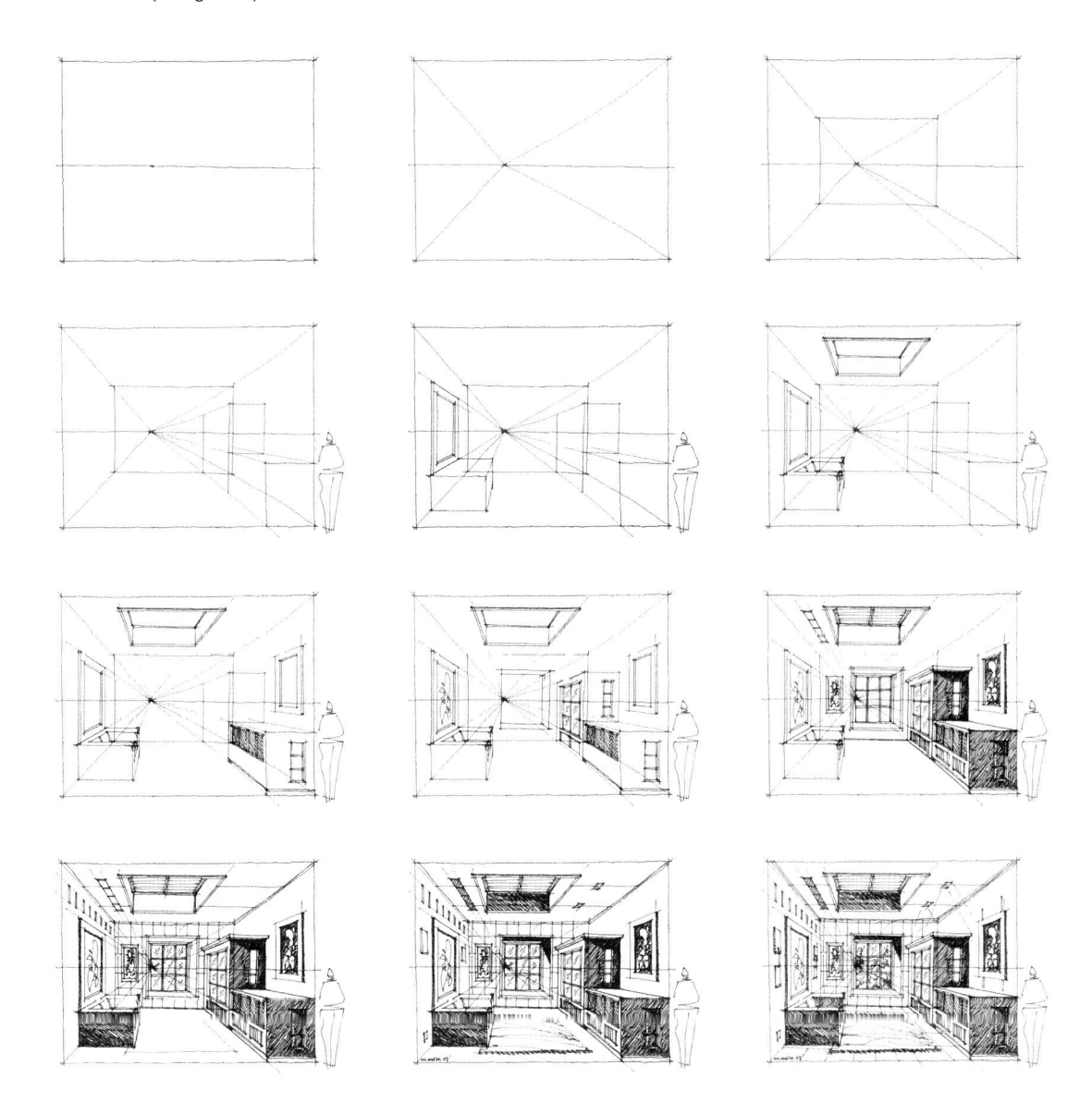

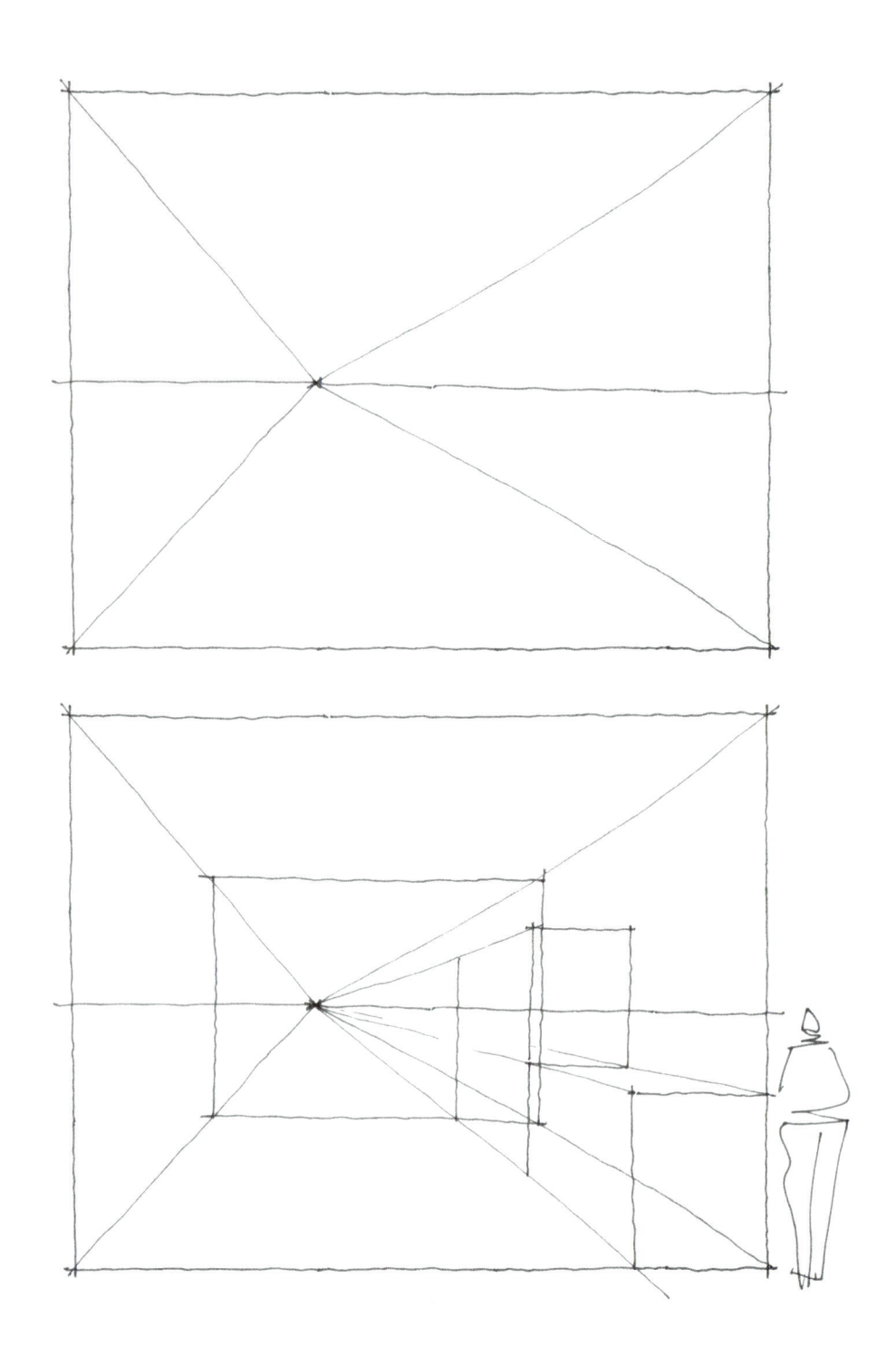

Step 1
The first step that needs to be done is to decide the type of view that is going to be used in the sketch, for instance, human eye view perspective. Then, based on the type of view, draw a box and set the horizon line and vanishing point.

Tip: *Be confident when you draw straight lines*

130 A STEP BY STEP PROCESS

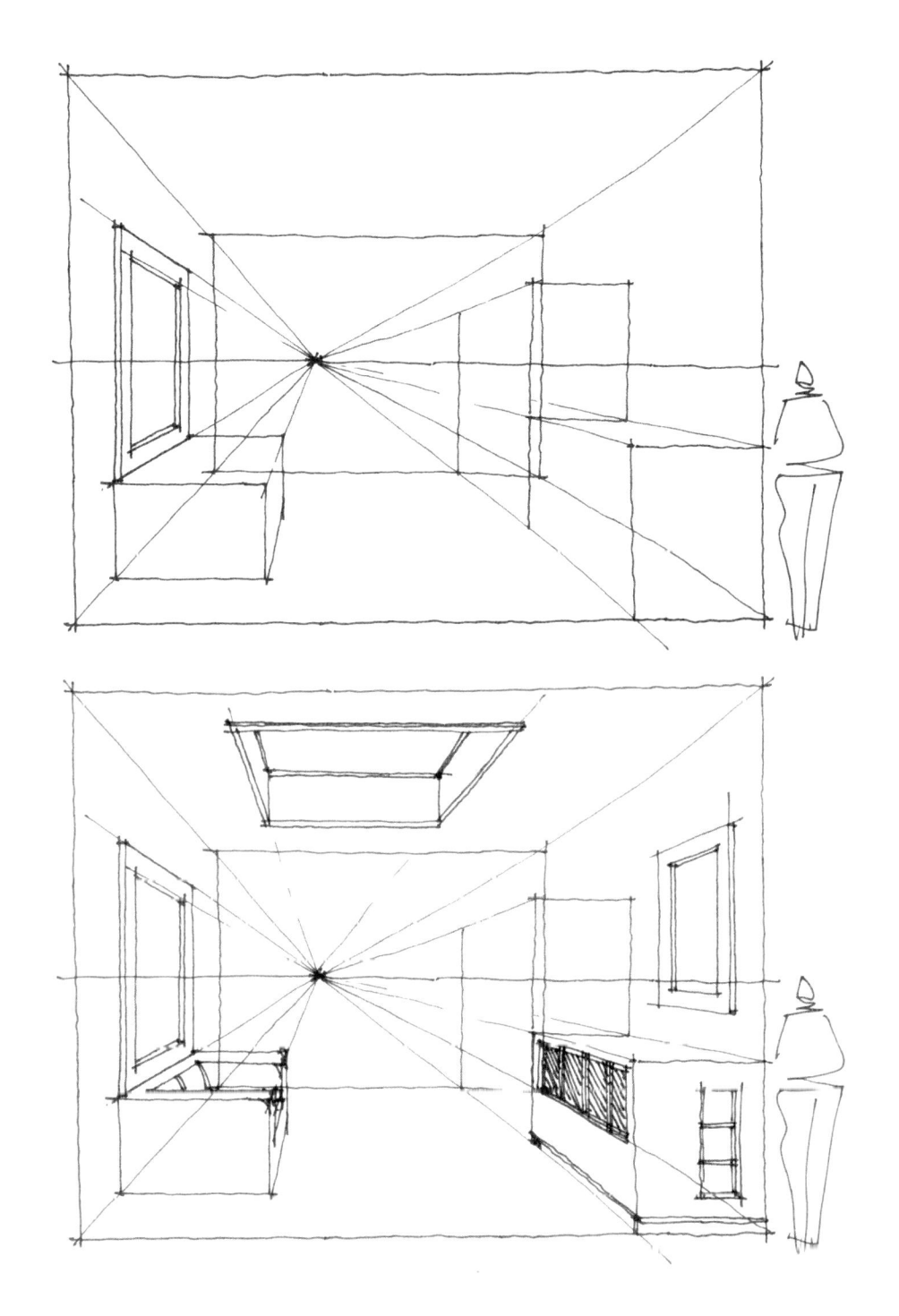

Step 2
Vanishing point is very important to produce a good sketch composition because every object's lines which are perpendicular to the horizon line will refer to this point.

Tip: *Always remember to refer to the vanishing point.*

A STEP BY STEP PROCESS 131

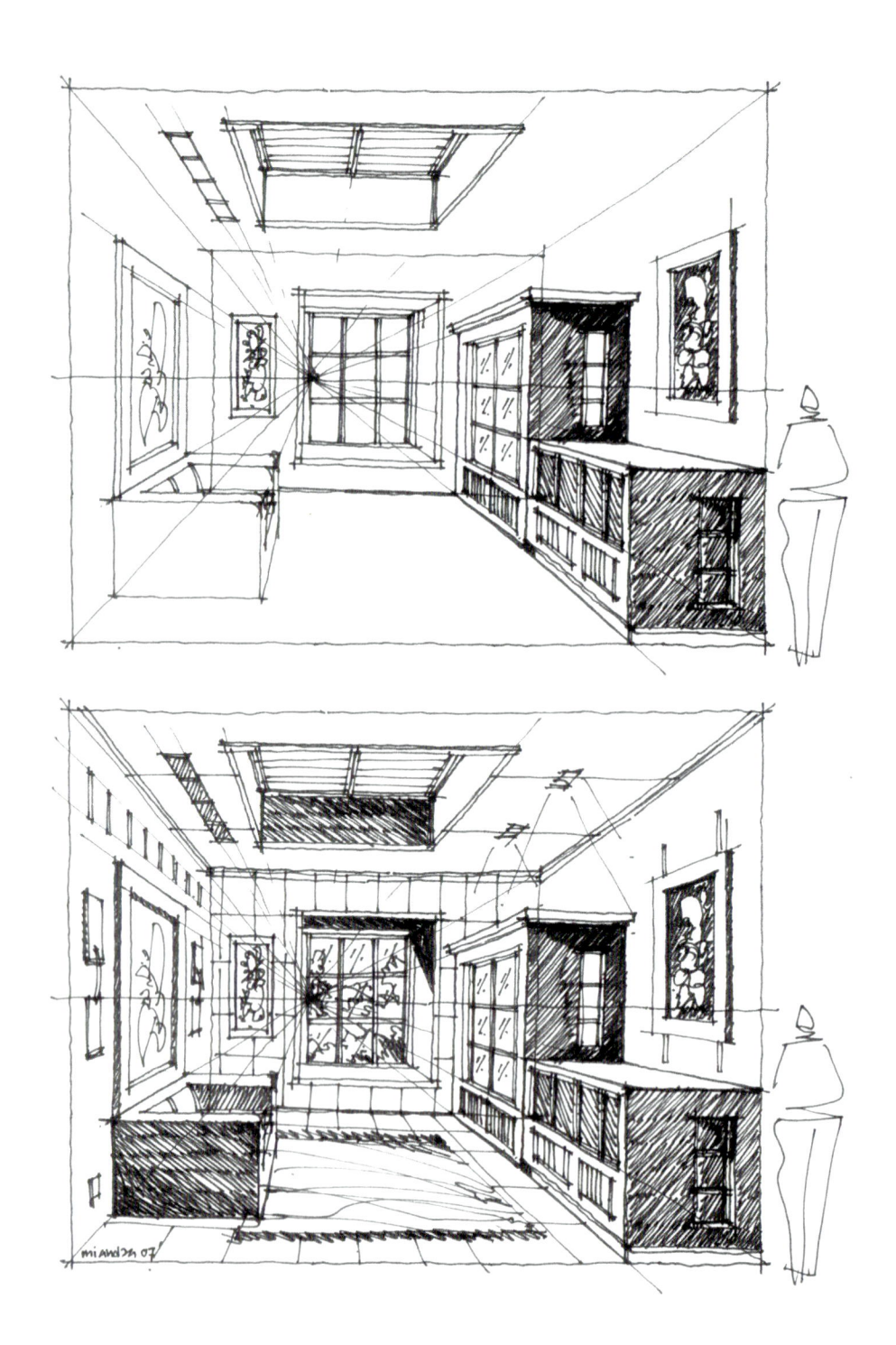

Step 3
Choose one of the suitable rendering techniques to render the sketch composition. Observe the process given to understand the rendering process. Do not over render because it will destroy the quality of the sketch composition.

Tip: *Do not over render the composition.*

• Interior 2 (Bedroom)

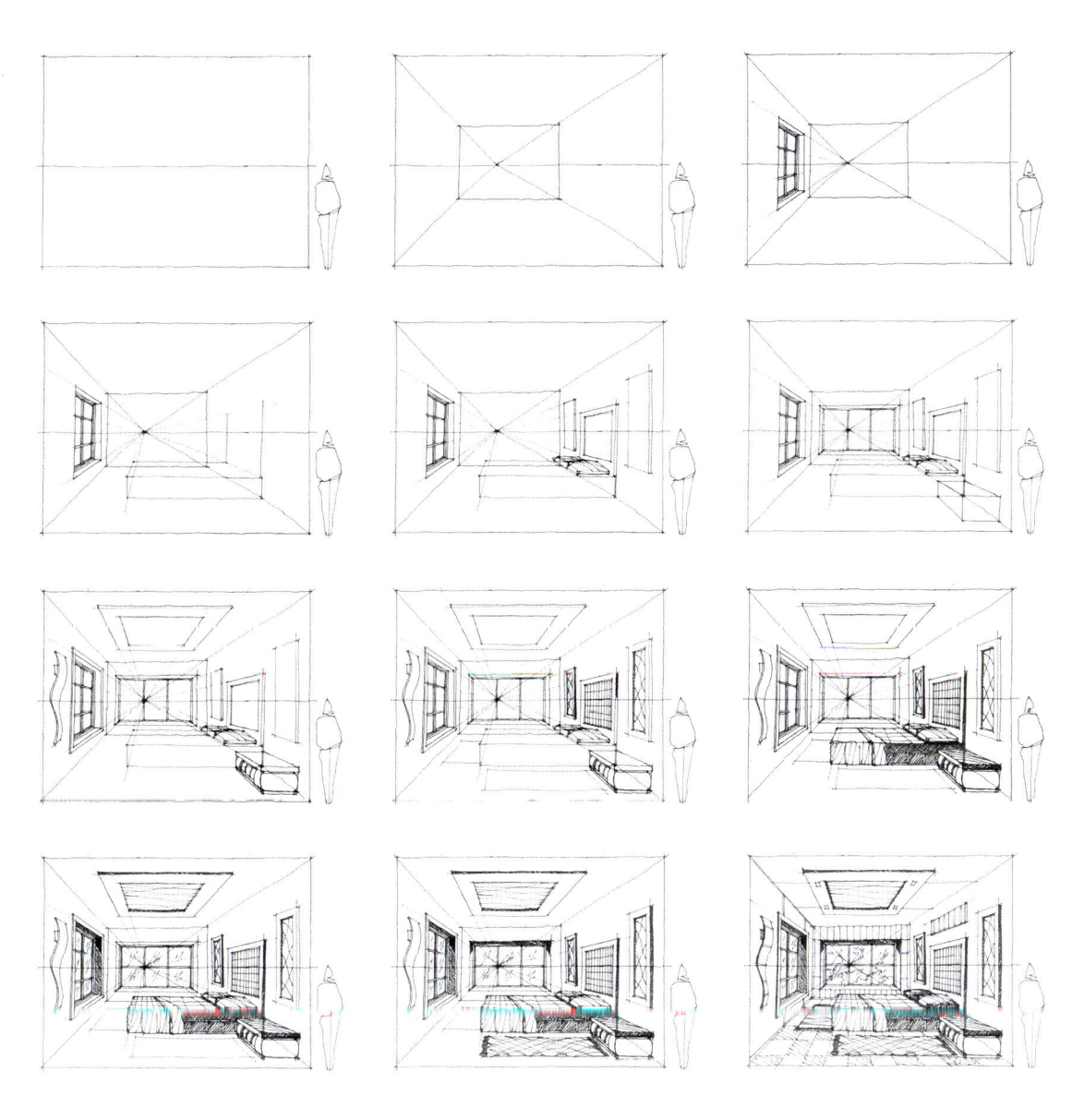

A STEP BY STEP PROCESS 133

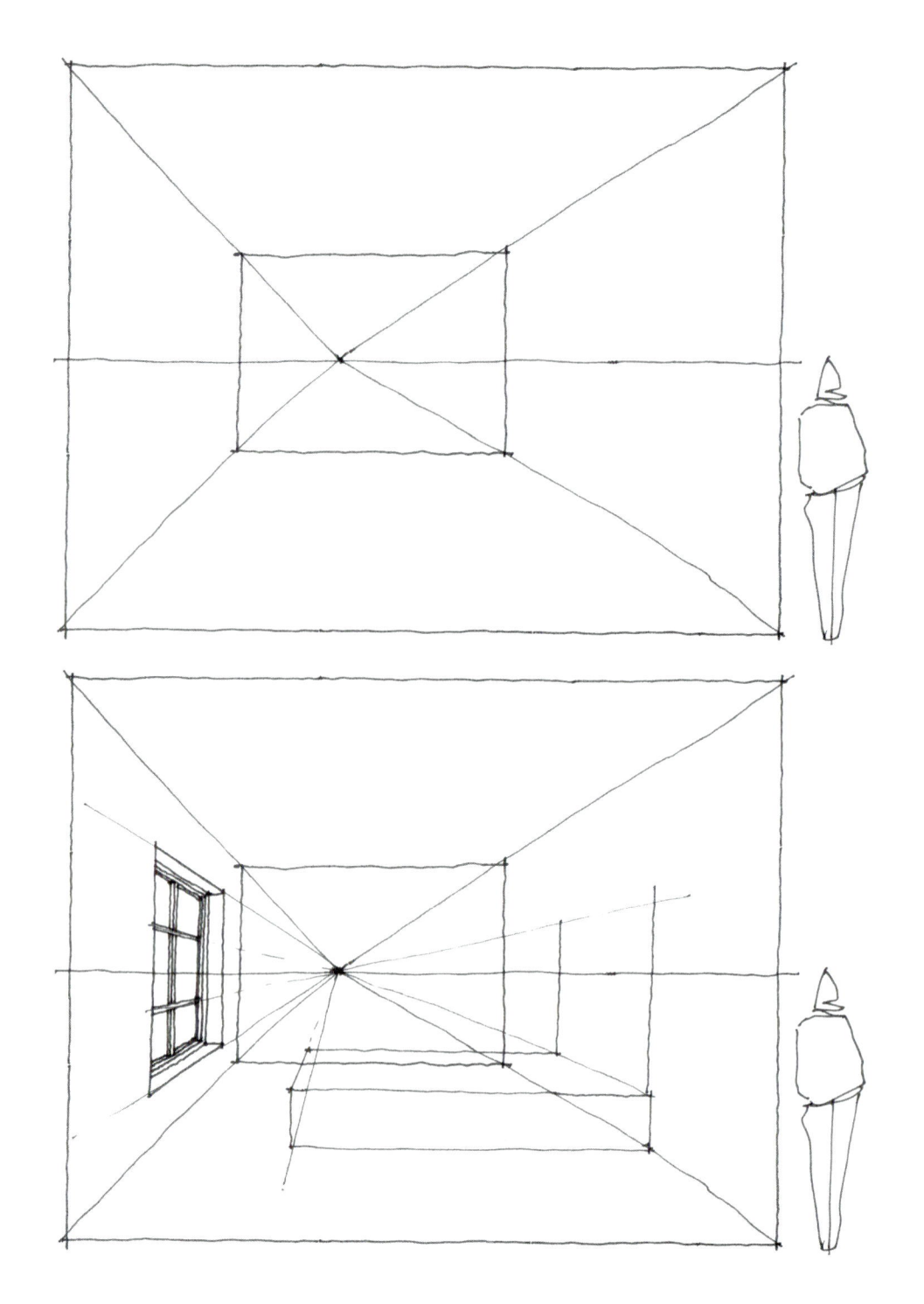

Step 1
Draw the horizon line based on the height of figure sketched by the box boundary. It is to set the eye level of the sketch composition.

Tip: *Horizon line is very important to determine the eye level of a sketch composition.*

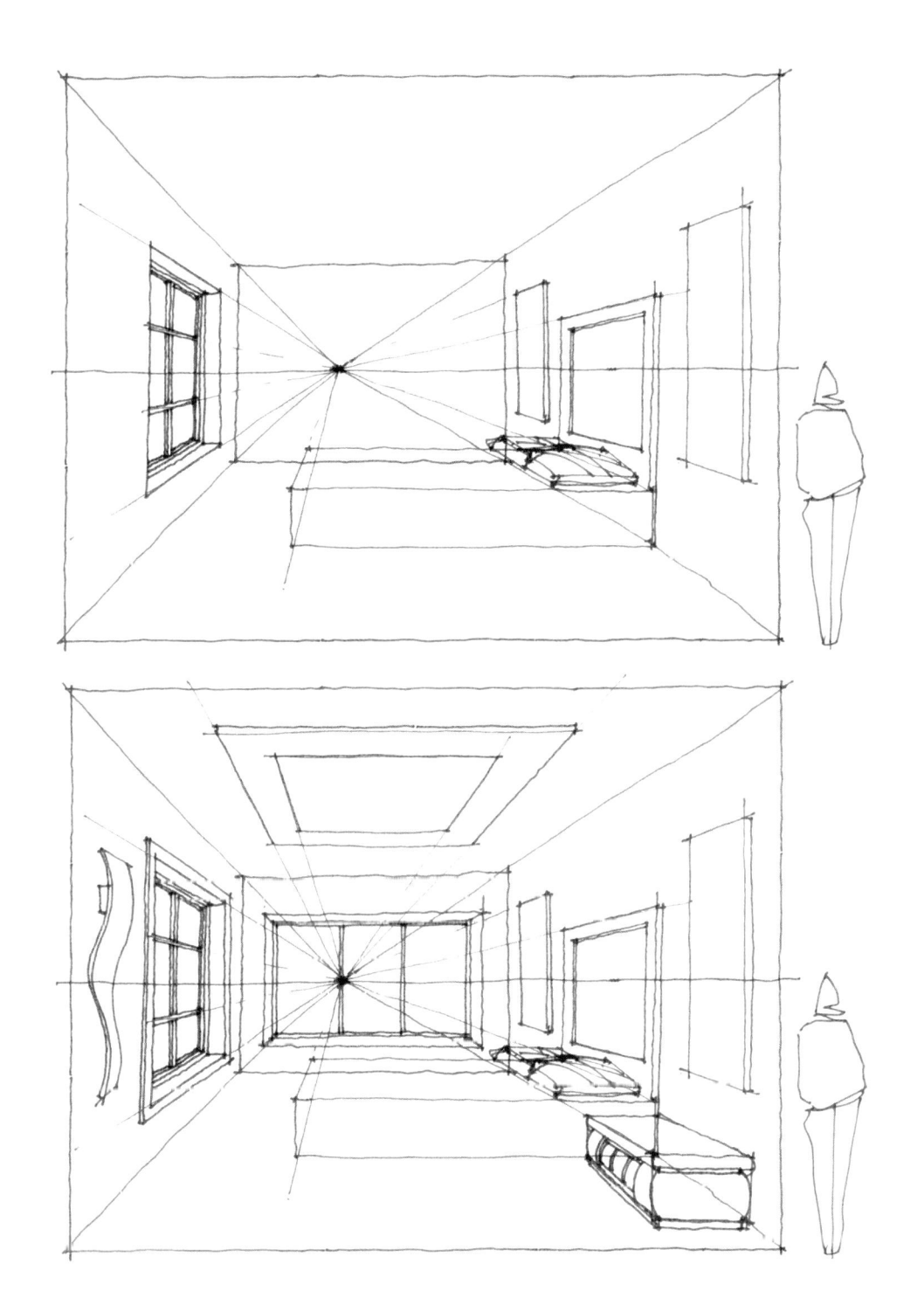

Step 2
Next step is to sketch the main objects to their position in the room setting followed by the secondary objects. It is important to do so because it will help to justify the position of other objects surrounding them.

Tip: Start sketching with the main objects in the room.

A STEP BY STEP PROCESS 135

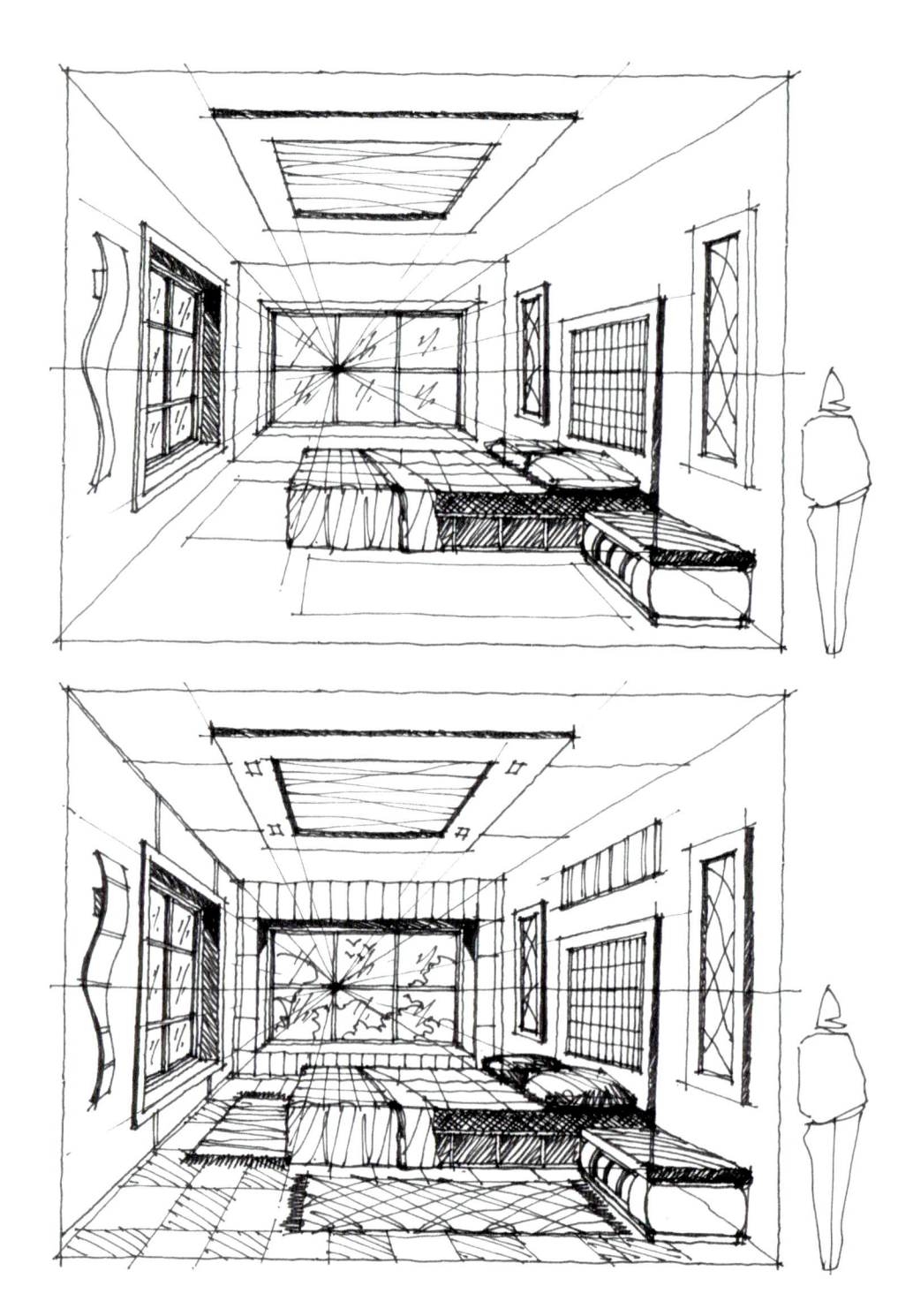

Step 3
The quality of the final sketch composition will be determined by your creativity in choosing and applying the rendering technique.

Tip: *Be creative in rendering your sketch composition.*

- Landscape setting 1

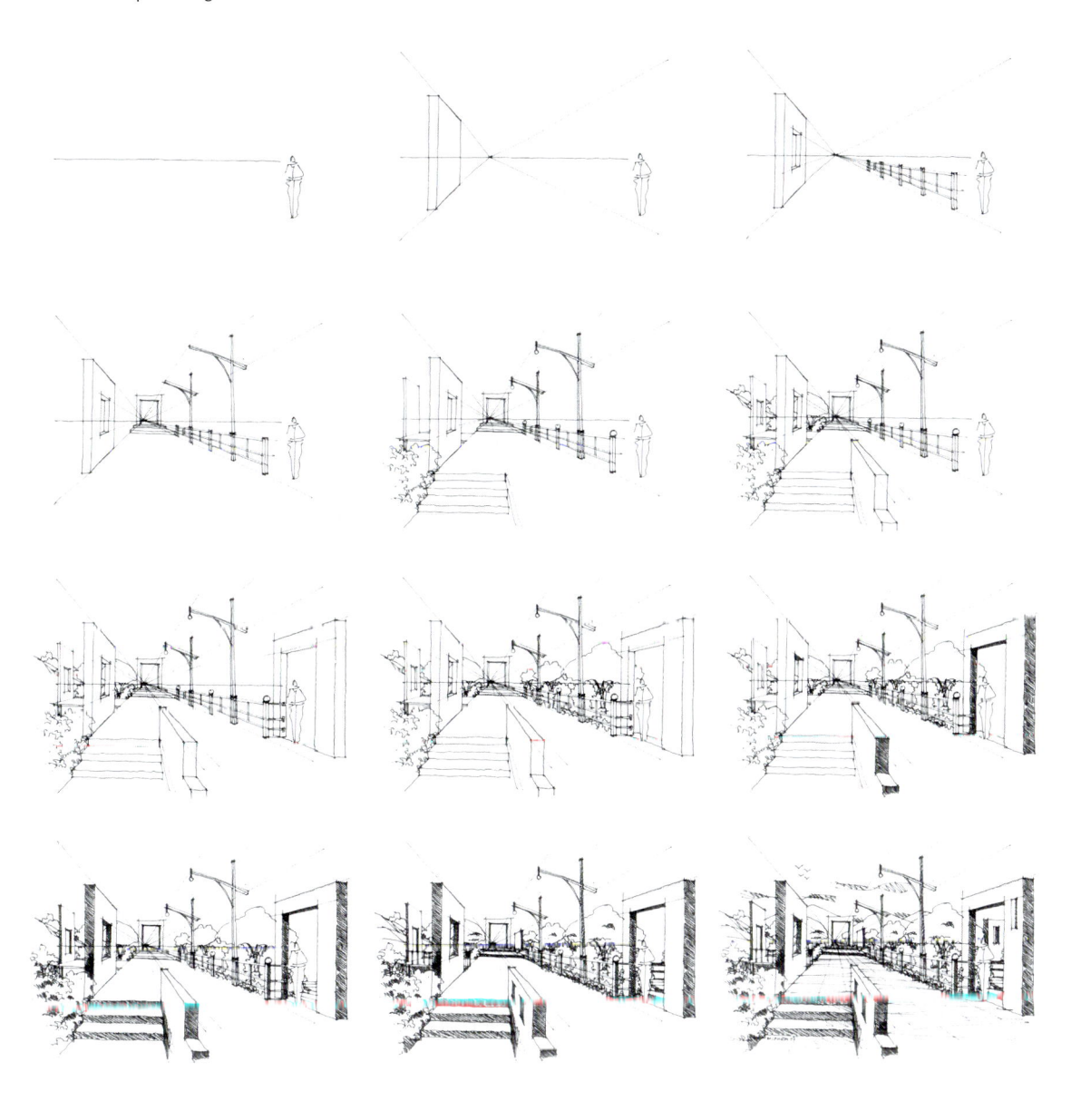

Step 1
Human figure is one of the important reference points in order to obtain the right scale and proportion for the sketch composition. Always refer to the human figure.

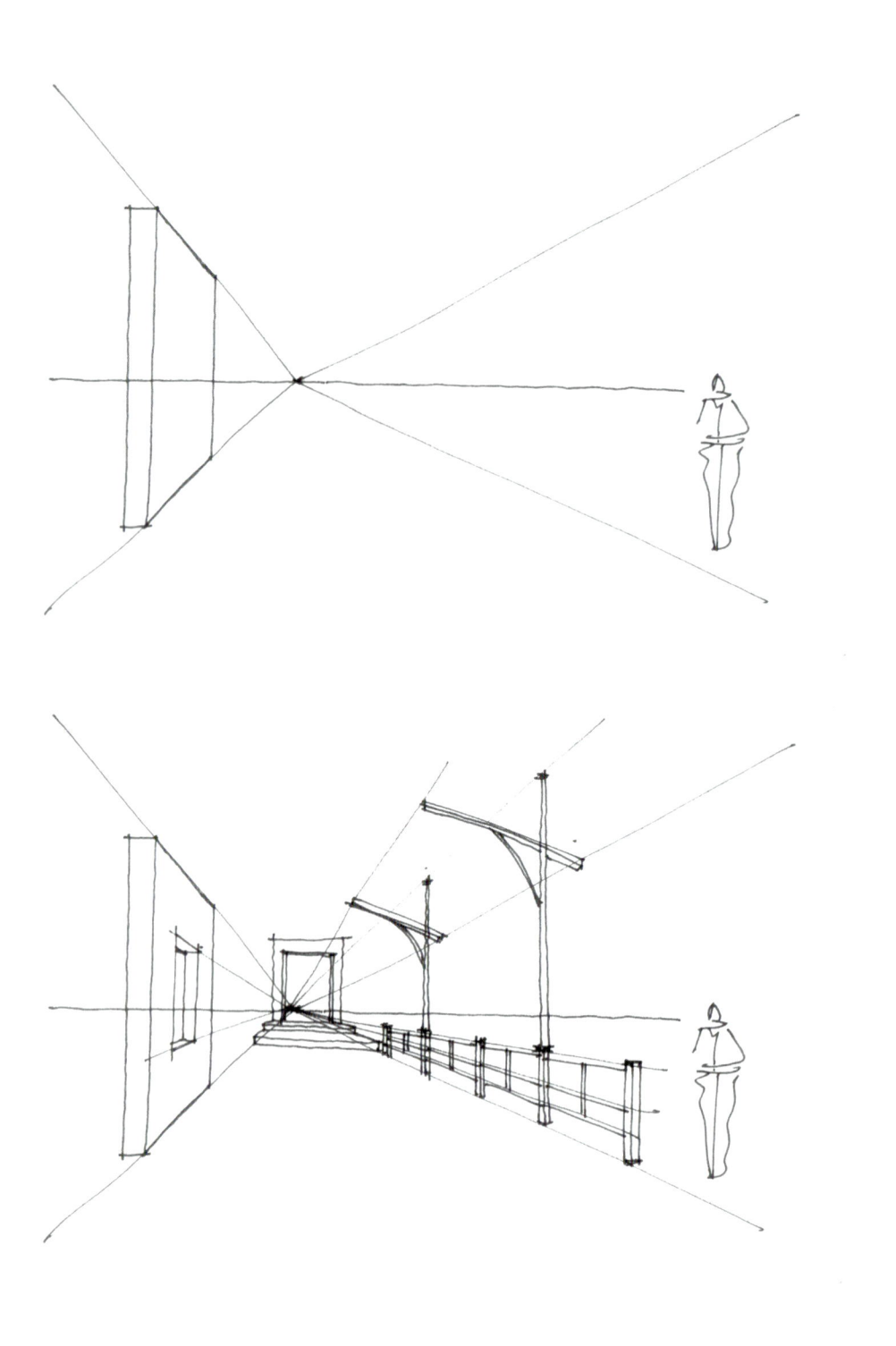

Tip: Create reference object, it can be a human figure, a wall or any other.

138   A STEP BY STEP PROCESS

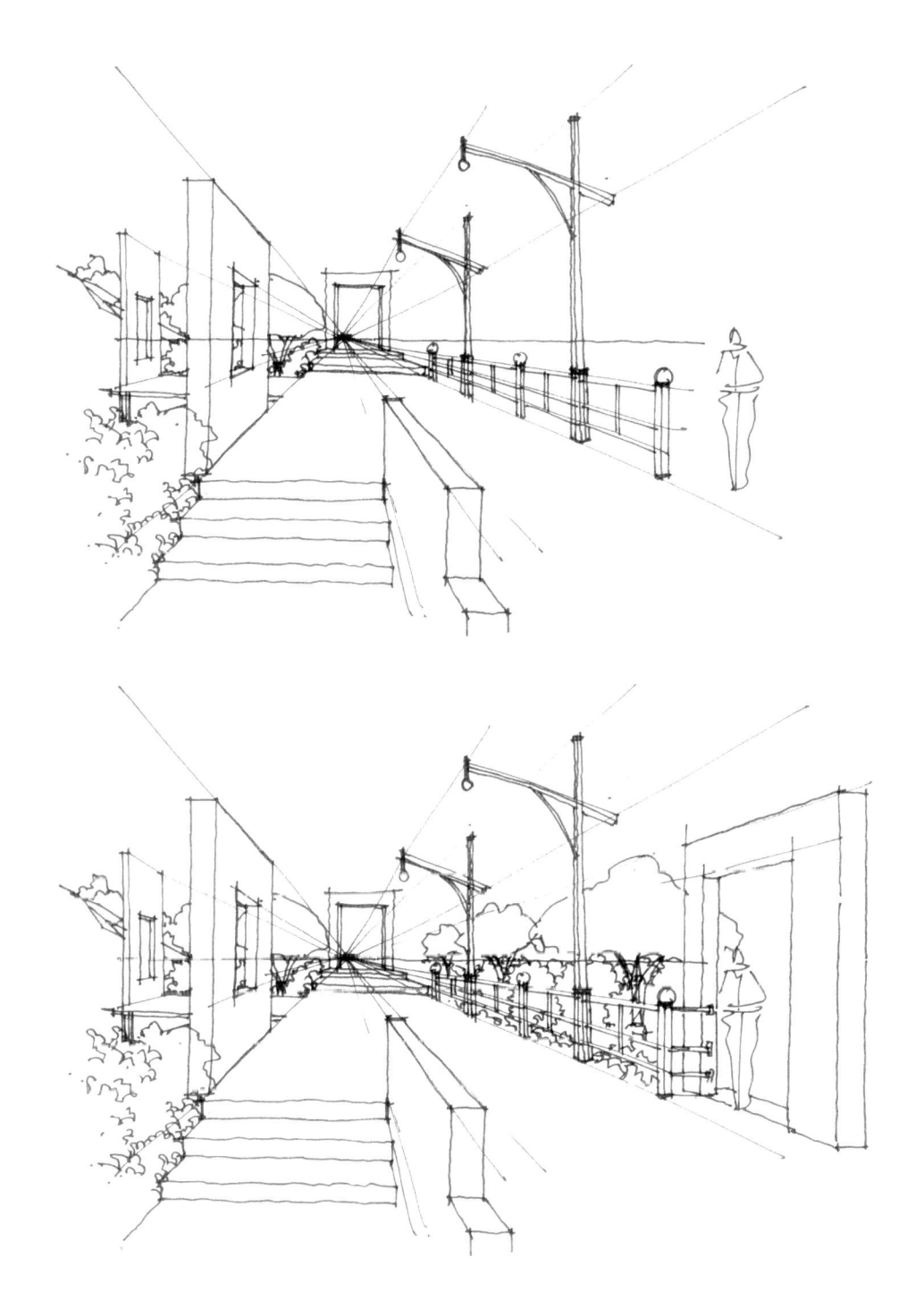

Step 2
Observe the process properly on how the secondary objects are added to the sketch without disturbing the main object composition.

Tip: *Identify the secondary objects.*

A STEP BY STEP PROCESS 139

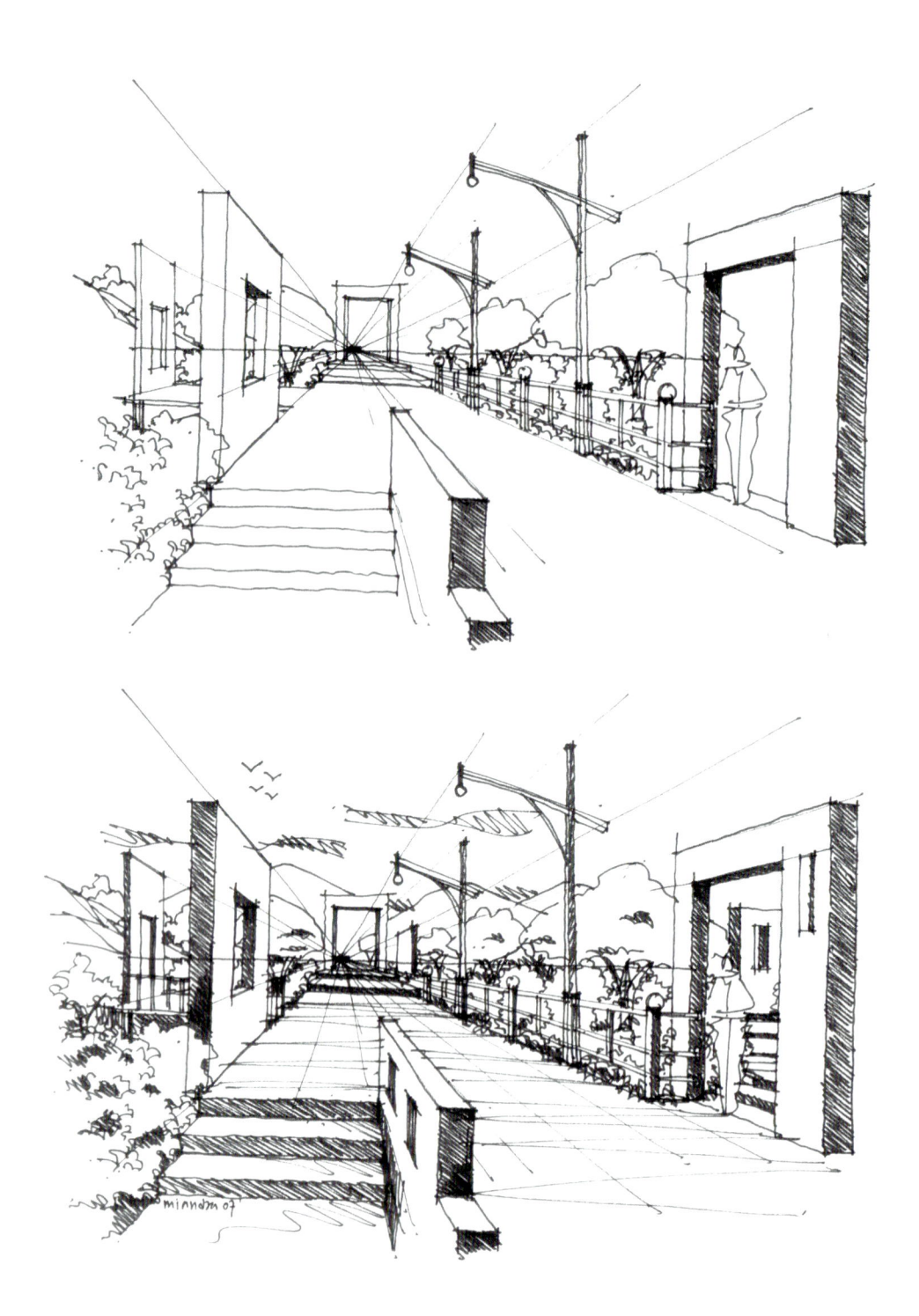

Step 3
Look at how the shades and shadows generate an interesting character to the sketch composition. Shades and shadows created from the pen rendering as shown in the examples.

Tip: Shades and shadows will generate a quality sketch.

• Landscape setting 2

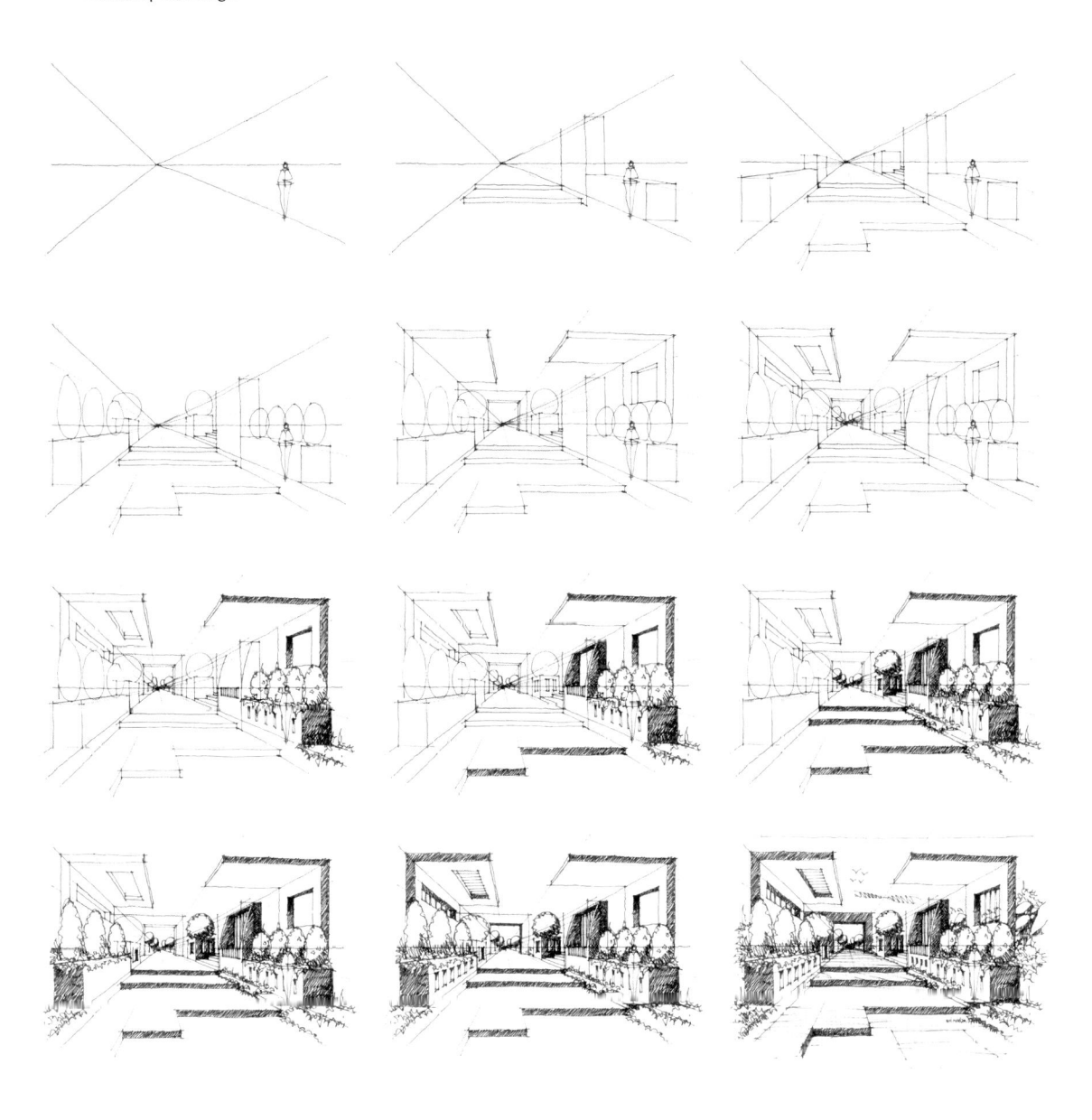

A STEP BY STEP PROCESS 141

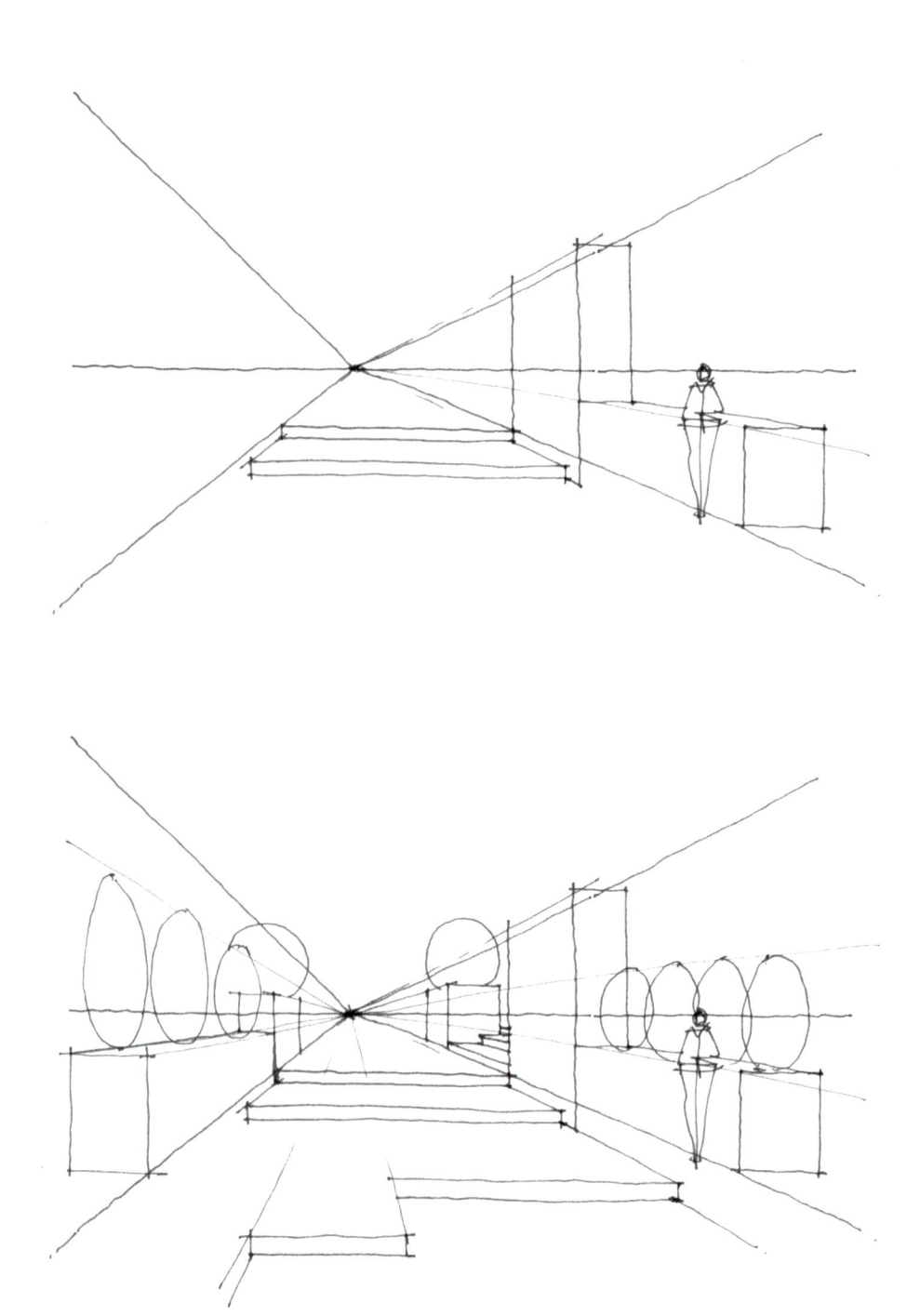

Step 1
The two steps given are the process of creating a sketch layout. The rough layout is needed to study the overall setting. It is important to get the right layout in the early stages.

Tip: *Make sure the right layout is sketched.*

142 A STEP BY STEP PROCESS

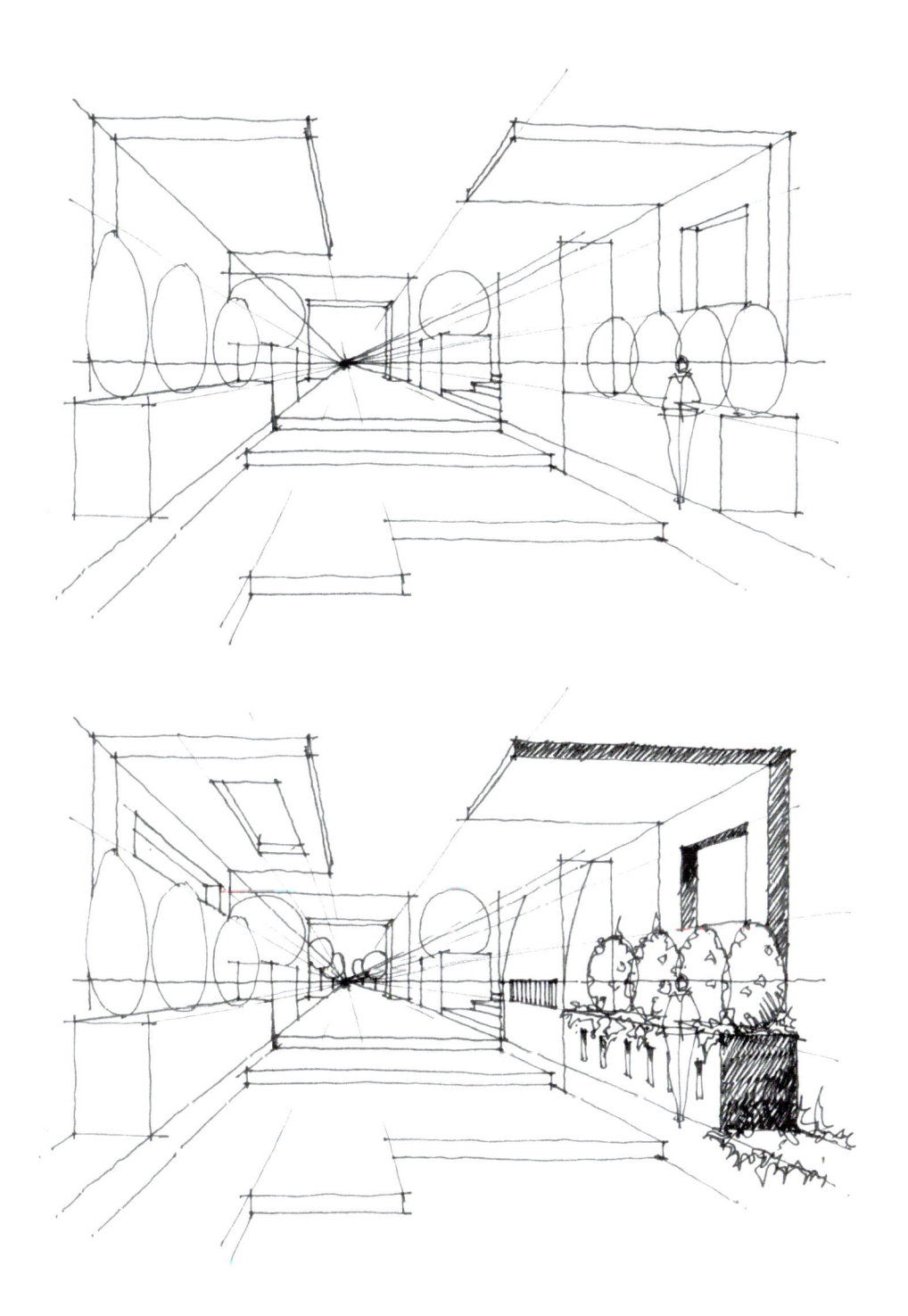

Step 2

The next step that needs to be done is to sketch the rough shape of all the main and secondary objects before proceeding to the final shape as shown in the sketch below.

Tip: Sketch the rough shape to get to the final shape.

A STEP BY STEP PROCESS 143

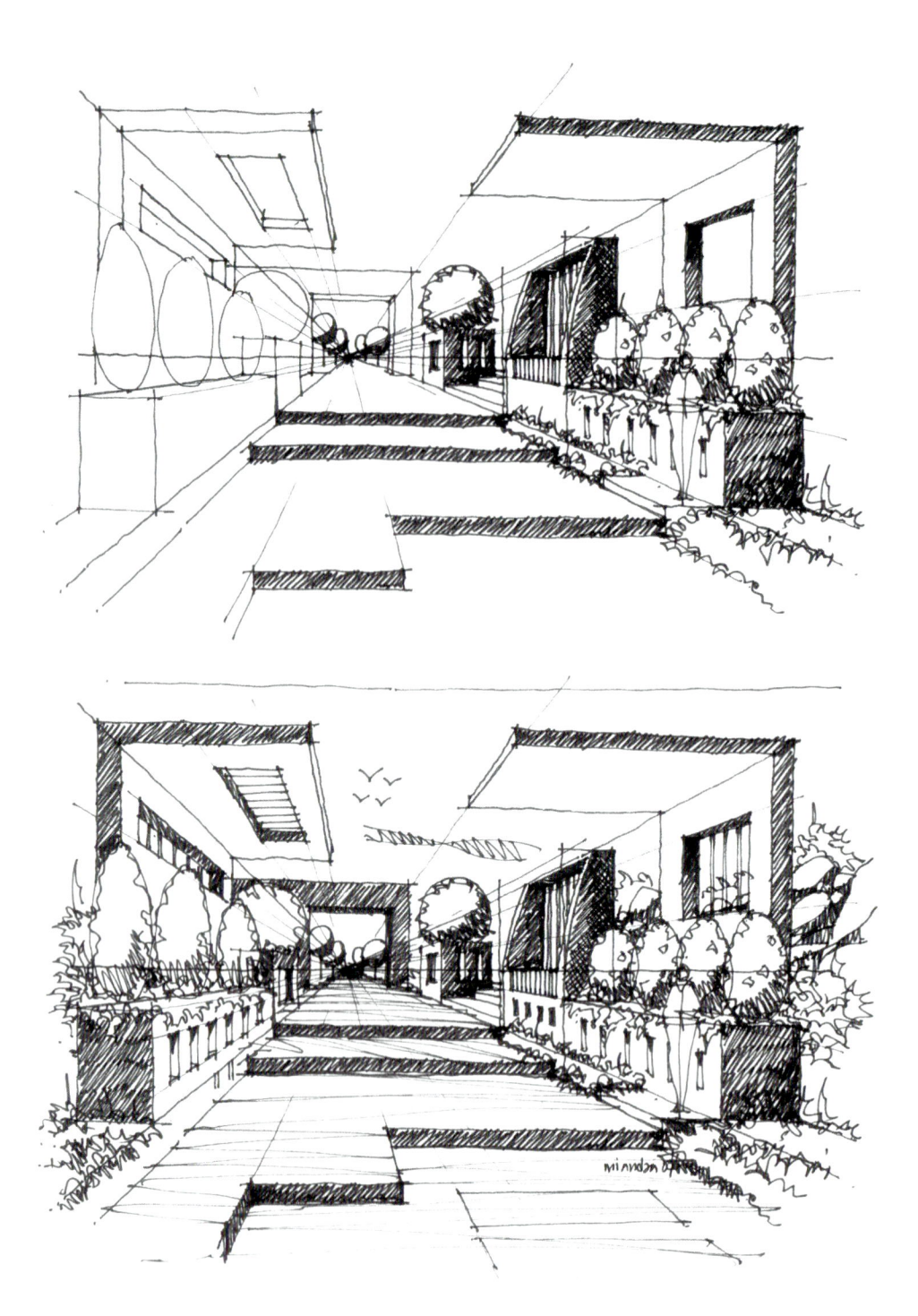

Step 3
After completing the rough layout, then start refining the shape as shown in the process.

Tip: *Do refine the composition to get a quality sketch.*

• Urban and architectural setting 1

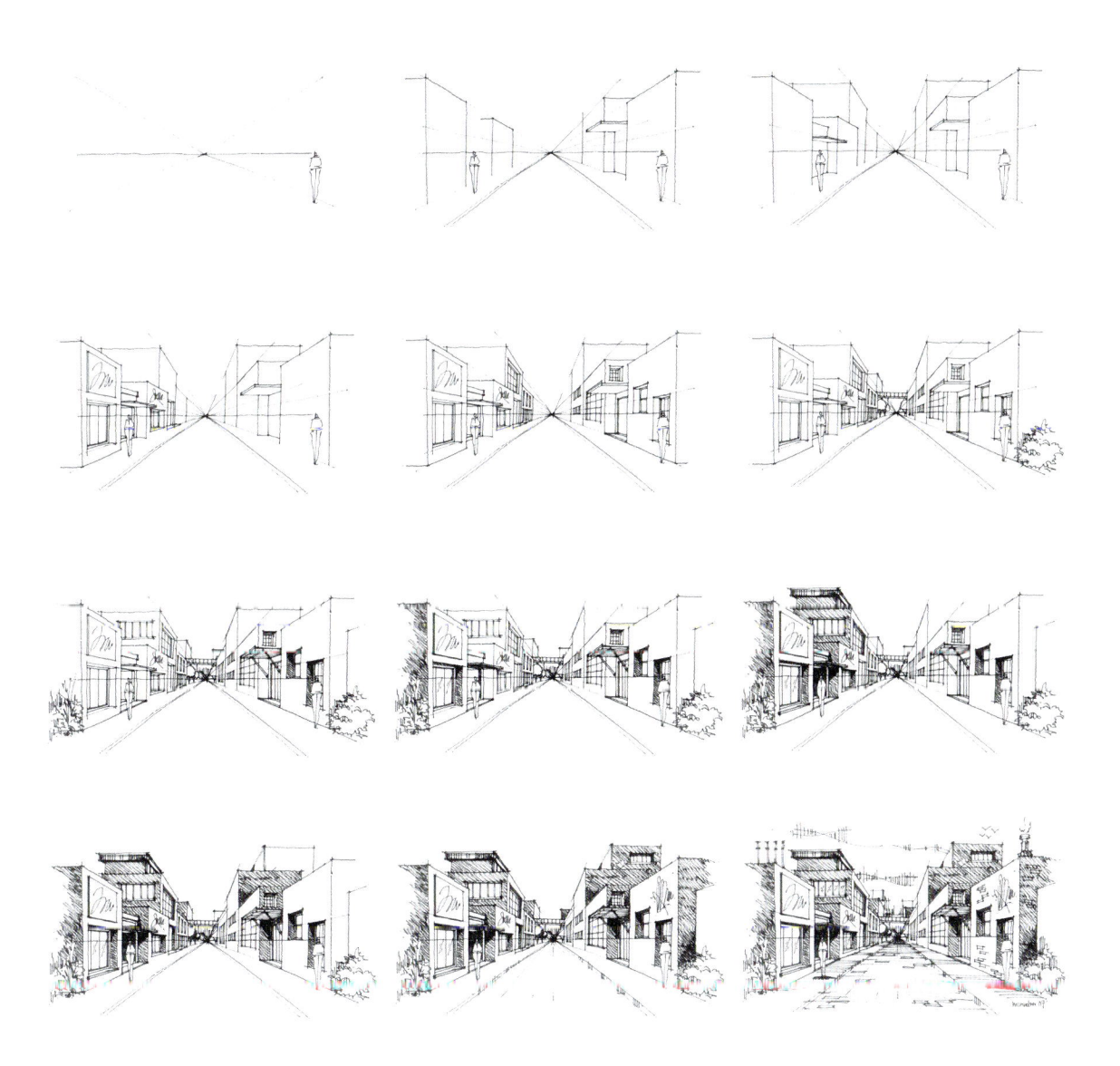

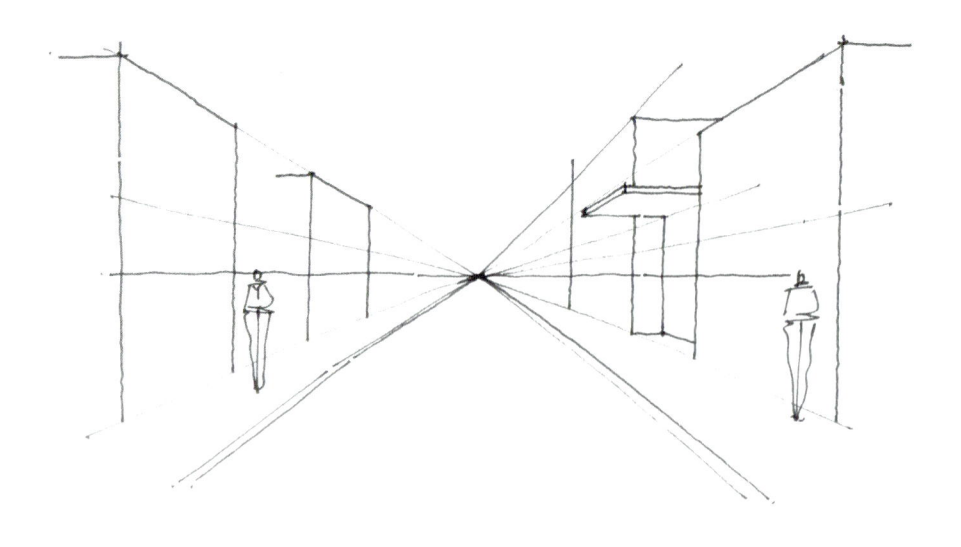

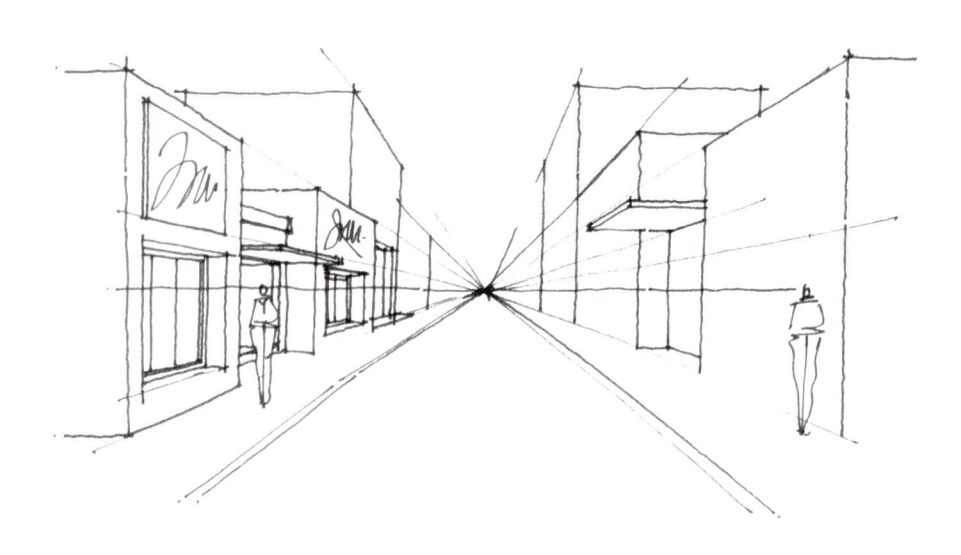

Step 1
Divide the street layout into several sections randomly as shown in the process. Make them interesting by applying different building heights.

Tip: Be creative to get a good street layout.

146 A STEP BY STEP PROCESS

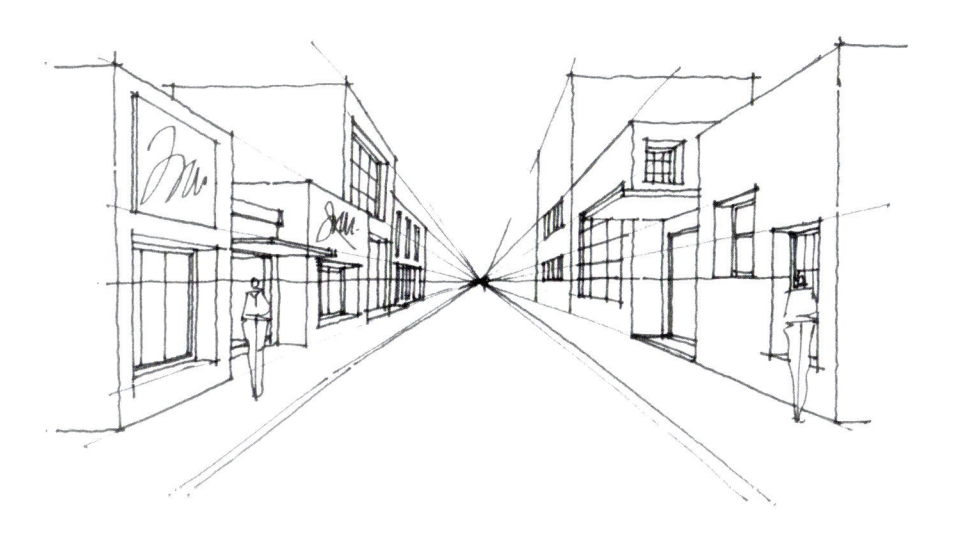

Step 2
Next, start sketching the entire street and buildings details such as windows, doors, signage and others.

Tip: Do observe existing street and buildings' details; they have their own image and characters to be understood.

A STEP BY STEP PROCESS 147

Step 3
What does a final touch-up mean? After rendering session is completed, there must be something that needs to be refined or corrected to make the composition more interesting such as sketching a graphic cloud or refining the surface rendering of any wall of the buildings.

Tip: *A good quality sketch needs a final touch-up.*

148 A STEP BY STEP PROCESS

• Urban and architectural setting 2

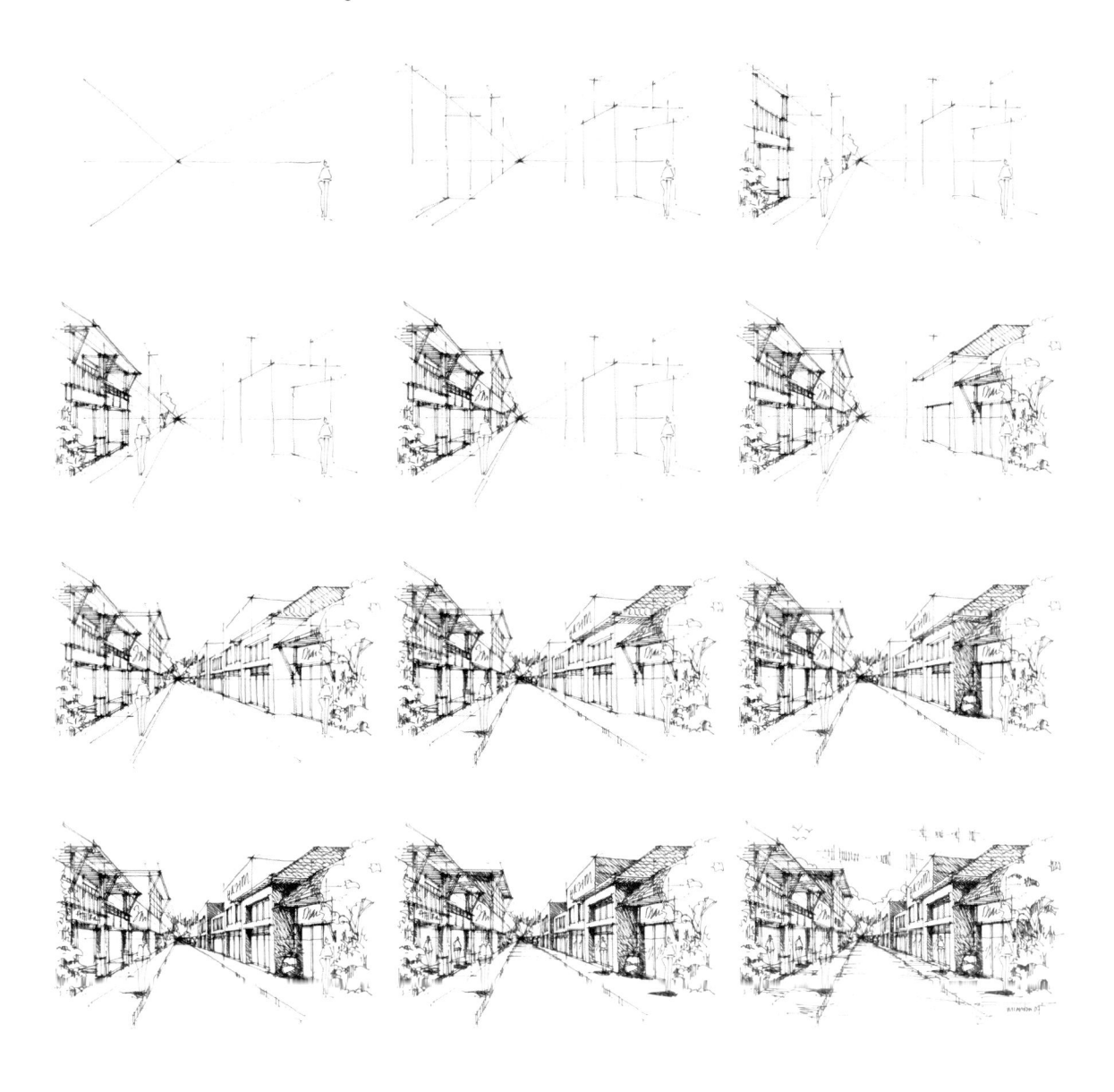

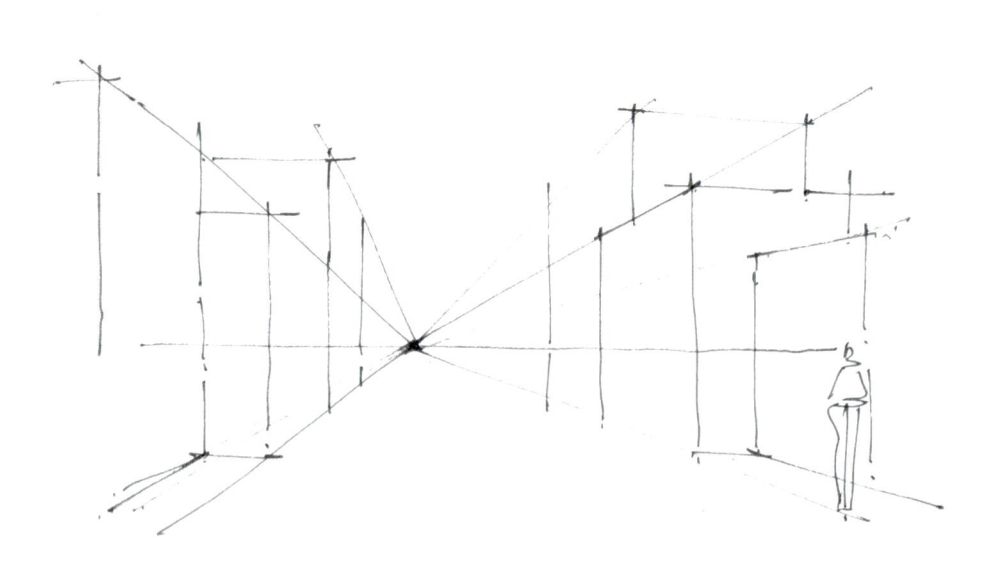

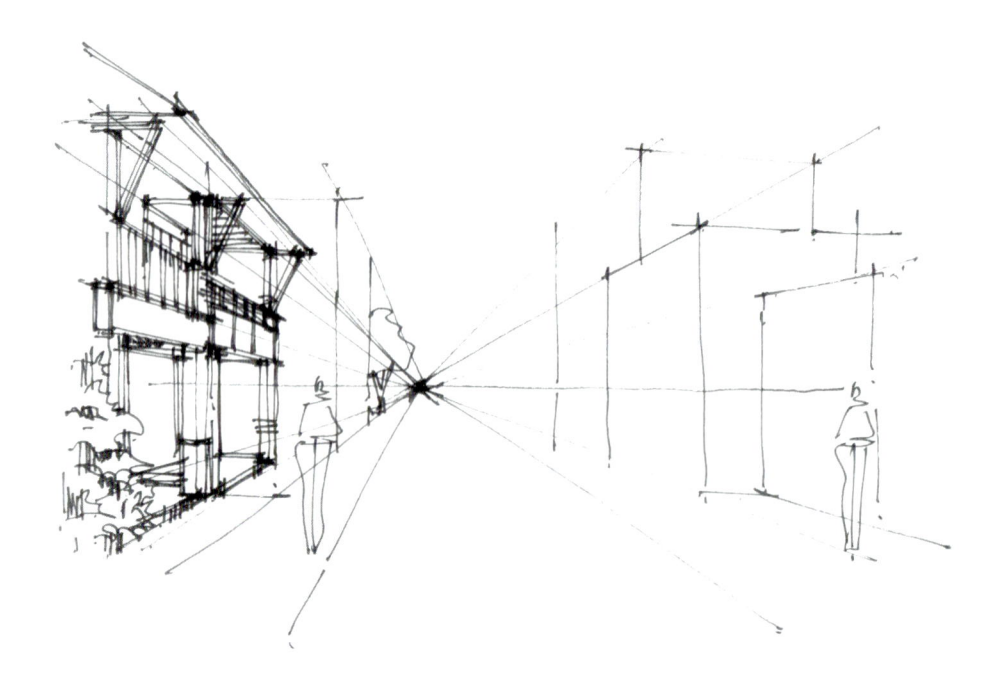

Step 1
Always start the sketch with rough layout and then concentrate on building character as shown below. This effort needs creativity because it is about giving a blank wall a totally new look.

Tip: *Build up your creativity in creating objects or layout characters.*

150   A STEP BY STEP PROCESS

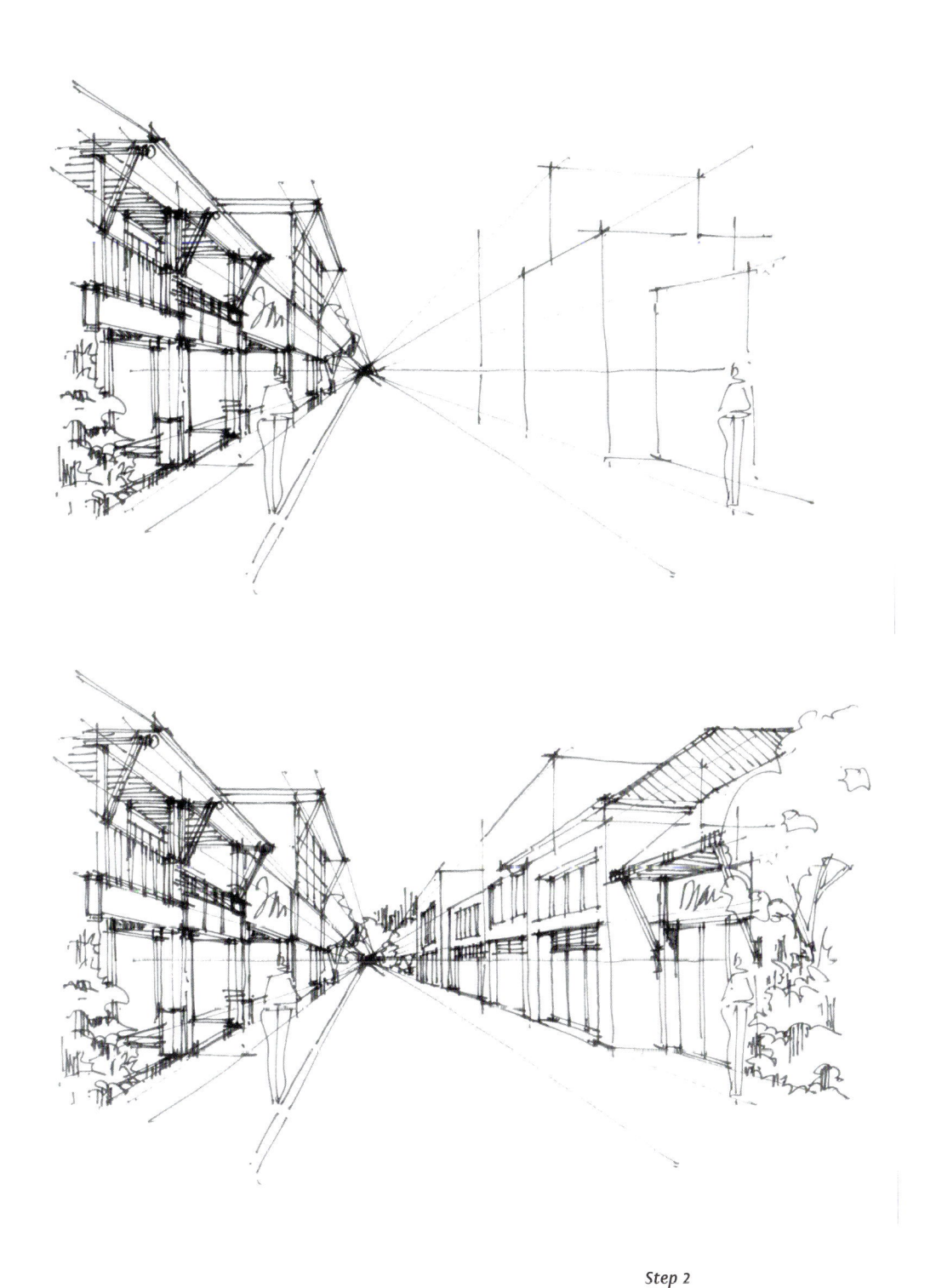

Step 2
Continue sketching the buildings and street character until everything is completed. Then, put some interesting details or special items to highlight the street layout such as plants or building ornamentation.

Tip: *Be creative in characterising the sketch composition.*

A STEP BY STEP PROCESS

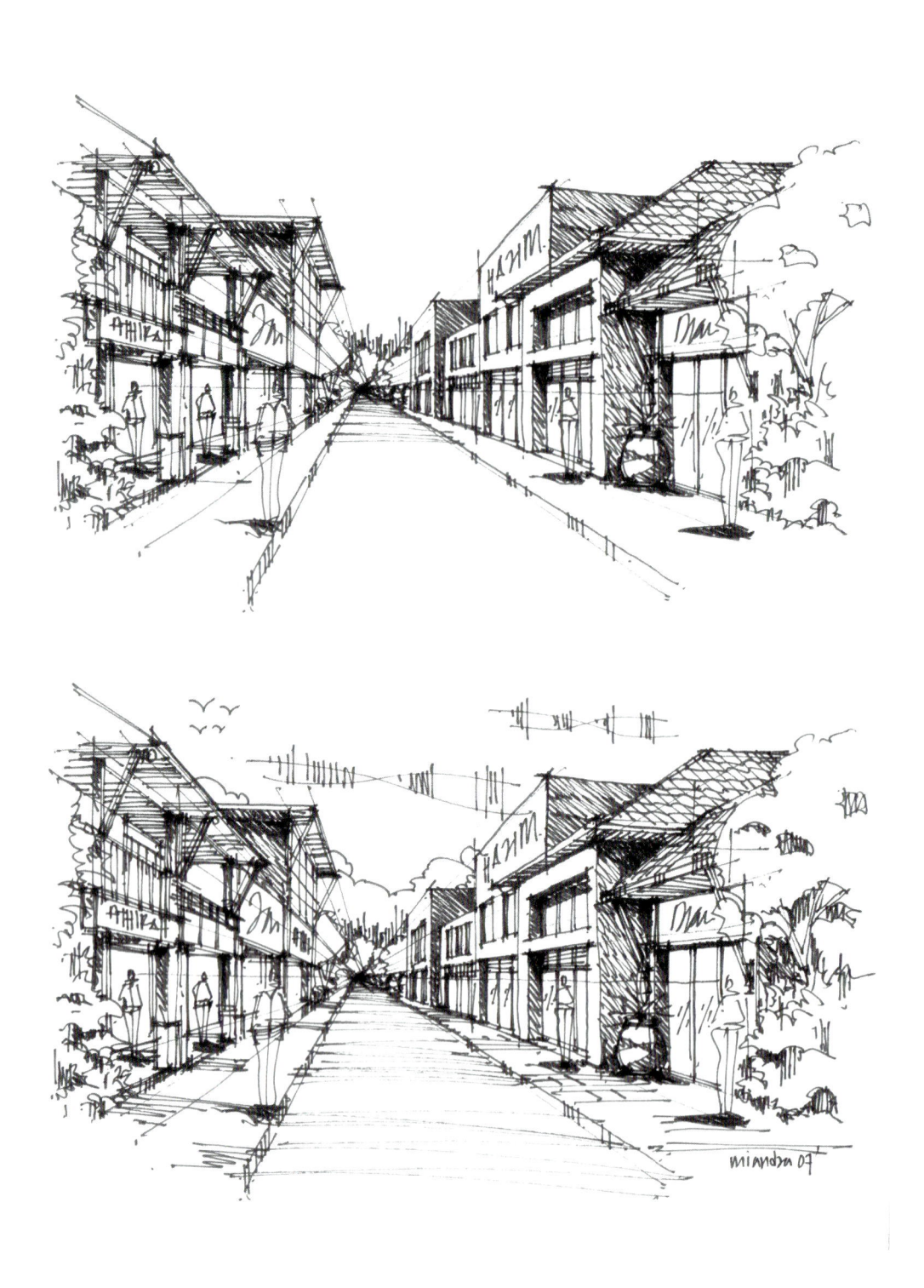

Step 3
Shades and shadows will give a very interesting impact to the sketch composition. Be careful not to over render, which will reduce the quality of the sketch.

Tip: Do master the shade and shadow technique.

• Height setting 1 (Bird's eye view)

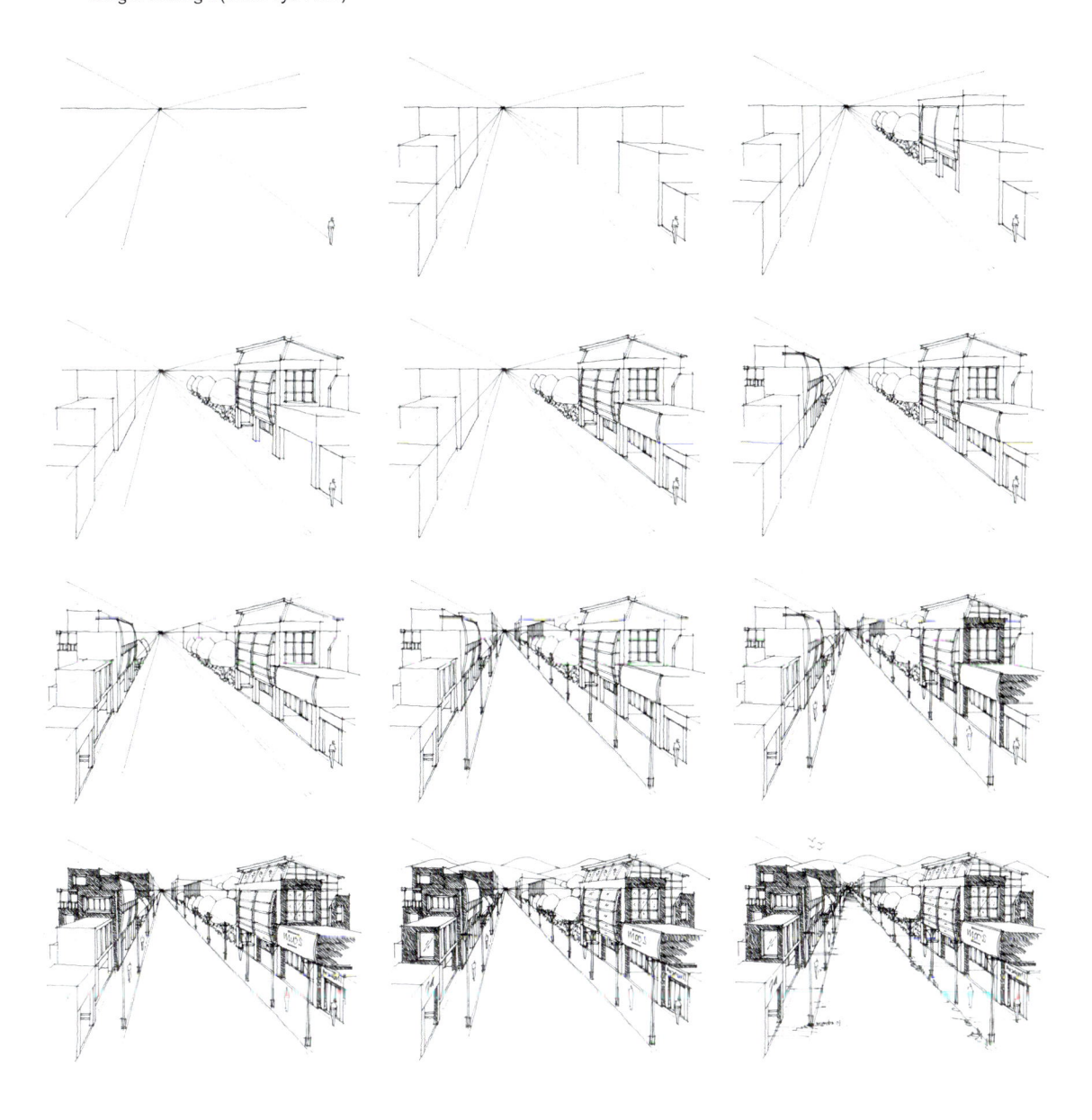

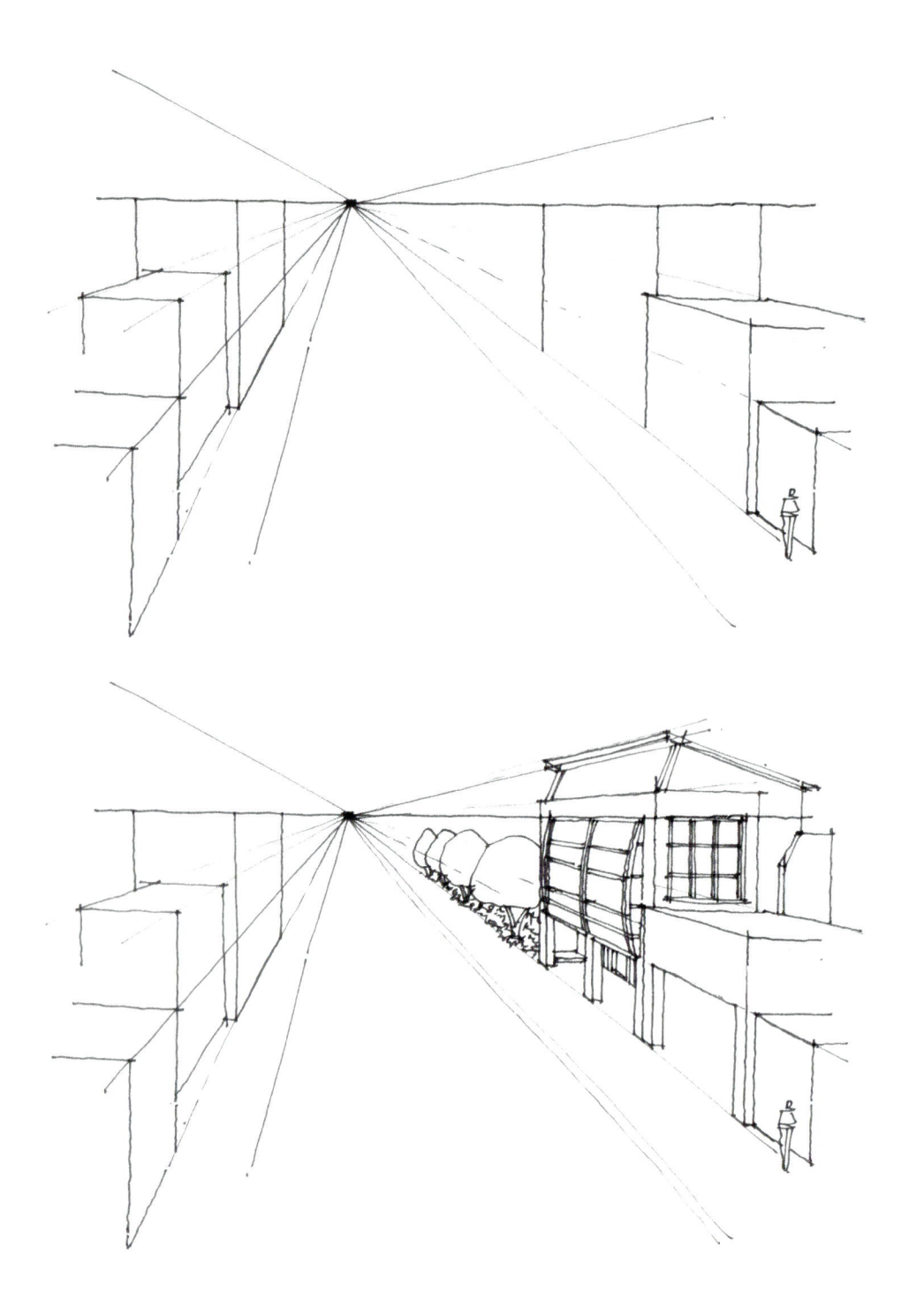

Step 1
In this process, the sketch is using the bird's eye view for eye level setting. Normally this type of sketch is used to get the overall view of a place such as a streetscape.

Tip: Understand on how the eye level works.

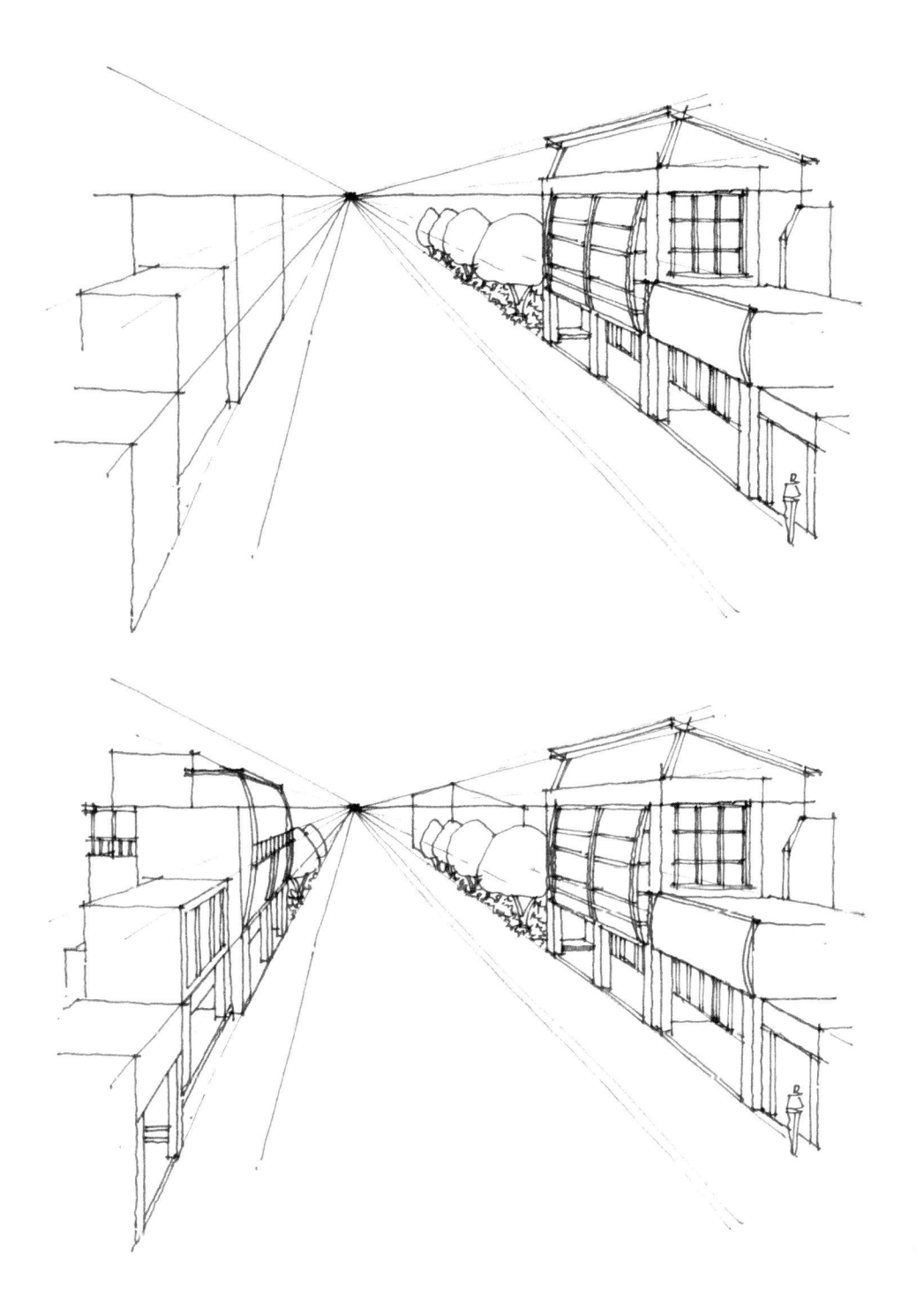

Step 2
Then sketch all the buildings and street layout following the one point perspective principle although the eye level has changed. Always refer to vanishing point and human scale.

Tip: *Always refer to vanishing point.*

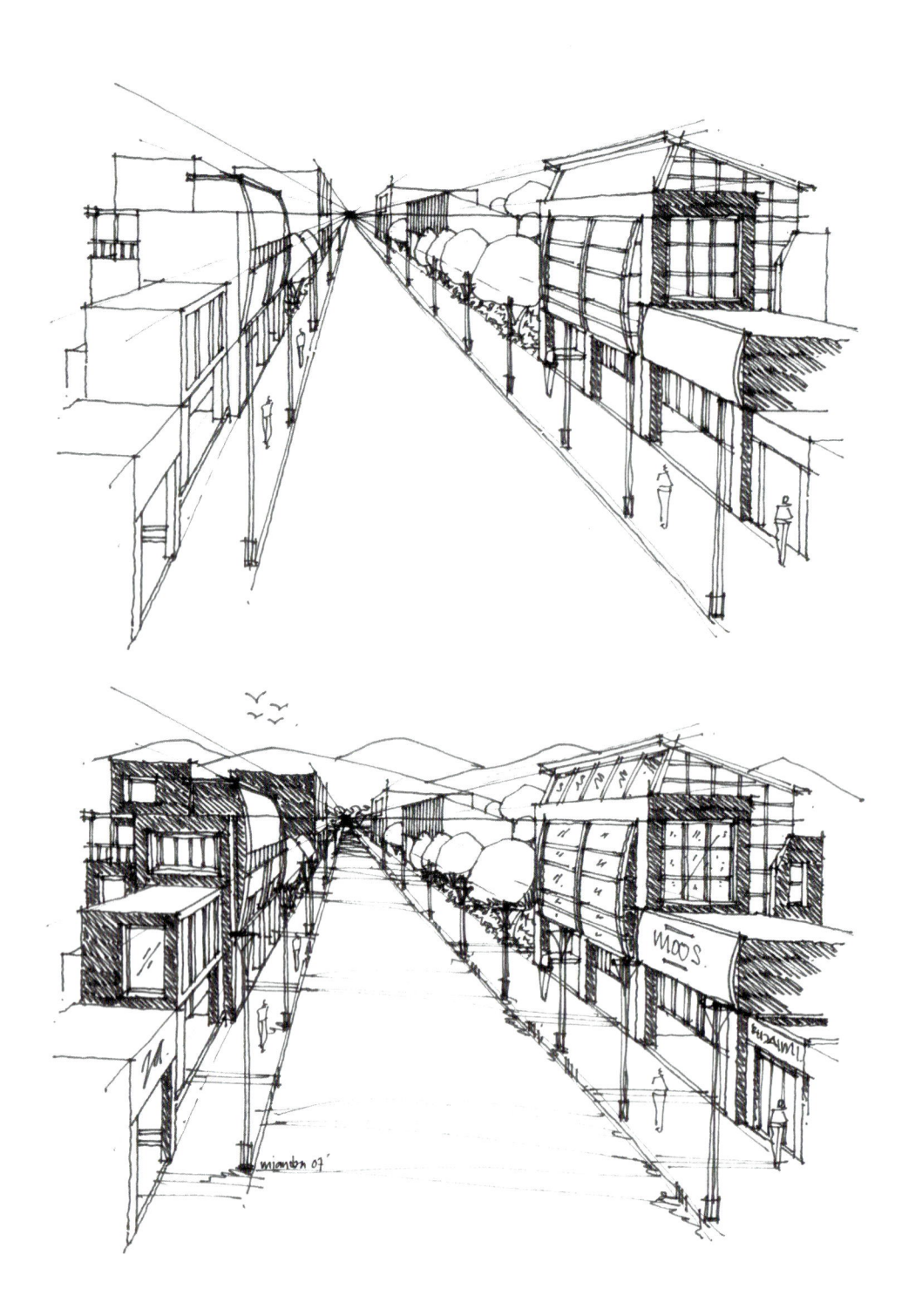

Step 3
Observe the process and identify the secondary elements that have been added to highlight the street layout such as light pole and trees. Look carefully at these items and how they have been treated to make them more interesting.

Tip: *Be creative in highlighting your sketch composition*

• Height setting 2 (Bird's eye view)

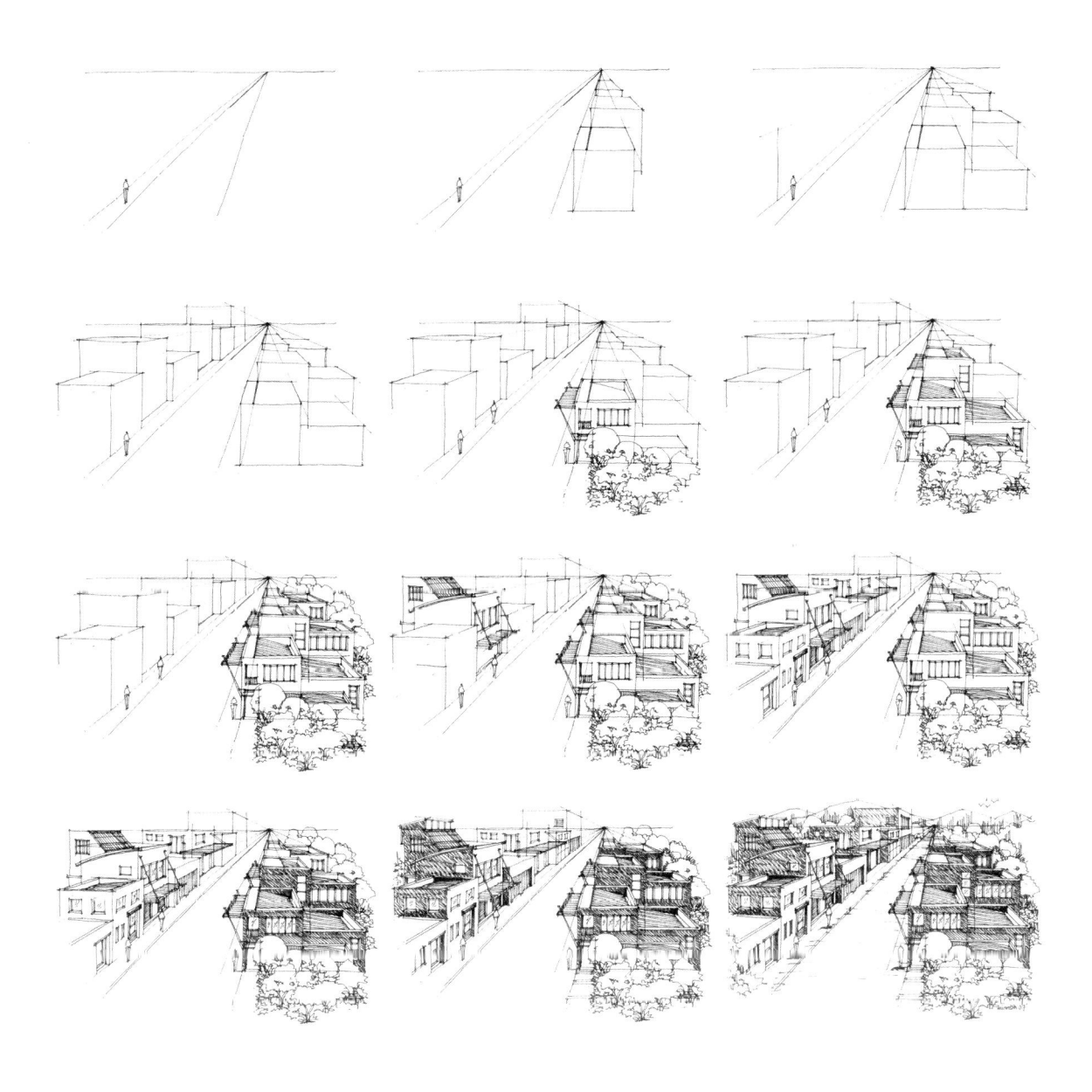

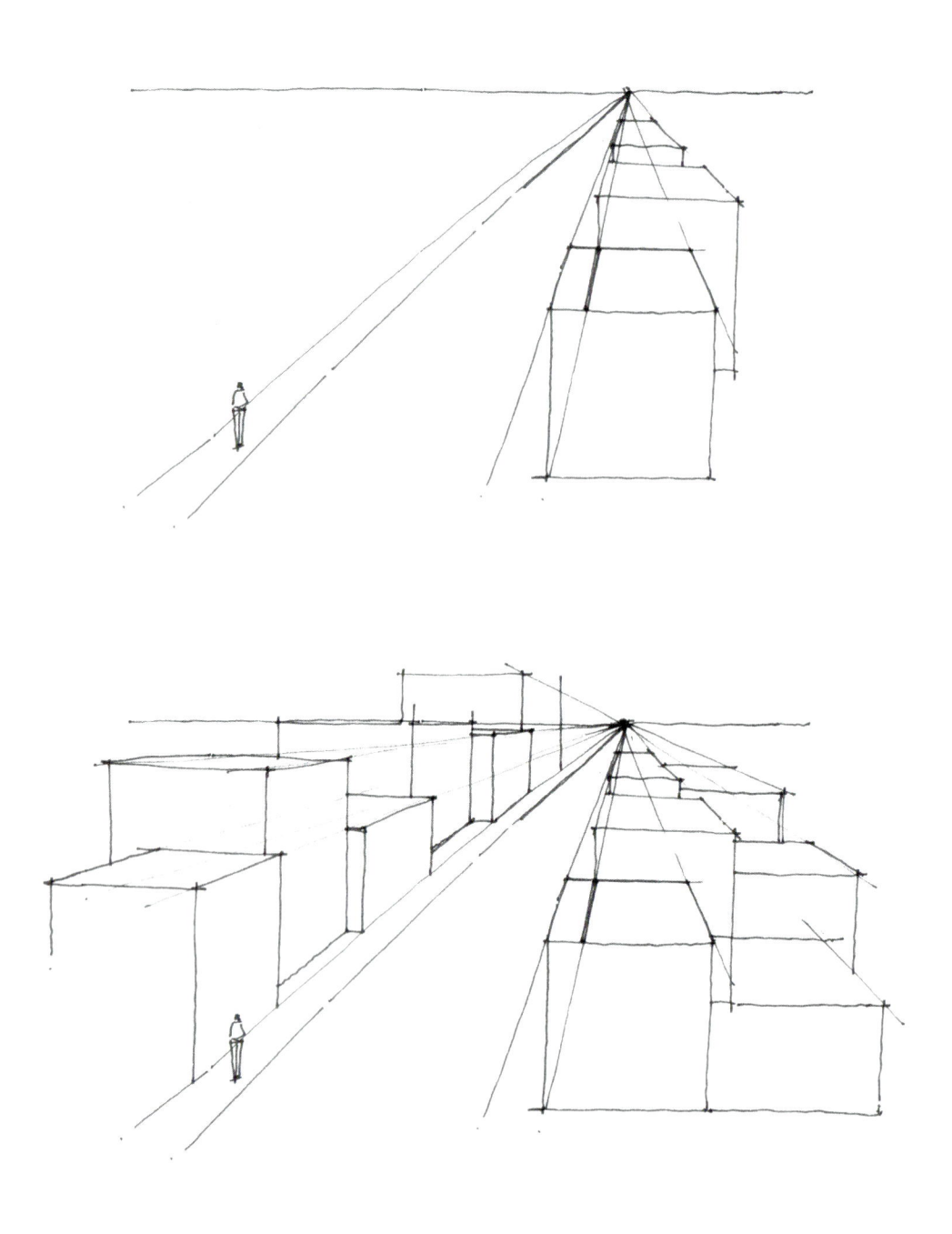

Step 1
Observe the sketch composition on how the human figure influences the street layout, buildings sizes and scale to get a quality sketch composition.

Tip: *Human figure is very important to determine the sketch composition in the right scale and proportion.*

Step 2

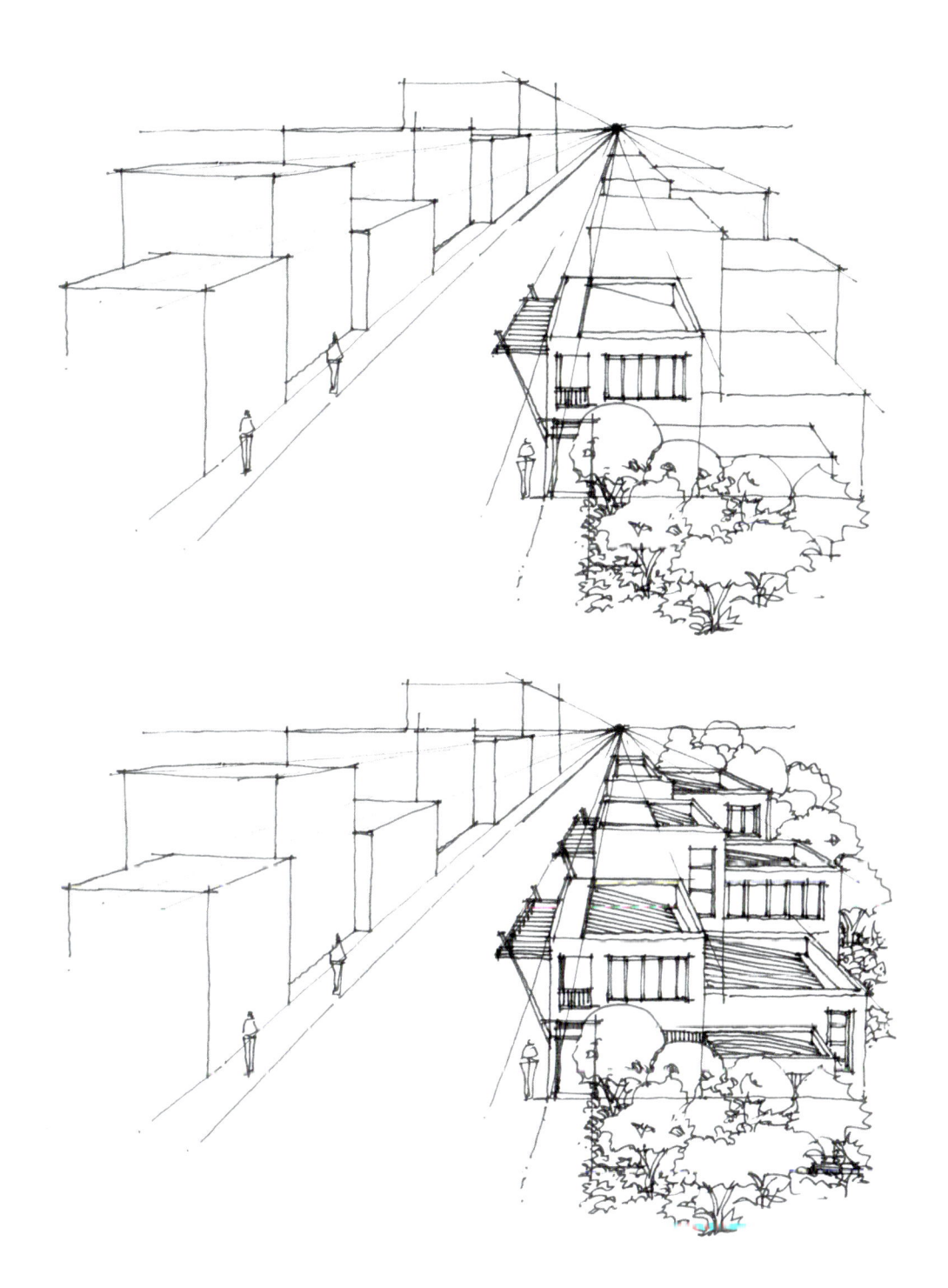

Refer to the sketch process. It is very important to understand how the object surface reacts when the eye level changes. In this case, the top buildings' surfaces are more highlighted compared to the side surfaces.

Tip: *Object surface changes when eye level changes.*

A STEP BY STEP PROCESS 159

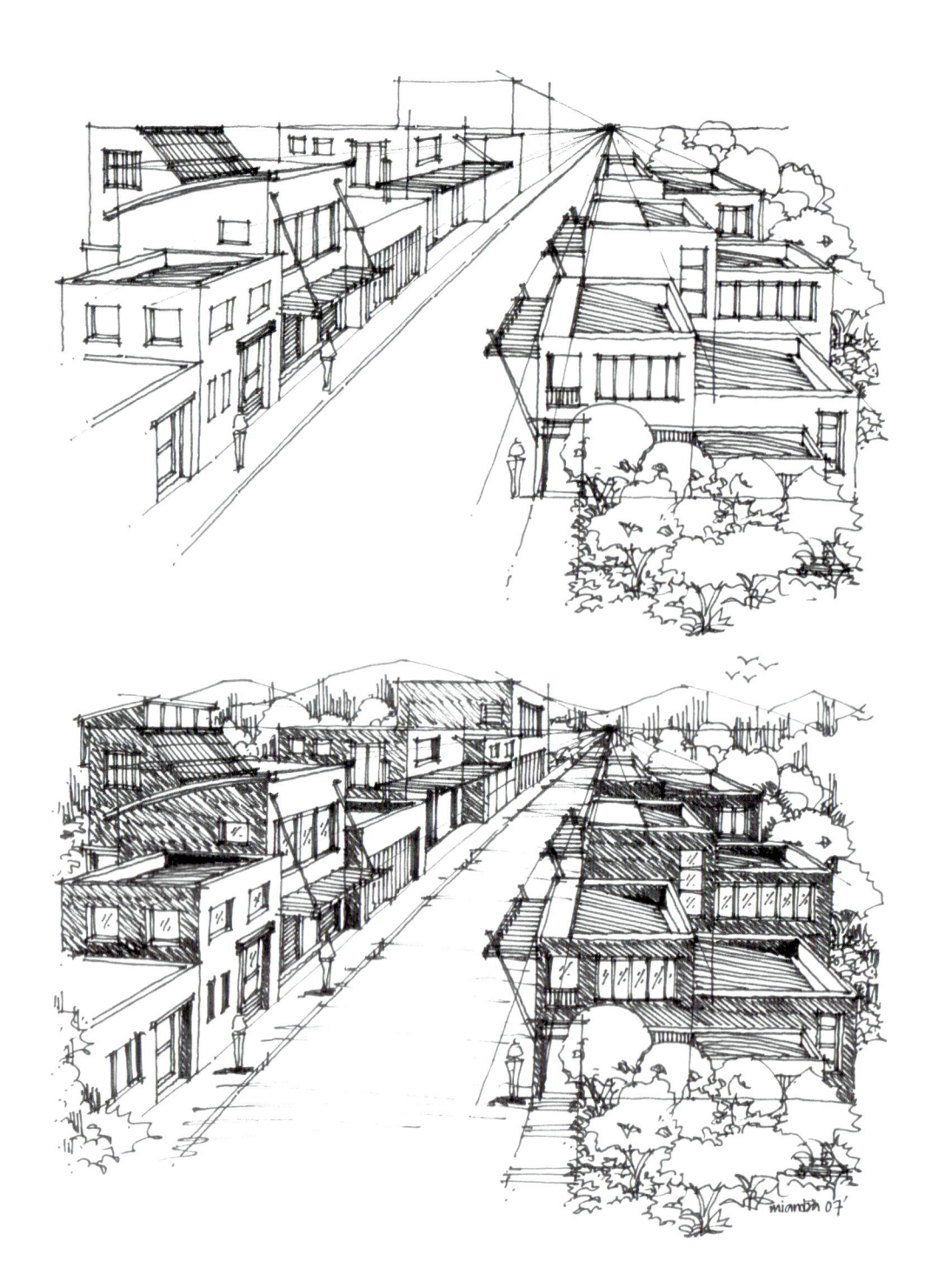

Step 3
You need to be creative when suggesting the background of any sketch composition. It will influence the quality of sketch if the background chosen does not really fit with the urban street setting.

Tip: *Choose the right background.*

• Level setting 1

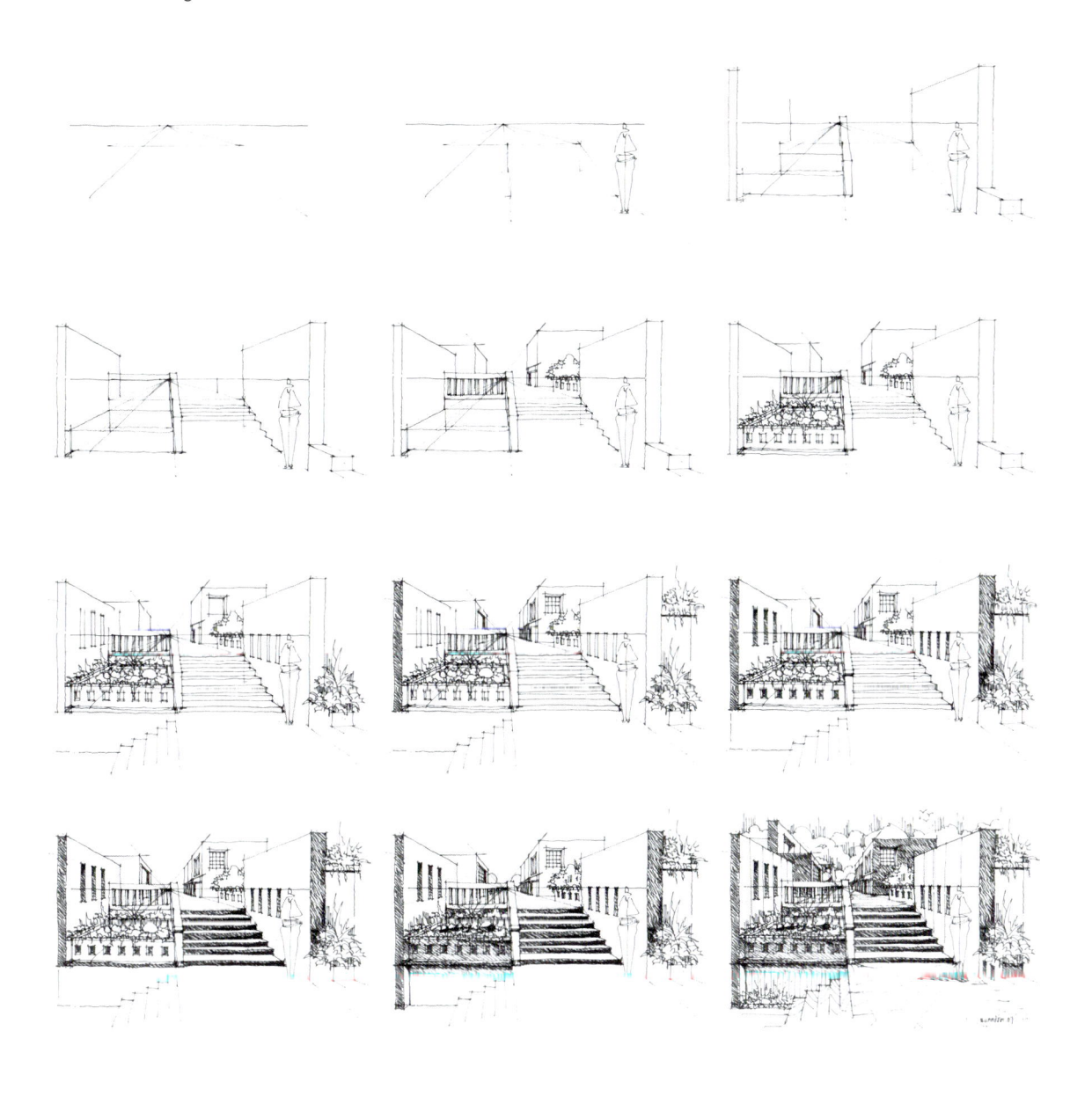

A STEP BY STEP PROCESS   161

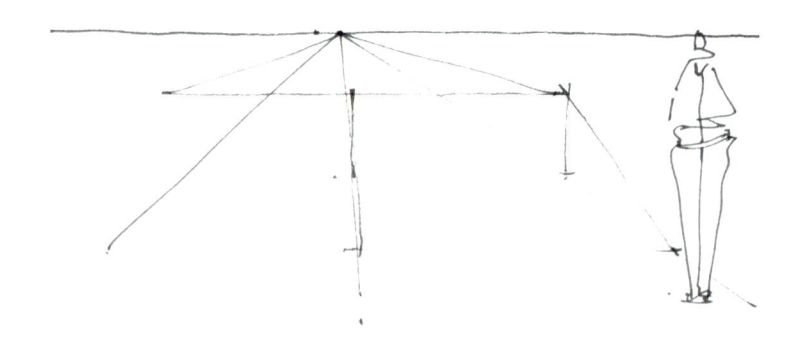

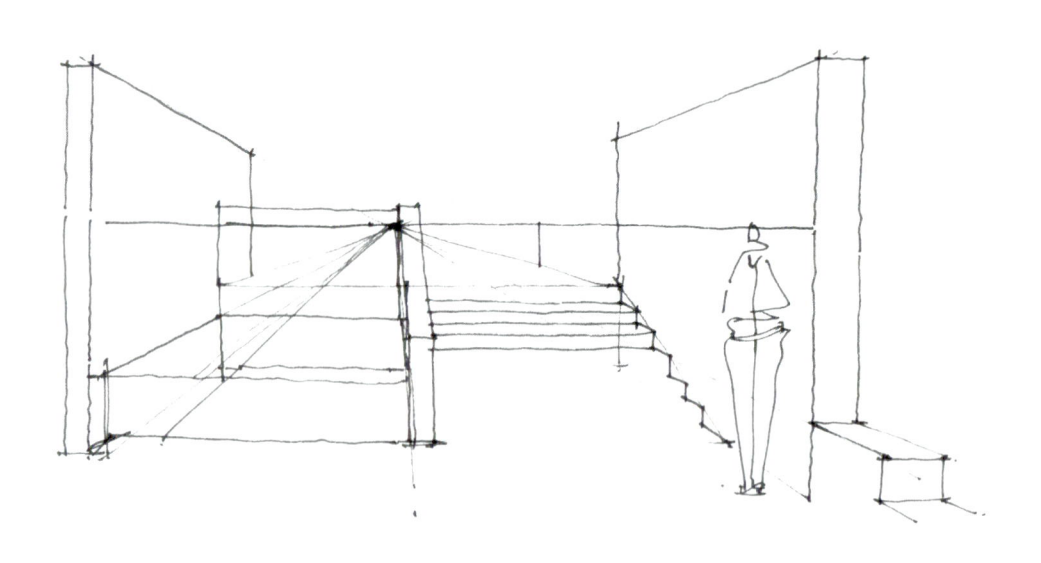

Step 1
This process is to demonstrate how to create levels in a sketch composition. Observe carefully and you will understand how to create levels as shown in the step by step process.

Tip: *Do learn to create levels.*

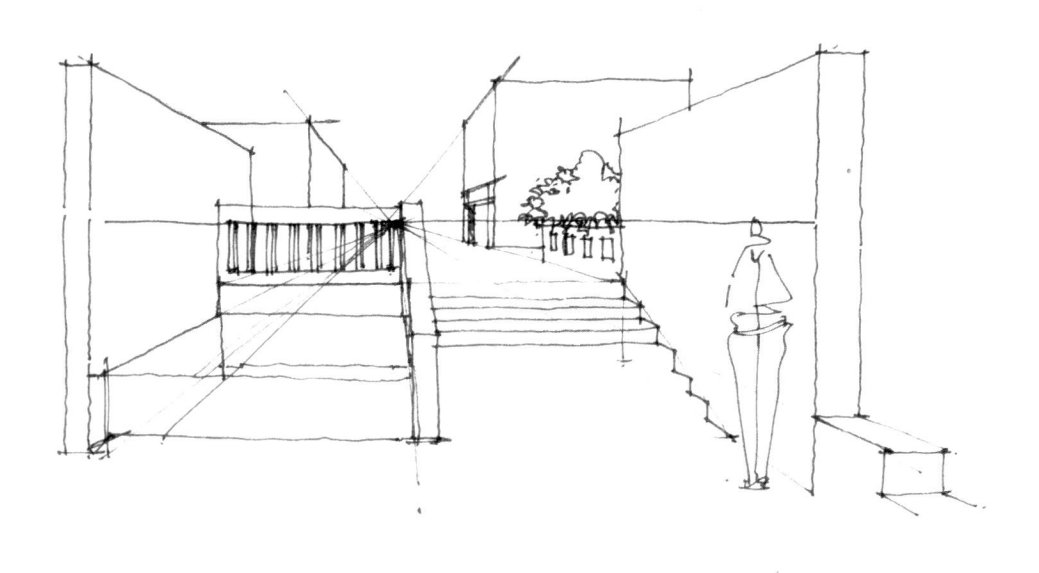

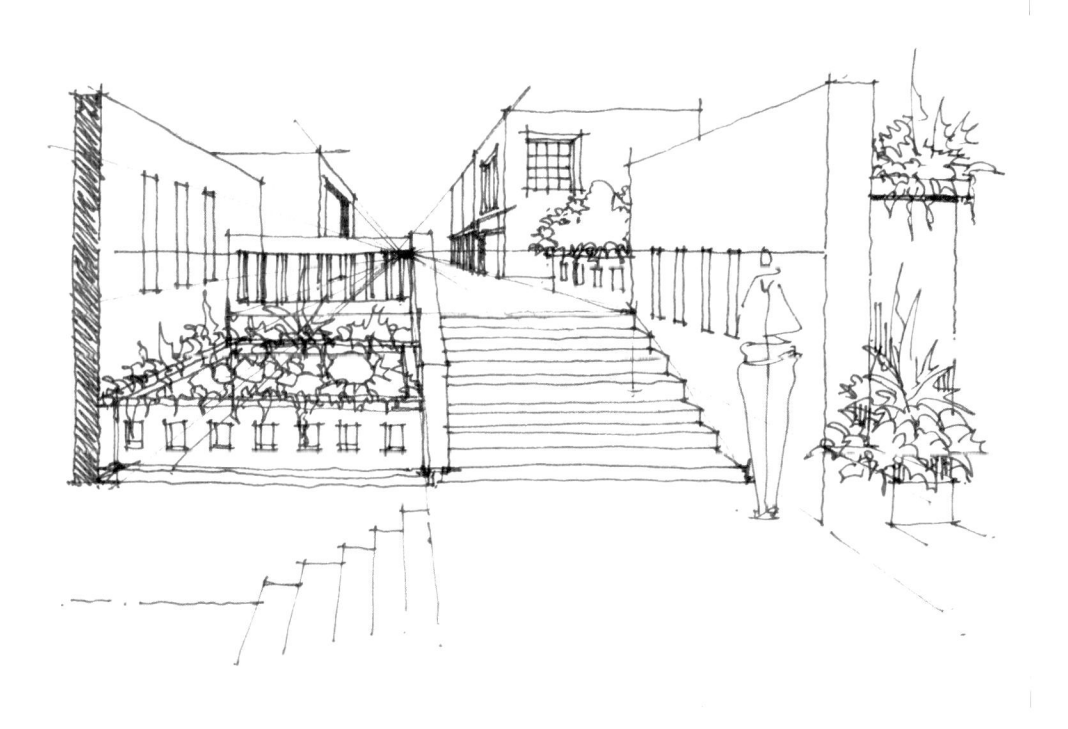

Step 2
Repeat the same process if you want to create another level as shown in the process and always refer to the vanishing point to connect the lines.

Tip: *Practise and practise.*

A STEP BY STEP PROCESS 163

Step 3
Observe the transformation of the sketch after the shades and shadows have been applied to the composition. You need to know the right surface to apply the shades and shadows. Always refer to the light source.

Tip: *Shade and shadow.*

• Level setting 2

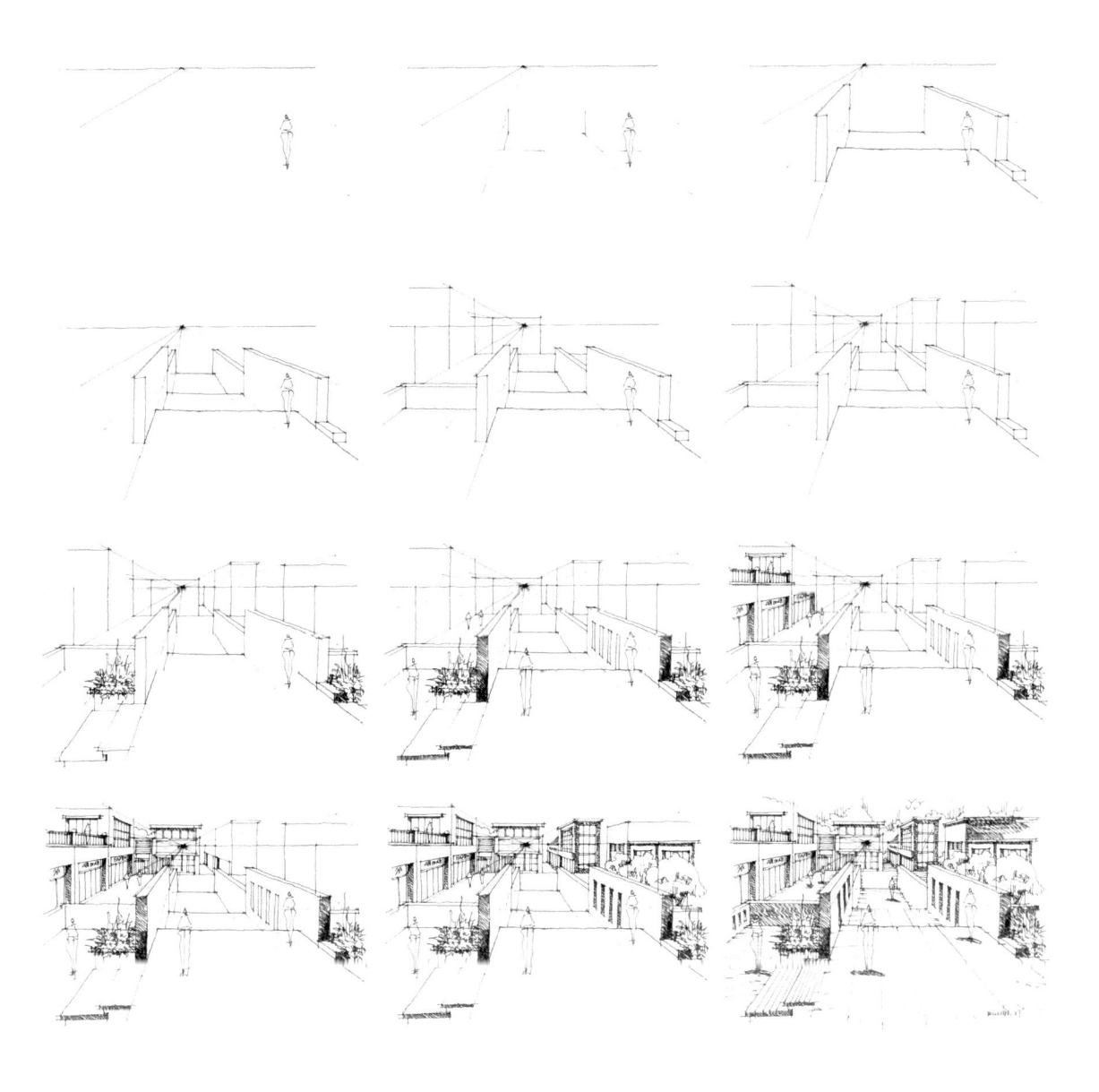

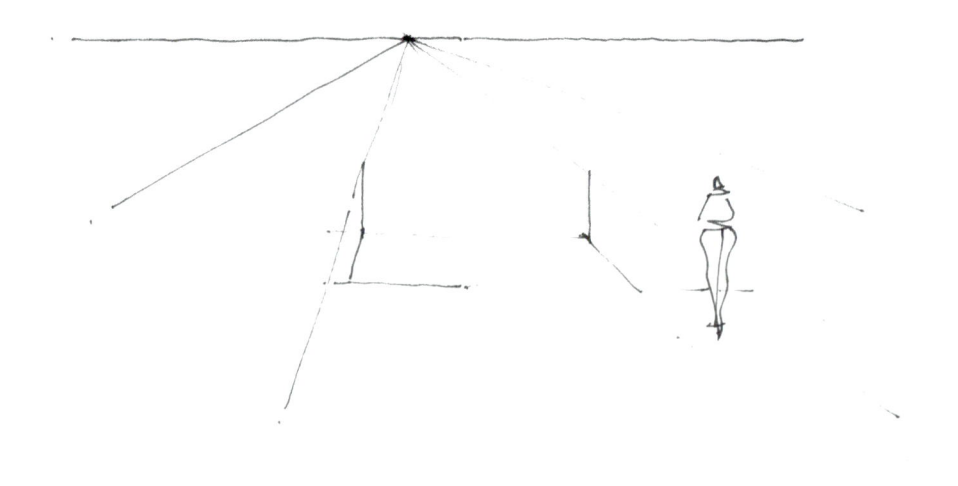

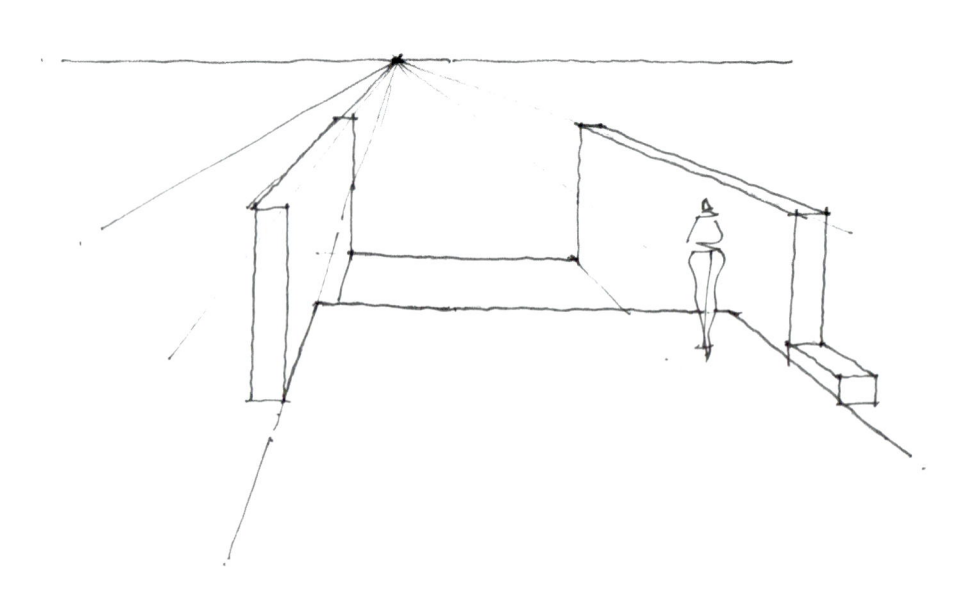

Step 1
This sketch will demonstrate the technique to sketch a drop level. Refer to the sketch and look carefully at the process. Repeat the same process to create another level. Always refer to the vanishing point and the human figure.

***Tip**: Check the eye level.*

166　A STEP BY STEP PROCESS

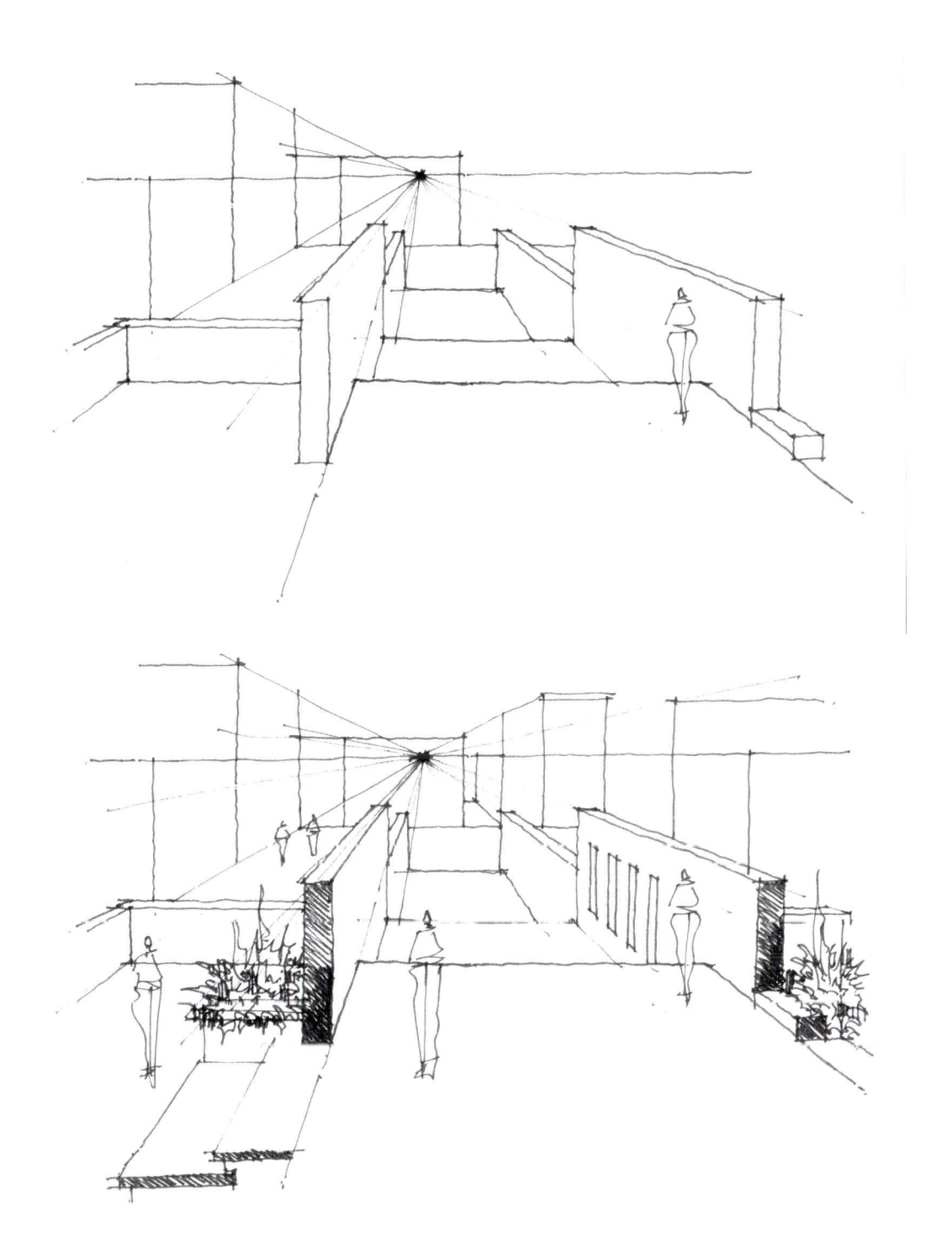

Step 2
Look at the transformation process of the sketch where the overall rough setting is transformed into a more detailed setting. Then, proceed by adding the plants and details of the objects.

Tip: *Creativity is needed when you deal with adding details and plants.*

A STEP BY STEP PROCESS

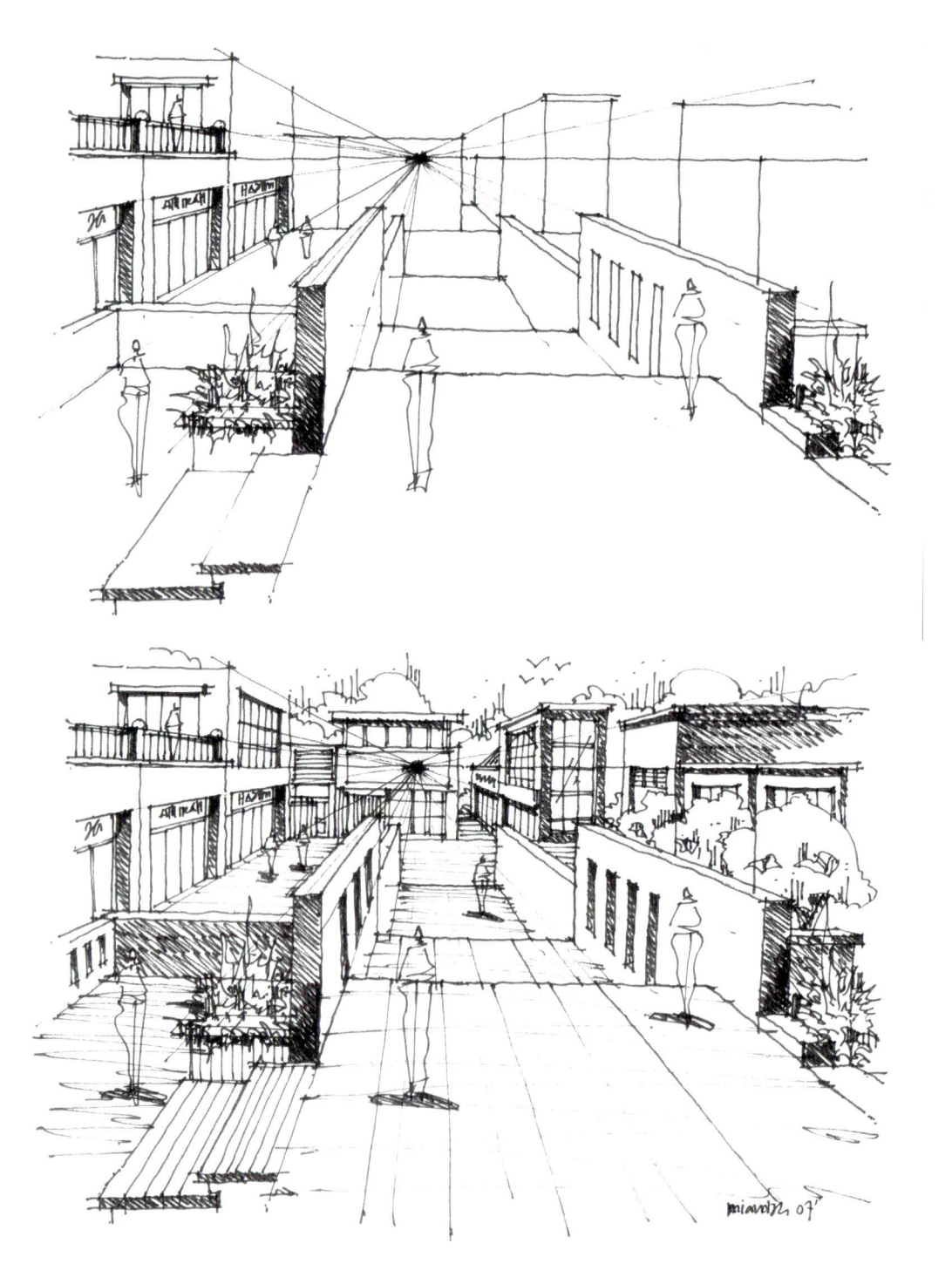

Step 3
Before proceed with rendering, make sure all the important elements have been sketched to their position.

Tip: *Do not proceed with rendering if the setting is not complete.*

6.3 TWO POINT PERSPECTIVE

- Object setting 1

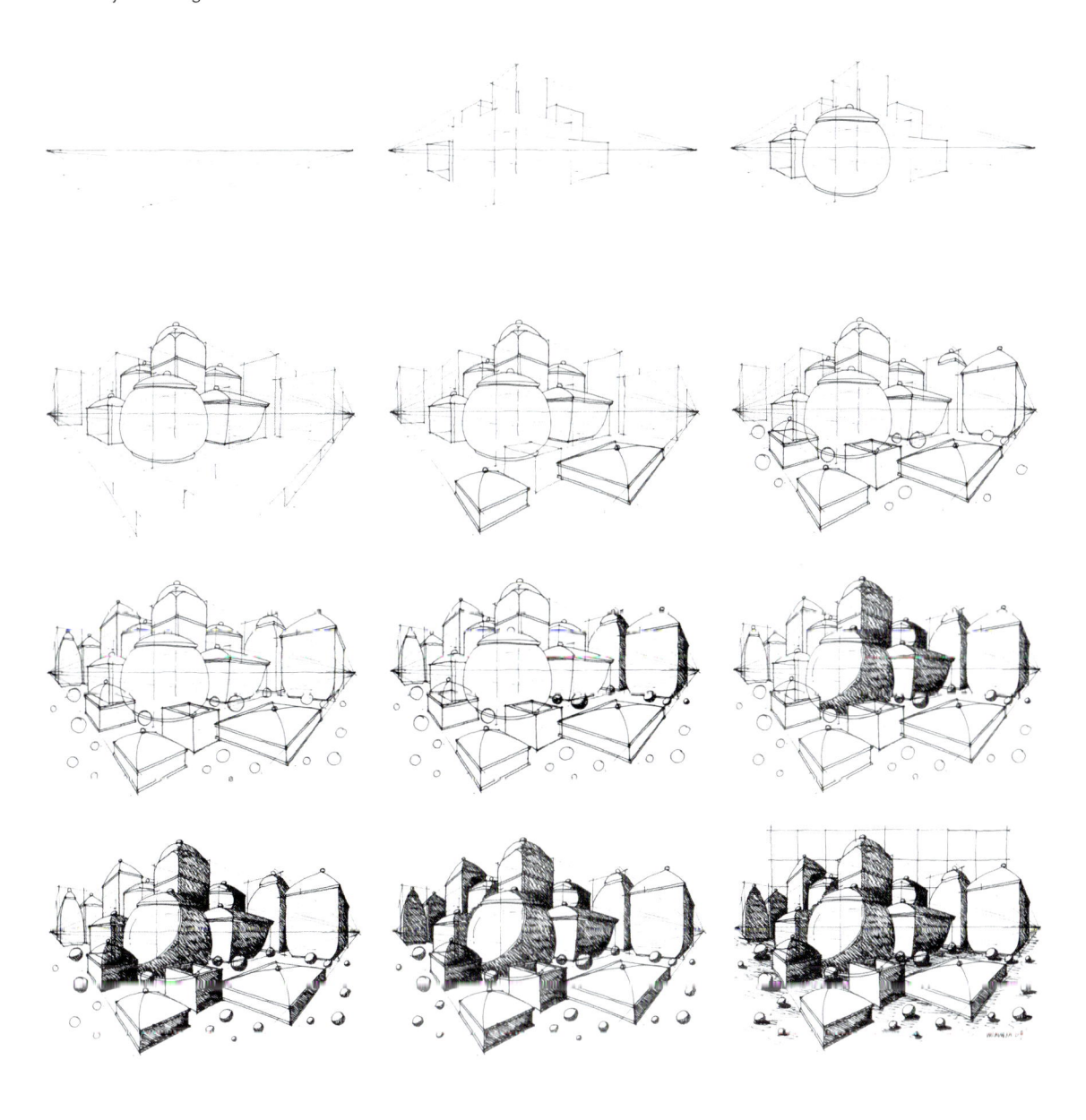

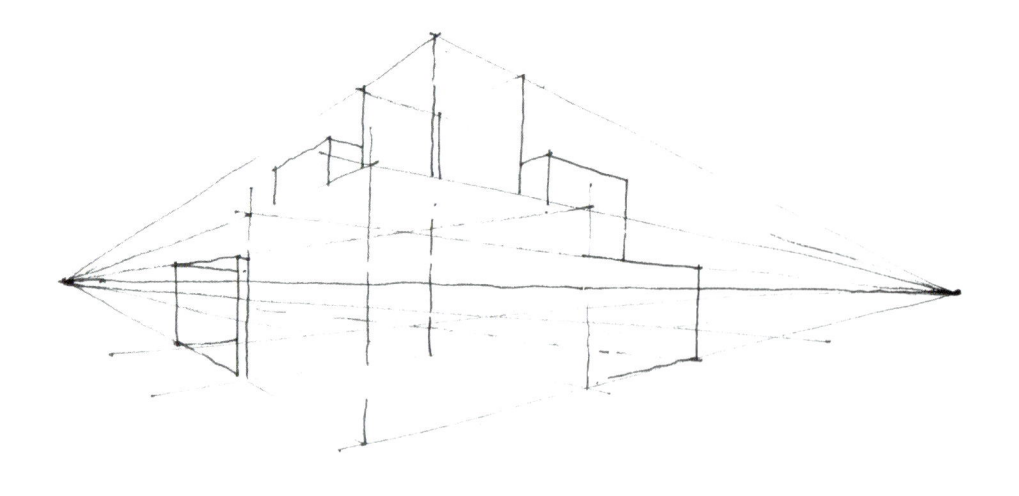

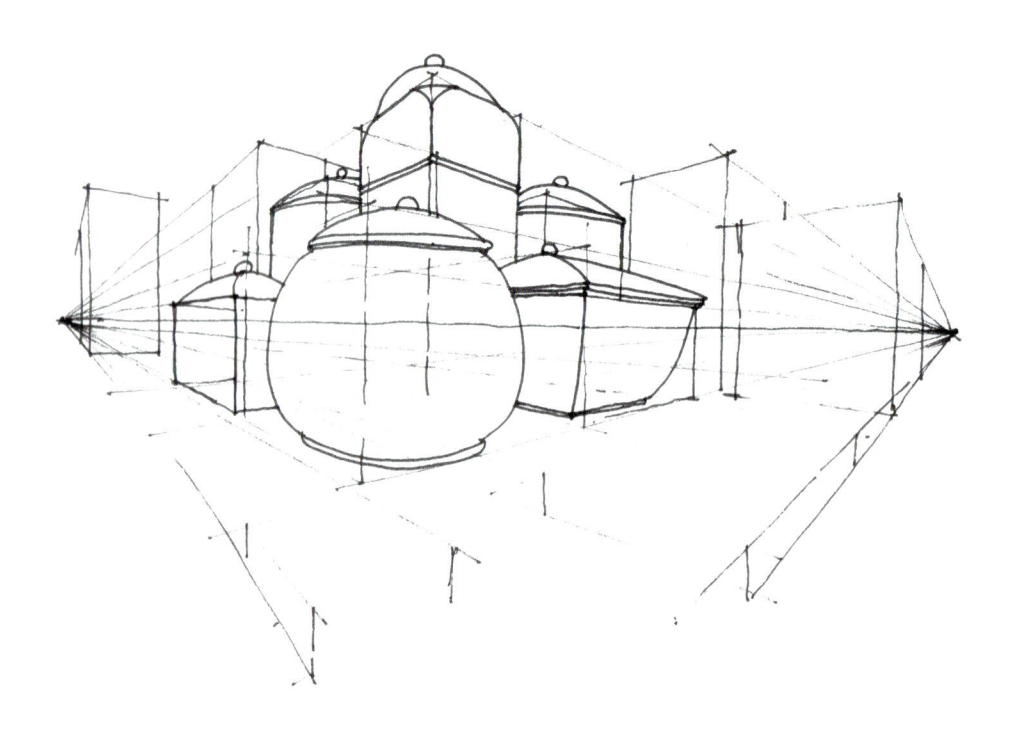

Step 1
It is important to finalise the desired angle of the sketch before setting up the two vanishing points. The angle will influence the view of the sketch.

Tip: *Set the desired angle.*

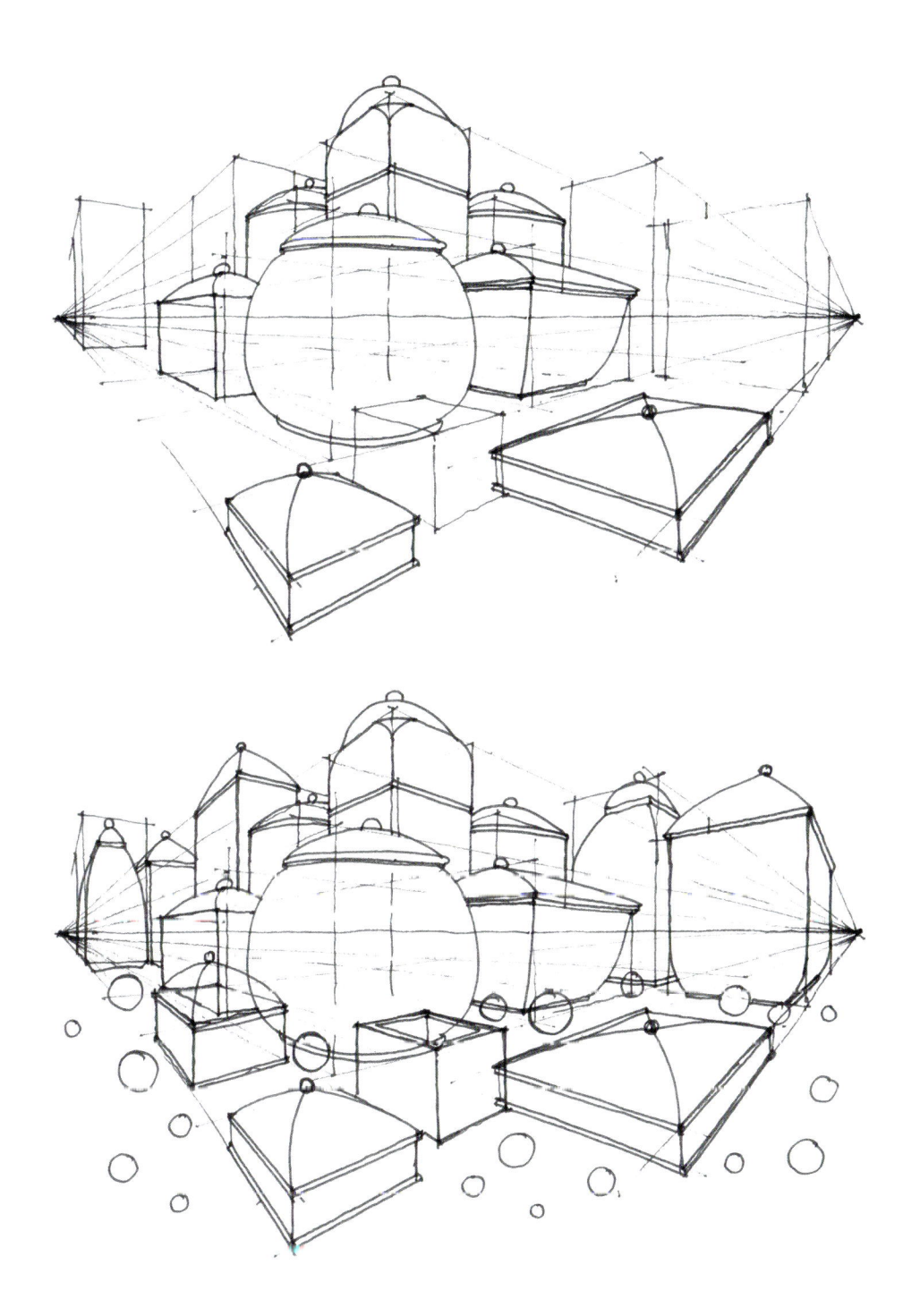

Step 2
Look carefully at the examples given; the perspective is called human eye view although the scales of the objects are smaller than the scale of human figure.

Tip: *The eye level will determine the perspective type.*

A STEP BY STEP PROCESS 171

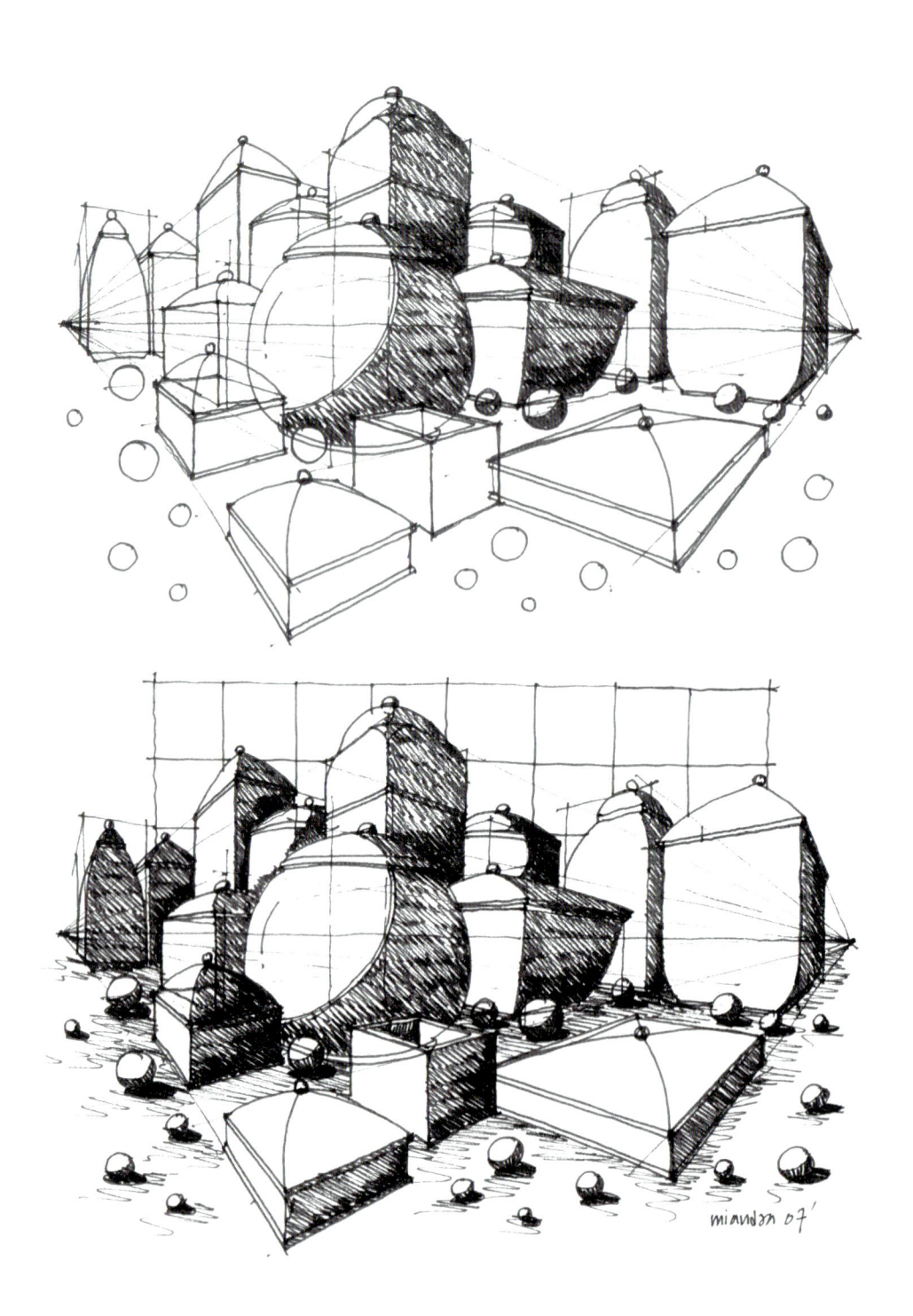

Step 3
Do a comparison between these two sketches. Look carefully at the shades and shadows on the objects' surfaces, they have different setting and criteria. For an example, the sphere surface has different shades than the square surface.

Tip: Shade and shadow.

• Object setting 2

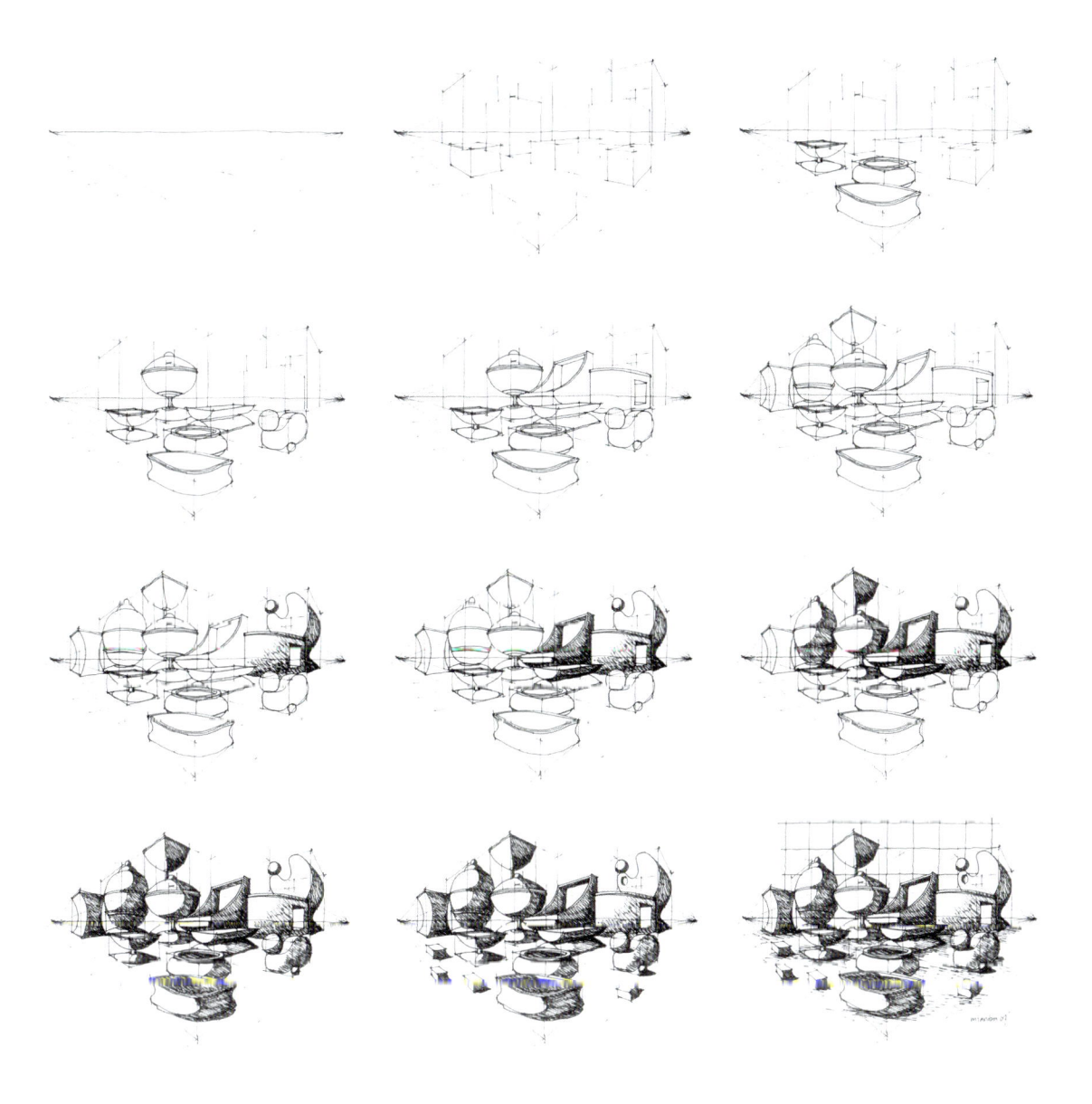

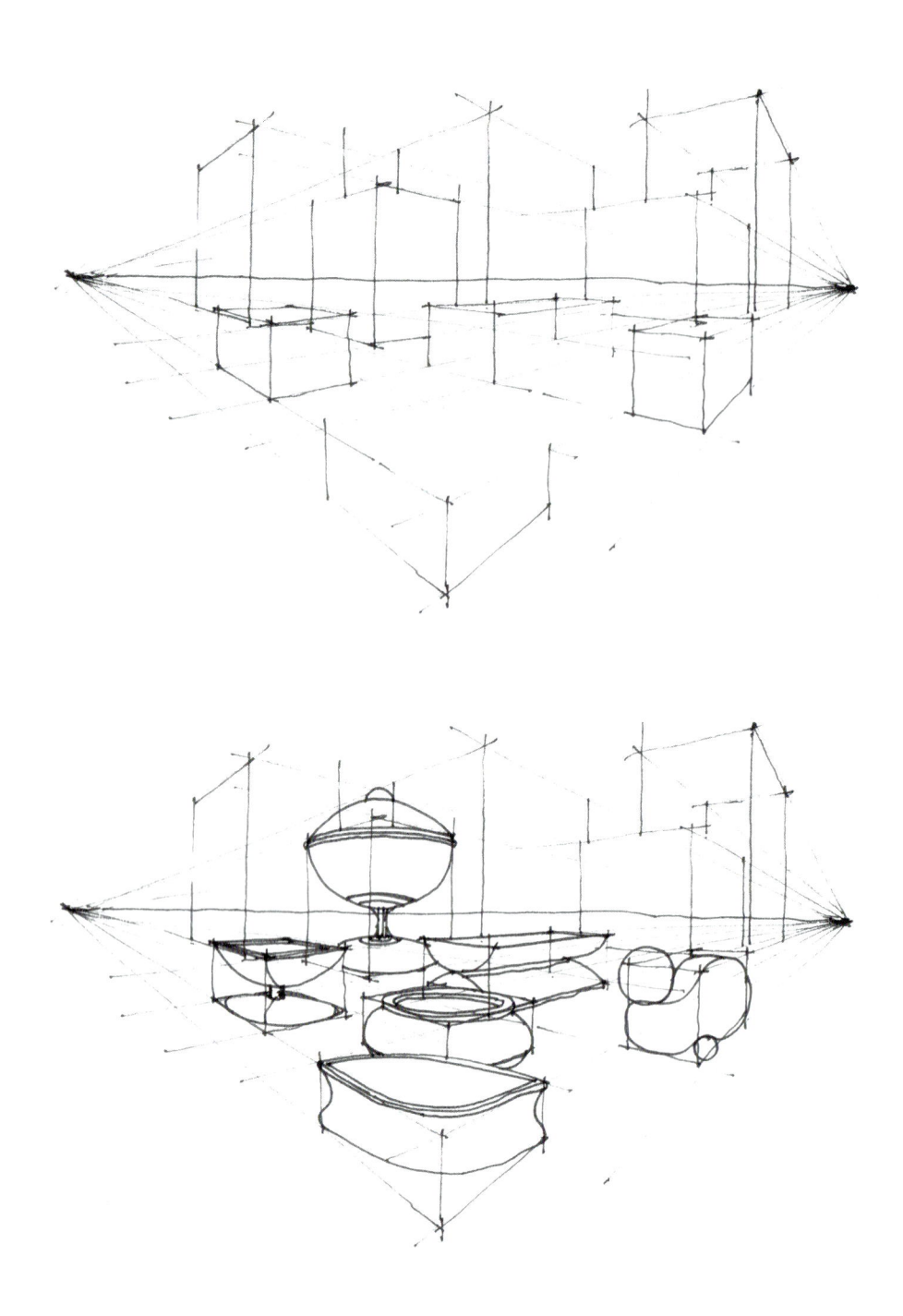

Step 1
Try to establish the way you start your sketch. The first thing to do is set the horizon line, then set the vanishing points and then the imaginary box. After that, sketch objects' setting.

Tip: *Establish the process.*

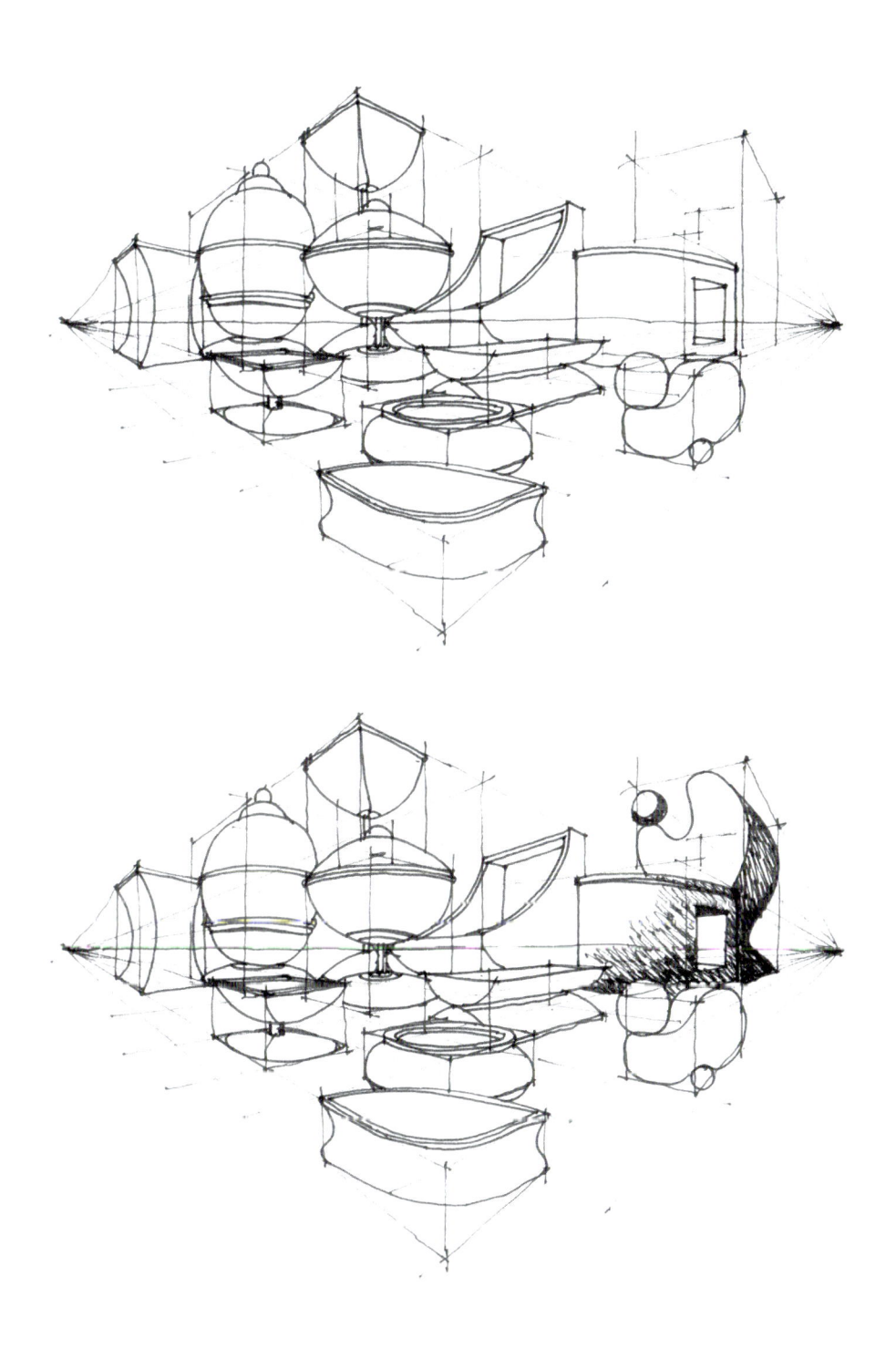

Step 2
The examples given show the process of sketching the objects' setting with different types of forms and shapes. Do observe the process and understand them properly.

Tip: *Study, understand and visualise an object surface before you start sketching them.*

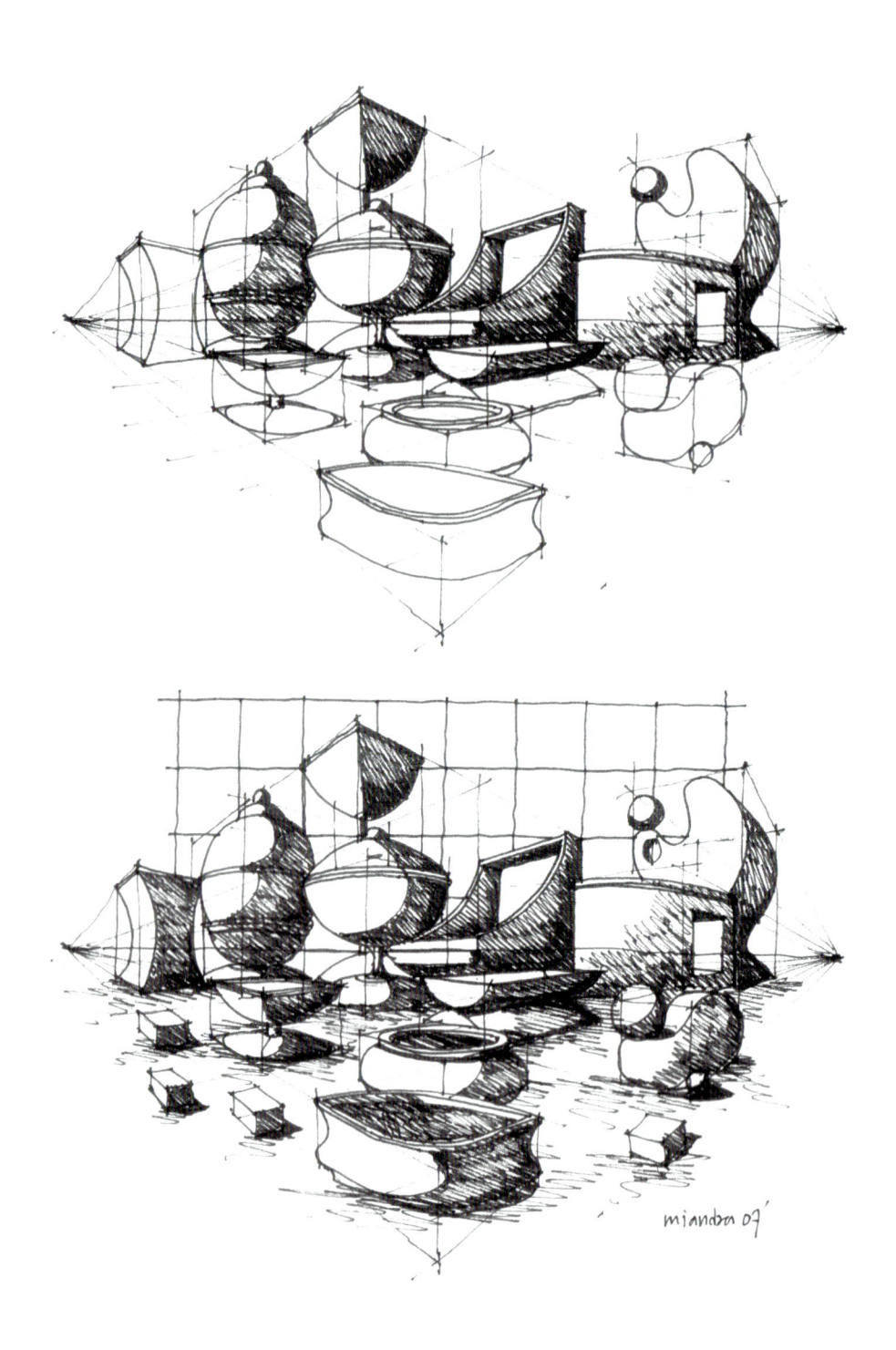

Step 3
The final touch-up is the last process that needs to be done. This process demands creativity from a designer because this creativity comes from self intuition and cannot be explained by process. Observe the concept discussed in the example given.

Tip: *Practice makes perfect.*

• Landscape setting 1

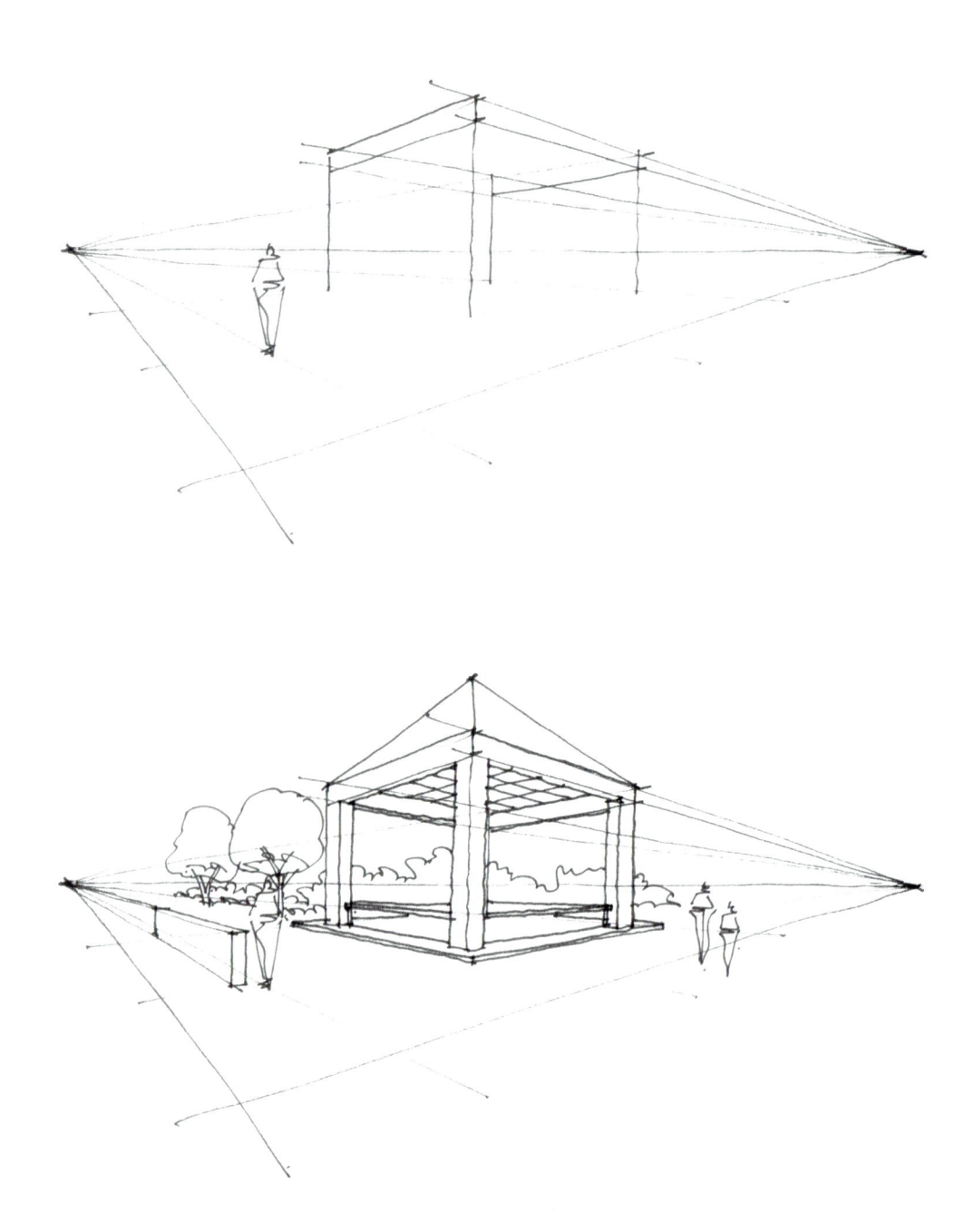

Step 1
The same process applies to any perspective. These three elements which are horizon line, vanishing point and construction lines are very important to create a quality perspective. Refer to the examples given.

Tip: Master these three elements.

178 A STEP BY STEP PROCESS

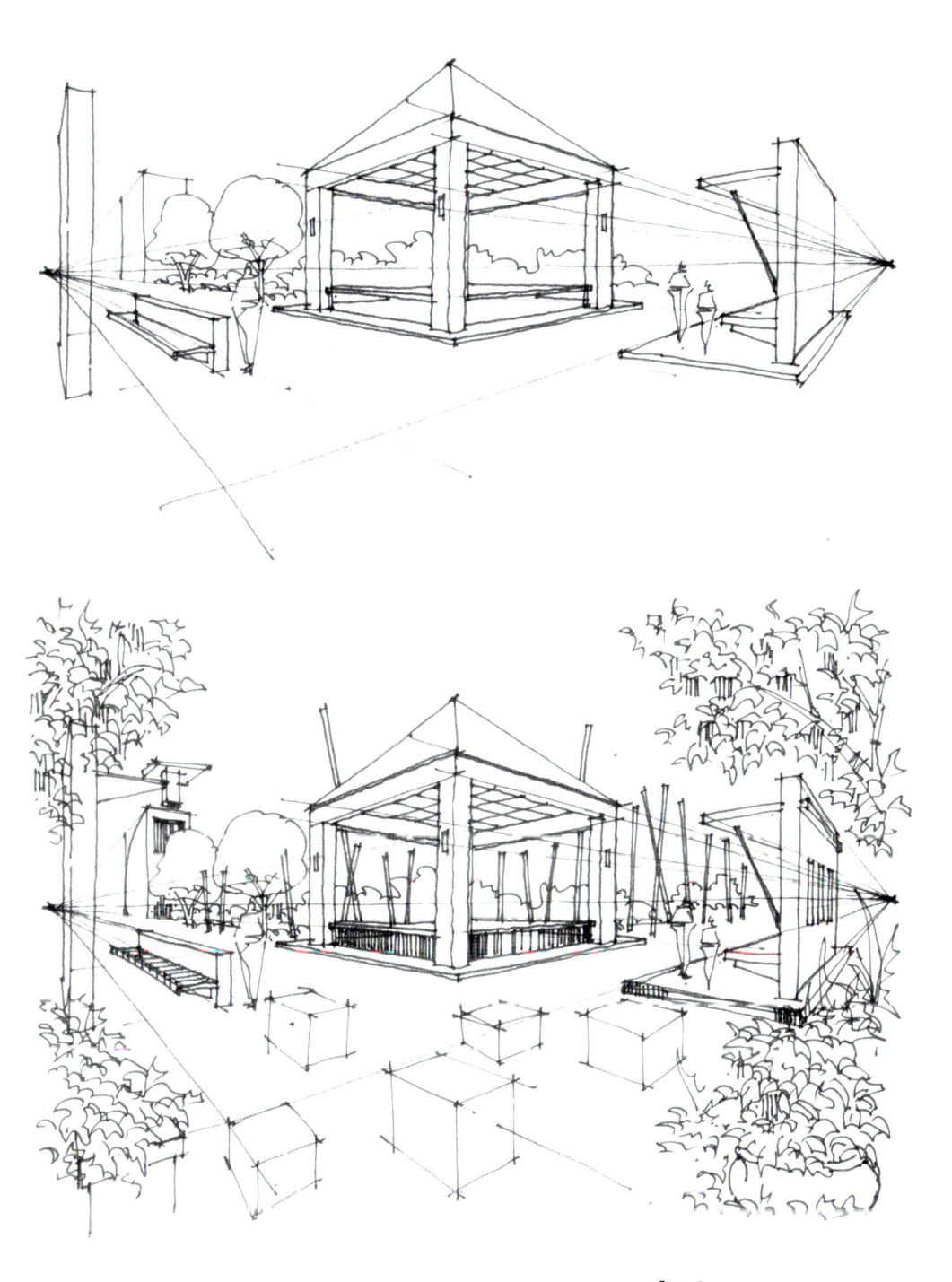

Step 2
This demonstration is to show the process of sketching secondary objects to complete the composition. Look at the examples on how the process is being implemented with suitable elements.

Tip: *Try to imagine the objects before sketching them on paper.*

A STEP BY STEP PROCESS 179

Step 3
Compare these two processes that explain the transformation of a sketch composition before and after the rendering process. The depth of the spaces in the sketch can be seen clearly in the final composition compared to the work before it.

Tip: Depth is very important to get a quality sketch.

180   A STEP BY STEP PROCESS

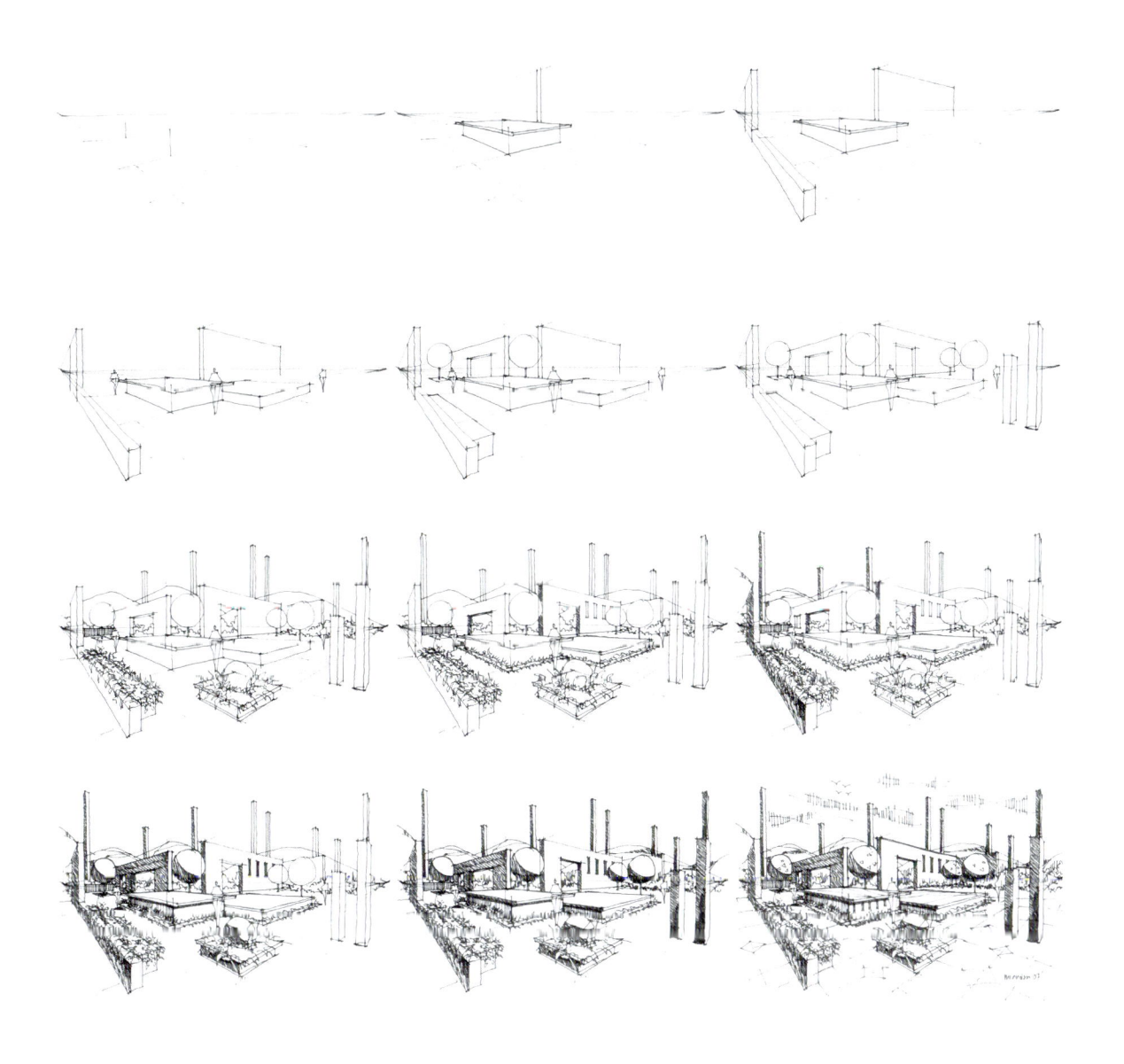

• Landscape setting 2

A STEP BY STEP PROCESS

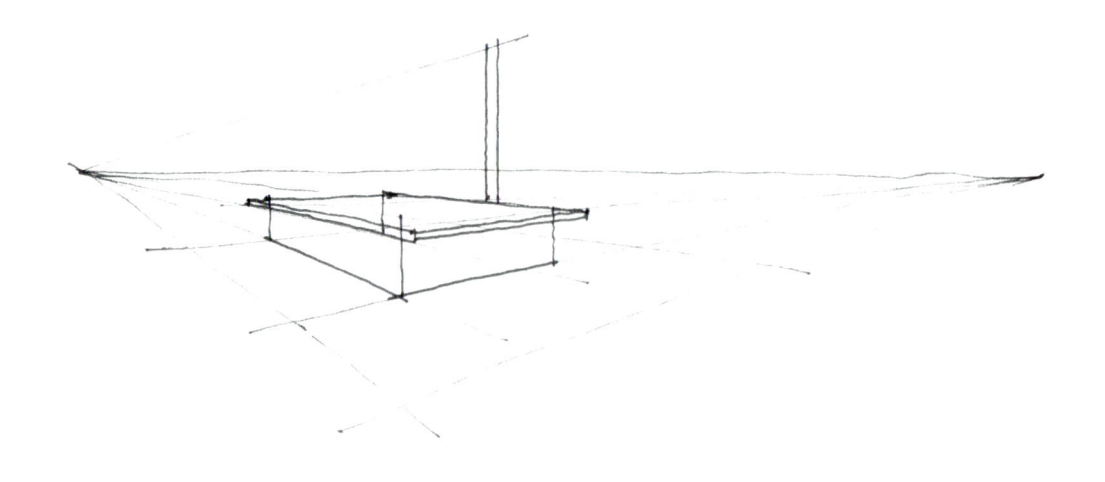

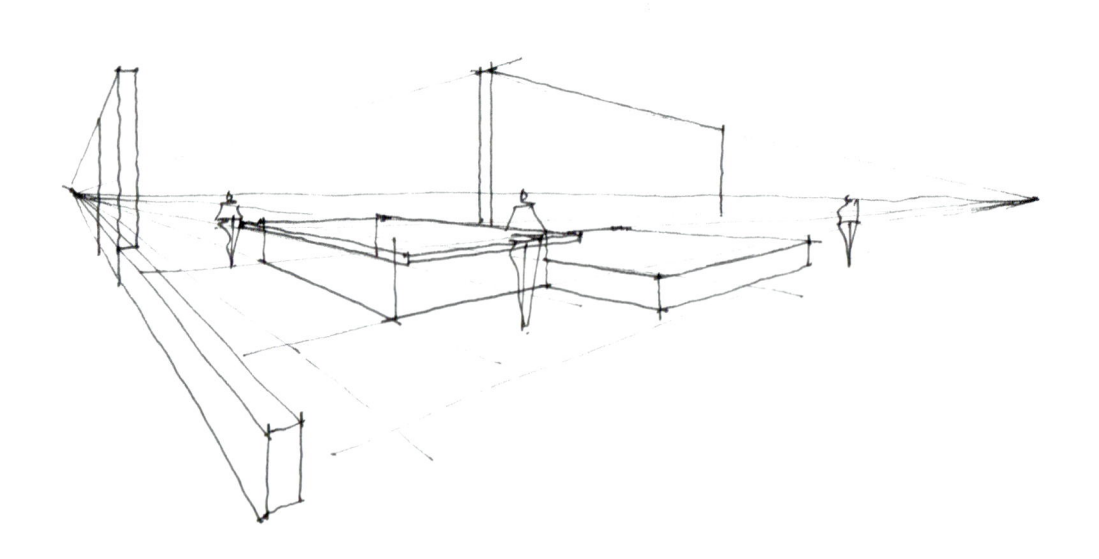

Step 1
The use of proper line types will help to highlight the sketch quality. Basic to complex compositions all need a good choice of line types. This example demonstrates a few line types that are used for sketching which differentiate object lines and construction lines.

Tip: Do learn different line types.

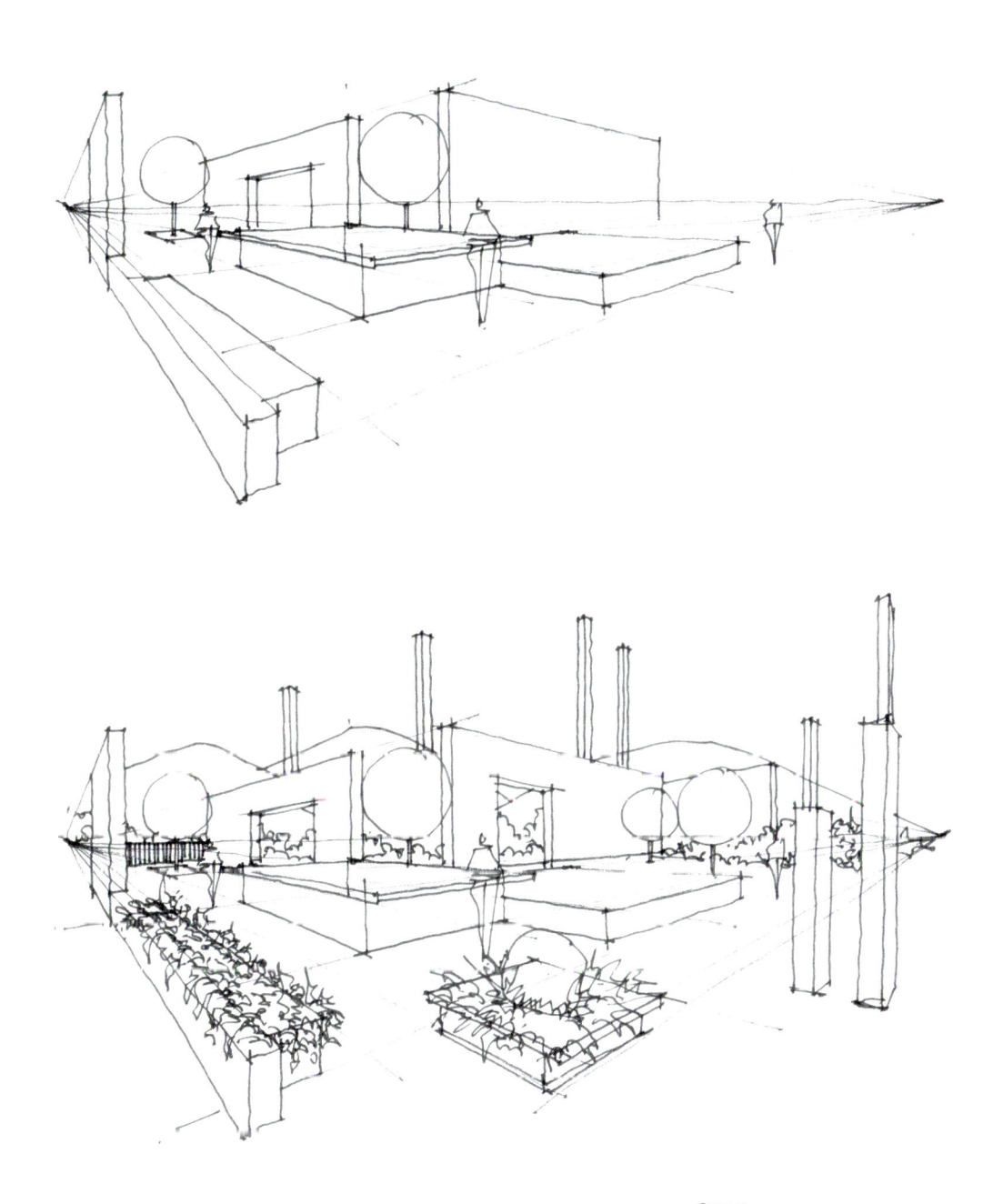

Step 2
Line quality is also important to produce a good quality sketch. Do observe and try to appreciate the line quality in the example given.

Tip: When sketching, a confident line is a quality line.

A STEP BY STEP PROCESS

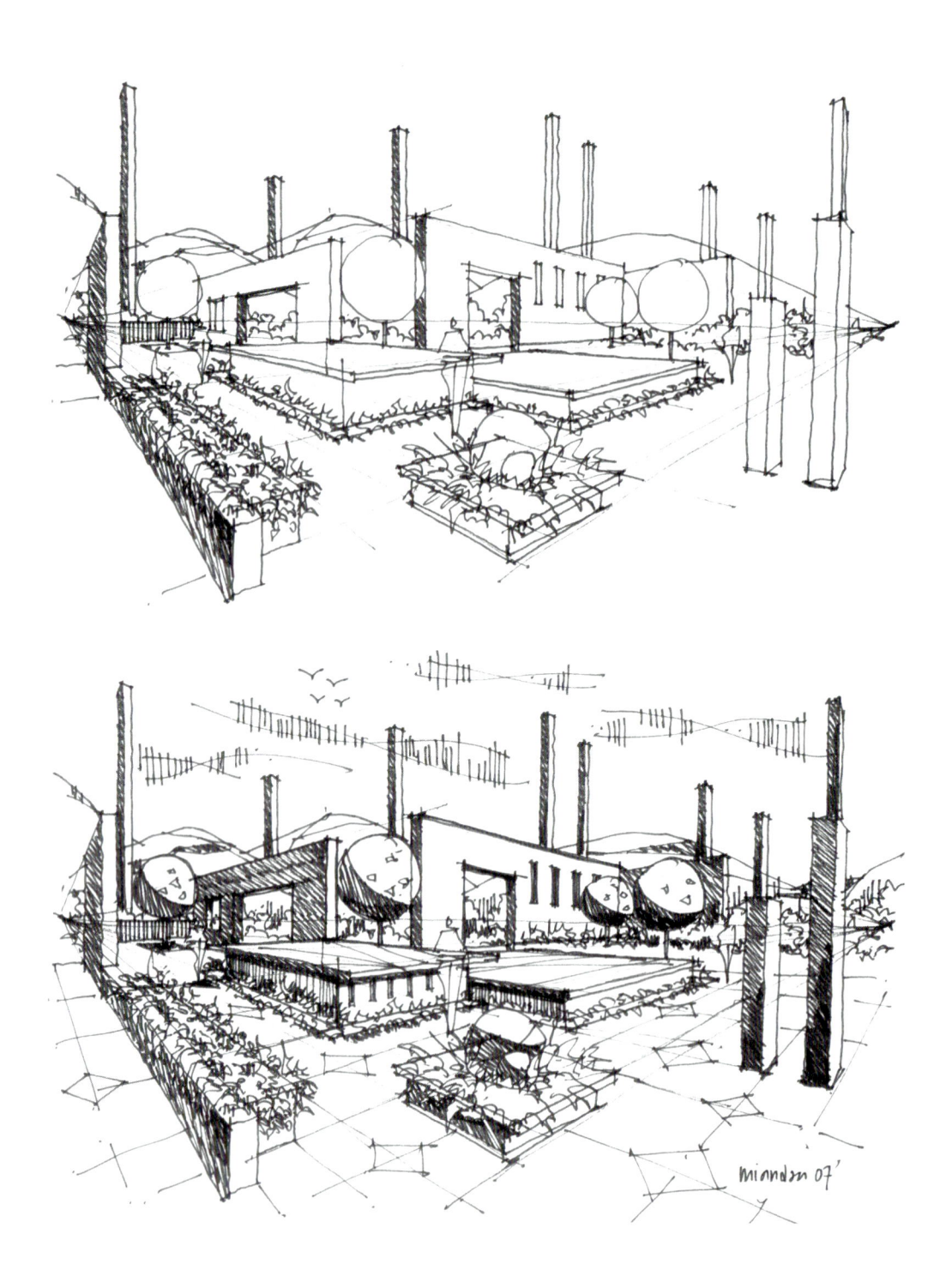

Step 3
Look carefully at the examples given; one of the factors to producing a quality sketch is the human factor. You must believe and have confidence in yourself that you can produce a quality sketch.

Tip: *Be confident.*

• Urban and architectural setting 1

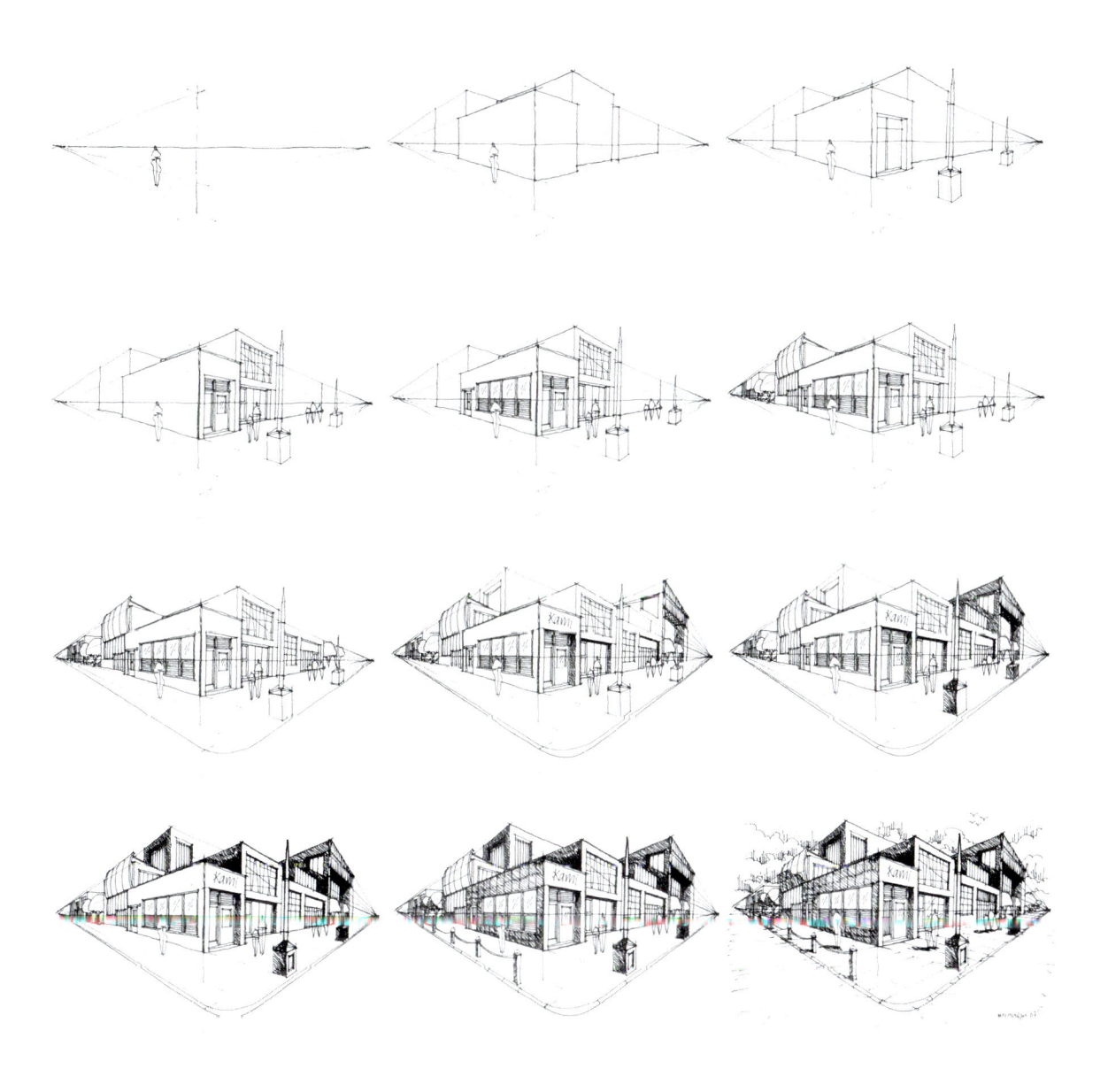

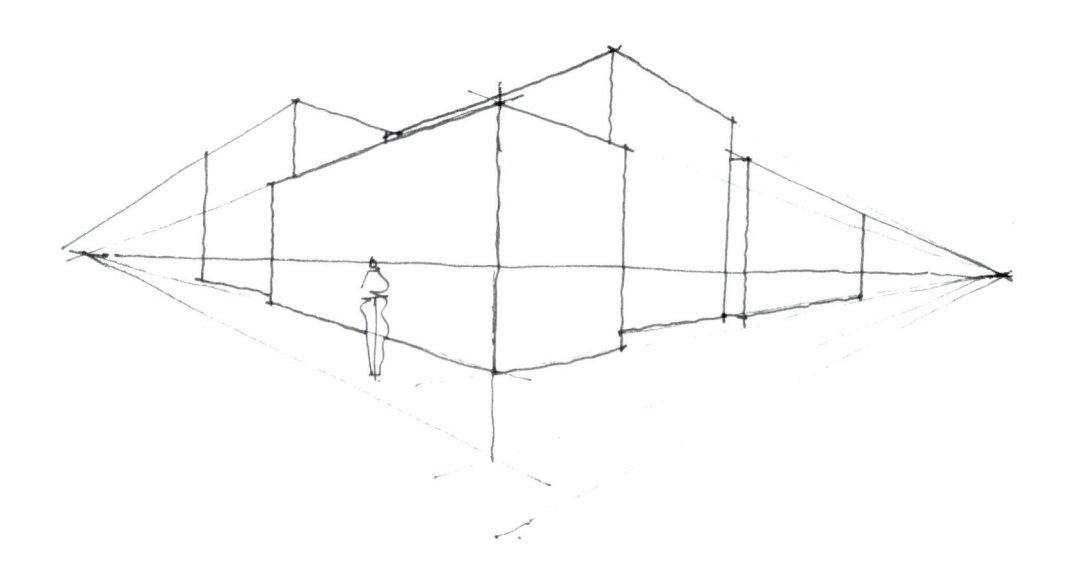

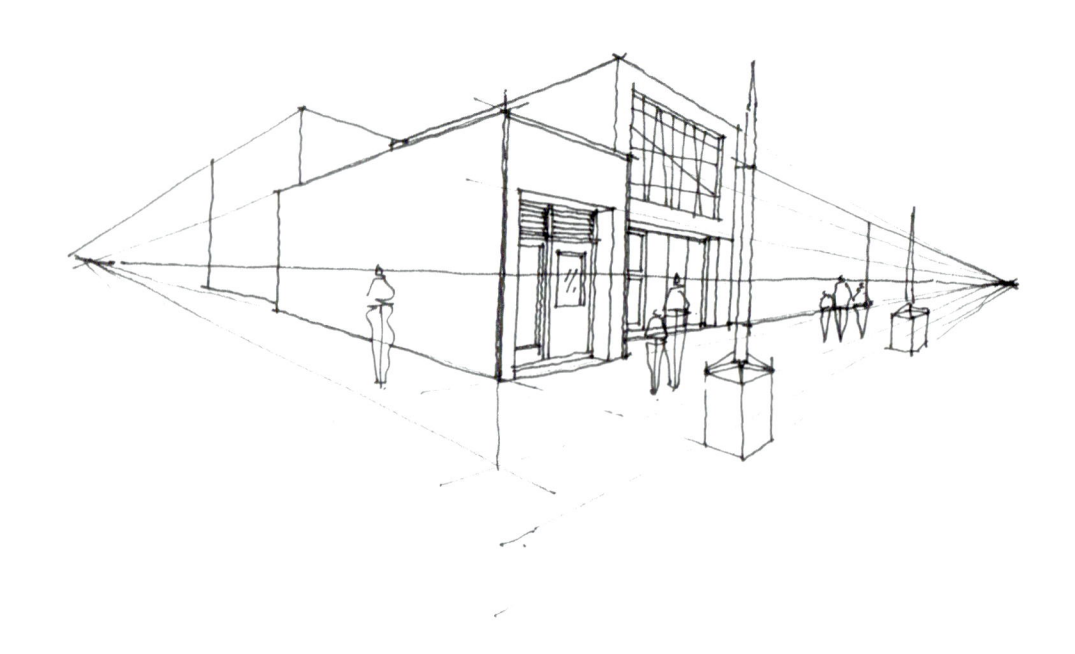

Step 1
Look carefully at the process given, there are two vanishing points that need to be considered before any line is drawn in the sketch. Do study the process and you will get the overall concept of these vanishing points.

Tip: *Always refer to the vanishing points.*

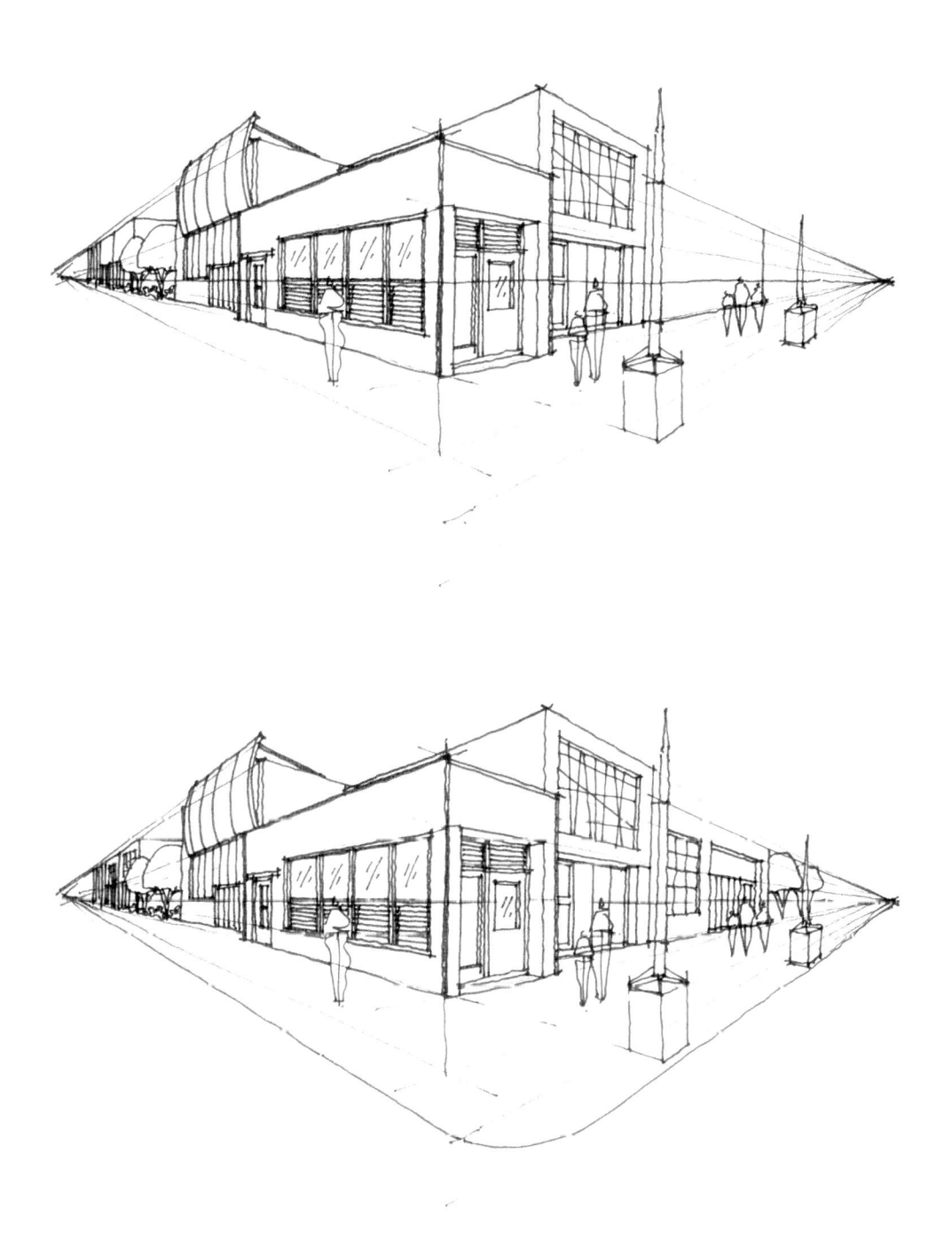

Step 2
Details are very important to making the setting interesting. The choice of details should come from the creativity of the artists or designers. Do refer to magazines or books to get more ideas.

Tip: *Refer to other sources to get more creative ideas.*

A STEP BY STEP PROCESS 187

Step 3
The last part of rendering process is to apply the composition background. Look at the process given; this is one of the graphic techniques that can be used to represent the cloud as the composition background.

Tip: *Background composition needs some creative graphic ideas.*

188 A STEP BY STEP PROCESS

- Urban and architectural setting 2

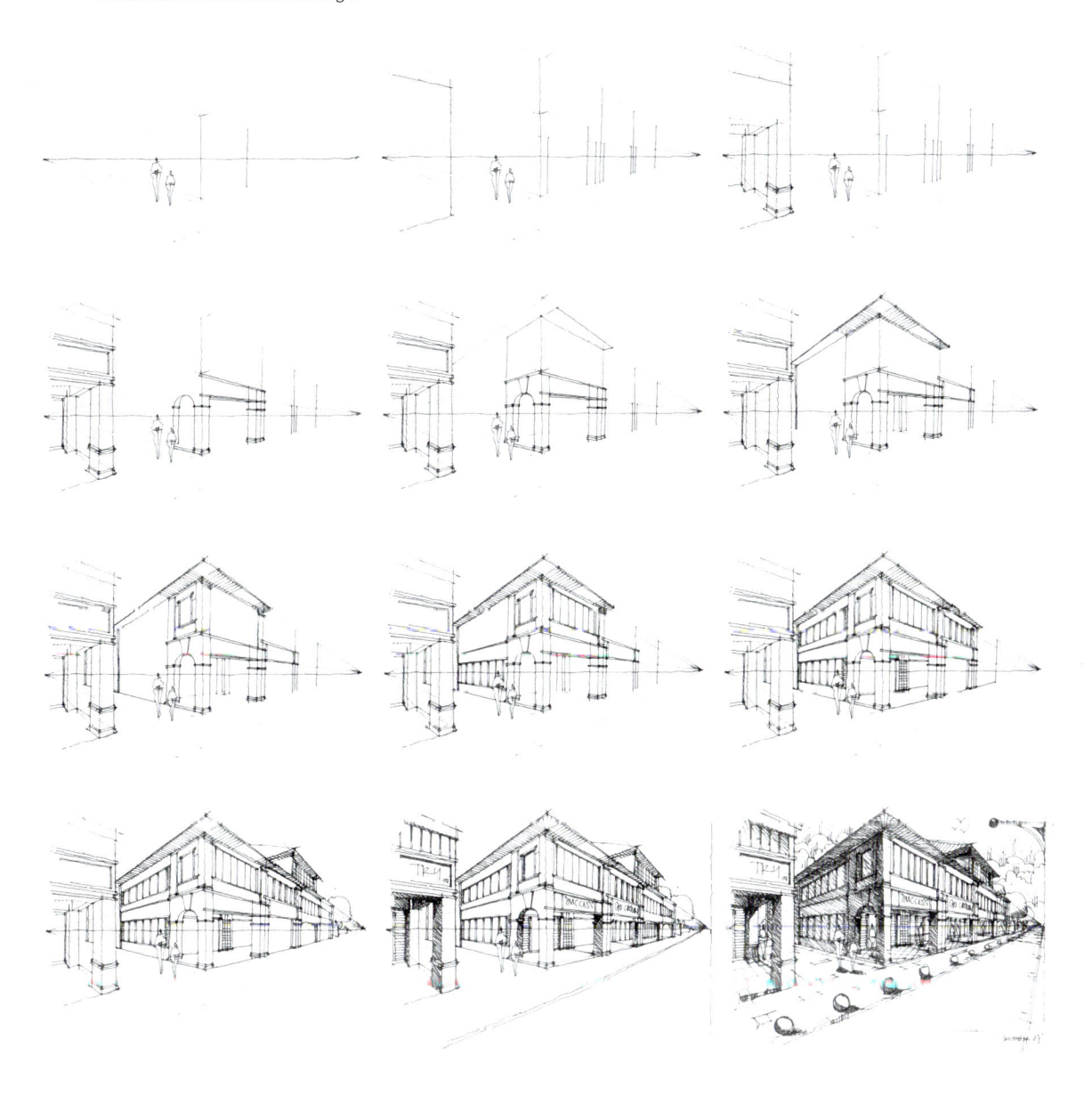

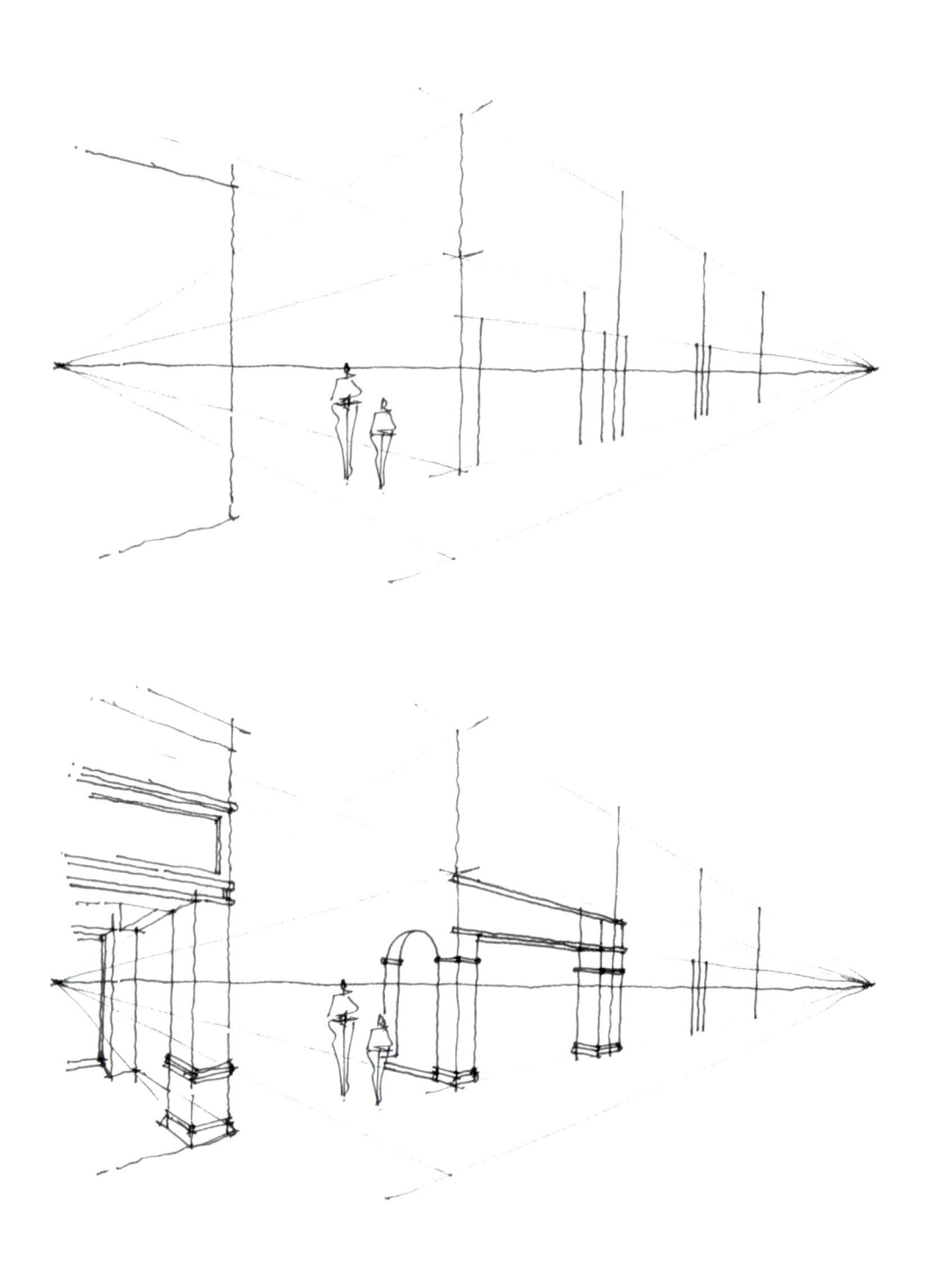

Step 1
The most difficult part in perspective is to make the proportion look good to the viewers. The artist's or designer's eyes play a very important role to achieve this target.

Tip*: Practise your skill of proportionating a sketch composition by referring to human figure or other reference objects.*

190   A STEP BY STEP PROCESS

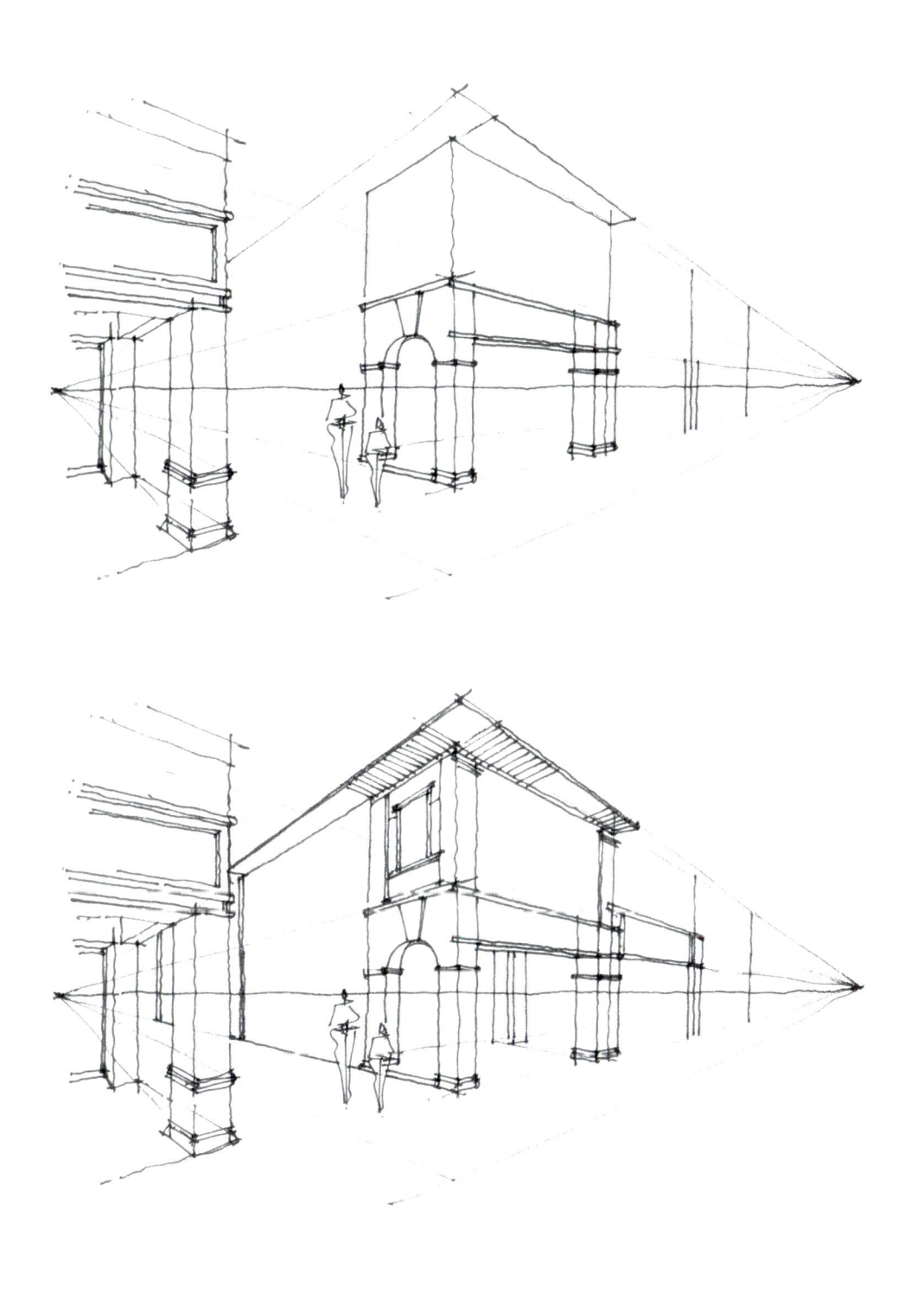

Step 2
Observe these two examples given; you will notice that there are added values to the buildings' facade details. These items must come from the artist's creativity.

Tip: *Always improve your knowledge of your surrounding.*

A STEP BY STEP PROCESS   191

Step 3
A quality rendering is based on shades and shadows. One of the factors that needs to be considered is the light direction. This idea can be portrayed by using the white surfaces for direct sunlight and the darkened surfaces for shaded areas. It is clearly demonstrated in the examples given.

Tip: Light direction is important to determine the quality of shades and shadows.

• Level setting 1

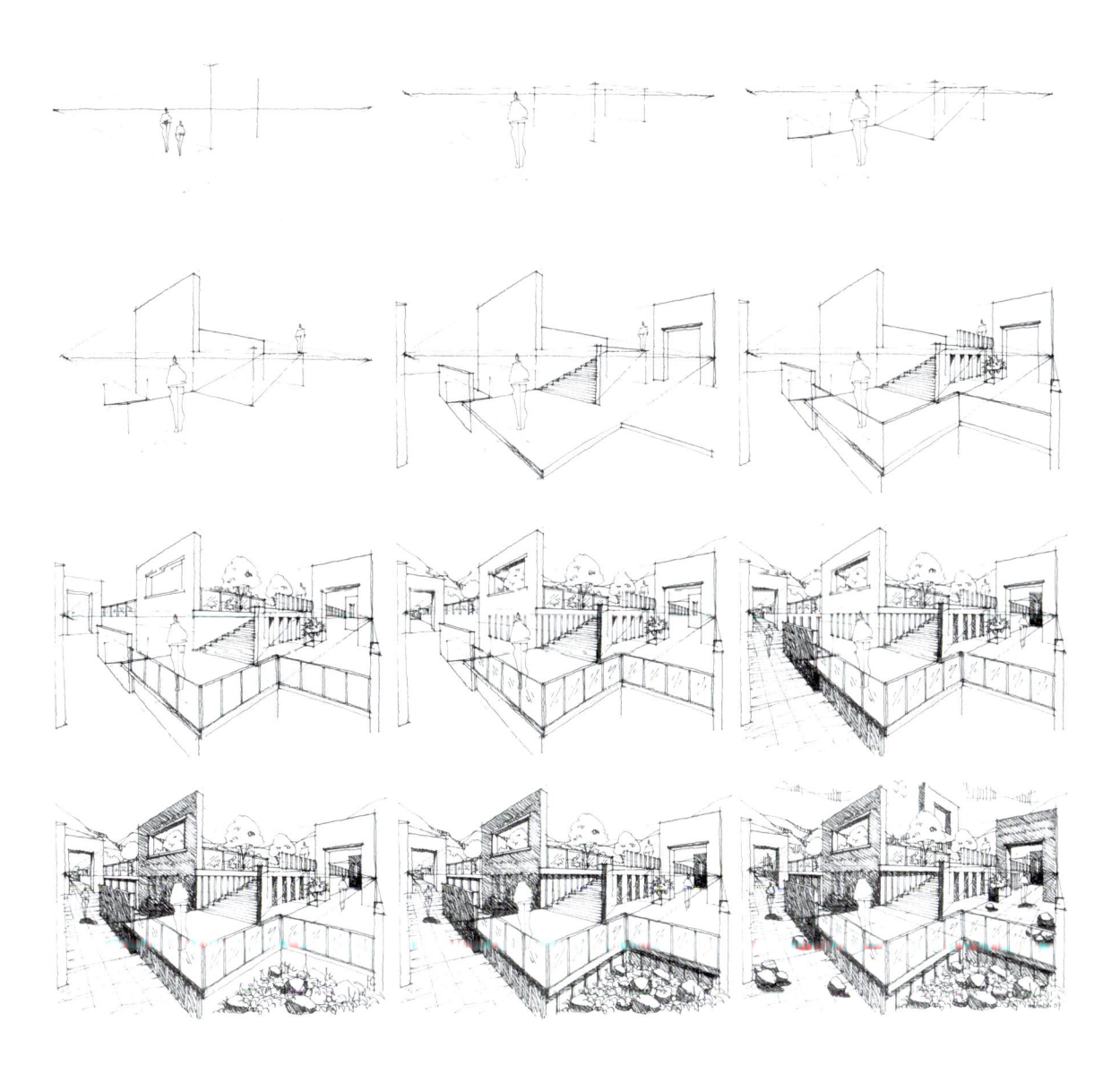

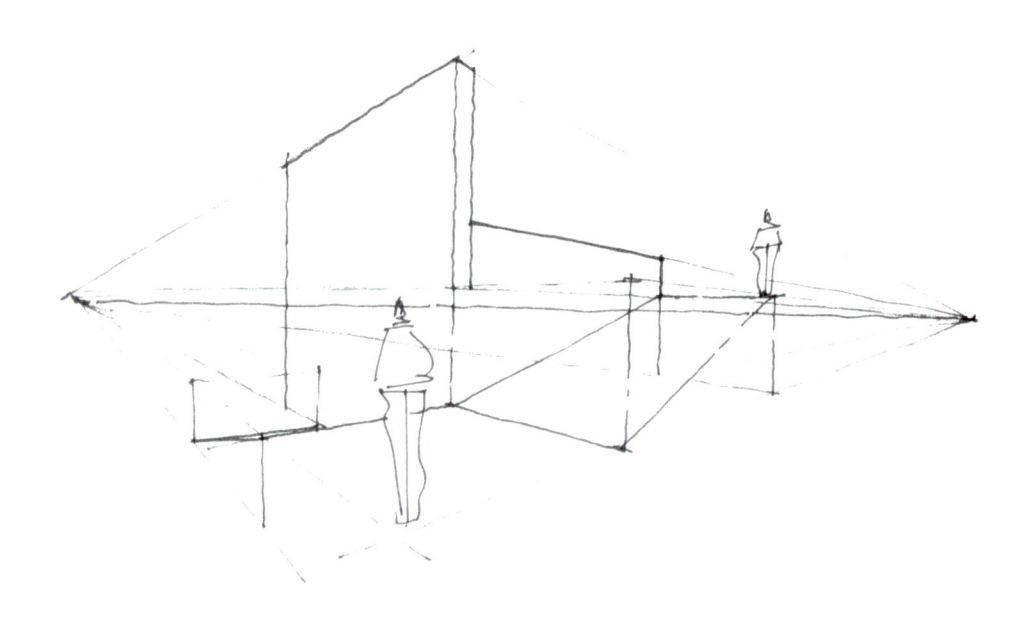

Step 1
Look carefully at these two processes to create levels in a perspective setting. Always remember the imaginary box to set the levels.

Tip: *Set the level by using the imaginary box.*

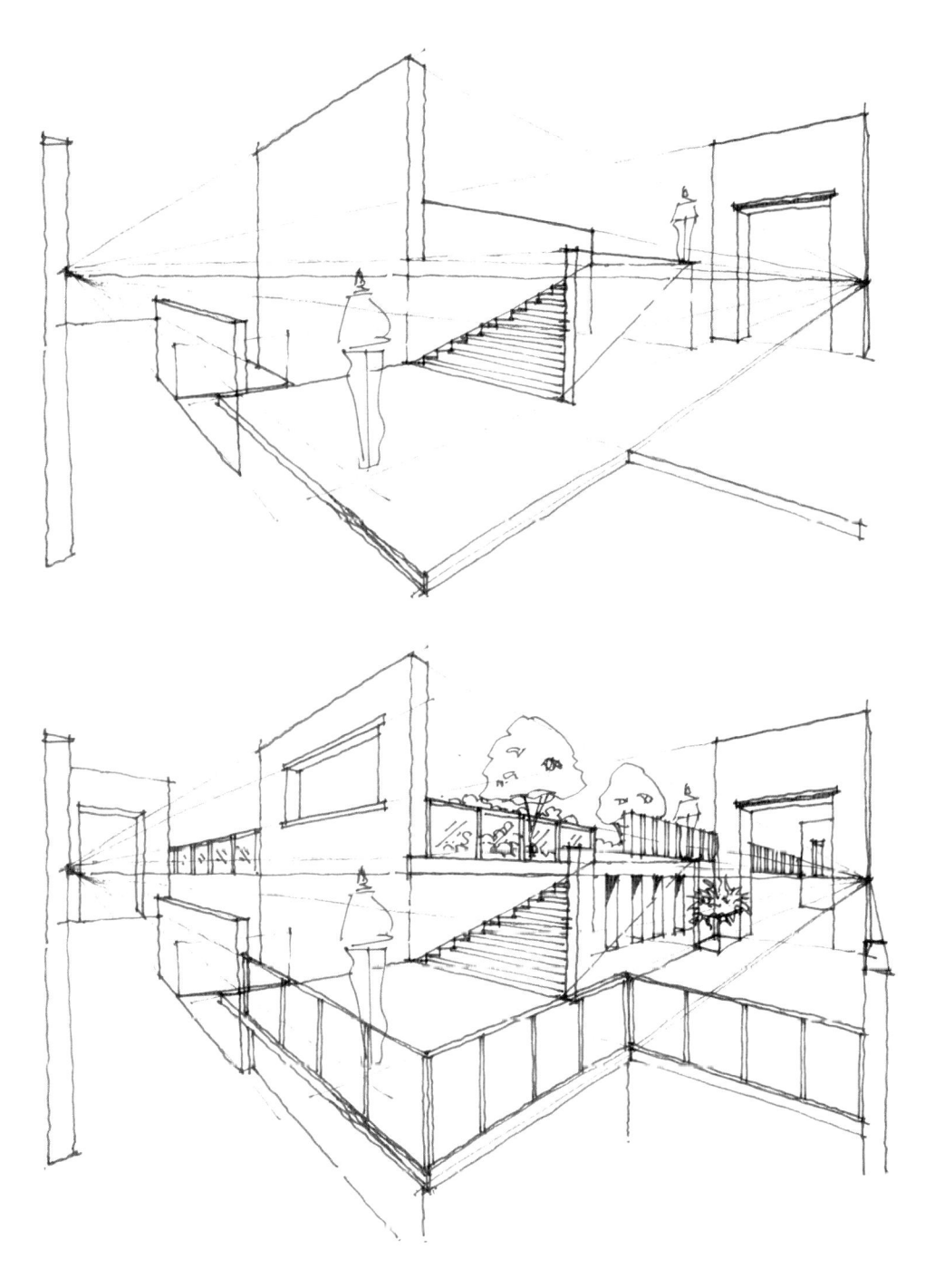

Step 2
Observe the technique used to create a staircase to join the two different levels using the imaginary box.

Tip: Create a staircase using the imaginary box.

A STEP BY STEP PROCESS

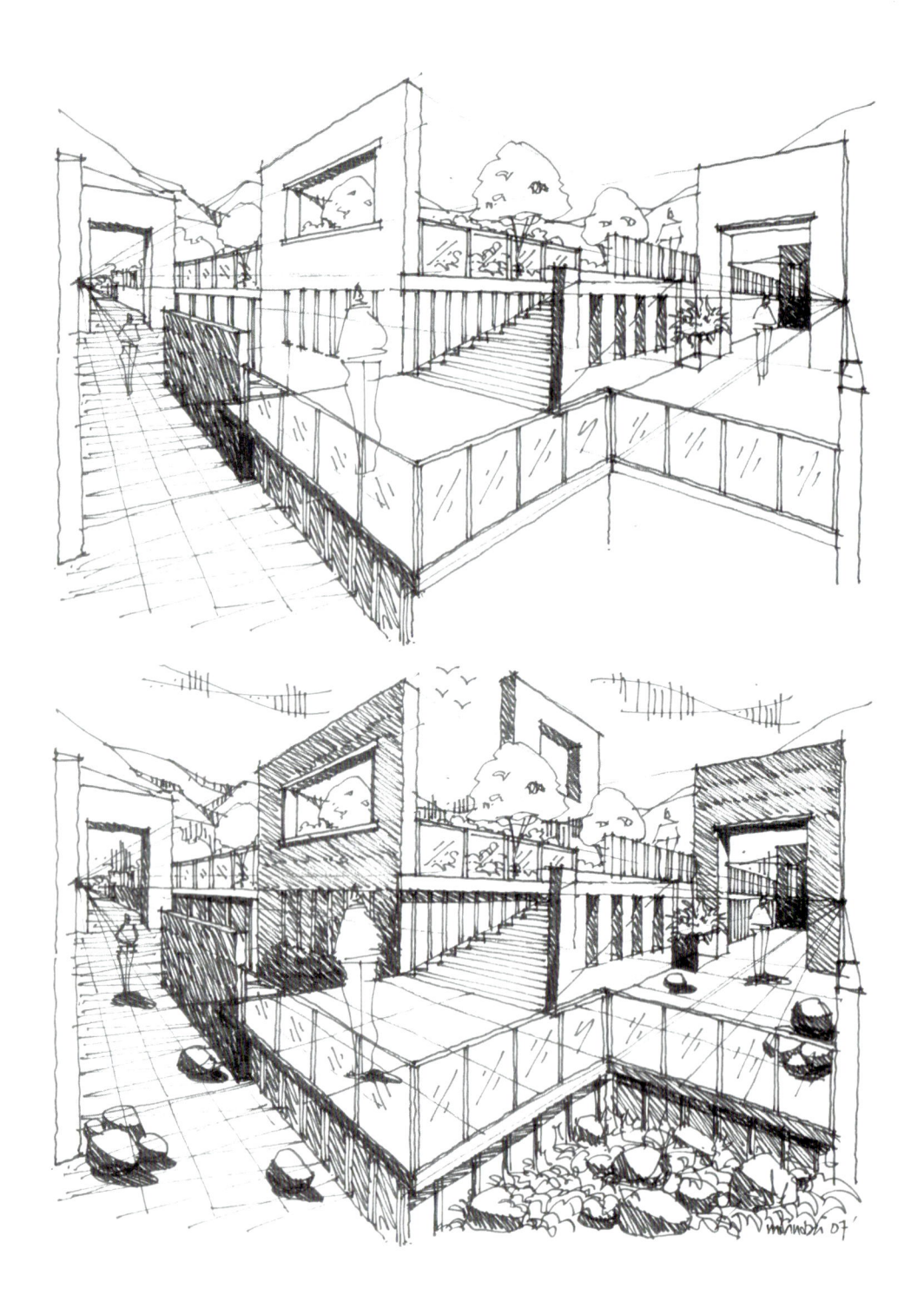

Step 3
Look carefully to see how to sketch the two different levels and put all the objects in their positions. The same principle is used to sketch and complete the composition.

Tip: Always refer to vanishing points as your guide.

• Level setting 2

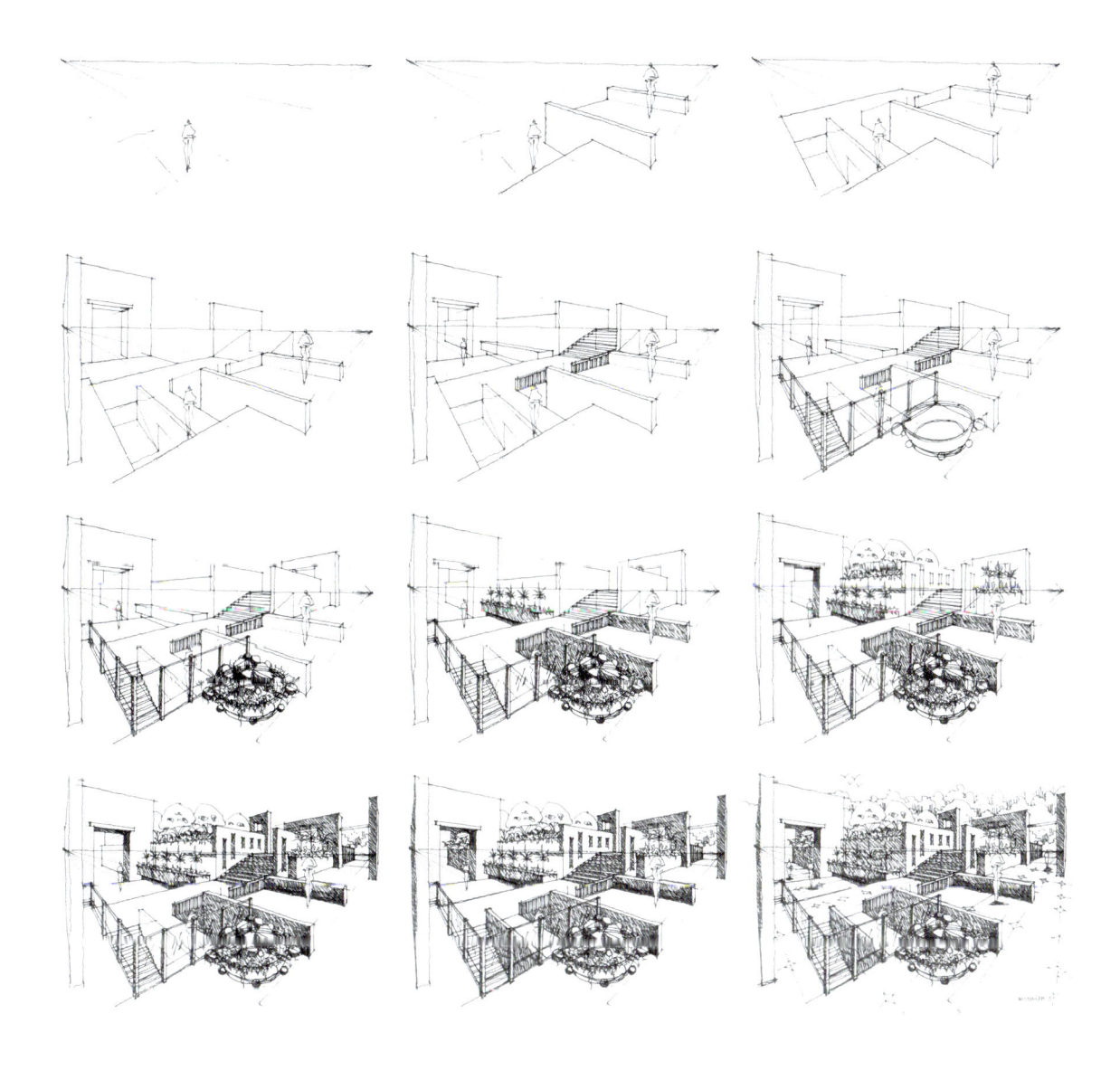

A STEP BY STEP PROCESS 197

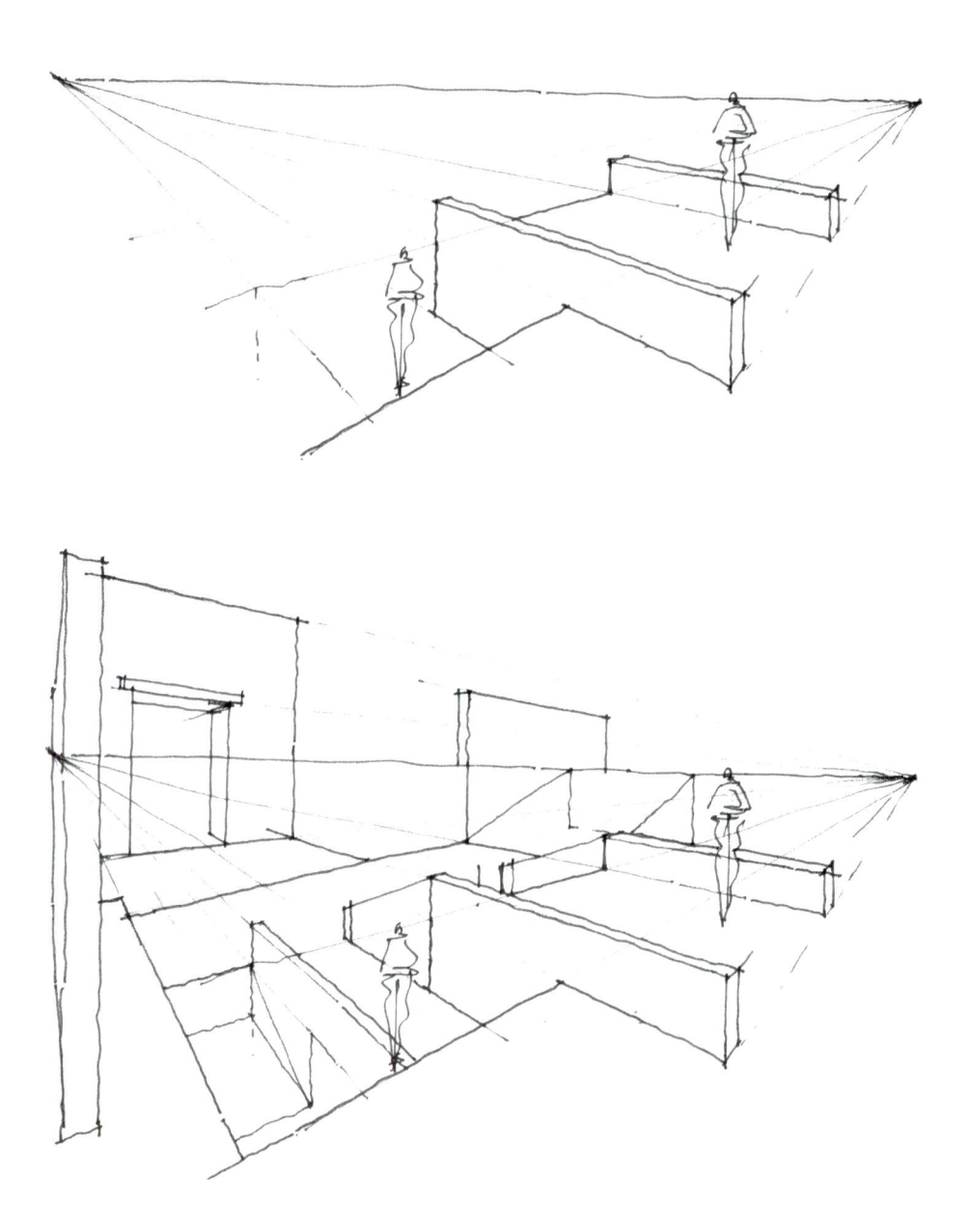

Step 1
Levels are one of the interesting elements that are sometimes very hard to sketch in perspective. To sketch a perspective composition that consists of many levels, the approach is the same as the one level perspective.

Tip: Always refer to vanishing points as your guide.

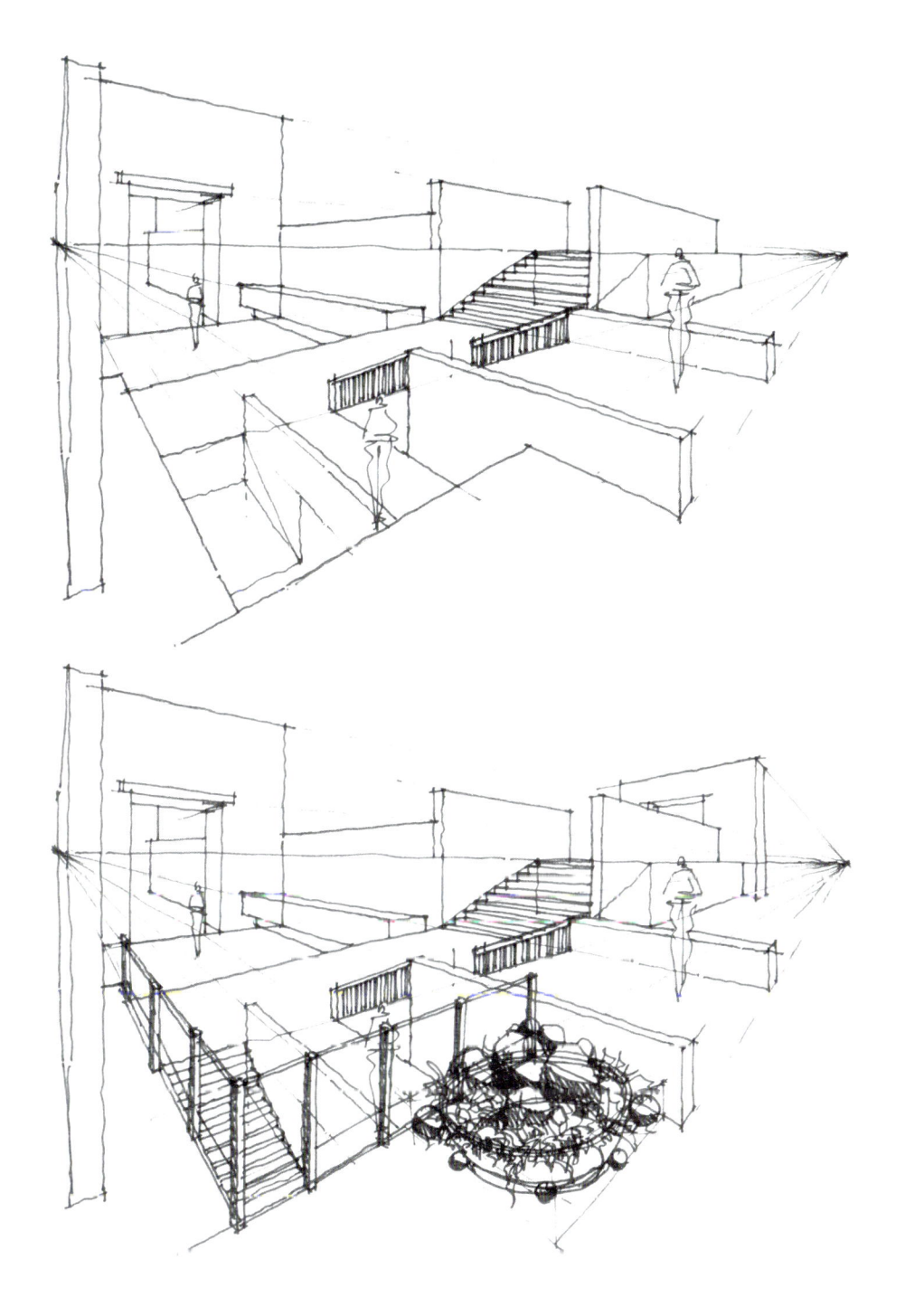

Step 2
The next step is to finalise the setting of the composition before proceeding to the rendering process.

Tip: *The setting is very important to getting a quality sketch.*

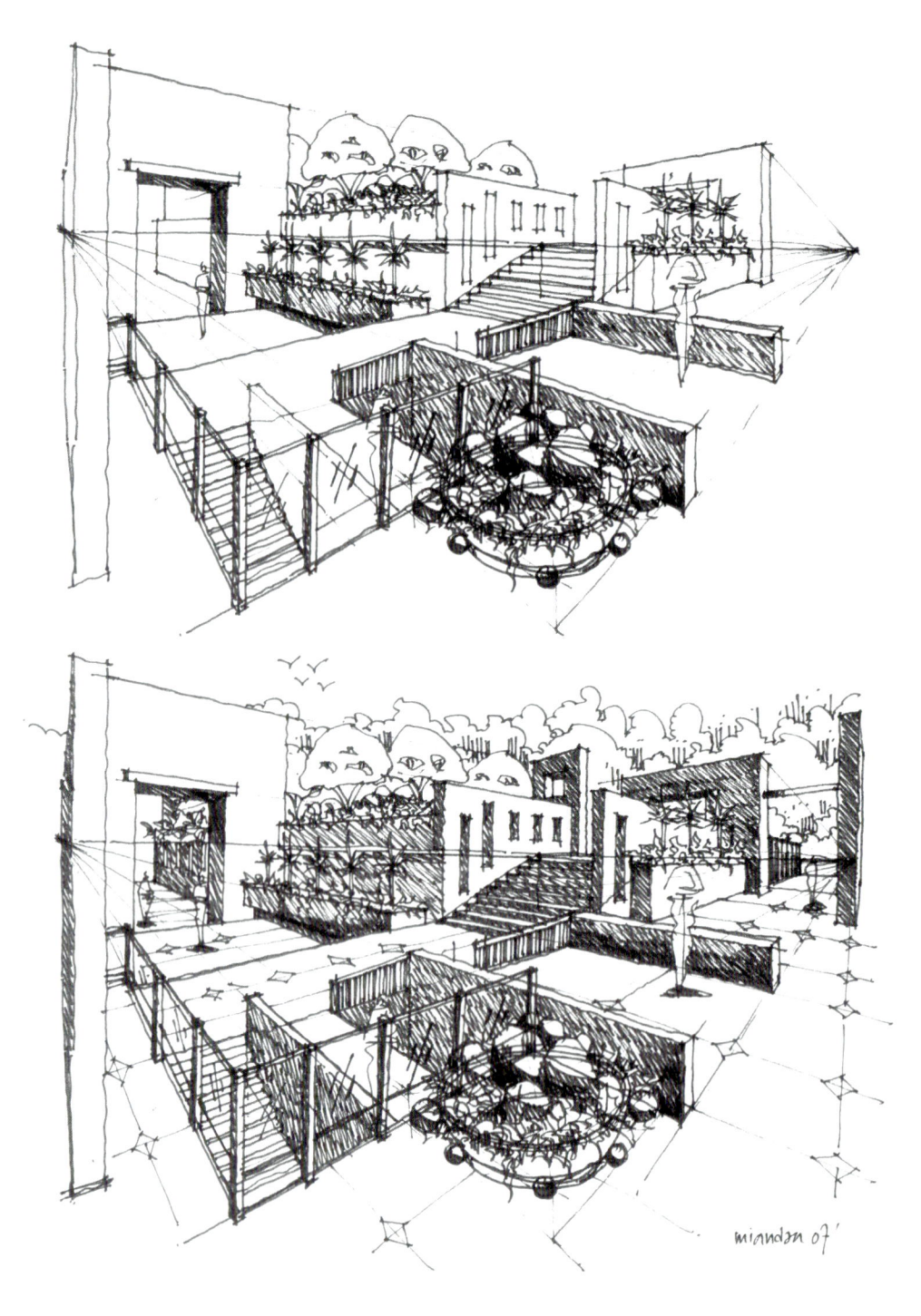

Tip: *Do render the floor surfaces.*

Step 3
One of the important elements that influences the quality of the sketch is the floor surface because it is one of the main surfaces of a sketch composition. Compare the two processes. The second process is of much better quality because the floor is well rendered. However, do not over render.

6.4 THREE POINT PERSPECTIVE

- Urban and architectural setting

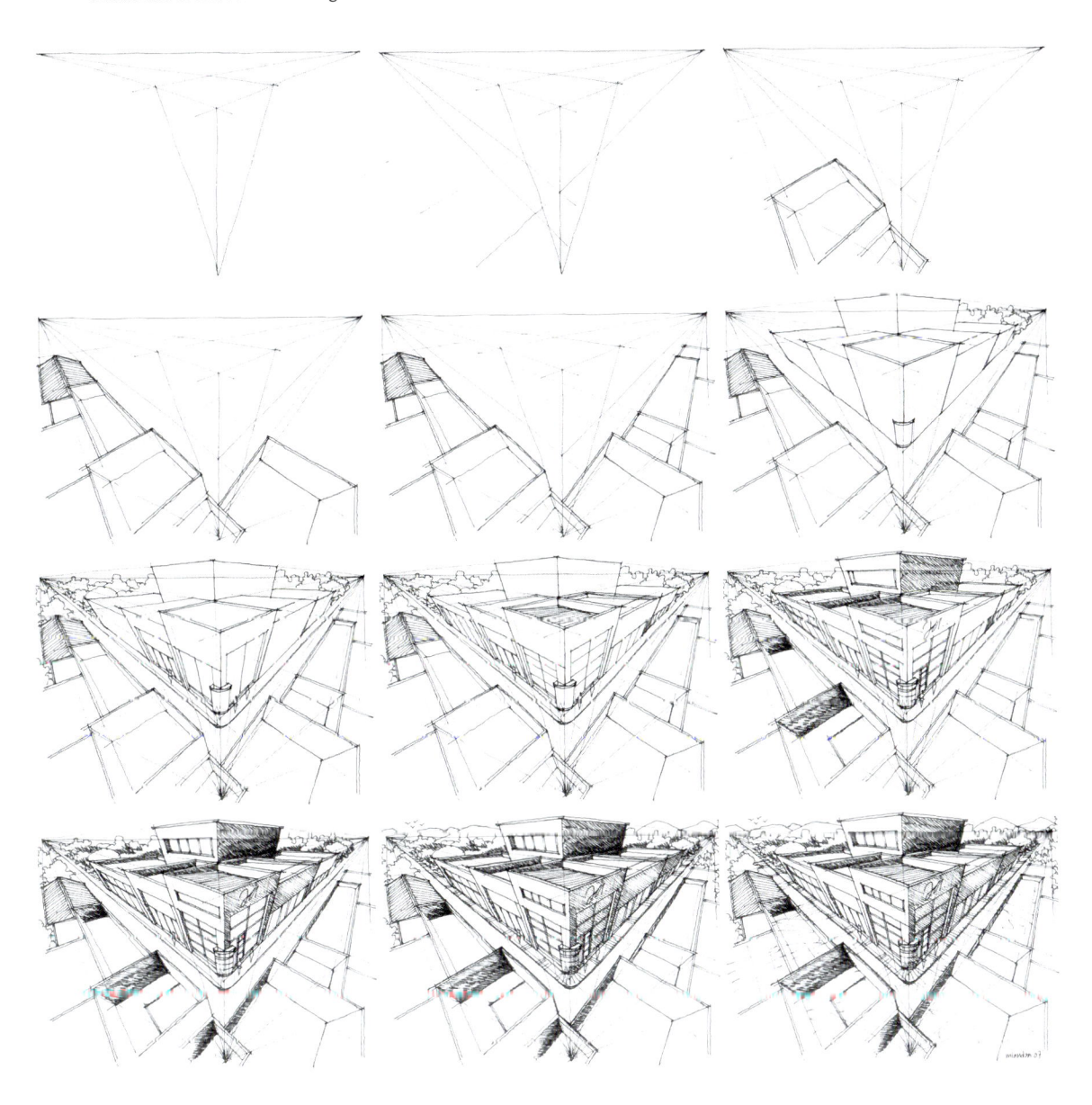

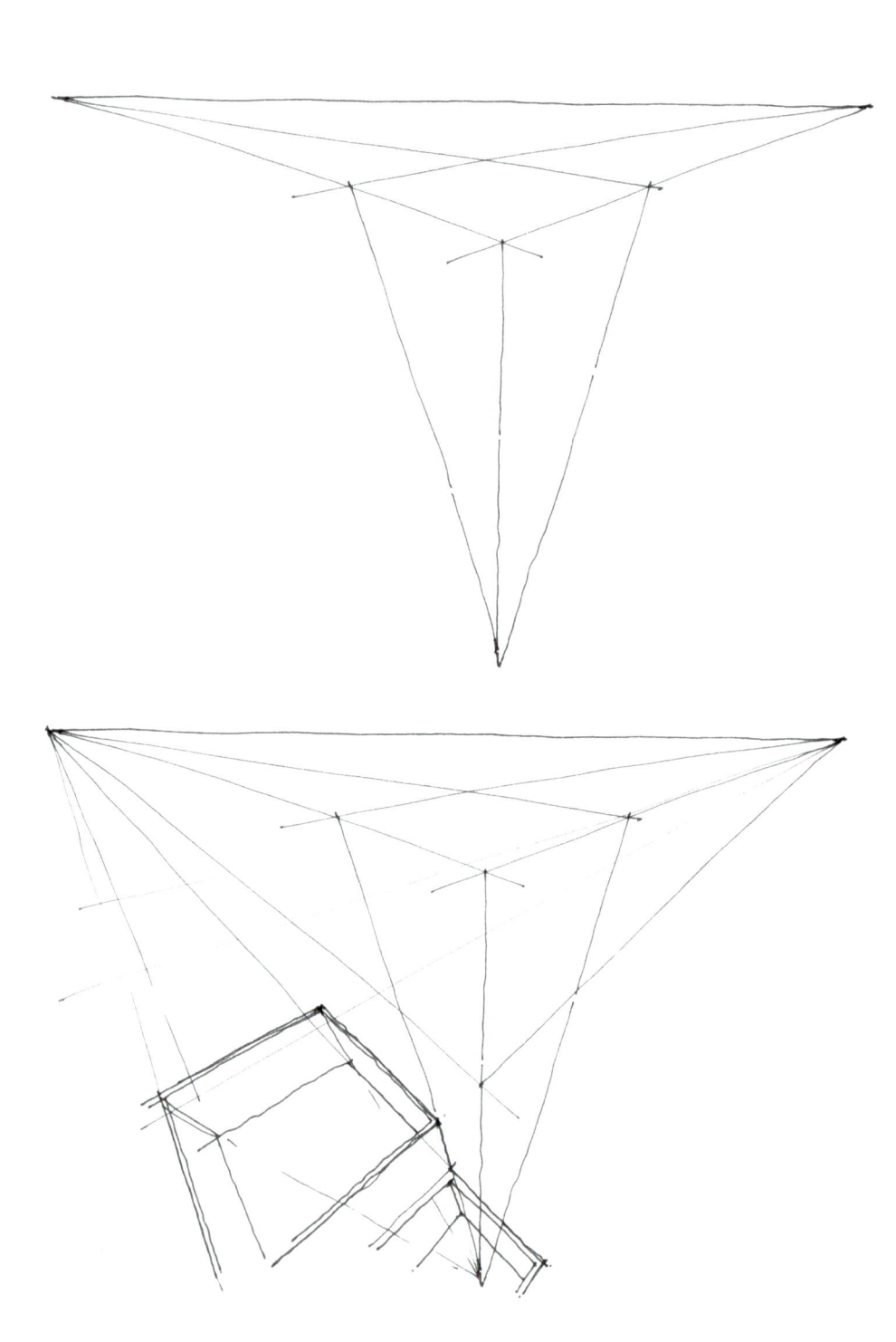

Step 1
The first thing to do is to understand how this perspective works. Observe the lines and their connection to each vanishing point.

Tip: *Understand the concept behind every perspective.*

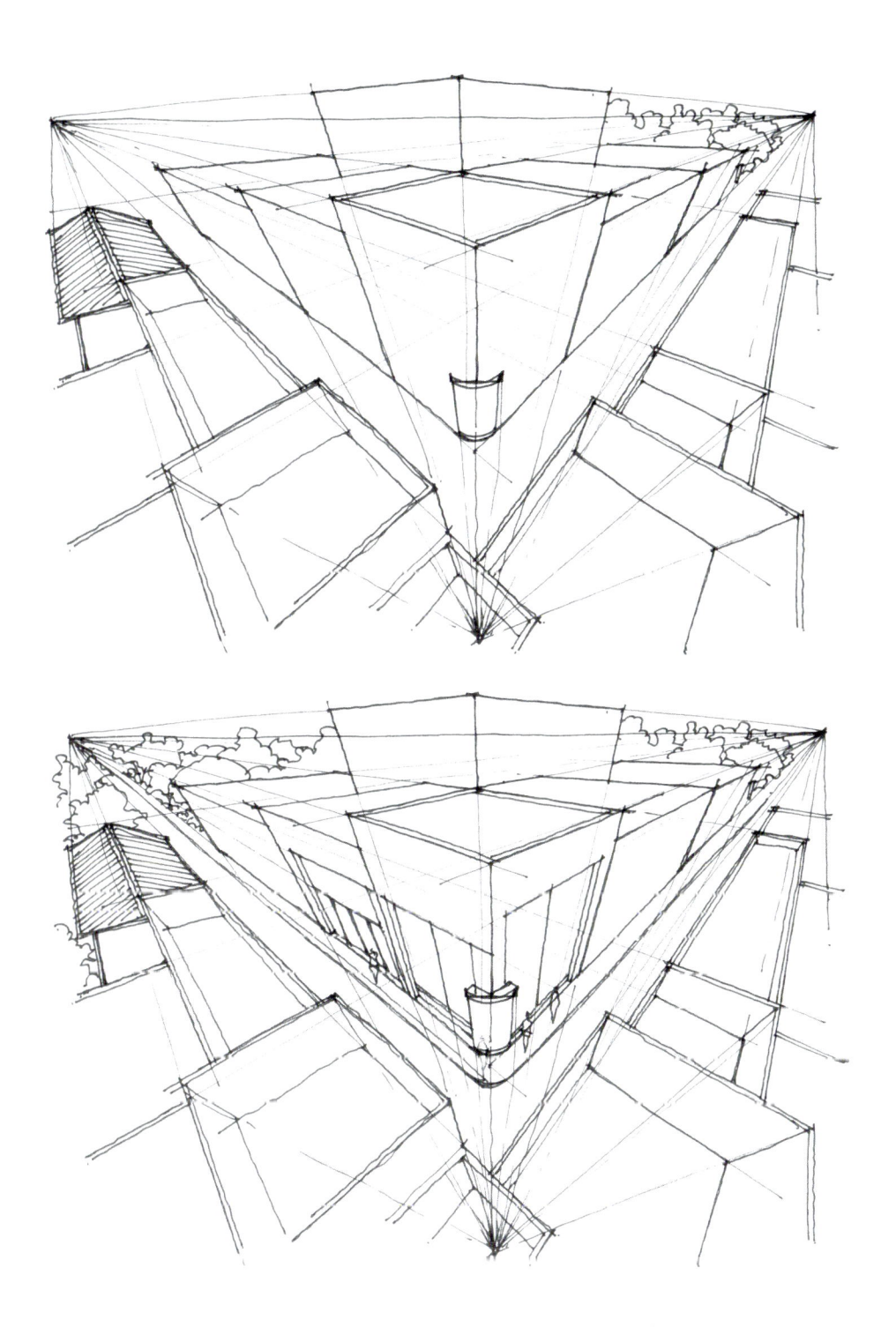

Step 2
Every line that is sketched is connected to vanishing points. Look carefully at the composition. All the buildings are sketched based on these three vanishing points.

Tip: Always refer to the three vanishing points.

A STEP BY STEP PROCESS 203

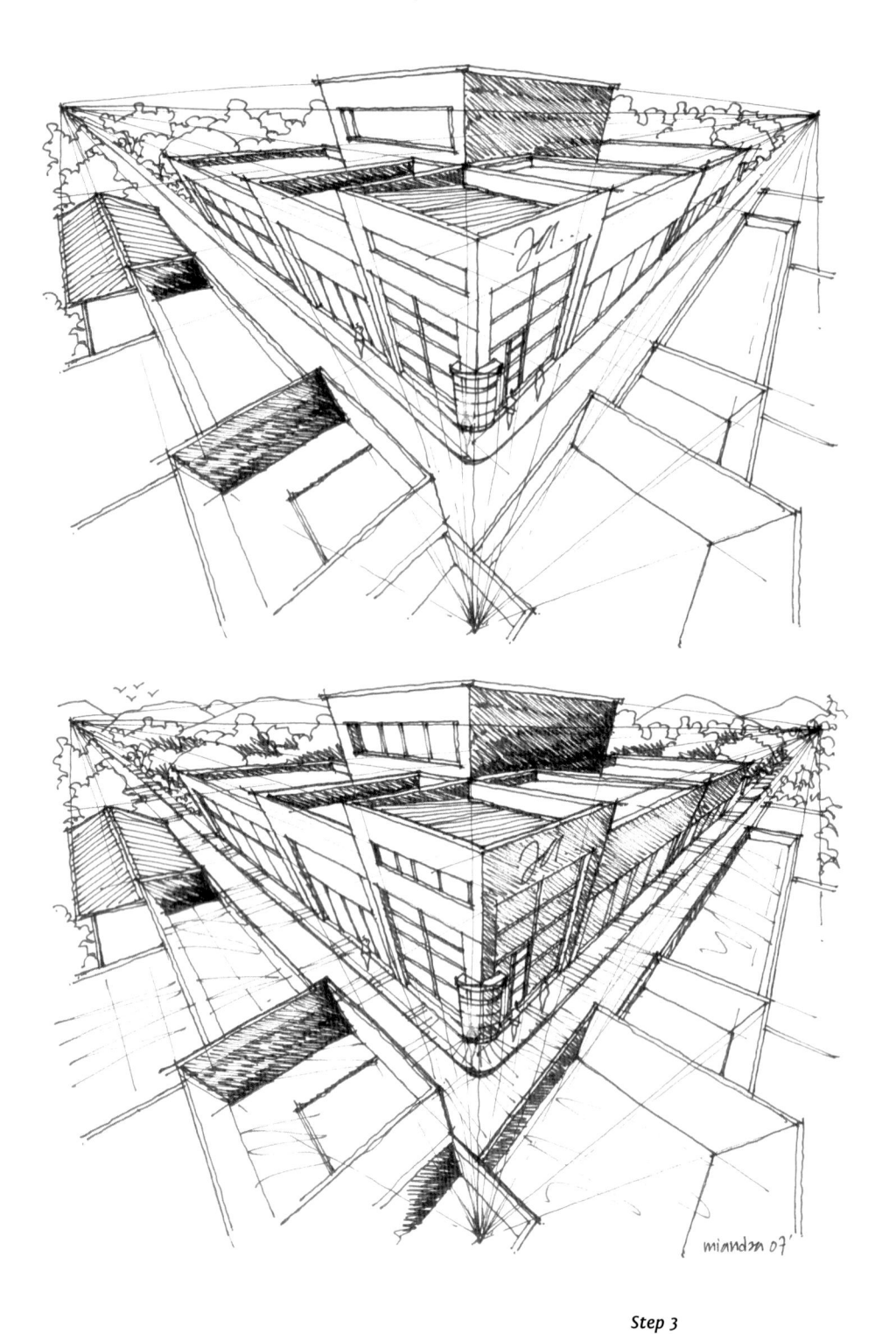

Step 3
This is very interesting sketch composition. It gives different dimensions of the environment, buildings' settings or street settings compared to the one or two point perspectives.

• Landscape setting 1

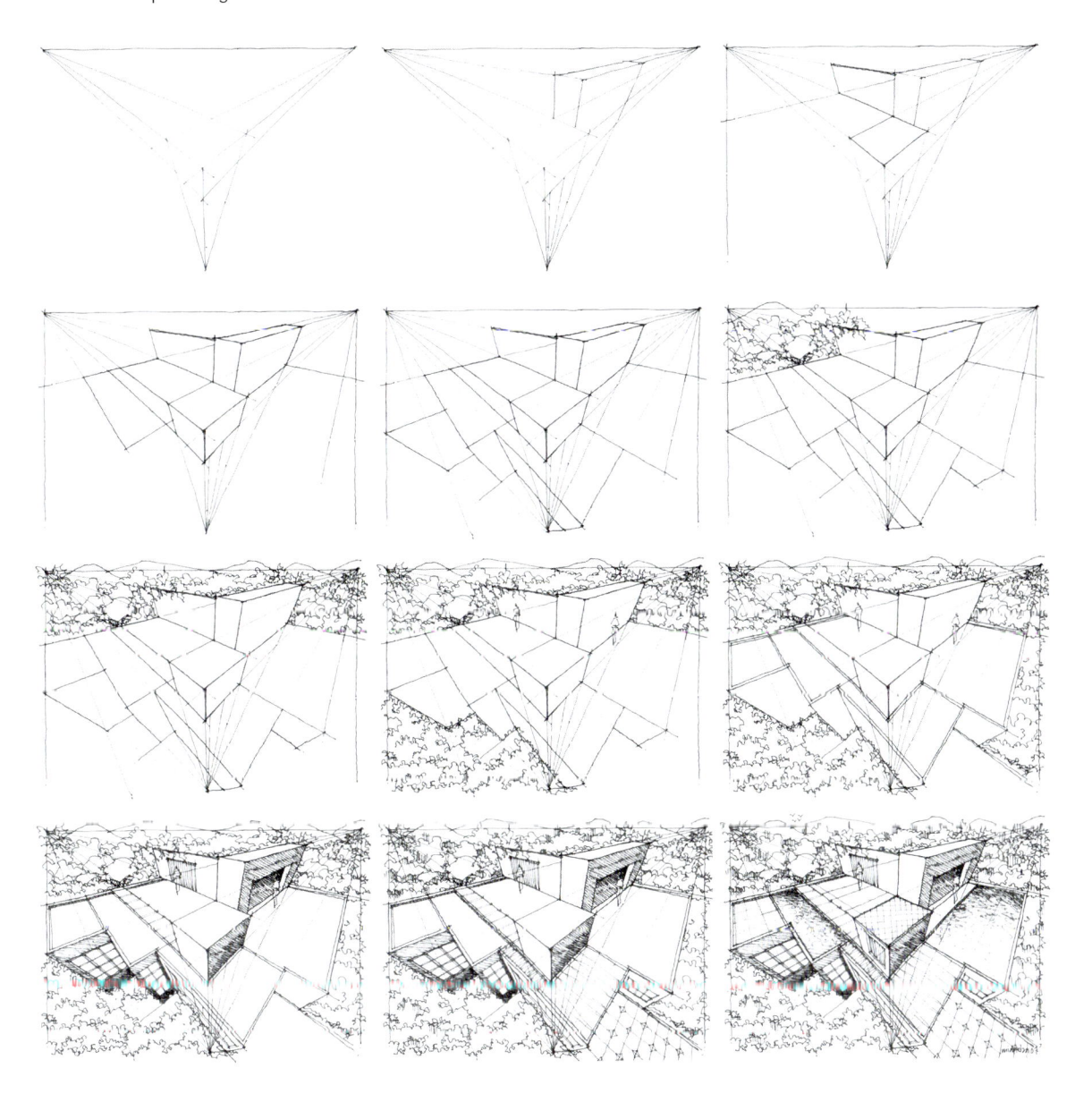

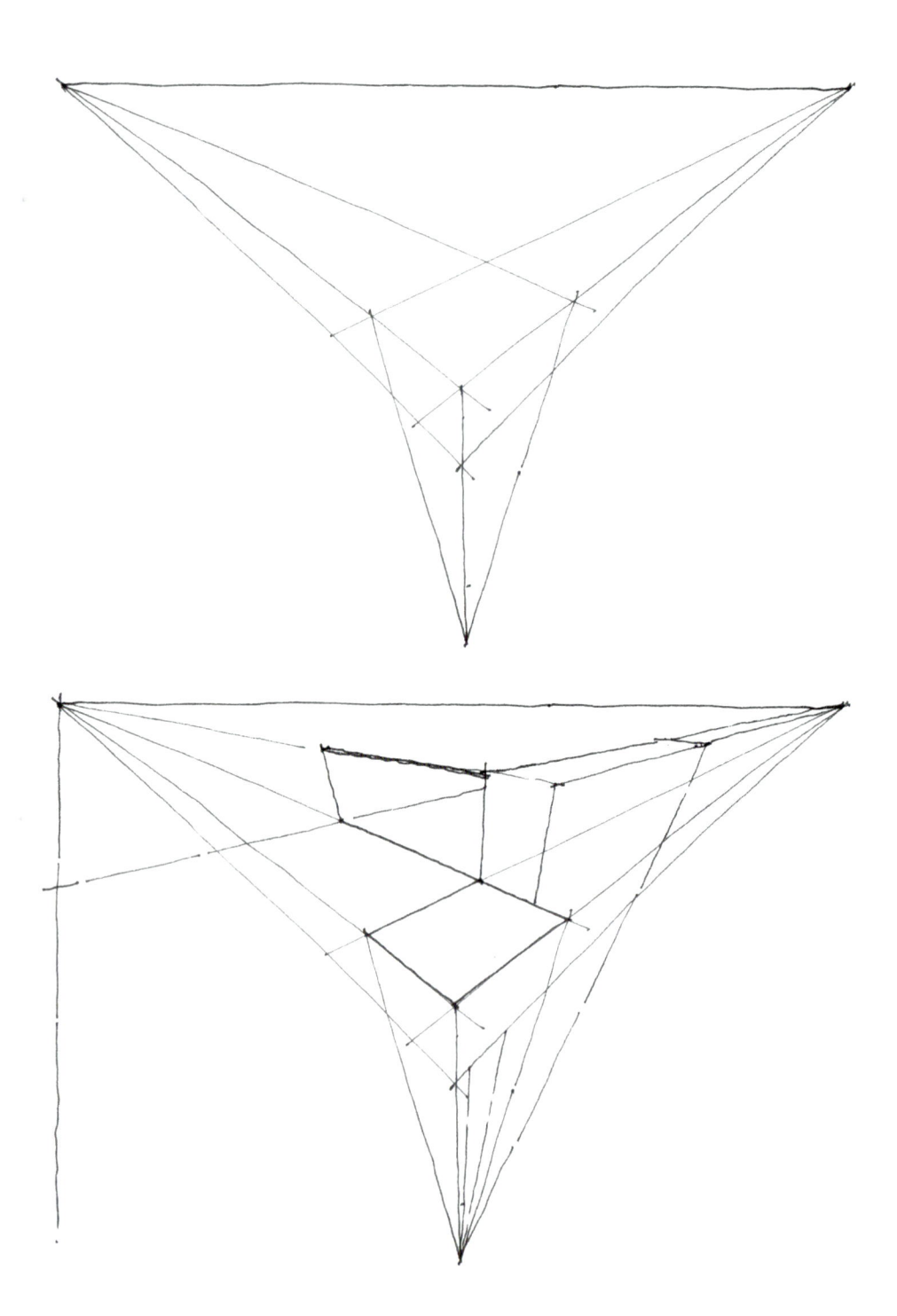

Step 1
Look carefully on how the lines and objects of the three point perspective are constructed based on these three vanishing points.

Tip: *The setting is important to getting a quality sketch composition.*

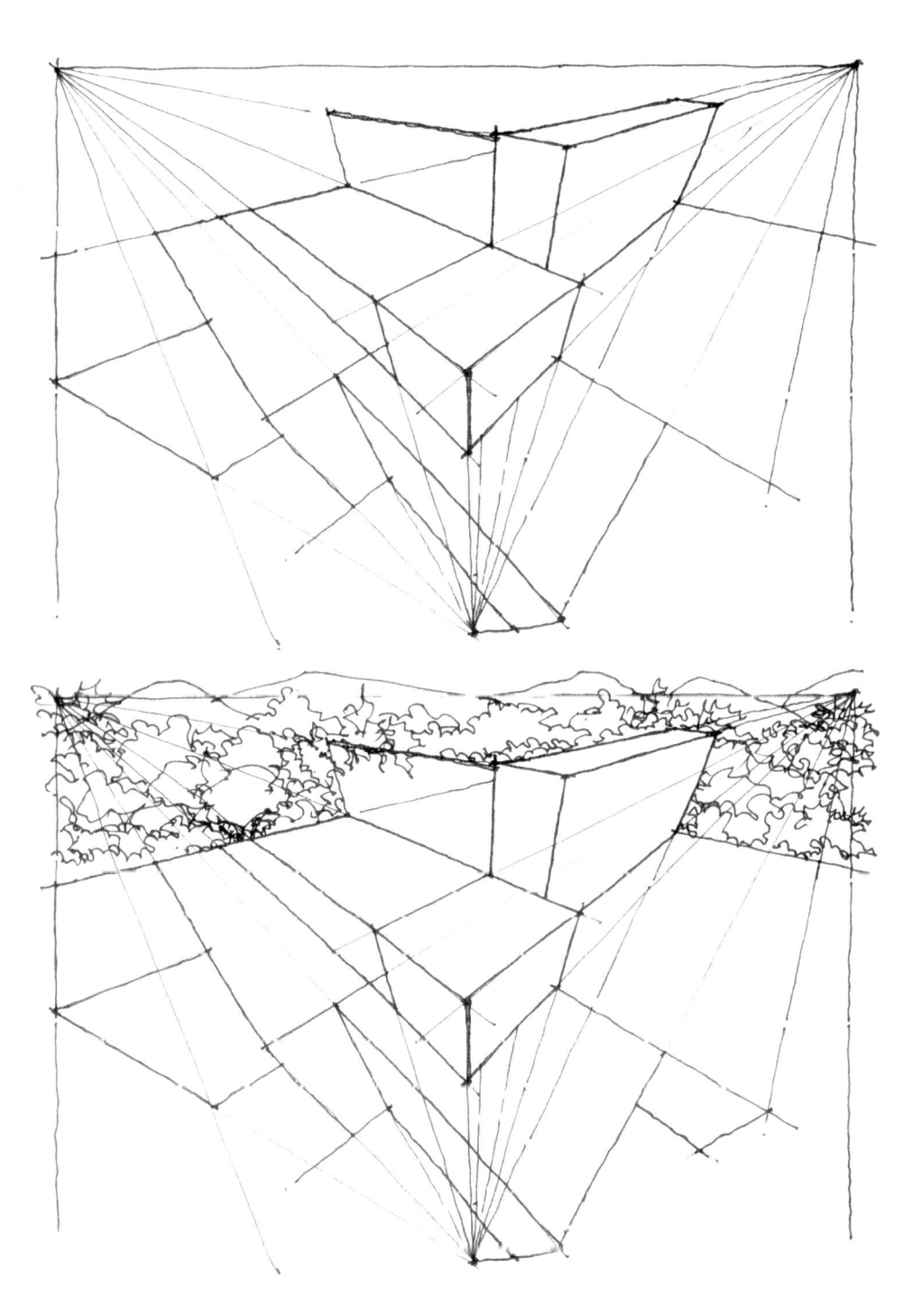

Step 2
Remember to set the main objects before setting the secondary elements. As an example, the building block (main object) is carefully set up before the landscape setting (secondary object) is applied to the composition.

Tip: *Do sketch starting with the main object.*

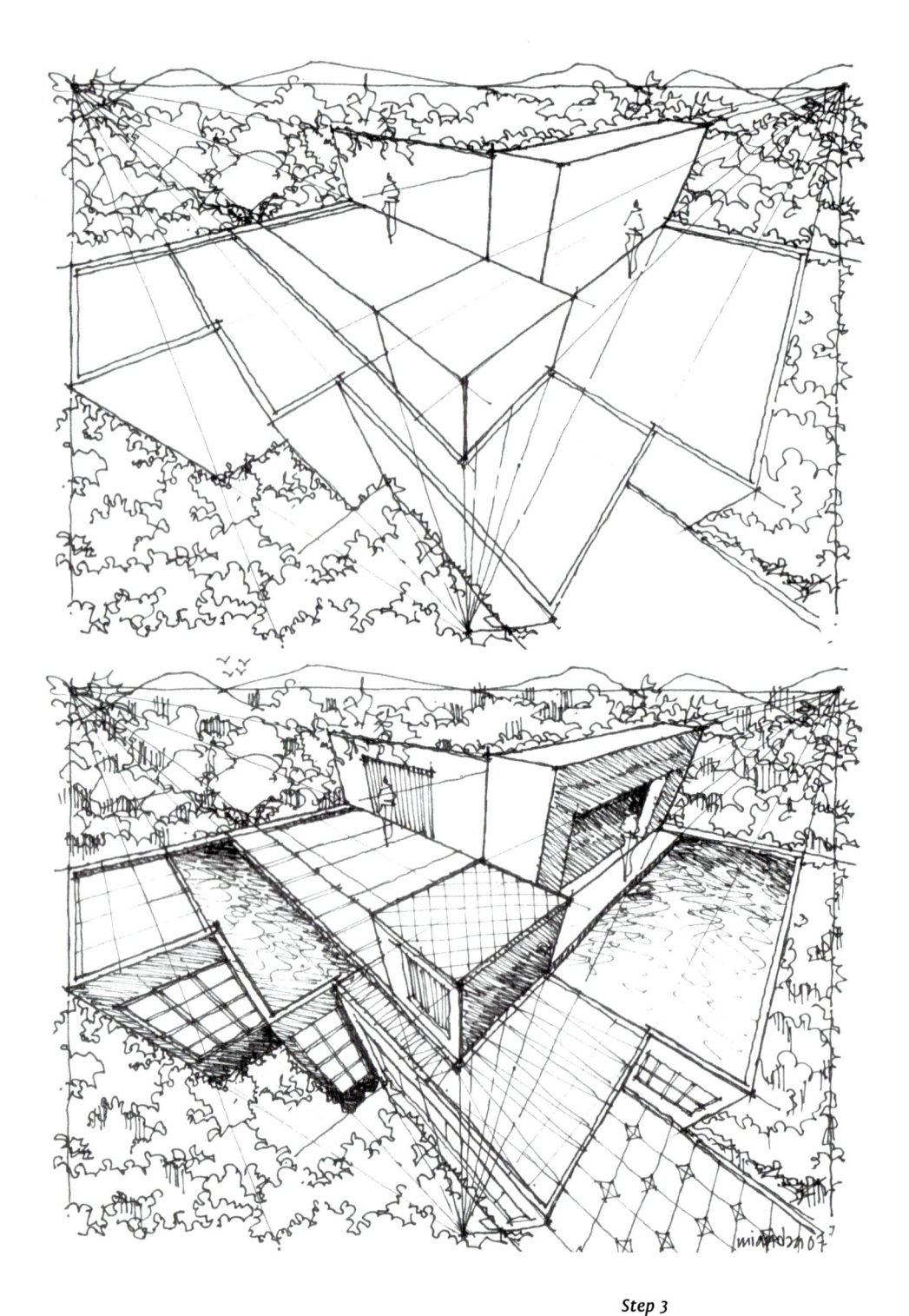

Step 3
Next step is the rendering process. Observe the examples given on how the rendering is applied in the process. Identify the surfaces that need shades and shadows but before that the sun direction must be confirmed.

Tip: *Shade and shadow is very important to get a quality sketch composition.*

208 A STEP BY STEP PROCESS

6.5 MULTI-POINT PERSPECTIVE

- Interior 1

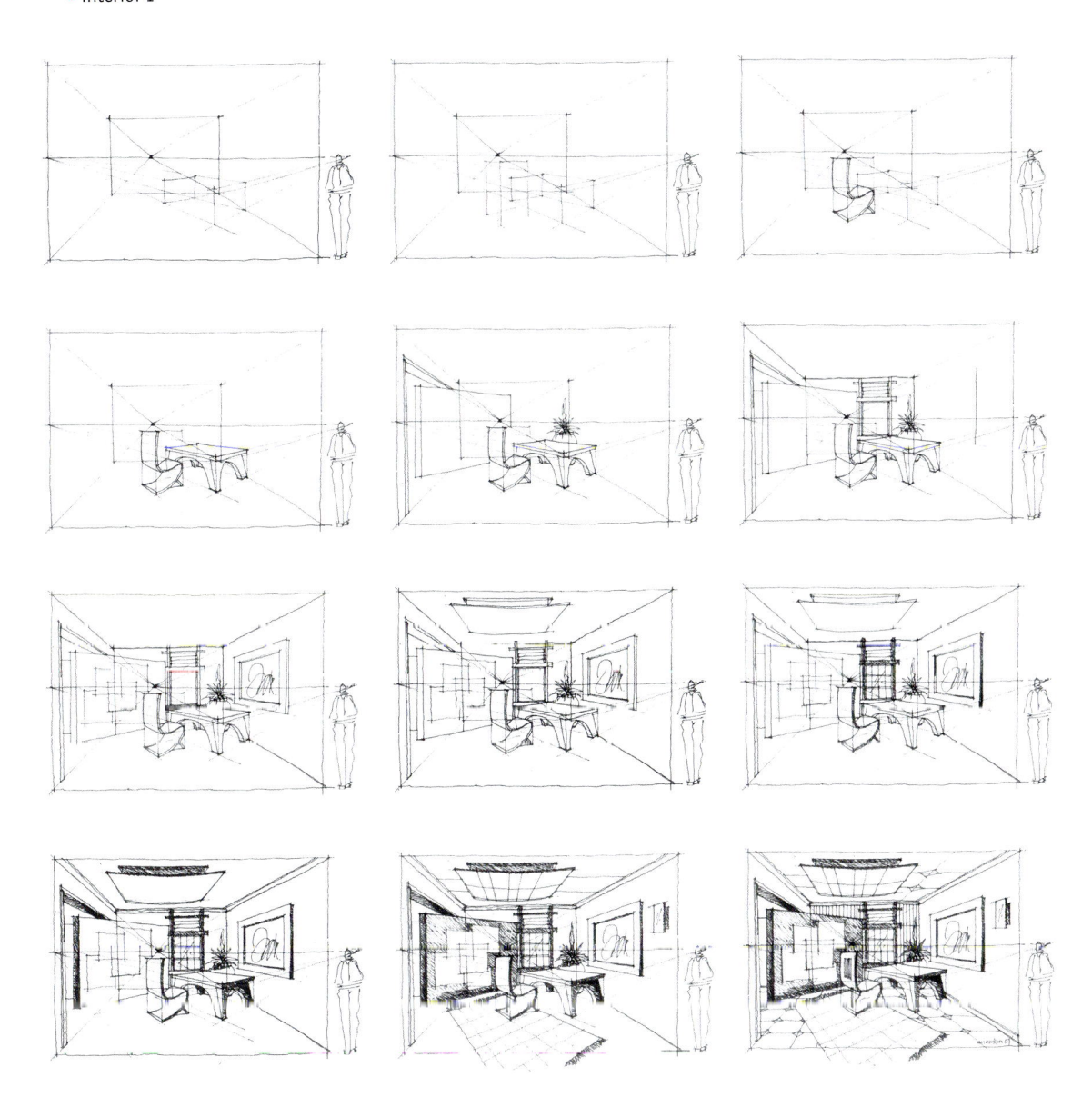

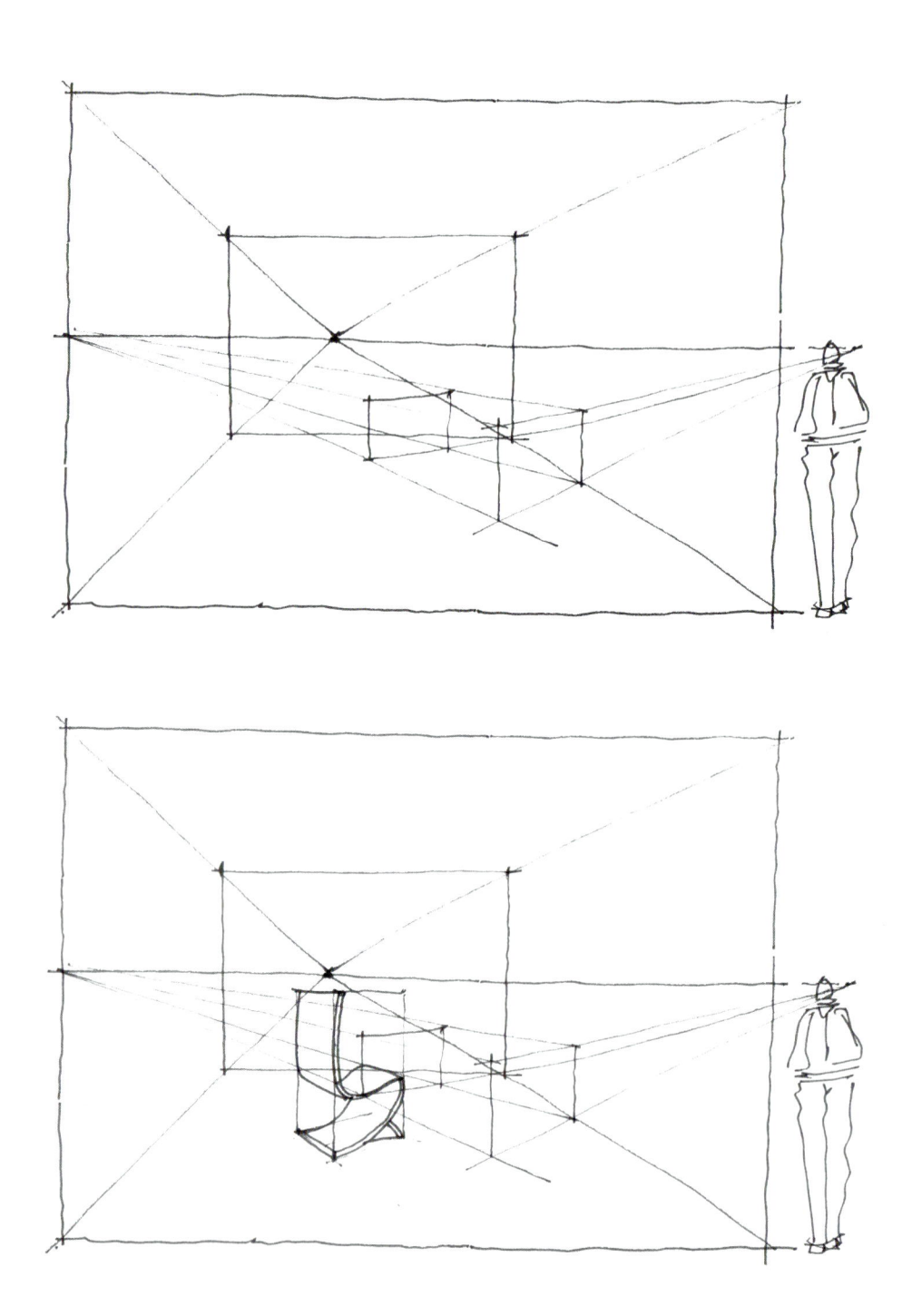

Step 1
The first step to do is set up the room boundary by using one point perspective. Then use the imaginary box to set the furniture positions. Do remember to refer to the vanishing points.

Tip: *Multi-point perspective still uses the same perspective principles.*

210   A STEP BY STEP PROCESS

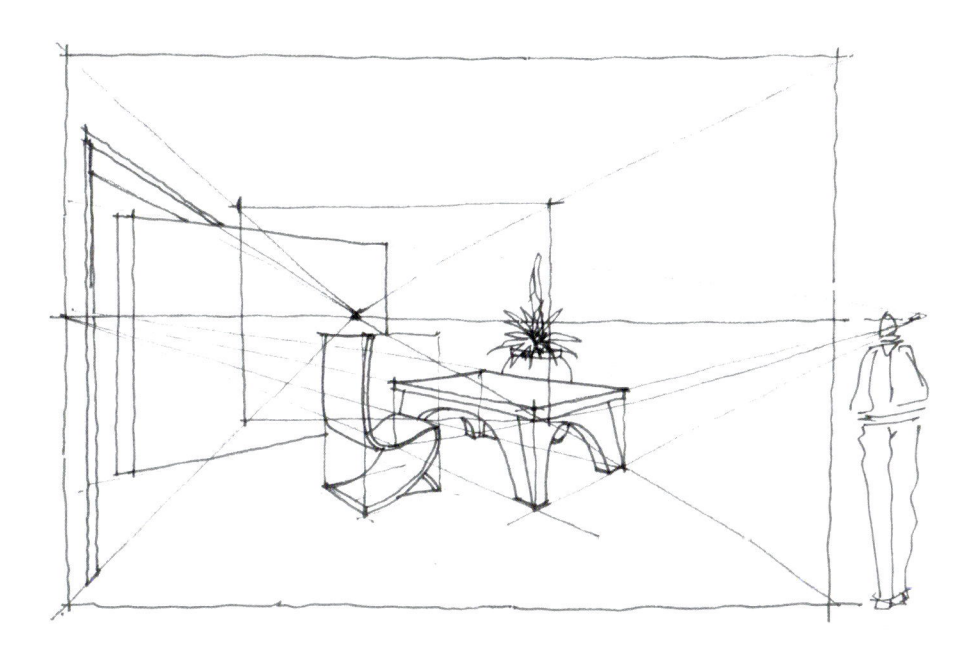

Step 2
Look carefully at how the positions of the objects are set by using multi-point perspective. Always use the imaginary box to position an object in perspective.

Tip: A good object setting and positioning will create a quality sketch composition.

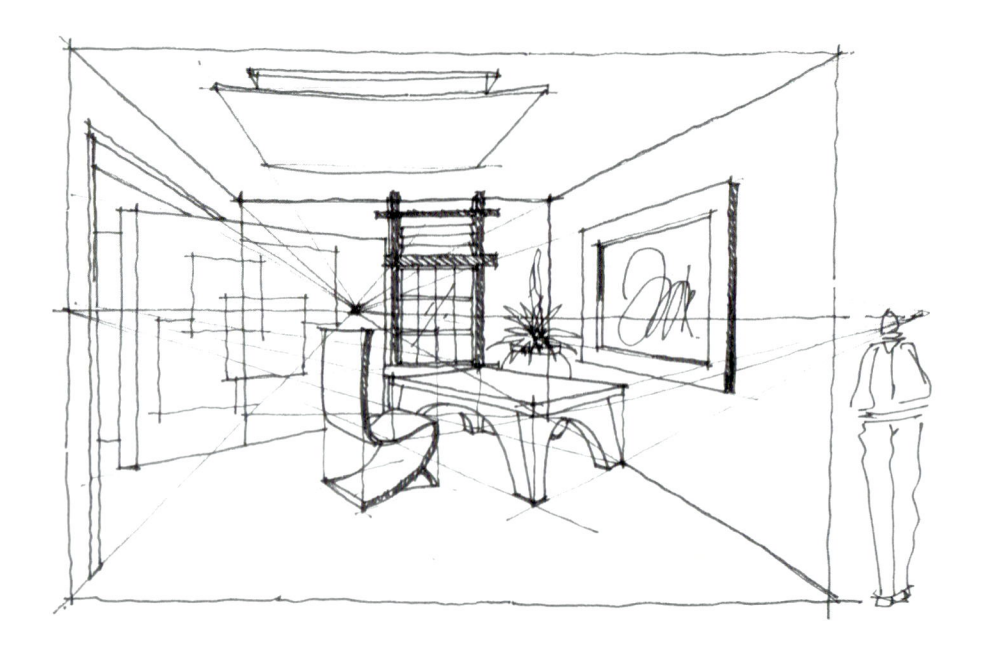

Step 3
Check the position of the free standing wall and the picture frame. They refer to the two sets of vanishing points but with the same horizon line. This means that there must be only one vanishing point in a multi-point perspective.

Tip: There must be one horizon line only.

• Landscape setting 1

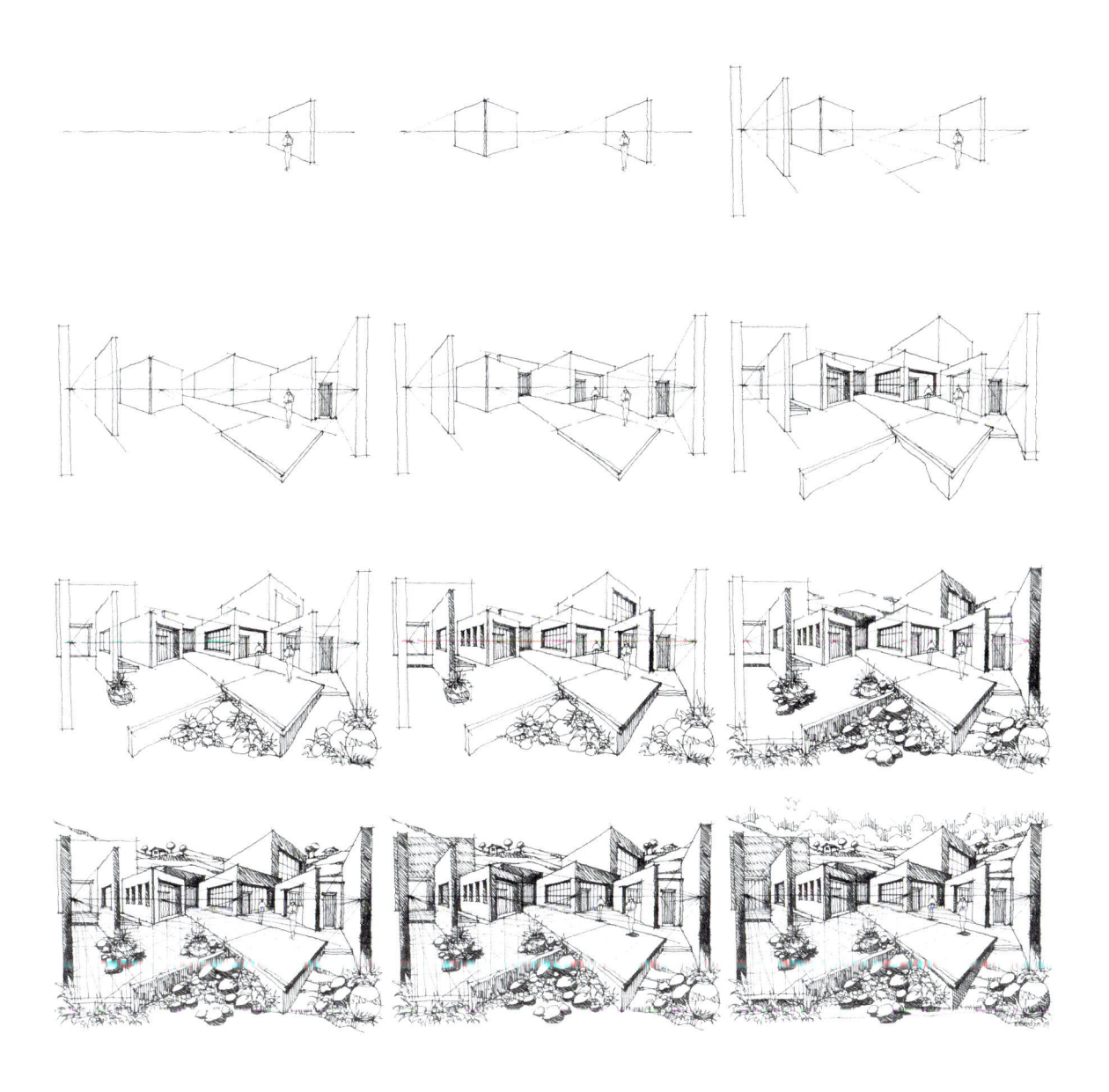

A STEP BY STEP PROCESS

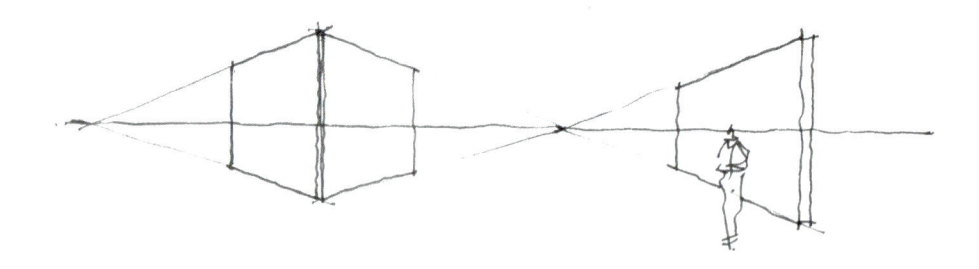

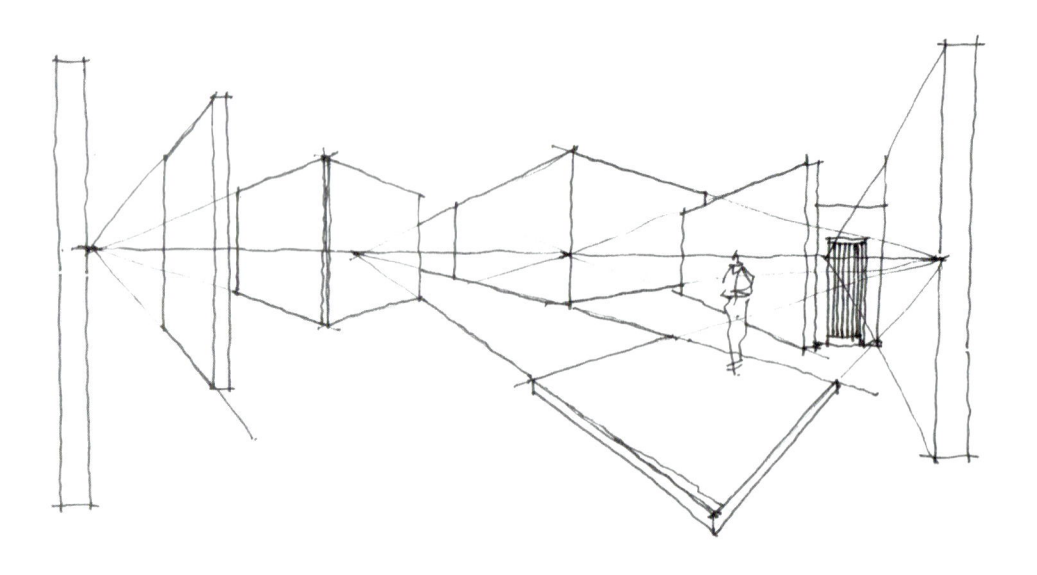

***Tip**: Visualise the view of the space before sketching the area.*

Step 1
These two examples will show the multi-point perspective used in the exterior area. As usual, the first thing to do is to draw the horizon line and then proceed to set vanishing points. The setting must refer to the desired angle and view. First imagine the composition that you want to sketch.

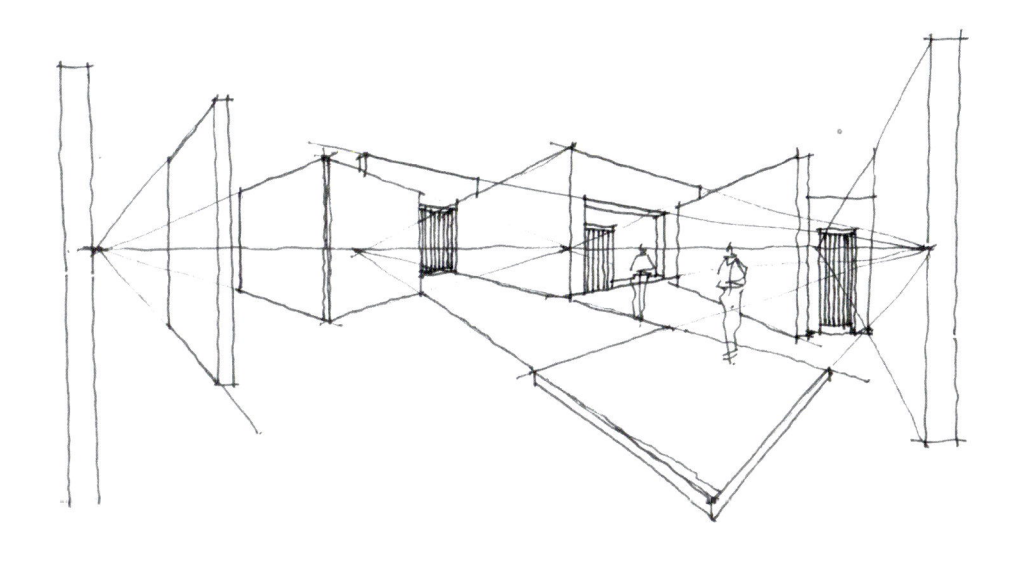

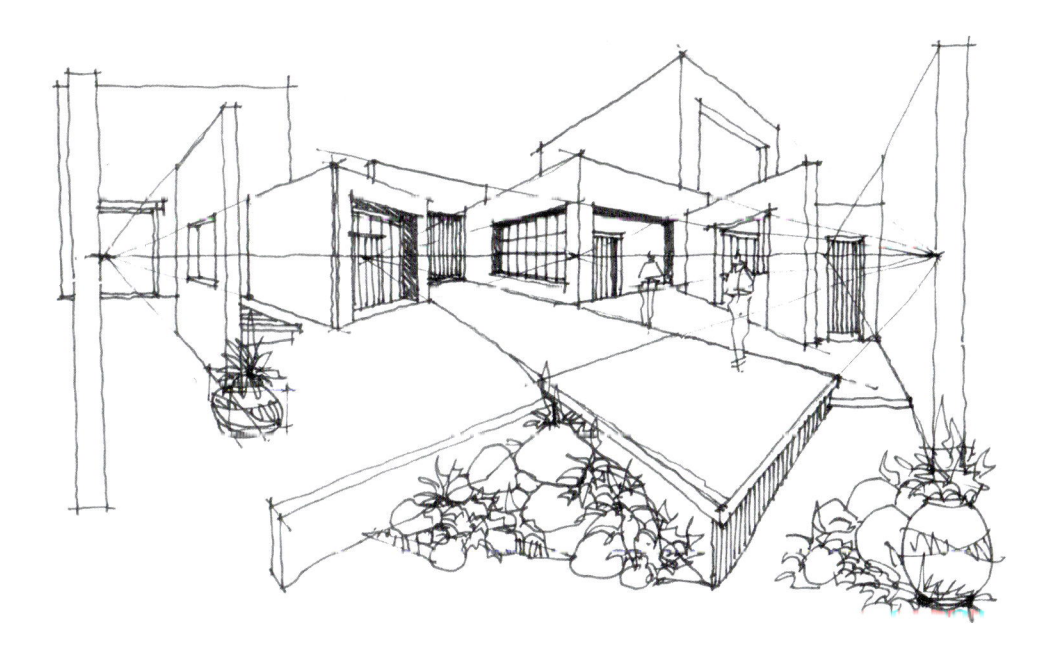

Step 2
Then, sketch the composition setting before putting details into them. Learn and observe how the composition is sketched.

Tip: Do remember to be confident in drawing lines.

A STEP BY STEP PROCESS   215

Step 3
Compare these two sketches to see the changes done by applying the rendering process. Try to find small surfaces to start your rendering before getting to the bigger surfaces.

Tip: Start rendering on small surfaces.

• Urban and architectural setting

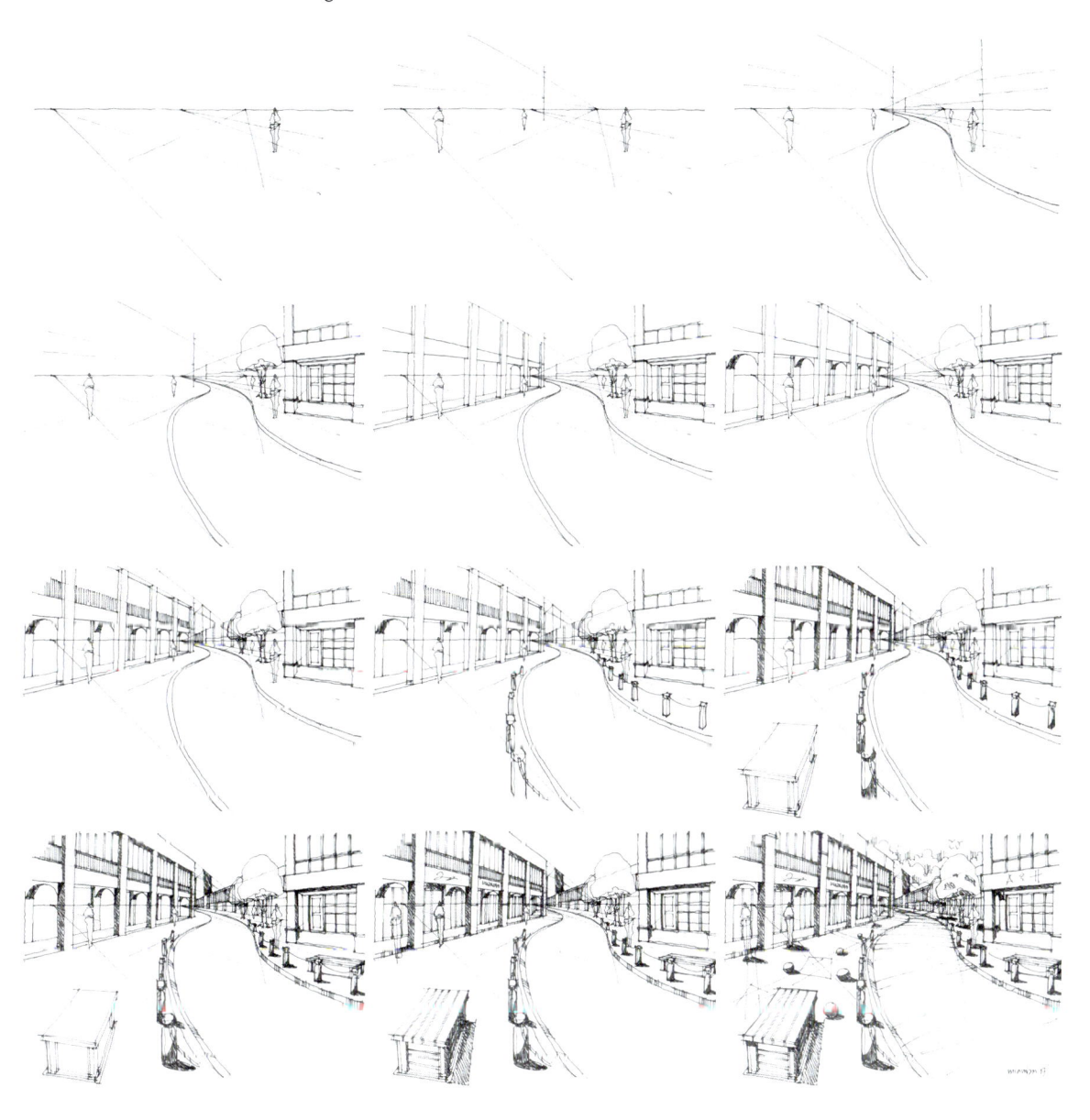

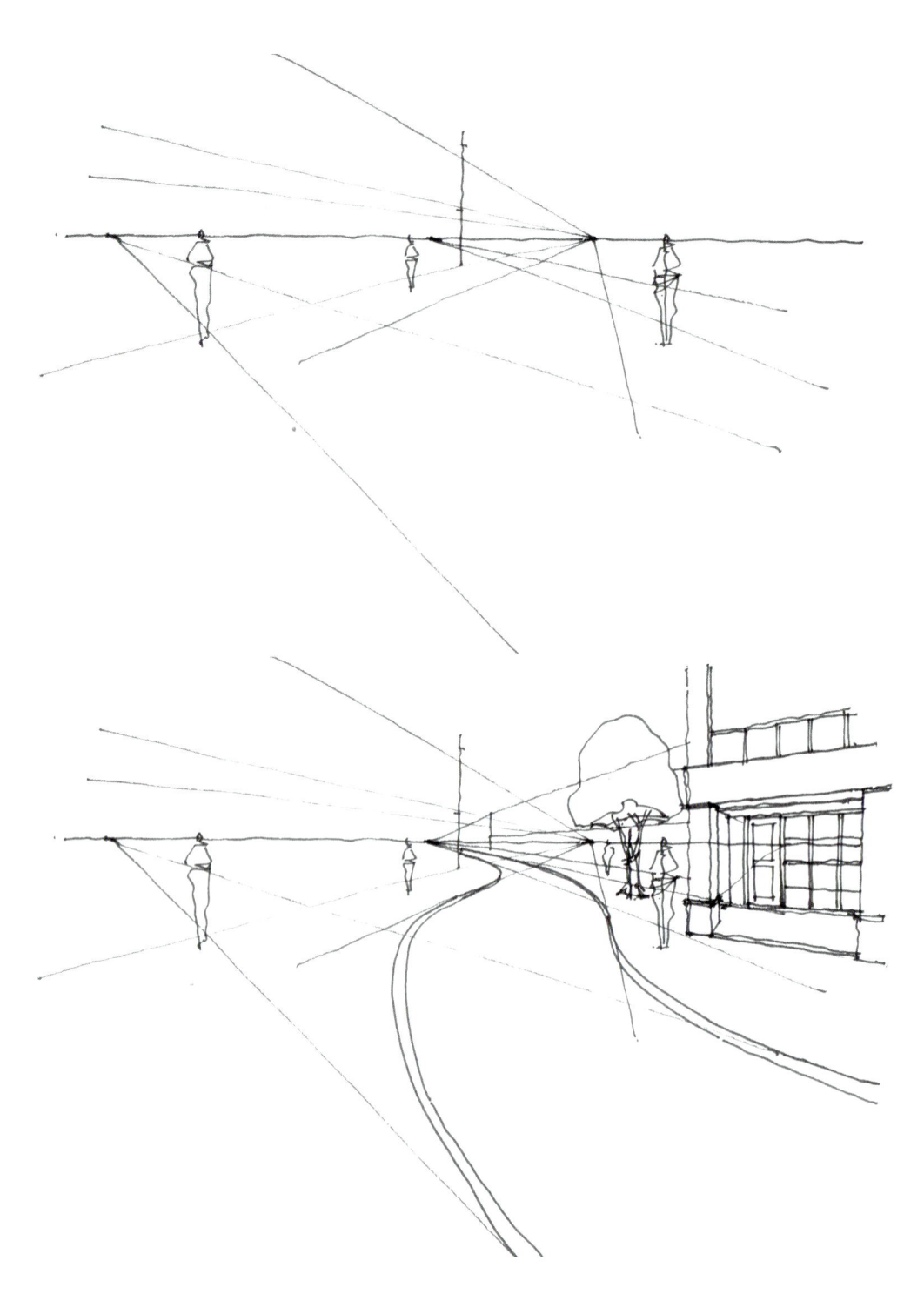

Step 1
The first step to do is to sketch the road and then follow with the buildings' setting. This demonstration will illustrate how to sketch a road by using a multi-point perspective. Look carefully at the process and then practise them.

Tip: Curvy roads need a multi-point perspective technique.

218   A STEP BY STEP PROCESS

Step 2

Next is to sketch all the buildings and road details before proceeding to the rendering process. Compare these two examples and look at the process of sketching details on the buildings and road.

***Tip**: Details should be properly sketched to get a quality composition.*

Step 3
The final step is to apply rendering and final touch-up. Look at the building facades and observe how to apply shades and shadows in their surfaces. These efforts will help to highlight the appearance of these facades.

Tip: *Details with shades and shadows will highlight the composition.*

• Level setting

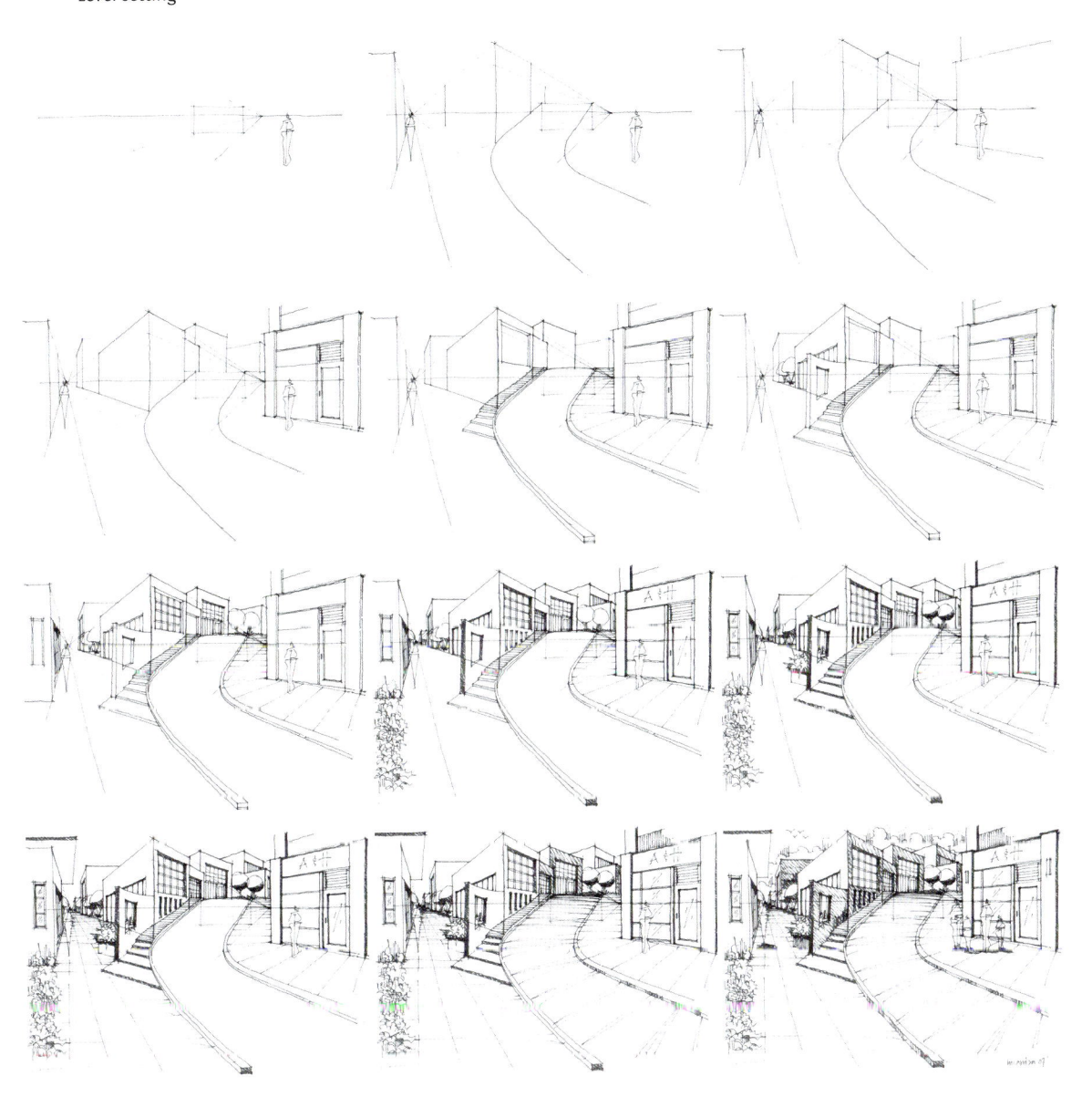

Tip: *Be confident with lines.*

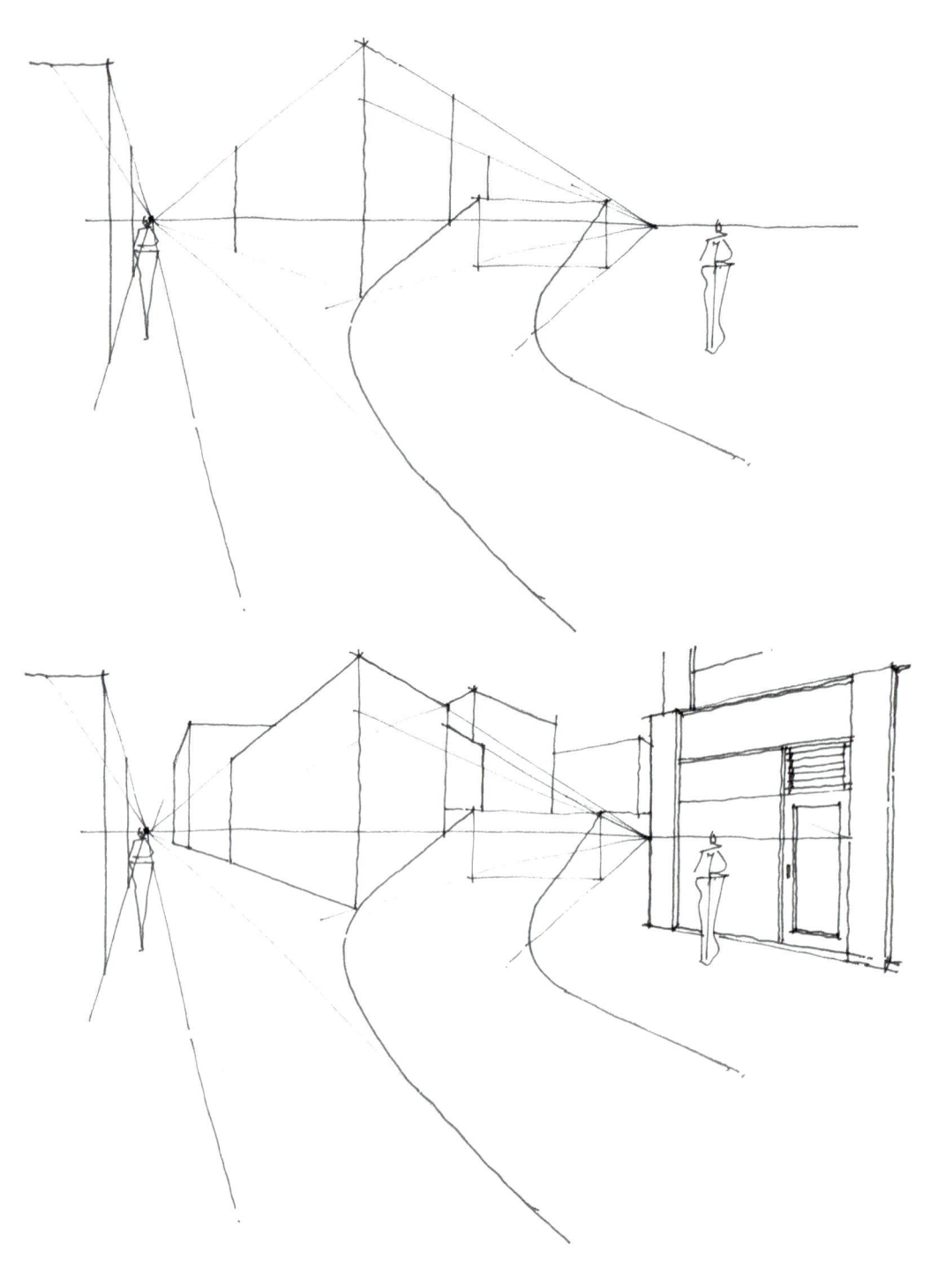

Step 1
The steps show the process of connecting a path from a higher level with another path from a different vanishing point using imaginary box and multi-point perspective. Sketch the box and join the lines as shown in the examples and look carefully at the joint area to see how the curvy path area is treated.

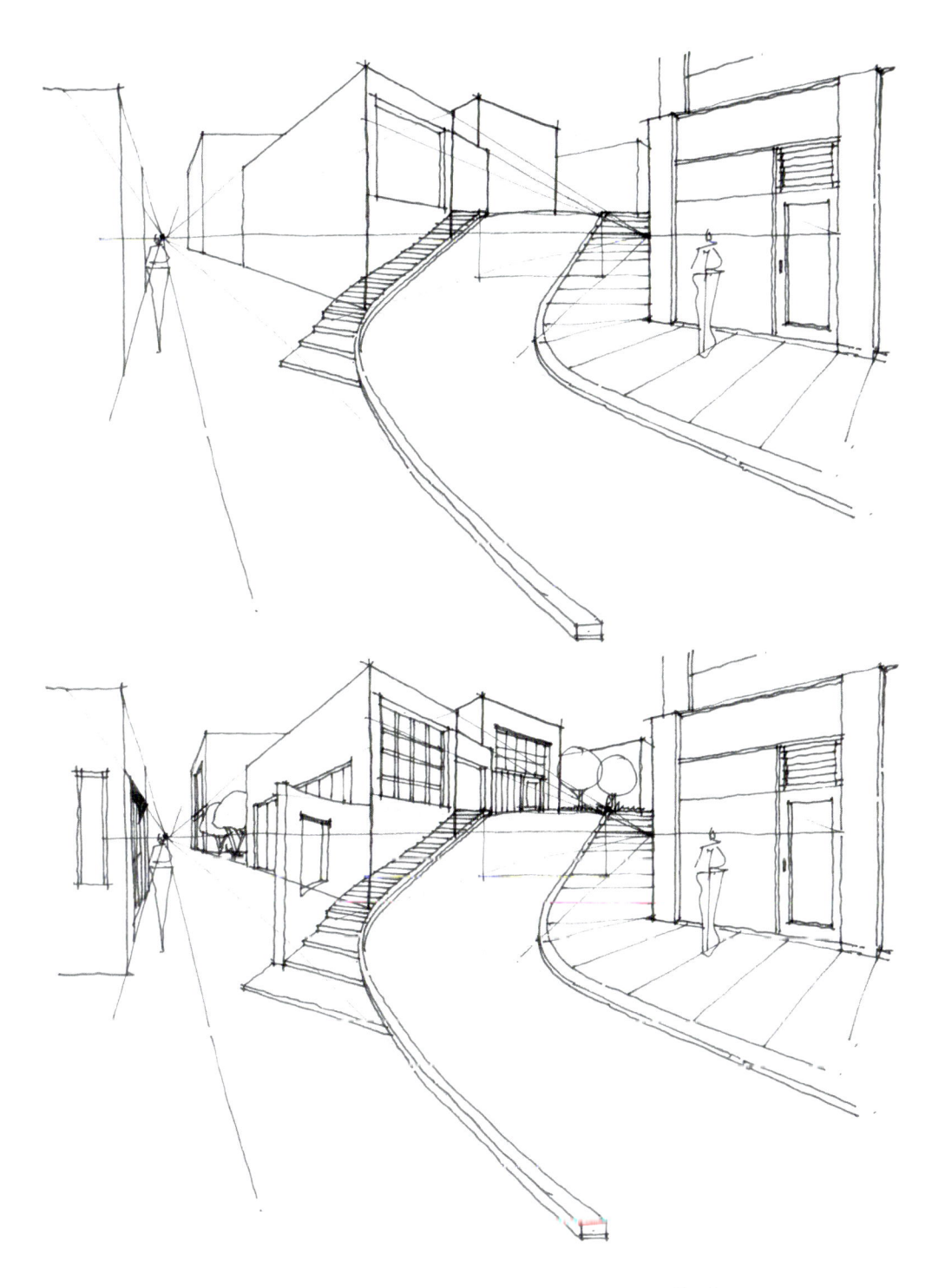

Tip: *Understand the curvy path process.*

Step 2
After getting a rough idea of the curvy path, continue your sketch by adding details on it. Look carefully at the curb's surface by the curvy path. The surface changes when the curvy line changes its direction. Master this process in order to make the sketch composition quality much better.

Step 3
This is the final step in sketching the curvy path which is the rendering process. Again, observe the curb surface and look at how the rendering technique is being applied. It is just a simple and random arrangement of vertical lines. This is one of the rendering examples that can be used for surfaces.

Tip: *Explore the rendering technique.*

REFERENCES

- Mike W. Lin, *Drawing and Designing With Confidence, A Step by Step Guide*, John Wiley & Sons. Inc, 1993.

- Ruzaimi Mat Rani, *The Sacred Garden, Exploration of Garden Design Through Mind Composition*, Pelanduk Publication, 2003.

- Angela Gair, *The Artist's Handbook, A Step by Step Guide to Drawing, Watercolor and Oil Painting*, Abbeydale Press, 1998.

- Francis D.K, Ching, *A Visual Dictionary of Architecture*, John Wiley & Sons. Inc, 1997.

- Kingsley K. Wu, *Freehand Sketching in the Architectural Environment*, Van Nostrand Reinhold, 1990.

- Paul Taggart, *Art Techniques from Pencil to Paint*, Sterling, 2003.

- Paul Laseau, *Graphic Thinking for Architects and Designers*, Van Nostrand Reinhold, 1989.

THE AUTHOR AND ILLUSTRATOR

Ruzaimi Mat Rani graduated with a Master of Landscape Architecture degree from Edinburgh College of Art (ECA), Heriot-Watt University and a bachelor's degree in Architecture from Universiti Teknologi Malaysia (UTM). His interest in sketching, drawing and painting started in primary and secondary school, continuing to higher education levels. His artworks have been exhibited in Bakat Muda Sezaman and PNB Art Exhibition.

His most important artworks are:
- 2003   Collection of 500 pieces of Edinburgh Old Town Sketches.
- 1999   Collection of 85 pieces of the Sacred Garden Collection.

CO- AUTHOR

Ezihaslinda Ngah is attached with Majlis Amanah Rakyat (MARA) as an educator for the subjects of English Language and English for Science and Technology. Throughout her number of years in the education line, she has had the opportunities to serve various MARA colleges. These include MARA Junior Science College (MJSC) Muar, Mersing and currently, Kuantan. She received her early education at Sekolah Rendah Tengku Bariah Kuala Terengganu. She then pursued her lower secondary education at Sekolah Menengah (A) Sheikh Abdul Malek and MARA Junior Science College Kuala Terengganu. For tertiary education, she was offered to continue her studies at Henley College, Coventry, United Kingdom for A-Levels and later her undergraduate degree B.Ed (Hons) TESOL at University of Warwick, Coventry, United Kingdom.